80-20 DEVELOPMENT IN AN UNEQUAL WORLD

'Like a phoenix, the revised 7th edition of *80-20 Development in an Unequal World* arises, not from the ashes but from the success of its predecessors. In appearance it is an elegant book; the content, however, speaks of the harsh reality of human rights abuses, poverty, gender disparities – in short, of the nadir of the human condition. Issues relevant to students of development studies are discussed and illustrated with appropriate case studies.

For students new to the field of study the book is a godsend; for lecturers it provides an excellent tool to unlock the complexities of social development in an unequal world. This book remains a compulsory companion for students in sociology, development studies, geography and in general all social sciences.'

Frik de Beer, *Professor Emeritus, University of South Africa, September 2016*

'The 7th edition of *80-20 Development in an Unequal World* is a pedagogical gem: one of those rare texts virtually guaranteed to capture the interest of students and involve them in lively and meaningful discussions of important issues. Critical, coherent, and multi-vocal, it makes superb use of both graphic and written materials to throw light on the structural sources of global violence and the possibilities of system-transformation. This book should be considered an indispensable part of the curriculum by teachers of international affairs and development, peace and conflict studies, human rights, political philosophy, and gender studies.'

Professor Richard E. Rubenstein, *School for Conflict Analysis and Resolution, George Mason University, USA*

'It is more important than ever that young people take a profoundly critical look at the way the world is headed. *80-20 Development in an Unequal World* features the latest theories and debates on current development, human rights and justice issues, and demonstrates their relevance to all of us involved in education. The accompanying support DVD of creative ideas, video clips, cartoons, blogs and practical activities gives us the confidence to explore these issues in the classroom alongside our students.'

Anne Kane, *Curriculum Adviser, Oxfam Scotland*

'As soon as I got to my ministerial position I was told I had to read this. I must say that those who read *80-20 Development in an Unequal World* find it a real eye-opener. It looks beyond tax avoidance to consider financial flows between the developed and the developing world in the round, pointing out the problems in the current rules of the game.'

Humza Yousaf, *Minister for External Affairs and International Development, Scotland, 2012*

'80-20 *Development in an Unequal World* is a seminal work in the field of development education. It is a one-stop-shop for those who want an informative and critical analysis of development and development education.'

Professor Claire Lyons, *Department of Learning, Society and Religious Education, Mary Immaculate College, Limerick*

A note on our cover

Our cover design seeks to reflect the many, inter-connected strands of human development in this, our highly unequal and unjust 80-20 world.

'*80-20 Development in an Unequal World* is a wonderful resource for teachers and learners alike. If we really believe that enabling young people to be 'responsible citizens' is a fundamental aim of the curriculum, then this book, with its in-depth analysis of a whole range of issues affecting people across the world, should become an essential resource in the 'learning classroom'. It is attractive, engaging, challenging and never simplistic or patronising and could allow schools to put global issues at the heart of the curriculum. It is particularly useful as schools seek to engage learners in inter-disciplinary learning.'

Professor Brian Boyd, *University of Strathclyde, Scotland*

'This resource is great for an overview of complex development topics, written in a critical yet accessible way. Either reading it cover-to-cover, or else 'dipping in' to each of the chapters… depending on my need…
80-20 was always there to enhance my knowledge!'

Grainne O'Neill, Irish NGO *Comhlámh*

'For any educator interested in bringing issues of global citizenship alive in the classroom, *80-20* is a tremendously versatile resource. It presents key concepts, timely and relevant data, pithy and perceptive insights and telling images in ways that inform, stimulate and encourage action. Whether the educator is experienced or just starting to teach development in an unequal world, *80-20* is likely to become a treasured and much used asset.'

Gerry Jeffers, *Education Department, Maynooth University, Ireland*

'Unlike many textbooks and articles, *80-20* references every quote, fact and figure which helps students to examine the validity of information. There is also onward referencing with suggested websites, books and people to research – excellent for older and more able and talented students and those who want to get involved in campaigning and taking action.'

Lucy Kirkham, *Geography subject leader, Bassaleg School, Newport, Wales*

'We have bought a huge number of these books in the past as we would use this as one of the resources in our teacher training courses; we also use them on a day to day basis to 'dip in' to when designing workshops etc. A key theme we promote in our training is critical literacy/thinking and this book is good at including a range of perspectives to challenge peoples thinking on global justice issues.'

Helen Henderson, *Children in Crossfire*

'High quality resources such as this publication are invaluable to assist students and the public in engaging on how best to achieve the Millennium Development Goals, tackle climate change and create a fair and just world for all. I believe it's important that students and the public have an opportunity to deepen their understanding of complex development challenges and the important role that Ireland plays in combating the causes and consequences of global poverty and hunger.
80-20 Development in an Unequal World, since its initial publication, has gained an enormous international reputation for the quality and clarity of its analysis and it is widely used in Ireland and internationally as an introduction for university students, teachers, youth and adult leaders as well as by NGOs. It has been consistently supported and part-funded by Irish Aid.'

Joe Costello, *Minister of State for Trade and Development at the launch of 6th edition of 80-20 in Dublin, 2012*

80-20

DEVELOPMENT IN AN UNEQUAL WORLD

7ᵀᴴ EDITION

Editors
Tony Daly, Ciara Regan and Colm Regan

Authors
Bertrand Borg, Mary Rose Costello, Tony Daly, Amal de Chickera, Michael Doorly,
John Dornan, Phil Glendenning, Lorna Gold, Omar Grech, Patrick Hayes, M. Satish Kumar,
Jerry Mac Evilly, Beatrice Maphosa, Grace McManus, Paul Power, Toni Pyke, Ciara Regan,
Colm Regan, Roland Tormey

Cartoons and illustrations
John 'Brick' Clark, Claudius and Martyn Turner

Photographers
Gareth Bentley, Elena Hermosa, Saiful Huq Omi and Amy Scaife

New Internationalist team
Chris Brazier and Dan Raymond-Barker

Design and graphics
Ray O'Sullivan Jr. (Pixelpress.ie) and Dylan Creane

Print Production: Pixelpress Ltd

Published in 2016 by
8⊕:2⊕ Educating and Acting for a Better World   **NewInternationalist**

Co-published by
80:20 Educating and Acting for a Better World, St. Cronan's BNS, Vevay Road, Bray,
Co. Wicklow, Ireland
New Internationalist, The Old Music Hall, 106-108 Cowley Road, Oxford, OX4 1JE, UK

www.8020.ie and www.newint.org

75:25 was first published by the Development Education Commission of Non-Governmental Organisations
for Overseas Development (CONGOOD) 1984
7th edition published in Ireland by 80:20 Educating and Acting for a Better World and the New Internationalist 2016

Disclaimer: the ideas, opinions and comments therein are entirely the responsibility of the authors and do not necessarily represent or
reflect the policies of Irish Aid, Trócaire or Concern Worldwide, our partners or of 80:20 and the New Internationalist.

Printed in Northern Ireland by GPS Colour Graphics Ltd (FSC and PEFC accredited)

A catalogue record for this book is available from the British Library
Library of Congress Cataloguing in Publication Data available

ISBN 978-1-78026-316-8
eBook edition available: ISBN 978-1-78026-317-5

*80:20 Educating and Acting for a Better World is committed to a sustainable future for our business, our readers and our planet.
This book is made from Forest Stewardship Council ™ certified paper.*

 @8020world   @our8020world

CONTENTS

Foreword by Senator Patrick Dodson   6

Editor's Introduction   8

Numbers, Perspectives and Politics   11

World Hunger: from the specific to the general – 'percentage to proportion'   12

PART ONE

1. **Wealth, Poverty and Human Development – New Extremes**   14
   by John Dornan and Colm Regan

2. **Development – the story of an idea**   34
   by Tony Daly, M. Satish Kumar and Colm Regan

3. **Sustainable Development – 'enough for all, for ever'**   54
   by Roland Tormey

4. **Human rights and Development – 'a right, not an act of charity'**   74
   by Omar Grech

5. **Justice and Development – 'an illusion of innocence…?'**   94
   by Colm Regan

6. **Development and Politics – two sides of the same coin?**   112
   by Toni Pyke

7. **From the Poor to the Rich**   128
   by Bertrand Borg and Colm Regan

8. **Women, Development and (dis)empowerment**   148
   by Ciara Regan

9. **Climate Change and Development**   166
   by Tony Daly, Lorna Gold and Jerry Mac Evilly

CONTENTS

PART TWO: ISSUES AND CHALLENGES

10. **Migration and Development**   190
    by Amal de Chickera, Phil Glendenning, Paul Power and Colm Regan

11. **International Trade and Development Today**   206
    by Bertrand Borg and Colm Regan

12. **Food is Power**   226
    by Michael Doorly and Patrick Hayes

13. **Basic Needs, Population and Development**   242
    by Beatrice Maphosa

14. **Debating Aid – moving beyond pantomime**   260
    by Mary Rose Costello and Colm Regan

15. **Making Change - ideas, experiences and arguments**   274
    by Tony Daly, Grace McManus and Ciara Regan

Index   304

EDUCATIONAL DVD AND SUPPORT MATERIALS

80-20 Development in an Unequal World is available with an accompanying education DVD from 80:20 Educating and Acting for a Better World.

The support DVD provides ideas and suggestions for using the resource creatively in different types of educational settings – a tutorial group, a school classroom, an adult learner group or a youth organisation. It contains:

- 20 'starter' activities to help get a discussion and debate underway
- A set of 'stimulus' sheets to generate debate
- 60 activities exploring the content and of the various chapters and topics
- A set of videos and poster resources to take issues further and reflect on key themes

For an expanded, interactive version of these materials and more visit **www.8020.ie**

DEDICATION

This edition is dedicated to the memory of two departed fellow activists:

Peadar Cremin – first Chairperson of 80:20 Educating and Acting for a Better World; trusted friend, colleague and so much more.

Aengus Cantwell – who brought style, grace and great humour to our lives.

ACKNOWLEDGEMENTS

80:20 would like to thank Concern Worldwide, Irish Aid and Trócaire for their invaluable support and funding.

Producing this, the 7th edition of *80-20 Development in an Unequal World* is a major task only made possible over many years by a network of individuals and organisations; we owe them a huge ongoing debt:

John Clark (Brick), Bertrand Borg, Anne Cleary, Dylan Creane, Mella Cusack, Valerie Duffy, Linda Cornwall, Frik De Beer, Michael Doorly, John Dornan, Gerry Fenlon, Anne Kane, Kevin Kelly, Úna McGrath, Tony Meade, Ray O'Sullivan Snr., Phil Glendenning, Omar Grech, Lorna Gold, Patrick Hayes, M. Satish Kumar, Valerie Lewis, Jerry Mac Evilly, Lydia McCarthy, Grace McManus, Josephine McLoughlin, Beatrice Maphosa, Jen Murphy, Paul Power, Antonella (Toni) Pyke, Patsy Toland, Roland Tormey, Martyn Turner, Gary Walsh and the dedicated members of the Management Committee of 80:20 - Mary Rose Costello, Vaughan Dodd, Gerry Duffy, Louise Gaskin, Gráinne McGettrick, Dermot O'Brien and Clifton Rooney.

Thanks to our many readers, users and critics in Ireland and internationally who took part in consultation events, who sent feedback on the 6th edition and who made many invaluable suggestions for improvement. We hope this edition adequately reflects your ideas.

To Frank Geary, Éimear Green and Susan Gallwey of the Irish Development Education Association for facilitating a consultation on this edition and to the members of the Association for sharing time, ideas and reflections. Thanks also to Deirdre Hogan and members of the Ubuntu Network, to the Association of Geography Teachers of Ireland, and to staff and students at the Department of Development Studies, University of South Africa for feedback.

It has been important to us to listen to and hear from colleagues who, not surprisingly have a lot to say.

As ever, our special thanks to Ray O'Sullivan Jr. and to Dylan Creane for their design work and general support and to Tony Meade for editorial support.

Thanks to Amanda Bell for an excellent indexing job and to Maeve Tierney, Anne Ivory, John O'Toole and the staff and community at St Cronan's BNS in Bray for their ongoing support.

Special mention must be made of the support of Michelle D'Arcy of Trinity College Dublin, Gerry Jeffers of Maynooth University, former Scottish Minister for External Affairs, Humza Yousef, Scott Sinclair, Eoin Heaney, Duncan Green in Oxfam, Phil Glendenning, Louise McRae of The Zoological Society of London and WWF for permission to use graphics, Miriam Dornan, Anthony Dornan and Liz Dornan for support in Scotland.

Special thanks must go to our family who have lived and breathed this journey with us over the past two years through many long days and late nights – Hilda, Anna and John and to Donny for reminding us of what's important.

About this book

Proceeds from this book contribute to the non-profit work of 80:20 Educating and Acting for a Better World and the New Internationalist.

FOREWORD

Clearly, there is work to be done.

I am a proud member of the Yawuru people of Broome in Western Australia. In the Yawuru language of my people there are three key concepts which shape our ways of knowing and understanding. They are:

Mabu ngarrung: a strong community where people matter and are valued

Mabu buru: a strong place, a good country where use of resources is balanced and sacredness is embedded in the landscape

Mabu liyan, a healthy spirit, a good state of being for individuals, families and community. Its essence arises from our encounter with the land and people.

These concepts are not newly minted nor are they unique to Australia; they come from the time before time began. We call this the *Bugarrigarra* - from when the earth was soft and yet to be moulded and given its form by the creative spirits. The *Bugarrigarra* encompasses the time well before Western philosophy, religion and laws existed or travelled to our lands in ships.

I draw your attention to these concepts for they capture much of the essence of what this compelling and rich book, *80-20* is all about. They provide a context and a perspective for analysing the world immediately around us and that world which appears to be far distant. These three concepts and the way they are explored in *80-20 Development in an Unequal World* remind us of the urgent need to recognise and recover the fundamental principles of respect for the diversity and richness of our various cultures in Australia and beyond – principles that remain at fundamental risk today worldwide. They serve to remind us of our shared humanity without which we will never overcome the challenges we face. 80-20 vividly captures the essence of the work that is before us.

The history of our people – the First Australians - is one of official denial and exclusion in our own land. My family, along with most Aboriginal families, carries the pain of this exclusion in our recent history. Australian law at that time was unarguably founded on a social outlook that was highly ethnocentric, even racist. Many of the laws were genocidal in intent, application and consequence. The same moral compass justified the American laws that mandated racial segregation in the US before the civil rights movement. Such views and laws led also to the horrors of Soweto and Robben Island and even the hate crimes of Nazi Germany. These systems of laws and regulation shared the same legal, intellectual and moral parentage. Such laws, worldviews and practices have their parallels across the world today with similar pain and suffering for their victims.

This exclusion continues to be challenged in Australia today just as it is challenged in very many ways across all regions of the world, especially among the world's poorest – a reality described in some detail in 80-20. Chapter after chapter, story after story, this book not only catalogues exclusion and its consequences; it also offers remarkable storytelling of change in today's world.

In reading *80-20 Development in an Unequal World*, I am reminded of the words of Australian anthropologist Bill Stanner who, in reference to official policy towards the First Australians, described it as '...*a cult of forgetfulness practised on a national scale*'. For the perceptive reader, 80-20 offers a clarion call to challenge the constant *'forgetfulness'* of the realities of inequality and exclusion effectively practiced on a world scale. It catalogues the denial of dignity and human rights of the many which, in turn undermines the humanity of all. Using extensive data, perceptive analysis and excellent graphics (alongside biting cartoons), *80-20* offers a compelling alternative storyline that not only highlights what is wrong today but also constantly suggests and debates solutions. In this regard, I endorse the observation made by Irish President Michael D. Higgins in his preface to the 6th edition that this is a book of '*hope and courage*'.

We know, as fact, that just as some Australian legislation in the past was founded on outmoded patterns of thought and belief, much of current official policy and practice on international development is not sustainable of people or planet. Our thinking, our laws and much of our practice remain locked in an ingrained paternalism and racial superiority (and behind those, a deep and abiding fear). Such mindsets and policies continue to justify repeated acts of greed that grab the lands, resources and lives of far too many people. They undermine not only our shared humanity but also our common future.

A dominant thread throughout this book is the recognition of that common humanity (and, all too often, inhumanity); it is catalogued in the discussions of justice and injustice, hunger and poverty, women's rights, human rights and climate change. Recognising this will serve to refresh our spirit (our '*liyan*'). It will enable us to move on from the many mistakes, poor policies, ignorance and outright racism that have bedevilled us to date

For many years now, my Aboriginal colleagues from Broome and myself have had a creative and productive partnership with the organisation 80:20 Educating and Acting for a Better World. Together, we have worked on the reconciliation agenda here in Australia and also in Ireland and beyond. I commend the energy, creativity and resilience that characterises 80:20 as an organisation and that is evident in the pages of this book. Our partnership continues to energise us for the work that lies ahead.

80-20 Development in an Unequal World reminds us that regardless of race, culture or gender, we all have a shared goal as global citizens - wanting to build a common, tolerant and flourishing future together. We urgently need a world unencumbered by a lack of respect and appreciation for the human dignity of all peoples and our planet. If we constantly build on what we have in common rather than what divides us, I believe that we can be better people; we can create a better world and, together, we can offer a better place to the coming generations. In the meantime, there is indeed work to be done.

I am very happy to endorse this educational resource for the story it tells; the analysis it offers and the vision it inspires.

Senator Patrick Dodson
Australian Aboriginal Leader

EDITOR'S INTRODUCTION

As he put pen to paper from his prison cell in Birmingham, Alabama, drafting a public response to a statement of concern issued by religious leaders who viewed his nonviolent demonstration activities against segregation as *'unwise and untimely'*, Martin Luther King Jr. would have had little doubt about how slow and unglamorous change could be. With hundreds of teenagers in jail for peacefully protesting segregation alongside King, he also had to deal with angry parents who demanded to know when their children would be bailed out.

Worldwide today, there are countless numbers of communities and individuals compelled to struggle on, urging others to do so too, understanding the challenges and the risks they face in posing uncomfortable questions. Berta Cáceres, the Honduran indigenous and environmental rights campaigner, was one of these people. Before her murder in March 2016, following threats to her life for opposing one of Central America's biggest hydropower projects, she spoke of her compulsion, her duty to act:

> *'We must undertake the struggle in all parts of the world, wherever we may be, because we have no other spare or replacement planet. We have only this one, and we have to take action.'*

The costs of confronting injustice have all too often been, as noted in previous editions of this book, extremely high. This has included Nigerian environmental and minority rights activists Ken Saro-Wiwa and the Ogoni Nine, murdered by his government for defending the Ogoni people and their homeland and school teacher Malim Abdul Habib, assassinated by the Taliban for insisting on the fundamental right of all girls to an education. Justice, when viewed from the perspective of the 1.5 million landless rural workers struggling for access to land in Brazil (and Honduras, and elsewhere), appears to be for the rich only; 'sustainability', corporate-speak for business as usual. But, as Martin Luther King Jr. asserted in his Letter from a Birmingham Jail, *Justice too long delayed is justice denied.'*

Learning about rights and wrongs; choosing to question, identifying alternatives is, at its core, what this book is all about. In daring to teach and to learn (and unlearn and relearn) literally millions of people have been speaking out, demonstrating and working to create a fairer, more equal and healthier world for present and future generations.

This 7th edition of *80-20 Development in an Unequal World* arrives at a moment of potential and urgent renewal for the planet as illustrated by the era of the Sustainable Development Goals, heralded as a new and ambitious framework for transforming our world for the better. The SDG agenda seeks to eradicate extreme poverty (defined at US$1.25 a day) by 2030; yet, given even the most optimistic growth rates and existing environmental limits, this target is well-nigh impossible. As a model of poverty eradication, *'trickle down'* economic growth-led development will not work; it hasn't before and it won't in the future. At US$1.25 a day, with the current model of capitalism, it would take 100 years to eradicate extreme poverty and at US$5.00 a day, it would take 207 years.

IN DARING TO TEACH AND TO LEARN (AND UNLEARN AND RELEARN) LITERALLY MILLIONS OF PEOPLE HAVE BEEN SPEAKING OUT, DEMONSTRATING AND WORKING TO CREATE A FAIRER, MORE EQUAL AND HEALTHIER WORLD FOR PRESENT AND FUTURE GENERATIONS.

THE RATIO BETWEEN THE WORLD'S RICHEST AND POOREST IN PER CAPITA TERMS NOW STANDS AT A STAGGERING 65:1; WE CAN NOW CALCULATE, WITH PRECISION, THAT INCOME AND WEALTH ARE BEING SUCKED UPWARDS TO THE TOP GEOGRAPHICALLY, POLITICALLY AND ECONOMICALLY.

The era of global development goals is further challenged by a more complex world – in preparing the ledger of winners and losers, the development balance sheet has never been more detailed. The ratio between the world's richest and poorest in per capita terms now stands at a staggering 65:1; we can now calculate, with precision, that income and wealth are being sucked upwards to the top geographically, politically and economically. The 'growth industry' of tax avoidance by wealthy individuals, companies and corporations continues in the shadows but is increasingly under strain from global tax justice and transparency movements.

The 21st Century has been characterised as an age of new extremes – extreme wealth, extreme climate, extreme inequality. Interrogating and challenging these baseline extremes in the 'development project' is no longer the sole preserve of 'development elites' (specialists, academics, policymakers, politicians etc.), it is now firmly in the public domain with education playing a pivotal role.

As the previous century once again demonstrated, nothing is as impermeable as it seems. Momentum and movements for change are quietly (and sometimes loudly) occurring, across the many spaces and places where justice remains denied. If you care to look and listen, you will see and hear them. Looking beyond the fatigue of the 24-news cycle and a hardening indifference to images of suffering, you will see these moments in the volunteer search and rescue White Helmet workers in Syria,

the Fairtrade towns and school committees, the divestment in fossil fuels campaigns, the indigenous communities and women's rights groups challenging traditional land and inheritance laws and customs in places like Kenya and India and in the onward journey of the human rights movement worldwide.

80-20 Development in an Unequal World is offered as an exploration of some of the most central global issues and debates of our time – a contested agenda to be struggled with. It is an agenda that we must not only learn but also dare to teach.

As long-standing fans of the New Internationalist magazine over the last four decades we are particularly delighted to have worked with them as publishing partners on this edition.

Tony Daly, **Ciara Regan** and **Colm Regan**

'ATLESS HOLDING UP the WORLD
(HELPED BY 'OMELESS, JOBLESS,
FOODLESS, WATERLESS' etc etc)

NUMBERS, PERSPECTIVES AND POLITICS

'SOMEBODY, SOMEWHERE, NEEDS TO SPEAK THE TRUTH, NEEDS TO SAY THAT THE POOR HAVE BEEN DRAMATICALLY BETRAYED.' THOMAS POGGE 2015

JUST AS POVERTY IS POLITICAL, SO TOO IS ITS DEFINITION
US$1.00 PER DAY, $1.25, $1.90, $2.00 OR MORE....?

US$1.00 A DAY

For decades, the shorthand definition of absolute poverty was 'a dollar a day' (roughly equivalent to the 1990 national poverty lines in the 22 countries used to build the data).

Given the very significant weaknesses in the data and its arbitrary nature, this line was always contested with many arguing that it was so basic and frugal as to be meaningless.

US$1.25/US$1.90 A DAY

In 2008, the World Bank re-defined the International poverty line at US$1.25 a day and in 2015, it re-defined it once again at $1.90 a day purchasing power parity (i.e. the equivalent cost in 2011 dollars of a bundle of goods across all countries – see page 28).

The Bank claimed that the latest figure is roughly equivalent to the old one, simply updated to current realities. For some, the figure is too high, for others too low while many reject the measurement of poverty as being defined solely against the cost of a minimum basket of goods.

US$6.00 A DAY

According to the Bank, US$1.90 is the average of poverty lines of the poorest countries but, for critics, it says little about poverty in most other countries (e.g. US$6 a day is deemed more accurate in Latin America).

US$1.90 a day enables the Bank to argue that the number living in extreme poverty is less than it is and, because of the 2015 re-definition, the numbers of the world's poor were reduced by 100 million overnight.

US$2.00/US$5.00/US$7.00 A DAY

In the past, many NGOs insisted that US$2.00 a day should have been the minimum but that now, it needs to be set at US$5.00 a day; others have argued for a *'morally defensible poverty line'* or a *'multidimensional poverty'* approach – if adopted these would generate a figure of up to US$7 a day.

4.2 BILLION OR 900 MILLION?

At the higher level up to 4.2 billion would live in poverty – at the Bank's new level it was 900 million in 2012 with an estimated figure of 700 million in 2015.

2030, 2115 OR 2222?

The SDG agenda seeks to eradicate extreme poverty by 2030 (defined at US$1.25 a day); given the most optimistic growth rates and environmental limits, critics argue that this target is impossible. As a model of poverty eradication, *'trickle down'* economic growth-led development will not work; it hasn't before and it won't in the future.

At US$1.25 a day, with the current model of capitalism, it would take 100 years to eradicate extreme poverty and at US$5.00 a day, it would take 207 years.

60% AND 5%

Just 5% of all income generated by global GDP growth from 1999 to 2008 went to the poorest 60% of humanity; the richest 40% received the remaining 95%; this clearly illustrates that *'trickle-down'* is a myth.

175

The number of times global GDP would have to increase if poverty were re-defined at US$5.00 a day – nothing like this has been achieved to date, and critics argue that such growth would 'destroy' the planet.

WORLD HUNGER:

FROM THE SPECIFIC TO THE GENERAL – *'PERCENTAGE TO PROPORTION'*

1994/460 MILLION

'...within a decade, no child will go to bed hungry' (Henry Kissinger, World Food Conference, Rome), then the FAO estimated there were 460 million hungry people in the developing world and that in 10 years it could reach 800 million.

788/1,023 MILLION

In 1996, the Rome Declaration on World Food Security was agreed (to cut the number of the world's hungry by half based on 1996 figures); the FAO then estimated some 788 million were hungry. By 2009, the number was 1,023 million (+30%).

1990?

When agreeing the MDG agenda in 2000, two important changes were introduced – 1990 became the year against which progress would be measured, not 1996 (making the figures look much better for a variety of reasons). A second change was even more significant – *'percentage'* of hungry people became *'proportion'* – again making the figures look better.

23% - 15%

The figures changed again in 2012 (FAO argued the methodology *'improved'*); the new figures argued that while 23% of the developing world was undernourished in 1990, a 'reduction' to 15% could be reported and progress declared.

1800 KILO CALORIES

Critics argue that the FAO definition of hunger is too narrow and too conservative; it hides realities and *'gravely underestimates'* the size of the problem (the FAO accepts some of this and rejects the rest). Critics argue the FAO only counts people as hungry when caloric intake reaches *'rock-bottom'* (around 1,800 calories per day – the minimum for a *'sedentary'* lifestyle; the FAO insists this is but one criteria). However, most of the poor do not live such lifestyles; they usually work hard physically and need far more than 1,800 (the FAO agrees but the definition remains).

1.5 – 2.5 BILLION

Based on calorie needs for 'normal' and 'intense' activity, there are between 1.5 and 2.5 billion hungry - and rising (FAO figures, 2-3 times the MDG figure). If China is removed from the equation (73% of reported progress on hunger was there, mostly in the 1990s before the MDGs), things are even worse. In reality, other developing countries have seen a *net increase* in hunger numbers.

3000 CALORIES EACH DAY

The SDG campaign needs to recognise that there are at least 2 billion people hungry (nearly one third of humanity) who cannot access adequate food while the world produces enough to feed everyone worldwide 3,000 calories per day.

> *'Just poor,' are the words thought by the global elite before the tragedy of misery scattered all over the world. With the lack of feeling of that which does not understand the suffering of its equals, the world economic elite does not consider human value in the faces of the poor, does not understand the sacrifice of destruction of human beings and commits the crime of destroying its own humanism.'*
>
> Brazilian Cristovam Buarque 2001

> *'This is not conscious corruption. It's a symptom of an institutional culture that has to prove it is achieving important progress. The 1990 change justifies the United Nations' efforts and jobs, as much as it quiets our consciences.'*
>
> Argentinian writer Martín Caparrós, author of El Hambre (on world hunger) in the New York Times September 28th, 2014

Sources (a limited selection):
Cristovam Buarque (2001) Opinion Piece www.brazzil.com/pages/p21jun01.htm
Martin Caparrós (2014) Counting the Hungry, New York Times, September 29th
Jason Hickel (2015) The hunger numbers: are we counting right? Guardian Newspaper July 17th (it is important to read the ensuing debate in the Guardian)
Tom Murphy (2015) World Bank draws a new-ish extreme poverty line, see www.humanosphere.org
Thomas Pogge (2010) Politics as Usual: What lies Behind The Pro-Poor Rhetoric, Cambridge, Polity Press
Martin Ravallion (2010) World Bank's $1.25/day poverty measure- countering the latest criticisms, see www.econ.worldbank.org
Martin Ravallion, Shaohua Chen and Prem Sangraula (2008) Dollar a Day Revisited
The World Bank, Development Research Group
David Woodward (2015) *Incrementum ad Absurdum:* Global Growth, Inequality and Poverty Eradication in a Carbon-Constrained World, World Economic Review 4: 43-62

'And even the rhetoric is appalling. At the 1996 World Food Summit in Rome, the world's governments grandly promised to halve the number of extremely poor people between 1996 and 2015, implicitly accepting 25,000 daily poverty deaths in 2015 and some 250 million such deaths in the interim. In the 2000 UN Millennium Declaration, they modified their promise - replacing 'number' by 'proportion' and extending the plan period backward to 1990. Taking advantage of rapid population growth and a huge poverty reduction in China during the 1990s, these clever modifications greatly dilute the target: the new promise, if fulfilled, would reduce the number of extremely poor people by only 19.5% between 1996 and 2015'

PHILOSOPHER THOMAS POGGE, GLOBAL JUSTICE PROGRAMME, YALE UNIVERSITY, 2012

CHAPTER 1

WEALTH, POVERTY AND HUMAN DEVELOPMENT - NEW EXTREMES

JOHN DORNAN AND COLM REGAN

This chapter explores the significance of the considerable progress made over recent decades in promoting the basic needs of the world's people – focusing on human development as the priority. It highlights improvements in poverty reduction, health, education, hunger, water and sanitation as they impact on the world's poorest. Such improvements have, however, taken place in the context of systematic and growing inequality that threatens to undermine the progress made. Using evidence and argument from a wide range of sources, the chapter also introduces other threats and challenges to human development including climate change, political exclusion and the inherent contradictions of development led by economic growth.

KEYWORDS:

EXTREME POVERTY NUMBERS; **UNDERNOURISHMENT;** CHILD MORTALITY; **PROGRESS ACHIEVED;** DEBATING POVERTY AND ITS MEASUREMENT; **WEALTH AND POVERTY;** THE 'BOTTOM BILLION'; **CLIMATE CHANGE;** THE POLITICS OF DEVELOPMENT

INTRODUCTION

The past three decades have witnessed substantial and life changing progress in a number of vital areas – poverty and hunger reduction, improved overall health (especially for women and children), rising literacy and schooling statistics, improved access to safe and clean water and sanitation, reduced gender inequality in some areas and generally improved human security. Despite ongoing debates about measurement (see chapter 2), the following snapshot illustrates key dimensions of the progress achieved as well as the scale of the injustices remaining.

- The absolute number of people living in extreme poverty (those living on less than US$1.25 per day) fell from an estimated 1.9 billion in 1990 to an estimated 1 billion in 2011 with a further 165 million lifted out of such poverty as of 2015 – yet 1 billion people (a likely underestimate) live in 'low human development'.

- The child mortality rate fell by more than half, while under-five deaths fell from 12.7 million to 6 million - yet 11 children under 5 years die every minute while an estimated 33 mothers die every hour.

- The number of people undernourished globally has declined from an estimated 1 billion in 1990/1992 to about 795 million people today - yet this figure still represents almost 10% of total world population.

- While there has been a major decline in 'inter-state wars' since the 1950s, a reduction in murder rates worldwide and a global spread of human rights culture, there continues to be a proliferation of civil wars involving devastating conflict (as in Palestine and Syria).

(Sources: UNDP Human Development Report 2015; Human Security Report 2013 and Freedom in the World 2016)

This snapshot highlights what has been achieved (especially since 1990) but, more importantly, what can be achieved. However, despite such a positive analysis, the progress achieved is highly uneven within and across regions and countries and is now increasingly under threat from political and economic fundamentalism as well as from growing and chronic inequality, escalating climate change and environmental degradation (fuelled by the overconsumption of some), and regional conflict. As has so often been the case, these trends and patterns affect the poorest, most vulnerable and least empowered most.

Despite talk of progress and equality, the richest countries today are exponentially richer than the poorest and the ratio between the world's richest and poorest in per capita terms now stands at a staggering 65:1. While the world is in so many ways increasingly globalised, interconnected and wealthier than ever before, it is simultaneously increasingly fragmented, unequal and is now at growing risk from its own internal mechanisms and contradictions.

Oxfam summarised this current reality in a 2016 briefing paper as follows:

> *'There is no getting away from the fact that the big winners in our global economy are those at the top. Our economic system is heavily skewed in their favour, and arguably increasingly so. Far from trickling down, income and wealth are instead being sucked upwards at an alarming rate.'*

(Oxfam, *An Economy for the 1% January 2016:3*)

This chapter explores and analyses key aspects of these realities setting the scene for much that follows in subsequent chapters. It places particular emphasis on poverty and wealth in the world today in addition to highlighting the progress in human development achieved over the past number of decades. It also explores some of the inherent contradictions 'hardwired' into current dominant development models and strategies.

MEASURING DEVELOPMENT

This section explores two frequently used ways of measuring and mapping development, as well as a range of other development indicators. At the end of the section, data for selected countries illustrates how these indicators compare and highlights many dimensions of progress in human development.

WEALTH

A number of similar indicators measure a country's wealth - Gross Domestic Product (GDP) measures the production of goods and services in a country while Gross National Product (GNP) includes GDP, plus income earned by residents from overseas investments minus income earned within the domestic economy by overseas residents. The World Bank now uses Gross National Income per capita (GNI) which is very similar to GNP. All are measured in US$; they are often expressed per capita, that is, proportional to a country's population.

Wealth per capita is widely used as a measure of development and is straightforward to understand. For example, it is used by the World Bank as a basis for its categorisation of low, lower middle, upper middle and upper income countries. This is a more sophisticated view of the world than the often simplistically used 'developed/developing' or 'north/south' divisions (see the discussions of 'labels' and terminology in Chapter 2). It is firmly linked with ideas of development as being primarily about wealth and, by comparing countries in this way, with a 'modernisation view of development' (see Chapter 2). It has little to say about the social, political and cultural aspects of development.

Wealth has a number of particular disadvantages as a measure of development; in common with other measures, it is an average for the country as a whole, so it does not show inequalities within countries. Perhaps more significantly, wealth data do not include those forms of production that are not accounted for, such as subsistence agriculture,

unpaid work (for example in the home), or work in the 'informal' economy. These aspects of the economy are likely to be comparatively more significant in Third World countries.

A further weakness is that comparisons in wealth are made between countries with huge differences in living costs; for example, you can buy much more for US$1 in India than in the US. So a variation is to make comparisons using Purchasing Power Parity, which accounts for differences in the cost of living (on this basis, China has already overtaken the US).

HUMAN DEVELOPMENT

The Human Development Index (HDI) was devised by the United Nations Development Programme (UNDP) as an alternative and is now widely used as an indicator of human progress and quality of life. It is based on a score derived from three measures: life expectancy, education (literacy and years of schooling) and income (purchasing power in parity US dollars). As HDI includes both social and economic aspects, it is widely accepted as a more satisfactory view of development than those based on economics alone. The HDI is focused on people and their needs, and so can be linked with views of development focused on social justice. UNDP uses the HDI to categorise the world into high, medium and low human development.

The 2015 Human Development Report predictably shows high HDI values in Western Europe, North America and Australasia, and low human development in much of Africa. However, parts of Central and South America, the Caribbean, the Middle East, East and South-East Asia also have high HDI scores. In 2014 Norway had the highest score and Niger the lowest (for more, see Tables 1.4 and 1.7).

In 2010, the HDI was amended to take inequality into account with the development of the Inequality Adjusted Human Development Index. Using this new measure highlights how inequality impacts on human development – for example, when adjusted for inequality, the US drops 20 places in the 2014 human development table. Regionally, it is estimated that the losses in human development due to inequality amount to 33% in sub-Saharan Africa, 29% in South Asia, 25% in Arab states and 24% in Latin America and the Caribbean.

Although in general the wealthiest countries have the highest levels of human development, there is not always a straightforward link between wealth and high HDI especially when reviewed over time. Some of the top movers in the HDI since 1970 include several countries in East and South Asia and the Arab States (in North Africa and the oil-rich Gulf region). Oman heads the top 10 list followed by China, Nepal and Indonesia. Reviewing the top 10 in non-income HDI terms highlights some interesting case studies; for example, Ethiopia, Iran and Algeria score highly in health and education improvements as distinct from those in income. Countries such as Botswana and India score highly on the income improvement dimensions of the HDI. This is because several countries make it into the top 10 listings as a result of their high achievements in health and education despite unexceptional economic performance.

A NOTE ON THE HUMAN DEVELOPMENT INDEX (HDI)

The HDI was developed in 1990 by a team led by Pakistani economist Mahbub ul Haq and influenced by the ideas of Nobel prize-winning economist Amartya Sen.

Expanding the choices people effectively have is central to the definition of well-being underpinning the concept of human development. In order to expand those choices, however, people must be empowered to do so – most notably by being healthy and by being educated. The HDI therefore takes these three dimensions (economic, health, and education) and creates a composite index by which a country's level of human development can be measured and compared to other countries. Thus, for the creators of the HDI, human development has three fundamental components – *well-being* (expanding real freedoms so that people can flourish), *empowerment and agency* (enabling people and groups to act and to generate valuable outcomes) and *justice* (expanding equity, sustaining outcomes over time and respecting human rights and other goals of society). These dimensions of development are explored further in the various chapters that follow.

A number of criticisms have been levelled at the HDI: that it fails to include any ecological dimension; that by focusing on individual nations and ranking them it fails to consider development from a global perspective; that it did not include an adequate gender dimension (though this has now been addressed). Some critics have considered the data on which it is based to be flawed, while others have not had a problem with the HDI itself, but believe it to be a reinvention of the wheel, showing nothing that wasn't evident prior to its creation.

In the 2010 report, the HDI indicators in education and income were modified and the collection method was also changed in four dimensions:

- Mean years of schooling replaced literacy.
- Gross enrolment is shown as expected years of schooling which gives the years of schooling that a child can expect to receive given current enrolment rates.
- Gross National Income (GNI) per capita replaced Gross Domestic Product (GDP) as income earned and remittances received as well as sizeable aid flows lead to large differences between the income of a country's residents and its domestic production.
- The data collection method in the three dimensions changed (from an arithmetic mean to a geometric mean) - as well as recognising that health, education and income are all important; poor performance in any dimension is now directly reflected in the reporting.

Other significant changes were also introduced in 2010 – the HDI focused increasingly on deprivation, vulnerability and inequality and included the *Inequality Adjusted Human Development Index* (this measures the losses in human development due to inequality in health, education and income); *the Gender Inequality Index* (this reveals gender-based disparities in reproductive health, empowerment and labour market participation) and the *Multi-Dimensional Poverty Index* (which identifies overlapping deprivations suffered by households in health, education and living standards). The changes reflect advances in knowledge and information and allow for innovation in measuring multidimensional inequality and poverty, which can then be applied internationally to enable comparisons to be made and to provide new understandings and insights on human development.

IN 2010, THE HDI WAS AMENDED TO TAKE INEQUALITY INTO ACCOUNT WITH THE DEVELOPMENT OF THE INEQUALITY ADJUSTED HUMAN DEVELOPMENT INDEX.

UNDER-FIVE MORTALITY

Another sensitive measure of human development is the under-five mortality rate which measures the number of children per 1,000 live births who die before their fifth birthday.

This is similar to the Infant Mortality Rate (IMR) which measures the proportion of children who die before their first birthday. UNICEF argues that these measures are important as they indicate the end result of the development process, as it impacts on children.

It is also a useful indicator of a population's health and nutritional status, and of social progress through health-care and educational programmes; high infant and under-five mortality rates closely correlate with high adult mortality and low life-expectancy. Use of these child mortality rates often derives from a 'basic needs' approach to development (see Chapter 13).

In 2015 (World Bank data), Iceland, Japan, Estonia, Andorra, Finland and Luxemburg had the lowest under-five mortality rates (at 2 per 1000) and Angola and Sierra Leone the highest (at 96 and 87 per 1000, although both of these figures represent hugely significant reductions on previous mortality rates).

However, overall mortality rates for sub-Saharan Africa and the world's Least Developed Countries continue to decline significantly from previous highs (the UN Population Division estimates these figures in 2015 at 64 and 57 respectively).

HUMAN DEVELOPMENT TODAY

According to the Human Development Report for 2015, between 1990 and 2014 the number of countries in the very high human development classification rose from 12 to 46 while the population in that group increased from 0.5 billion to 1.2 billion. In the same period the number of countries in the low human development classification fell from 62 to 43 and the population numbers in that group fell from 3.2 billion to 1.2 billion. Progress on the Human Development Index has also been significant at the individual country level; for example, Ethiopia increased its HDI value by more than half; Rwanda by nearly half; five countries, including Angola and Zambia, by more than a third and 23 countries (including Bangladesh, the Democratic Republic of the Congo and Nepal,

by more than a fifth). The Report also notes that the fastest progress was among many low human development countries.

Over the past decades, Human Development Reports have highlighted the fact that there is no automatic link between income and human development. While income is of key importance in the HDI it remains just one of its four indicators - economic growth does not automatically translate into higher human development. For example, Equatorial Guinea and Chile have similar gross national incomes per capita (in Purchasing Power Parity terms) but different HDI values; by contrast, Gabon and Indonesia have different incomes but similar HDI values.

TABLE 1.1 Similar human development, different income 2014

COUNTRY	HDI	GNI PER CAPITA (PPP US$)
Australia	0.935	42,261
Switzerland	0.930	56,431
South Africa	0.666	12,122
Vietnam	0.666	5,092
Burkina Faso	0.402	1,591
Burundi	0.400	758

Source: UNDP Human Development Report, 2015

TABLE 1.2 Similar income, different human development 2014

COUNTRY	GNI PER CAPITA (PPP US$)	HDI
Canada	42,155	0.913
Bahrain	38,599	0.824
Sri Lanka	9,779	0.757
Indonesia	9,788	0.684
Zimbabwe	1,615	0.509
Haiti	1,669	0.483

Source: UNDP Human Development Report, 2015

Based on information from the annual Credit Suisse databook, the table below illustrates the changes in household wealth by region for 2015 highlighting global disparities further.

Table 1.3 | Change in Household Wealth 2015 by Region

Region	Total Wealth 2015 US$ bn	% of Total	Change in Total Wealth 2013 US$ bn	% Change	% Change in Wealth Per Adult
Africa	2,596	1.03	- 223	- 7.9	- 10.3
Asia Pacific	45,958	18.37	- 5,355	- 10.4	- 12.0
China	22,817	9.1	+ 1494	+ 7.0	+ 5.9
Europe	75,059	30.0	- 10,664	- 12.4	- 12.5
India	3,447	1.38	- 35	- 1.0	- 3.1
Latin America	7,461	2.98	- 1,535	- 17.1	- 18.5
North America	92,806	37.1	+ 3,897	+ 4.4	+ 3.2
World	250,145		12,420	4.7	6.2

Source: James Davies, Rodrigo Lluberas and Anthony Shorrocks, Credit Suisse Global Wealth Databook 2015

FIGURE 1 | EXTENT OF HUMAN DEPRIVATION IN THE WORLD

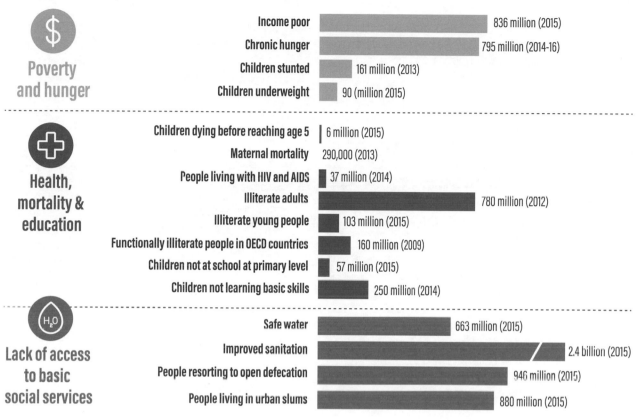

Poverty and hunger

Income poor	836 million (2015)
Chronic hunger	795 million (2014-16)
Children stunted	161 million (2013)
Children underweight	90 (million 2015)

Health, mortality & education

Children dying before reaching age 5	6 million (2015)
Maternal mortality	290,000 (2013)
People living with HIV and AIDS	37 million (2014)
Illiterate adults	780 million (2012)
Illiterate young people	103 million (2015)
Functionally illiterate people in OECD countries	160 million (2009)
Children not at school at primary level	57 million (2015)
Children not learning basic skills	250 million (2014)

Lack of access to basic social services

Safe water	663 million (2015)
Improved sanitation	2.4 billion (2015)
People resorting to open defecation	946 million (2015)
People living in urban slums	880 million (2015)

Source: UN 2015; UNAIDS 2015; UNESCO 2013, 2014

INTERPRETING INFORMATION

Table 1.4 on the page opposite shows data for 21 countries, chosen to highlight a geographical range, as well as high, medium and low levels of human development and a variety of different paths to development.

This data has many important limitations:

- It highlights only just over 10% of the countries represented in the main pages of the UNDP Human Development Report, and only a tiny fraction of the huge range of statistics available for them.

- Statistics such as these are also subject to the weaknesses and inaccuracies inherent in presenting each country as the 'average' of its people.

- The statistics routinely include inaccuracies and bias in the collection and presentation of information.

- Most of the statistics are a snapshot in time and tell a limited amount about short or long term trends or progress (or dis-improvement) in development, particularly in countries such as China or Brazil that are changing fast.

So, although in some ways this data represents our best guess at presenting some key information about development in a single table, it is important to remember what it does not tell us about the world, and to remember that different sets of data – for example those for wealth and health - serve different purposes and tell very different stories about development.

So when exploring information, think about these ideas:

- Use questions to help guide your inquiry; for example, which countries seem to have lower/higher HDI scores?

- Look for patterns and trends, perhaps by ranking countries in one category; for example, which countries seem to have the best record in primary education?

- Look for interesting exceptions to patterns that you might investigate further, for example in the data for child mortality.

- Try focusing on one or two data sets, or just compare a few countries; for example, compare the picture for HDI and GNI in the six African countries.

- Investigate whether two data sets correlate; for example, does good access to safe water match with high life expectancy?

- Use some of the websites at the end of this chapter to find other sets of data that might tell a different story, or add to the picture; for example, what might data on debt or aid tell us?

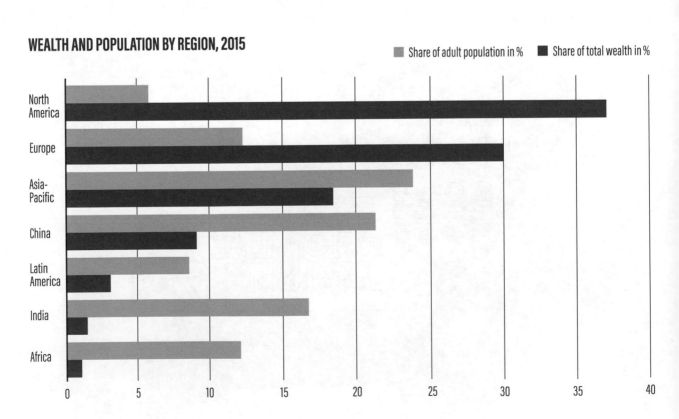

WEALTH AND POPULATION BY REGION, 2015

Legend: Share of adult population in % · Share of total wealth in %

TABLE 1.4 Human development worldwide 2015

Country	Quality of Life HDI value 2014	Gross national Income per capita US$ 2014	Life Expectancy (years) 2014	Maternal Mortality Rate per 100,000 live births 2013	Under 5 Mortality Rate per 1,000 live births 2013	Adult Literacy Rate, % of Adults 15 and over 2005-2013	Gender Inequality Index Rank 2014	% with access to Improved sanitation 2015	Carbon Dioxide Emissions in tonnes per capita, 2011
Norway	0.944	64,992	81.6	5	2.8	-	9	98	9.2
Ireland	0.916	39,568	80.9	8	3.8	-	21	90	7.9
USA	0.915	52,947	79.1	14	6.9	-	55	100	17.0
Canada	0.913	42,155	82.0	7	5.2	-	25	100	14.1
UK	0.907	39,267	80.7	9	4.6	-	39	99	7.1
Japan	0.891	36,927	83.5	5	2.9	-	26	100	9.3
Czech Republic	0.870	26,660	78.6	4	3.6	-	15	99	10.4
Qatar	0.850	123,124	78.2	13	8.2	96.7	116	98	43.9
Saudi Arabia	0.837	52,821	74.3	12	15.5	94.4	56	100	18.7
Argentina	0.836	22,050	76.3	52	13.3	97.9	75	96	4.7
Iran	0.766	15,440	75.4	25	16.8	84.3	114	90	7.8
Mexico	0.756	16,056	76.8	38	14.5	94.2	74	85	3.9
Brazil	0.755	15,175	74.5	44	13.7	91.3	97	83	2.2
Botswana	0.698	16,646	64.5	129	46.6	86.7	106	63	2.4
South Africa	0.666	12,122	57.4	138	43.9	93.7	83	66	9.3
India	0.609	5,497	68.0	174	52.7	62.8	130	40	1.7
Zambia	0.586	3,734	60.1	224	87.4	61.4	132	44	0.2
Bangladesh	0.570	3,191	71.6	176	41.1	58.8	111	61	0.4
Nigeria	0.514	5,341	52.8	814	117.4	51.1	-	29	0.5
Ethiopia	0.442	1,428	64.1	353	64.4	39.0	129	28	0.1
Liberia	0.430	805	60.9	725	71.1	42.9	146	17	0.2
World	0.711	14,301	71.5	216	45.6	81.2		68	4.6

UNDP (2015) Human Development Report 2015: UNICEF and WHO (2015) 25 Years Progress on Sanitation and Drinking Water: 2015 Update and MDG Assessment: UNICEF Database 2015

WHERE THE WEALTH IS

According to a briefing paper published by Oxfam in January 2016 (echoing the analysis and concerns of others including the World Bank, UNDP, UN MDG Annual Reports and the UN High Commissioner for Human Rights):

'The global inequality crisis is reaching new extremes. The richest 1% now have more wealth than the rest of the world combined. Power and privilege is being used to skew the economic system to increase the gap between the richest and the rest. A global network of tax havens further enables the richest individuals to hide US$7.6 trillion.'

- In 2015, just 62 individuals had the same wealth as 3.6 billion people – the bottom half of humanity. This figure is down from 388 individuals as recently as 2010.

- The wealth of the richest 62 people has risen by 44% in the five years since 2010 – that's an increase of more than half a trillion dollars (US$542bn) to US$1.76 trillion.

- Meanwhile, the wealth of the bottom half fell by just over a trillion dollars in the same period – a drop of 41%.

- Since the turn of the century, the poorest half of the world's population has received just 1% of the total increase in global wealth, while half of that increase has gone to the top 1%.

- The average annual income of the poorest 10% of people in the world has risen by less than US$3 each year in almost a quarter of a century. Their daily income has risen by less than a single cent every year.

- Today, a significant majority of the world's population lives in societies that are more unequal today than 20 years ago with the sharpest increases in inequality in economically successful developing countries.

- According to the IMF, the United States was the world's largest economy in 2015 (GDP US$17,968 billion), while Luxemburg had the highest GDP per capita in 2014 (US$116,664) and Burundi the lowest (US$315). The world map opposite, based on countries' share of world GDP, shows vividly the distribution of the world's wealth, now dominated by USA, Western Europe and China.

- China has grown rapidly and has become the second largest world economy and is expected to shortly overtake the US.

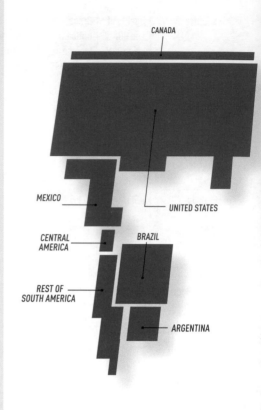

DISTRIBUTION OF WORLD WEALTH (2015)

PERCENT OF TOTAL, WITH QUINTILES OF POPULATION RANKED BY HOUSEHOLD WEALTH

RICHEST (1ST) QUINTILE	93.8%
2ND QUINTILE	4.2%
3RD QUINTILE	1.3%
4TH QUINTILE	0.5%
POOREST (5TH) QUINTILE	0.12%

THE DISTRIBUTION OF WORLD GDP (PPP)

Source: World Development Indicators database, World Bank - 2015

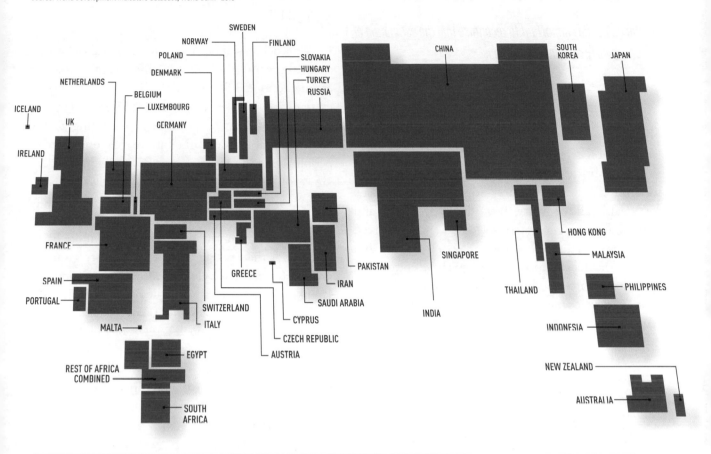

DISTRIBUTION OF WORLD WEALTH AND POPULATION

Source: James Davies, Rodrigo Lluberas and Anthony Shorrocks, Credit Suisse Global Wealth Databook 2015

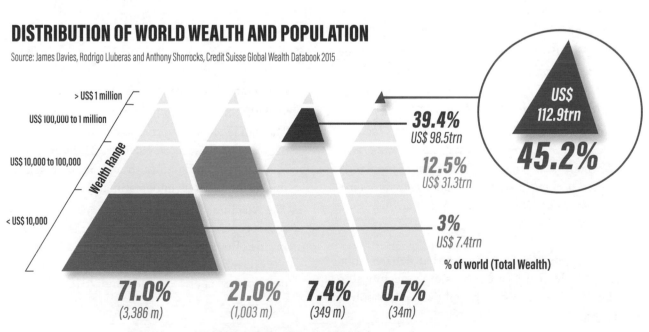

POVERTY AND WEALTH TODAY

'At the outset it is important to recognise that the estimation of global poverty remains contentious'

(Peter Edward and Andy Sumner
The Future of Global Poverty in a Multi-Speed World, 2013:9)

The measurement of poverty, wealth and income distribution remains not only contentious but also highly political; the reasons are, in turn technical, definitional and ultimately ideological. The issue of wealth and poverty, how they have been and continue to be generated, sustained and reinforced has been the stuff of history, politics, economics, and ethics. The debates around the topic have epitomised broader debates about the nature of power, ideology, human development and human rights. The debates have incorporated arguments about:

- **Definition** *(what do we mean by poverty? is it just about income and economics, a quantitative 'poverty line'? Who defines it and how does our definition relate to policy and the politics of change?)*

- **Data collection and measurement** *(survey design; sample selection; data collection and reliability, especially regionally in Africa and Asia; how to access 'hard to obtain' information on wealth)*

- **Aggregating upwards from sample surveys** *(how to scale upwards regionally, nationally and internationally from sample studies; accounting for international currency differences etc.)*

- **Policy and political implications** *(how do wealth and poverty intersect? What is the priority in tackling poverty? How do wealth and poverty affect inequality and its implications for human development? What are the environmental, gender and class dimensions?)*

It is clear from the very outset that debates about poverty and wealth are not simply technical or academic – they are deeply political, philosophical and ethical.

THE 'BOTTOM BILLION' AND WORLD POVERTY

Leaving debates about measurement and definition aside momentarily, it is broadly accepted that an estimated one billion people continue to live in extreme poverty, on less than US$1.25 a day, and one-third of them are children. According to the International Labour Office, more than one-third of people living in poverty (some 375 million) in 2014 are working but are surviving on less than US$1.25 a day; some two-thirds of these are smallholder farmers (many of them women). Members of ethnic- and religious-minority groups are much more likely to be poor than people from the majority group or groups (even in developed countries). Economist Branko Milanovic also argues that despite the progress made in tackling poverty even in the poorest countries, as much as 60% of the difference between real incomes globally can be explained by country of citizenship – where you live definitely matters. Table 1.5 opposite presents an overview of data on poverty worldwide by region for the period 1990 – 2015.

Using the international poverty line of US$1.25 a day:

- The numbers in absolute poverty are equivalent to approximately 1 in every 7 of the earth's inhabitants or just under one fifth of the developing world's population.

- The incidence of poverty has declined from 52% of global population in 1981 to 22% in 2005 and to about 16% in 2015 (although many consider this to be a serious underestimate).

- The decline in poverty varies considerably across regions; led by China, the East Asia and Pacific Region has made dramatic progress, with poverty incidence dropping from 56% to a projected 8% between 1981 and 2015.

Table 1.5 Regional Breakdown of Poverty Incidence and Estimates for 2015

Poverty rate (% of the population living below $1.25 a day)	1990	1999	2008	2015
East Asia and Pacific	56.2	35.6	14.3	7.7
Europe and Central Asia	1.9	3.8	0.5	0.3
Latin America and Caribbean	12.2	11.9	6.5	5.5
Middle East and North Africa	5.8	5.0	2.7	2.7
South Asia	53.8	45.1	36.0	23.9
sub-Saharan Africa	56.5	58.0	47.5	41.2
Total	43.1	34.1	22.4	16.3
Number of poor (millions living below $1.25 a day)				
East Asia and Pacific	926.4	655.6	284.4	159.3
Europe and Central Asia	8.9	17.8	2.2	1.4
Latin America and Caribbean	53.4	60.1	36.8	33.6
Middle East and North Africa	13.0	13.6	8.6	9.7
South Asia	617.3	619.5	570.9	418.7
sub-Saharan Africa	289.7	376.8	386.0	397.2
Total	1908.6	1743.4	1289.0	1019.9

Source: Shaohua Chen and Martin Ravallion, 2010 and World Bank, 2012

- At the other extreme is sub-Saharan Africa where the poverty rate has declined but still remains at 41% in 2015, ensuring the number of Africans in poverty continues to rise.

- The largest numbers of the world's absolute poor are still in South Asia, most of them in India. Despite current debates on the scale of poverty in middle-income countries, it is estimated that over the next two decades, at least the majority of the world's poor will be concentrated in low-income countries.

The more recent UNDP Multi-Dimensional Poverty Index (this identifies those who are experiencing deprivation in a third or more of 10 weighted indicators thus highlighting the extent of their poverty) identified the countries with the highest numbers in such poverty as: Ethiopia 79 million (2011), Nigeria 88 million (2013), Bangladesh 76 million (2011), Pakistan 83 million (2012-13) and China 72 million (2012).

The poverty line of US$1.25 a day represents the benchmark for poverty in the poorest countries in the world. A less basic standard would be at least US$2 per person per day (the median poverty line for all developing countries) or if they were to realise their most basic needs and achieve normal human life expectancy it would need to be nearer to US$5 per day. These latter figures are therefore more appropriate for middle-income countries and regions such as Latin America and much of Eastern Europe. According to the US-based Pew Research Centre, the share of global population living below US$2 per day (at 2005 prices) has fallen to an estimated 15% in 2011, yet the World Bank estimates 2 billion people lived below US$2 per day in 2015. At the next level of low income, it is estimated that 84% of the world's population lives on less than US$20 per day or US$7,300 per year.

As highlighted further below, if human development remains primarily dependent on economic growth (with an assumed 'trickle down' to the poor) and if it is assumed that it is possible to maintain the fastest rate of income growth that the poorest 10% of the world's population have enjoyed over the past few decades (between 1993 and 2008 at an average of 1.29% per annum), it would take 100 years to bring the world's poorest above the poverty line of US$1.25 per day. A growing number of analysts are beginning to point out that US$1.25 per day is insufficient for people to survive on; if the threshold of US$5 were used instead, it would take an estimated 207 years to eradicate such poverty (on this debate, see David Woodward (2015) 'Incrementum ad Absurdum: Global Growth, Inequality and Poverty Eradication in a Carbon-Constrained World', World Economic Review 4: 43-62).

Table 1.6 | 'The Bottom 20'

Country	GDP per capita (2011 PPP$) 2014	% Pop in severe multi-dimensional poverty and year	% Pop. Living on degraded land and at risk environmentally
South Sudan	1,965	69.6 – 2010	-
Senegal	2,170	30.8 – 2014	16.2
Afghanistan	1,884	29.8 – 2010/11	11.0
Cote d'Ivoire	3,171	32.4 – 2011/12	1.3
Malawi	755	29.8 – 2010	19.4
Ethiopia	1,336	67 – 2011	72.3
Gambia	1,608	31.7 – 2013	17.9
Congo (Dem. Rep.)	783	36.7 – 2013/14	0.1
Liberia	850	34.4 – 2013	-
Guinea Bissau	1,362	58.4 – 2006	1.0
Mali	1,589	55.9 – 2012/13	59.5
Mozambique	1,070	44.1 – 2011	1.9
Sierra Leone	1,495	43.9 – 2013	-
Guinea	1,213	49.8 – 2012	0.8
Burkina Faso	1,582	63.8 – 2010	73.2
Burundi	747	48.2 – 2010	18.5
Chad	2,022	67.6 – 2010	45.4
Eritrea	1,157	-	58.8
Central African Republic	584	48.5 – 2010	-
Niger	887	73.5 – 2012	25.0

Gross National Income (GNI) measures the value of the gross domestic product (the market value of all goods and services produced in a country in a given period) together with income received from other countries (e.g. interest and dividends), less similar payments made to other countries.

PPP = Purchasing Power Parity is a measure that indicates what this income will actually buy locally; it equalises local currencies against the cost of a given basket of goods in terms of US dollars.

Human Development Index combines the indicators of life expectancy, educational attainment and income into one composite 'human development' index. The HDI sets a minimum and a maximum for each of 3 dimensions - health, education and living standards - and then shows where each country stands in relation to these.

The education component is measured by mean of years of schooling for adults aged 25 years and expected years of schooling for children of school going age. Life expectancy at birth is calculated using a minimum value of 20 years and maximum value of 83.2 years (the recorded maximum value among countries for the period 1980 to 2010). The decent standard of living dimension is measured by GNI per capita (PPP US$) instead of GDP per capita (PPP US$).

The scores for the three dimensions are then compiled together into a composite index.

Table 1.7 | The Human Development Index – bottom and top 5 countries compared

Source: Human Development Report 2015, UNDP

Country	HDI	Life Expectancy at Birth (years)	Mean Years of Schooling (Years)	Expected Years of Schooling (Years)	GNI Per Capita US$ 2014
BOTTOM 5					
Burundi	.400	56.7	10.1	2.7	758
Chad	.392	51.6	7.4	1.9	2,085
Eritrea	.391	63.7	4.1	3.9	1,130
Central African Republic	.350	50.7	7.2	4.2	581
Niger	.348	61.4	5.4	1.5	908
TOP 5					
Norway	.944	81.6	12.6	17.5	64,982
Australia	.935	82.4	13.0	20.2	42,261
Switzerland	.930	83.0	12.8	15.8	56,431
Denmark	.923	80.2	12.7	18.7	44,025
Netherlands	.922	81.6	11.9	17.9	45,435

IS 'DEVELOPMENT' SUSTAINABLE?

The future character and direction of development based upon the (apparently often contradictory) patterns and trends of the past three decades is now a matter of intense debate and disagreement. While those who argue that, as before, economic growth remains the driving force for human development remain dominant (albeit with the promise of greater emphasis on those 'left behind'), their analysis and strategies have been the subject of intense criticism from a variety of perspectives and sources.

Essentially, the critique of 'economic growth led' human development boils down to a core argument – whatever the evidence from the recent past, this model of human progress is no longer sustainable as it is rapidly reaching its limits in terms of its environmental and human costs as well as its own internal contradictions. While there are many divergent critical views of the dominant (Western) model of growth, a number of common themes emerge:

- While development based on economic growth has led to very significant progress for a majority of people (including many of the poor and poorest), it continues to leave far too many behind and is based on a level of (growing) inequality that is unacceptable morally, economically and politically and that threatens to undermine the progress achieved to date.

  This view is shared to a greater or lesser degree by a very wide range of commentators and organisations from the World Bank and UNDP to UNCTAD and NGOs as well as independent commentators and analysts. It has long been a core strand of critique from a majority of analysts from the developing world.

  The critique is succinctly expressed by Oxfam in its analysis of the harmful consequences of inequality *Even It Up: Time to End Extreme Inequality*:

  'Extreme economic inequality has exploded across the world in the last 30 years, making it one of the biggest economic, social and political challenges of our time. Age-old inequalities on the basis of gender, caste, race and religion – injustices in themselves – are exacerbated by the growing gap between the haves and the have-nots.' (2014:8)

- The economic-growth model is rapidly reaching (many argue it has already reached and exceeded) its environmental and resource limits and is no longer sustainable. As our measurement and understanding of the impact of climate change and related processes rapidly expands, so too has the recognition that the planet simply cannot sustain the demands placed on its resources and capacity by the dominant model of economic growth. The concept of Earth Overshoot Day captures the reality neatly; it marks the day when humanity has exhausted nature's budget for that year after which we are in 'overshoot' and in 2016 that date was August 8th. From that date onwards we are borrowing resources from future generations with little prospect of repayment.

  The issue of climate change and sustainability was highlighted by the International Panel on Climate Change in 2014:

  'Continued emission of greenhouse gases will cause further warming and long-lasting changes in all components of the climate system, increasing the likelihood of severe, pervasive and irreversible impacts for people and ecosystems. Limiting climate change would require substantial and sustained reductions in greenhouse gas emissions which, together with adaptation, can limit climate change risks.'

  IPCC 5TH SYNTHESIS REPORT 2014: 56

'Let's assume that we can maintain the fastest rate of income growth that the poorest 10% of the world's population have ever enjoyed over the past few decades. That was between 1993 and 2008 ...during that period their incomes increased at a rate of 1.29% each year.

So how long will it take to eradicate poverty if we extrapolate this trend? 100 years. That's what it will require to bring the world's poorest above the standard poverty line of US$1.25/day... as if the 100-year timeline isn't disappointing enough, it gets worse. A growing number of scholars are beginning to point out that US$1.25/day... is actually not adequate for people to survive on. In reality, if people are to meet their most basic needs and achieve normal human life expectancy, they need closer to $5/day. How long would it take to eradicate poverty at this more accurate line? 207 years.

Jason Hickel, London School of Economics, Guardian, March 30th, 2015

'People perceive – correctly – that their individual actions will not make a decisive difference in the atmospheric concentration of CO_2; by 2010, a poll found that "while recycling is widespread in America and 73 percent of those polled are paying bills online in order to save paper," only four percent had reduced their utility use and only three percent had purchased hybrid cars. Given a hundred years, you could conceivably change lifestyles enough to matter - but time is precisely what we lack.'

Environmental activist Bill McKibben Rolling Stone magazine, July 19th 2012

'Those least responsible for climate change are worst affected by it.'

Indian biologist Vandana Shiva (2008) Soil Not Oil: Environmental Justice in an Age of Climate Crisis

- The progress in human development in recent years, even in circumstances of very limited or no economic growth, has illustrated that human development can be 'delinked' from economic growth and is by no means dependent on it. Our priority focus should change from growth to directly delivering human development per se.

Despite the development and aid pessimists (and much popular opinion) very significant and life-changing progress in the basics of human development has occurred, especially in the last three decades, even in many of the world's poorest countries. As highlighted earlier in this chapter, the number of countries in the very high human development category between 1990 and 2014 increased (as did the population in general in that group), the number of countries in the low human development category fell from 62 to 43 and the population numbers in that group fell from 3.2 billion to 1.2 billion.

The view was outlined by World Bank economist Charles Kenny in his book *Getting Better: Why Global Development Is Succeeding - And How We Can Improve the World Even More* (2012:4):

'While Africa and many other parts of the planet have lagged behind in terms of economic growth, they have also seen unprecedented improvement in health and education, gender equality, security and human rights ...too narrow a focus on one indicator of success - income - has blinded many to these broader advances and that is a potential tragedy.'

- While many traditional divisions and patterns remain, the 'old international world order' is changing with the rise of Brazil, Russia, India, China and others (the BRICS) and a new 'multipolar' world is taking shape with significant potential results - the traditional 'North-South' divide, while by no means eliminated, is now more complex.

'One of the central questions concerning 21st Century world order is how the machinery of global governance will change as a result of the economic and political decline of the United States and Western Europe and the emergence of influential states from the Global South, such as China, India, Brazil and South Africa ... which challenge the hierarchical and Northern-led model of global governance. The formal organizations of the post-1945 order, the Bretton Woods system and the United Nations, are the main focus of their collective efforts to increase developing countries' participation in key decision-making structures.'

MARCO VIEIRA, UNIVERSITY OF BIRMINGHAM 2011

- New political patterns and trends are challenging traditional models with new technologies playing an important role in this - popular movements worldwide threaten the 'old order' of the 'development project' as conceived post 1945. Overall, the world is far less 'traditionally' oppressed, more literate, educated, healthy, urbanised, informed and connected, with greater expectations and demands, yet it remains fractured, unequal and impatient - the *'political'* in development remains central.

Conclusion

Throughout such debates a constant theme emerges - despite ongoing change, core human 'development' challenges remain - reducing and eradicating poverty; delivering basic needs in healthcare, education, food, water and sanitation; struggling for equality at all levels and challenging inequality; confronting and resolving conflict and building democracy through supporting communities worldwide in holding states and institutions accountable.

READING

Human Development Report 2015: *Work for Human Development*, New York, UNDP

Richard Wilkinson and Kate Pickett (2009) *The Spirit Level: Why More Equal Societies Almost Always Do Better,* London, Penguin.

Amartya Sen (1999) *Development as Freedom*, Oxford University Press

Michel Chossudovsky (2003) *The Globalization of Poverty and the New World Order*, Ontario, Global Outlook

Wayne Ellwood (2015) *NoNonsense Globalization: Buying and Selling the World,* Oxford, New Internationalist

Maggie Black (2015, 3rd edition) *NoNonsense International Development: Myth and Reality,* Oxford, New Internationalist

Angus Deaton (2013) *The Great Escape: health, wealth, and the origins of inequality,* Princeton university Press

Arturo Escobar (2012 ed.) *Encountering Development: The Making and Unmaking of the Third World,* Princeton University Press

MORE INFORMATION AND DEBATE

www.fao.org/publications/sofa – Food and Agriculture Organisation *State of World Food Insecurity* (the 2015 Report provides a detailed global overview and an assessment of progress on International hunger 'targets'; the 2016 report provides a detailed overview and assessment of climate change, agriculture and food security adaptation and mitigation strategies)

www.socialwatch.org/publications – Instituto del Tercer Mundo *Social Watch Report* (a Third World perspective released every two years– the 2014 report has a revealing essay on 'eradicating poverty by lowering the bar')

www.hdr.undp.org – UNDP *Human Development Report* (annual since 1990)

www.wdronline.worldbank.org – World Bank *World Development Report* (annual since 1970)

www.unicef.org/sowc – UNICEF *State of the World's Children Report* (annual since 1996)

www.freedomhouse.org – Freedom House *Freedom in the World* (annual since 2005)

www.credit-suisse.com/researchinstitute – Credit Suisse Global Wealth Report (annual since 2009)

HUMAN DEVELOPMENT: A SNAPSHOT

RECENT PROGRESS

ONGOING DEPRIVATION

HUMAN DEVELOPMENT

Between 1990 and 2014 the number of countries with very high human development rose from 12 to 46.

In the same period the number of countries with low human development fell from 62 to 43.

In 2012, the number of people living in low human development was 1,185 million; this figure is expected to increase to 1,693 million by 2030.

LIFE EXPECTANCY

In 2014, life expectancy at birth in the countries with highest levels of human development had reached 80.5 years and for countries with high human development, 75.1

In 2014, life expectancy at birth in the countries with lowest levels of human development was 60.6 while in sub-Saharan Africa is was 58.5 and in the Central African Republic just 50.7.

HEALTH

The child mortality rate fell by more than half while under-five deaths fell from 12.7 million to 6 million.

Between 1990 and 2013, the number of children affected by stunting declined from 257 million to 161 million - 37%.

11 children under 5 years of age die every minute while an estimated 33 mothers die every hour. The highest maternal mortality ratio is in sub-Saharan Africa (510 deaths per 100,000 live births), followed by South Asia (190).

EDUCATION

Between 2009 – 2014, the attendance ratio for those eligible for primary school had risen to 85% for males and 83% for females (for secondary school, 62% and 58%). In the same period, the youth (15-24) literacy rate had reached 93% for males and 89% for females.

While the world average literacy rate was 82.1% for those aged 15 years+, in countries with the lowest levels of human development it was just 57.1%. The number of illiterate adults worldwide was 780 million in 2012.

If current trends persist, the world is off-track to reach primary and secondary education for all by 2030.

Sources

UNDP Human Development Report 2015
WHO World Health Statistics 2015
UNICEF State of the World's Children 2016

UNDESA World's Women: Trends and Statistics 2015
Amnesty International Annual Report 2014
UNHCR Global Trends Report 2015

Institute on Statelessness and Inclusion, The World's Stateless, 2014
Freedom House Freedom in the World Report 2016
UNESCO Education for All 2000-2015 Achievements and Challenges

INCOME

In 2015, 62 individuals had the same wealth as 3.6 billion people – the bottom half of humanity. The wealth of the richest 62 people has risen by 44% since 2010.

Since 2010, the wealth of the bottom half of humanity fell by 41%. Since the turn of the century, the poorest half of world population received just 1% of the total increase in global wealth while half of that increase has gone to the top 1%.

FOOD AND NUTRITION

Estimates of the number of people undernourished globally suggest a decline from 1,009 million in 1990/1992 to 795 million today.

Approximately 10% of the world's people remain undernourished.

POVERTY

The number of people living in extreme poverty (<US$1.25 per day) fell from an estimated 1.9 billion in 1990 to an estimated 1 billion in 2011 with a further 165 million lifted out of such poverty as of 2015.

1 billion people continue to live in absolute poverty; just under one fifth of the developing world's population; one-third of them are children.

CIVIL AND POLITICAL RIGHTS

102 of the world's 195 states and territories have completely abolished the death penalty. More than 970 million people – 62% of them in low and lower middle-income countries, 12% in upper middle-income countries and 26% in high-income countries – engage in volunteer work each year.

Despite the 1987 the UN Convention Against Torture signed by 159 states, 141 states still use torture. For the first time since 1945, the number of forcibly displaced people worldwide reached 50 million with an estimated 15 million people deemed to be 'stateless'. 78 countries criminalise sexual acts between adults of the same sex.

WOMEN

By 2015, some 119 countries had passed laws on domestic violence, 125 had laws on sexual harassment and 52 had laws on marital rape. Women's representation at lower or single houses of parliament has increased from 12% in 1997 to 22% in 2015; the number of female Heads of State or Government has increased from 12% in 1995 to 19% in 2015.

In 29 countries in Africa and the Middle East, more than 125 million girls and women alive today have been subjected to female genital mutilation. In nearly a third of developing countries, laws do not guarantee the same inheritance rights for women and men, and in an additional half of countries discriminatory customary practices against women persist.

'Today's 'developers' are like the alchemists of old who vainly tried to transmute lead into gold, in the firm belief that they would then have the key to wealth. The alchemists disappeared once it was realized that true wealth came from elsewhere – from people and from trade. When will we realize that well-being does not come from growth?'

GILBERT RIST (2008) HISTORY OF DEVELOPMENT: FROM WESTERN ORIGINS TO GLOBAL FAITH

CHAPTER 2

DEVELOPMENT – THE STORY OF AN IDEA

TONY DALY, M. SATISH KUMAR AND COLM REGAN

This chapter explores current thinking and debates about the nature and scope of development. It sketches out the evolution and definitions of the term from early world views via colonialism, the decolonisation process and the emergence of the 'age of development' following the Second World War. Modernisation theory, dependency theory and broader 'Third World' critiques of the theory and practice of development are also explored and debated. The era of the MDGs and SDGs and the associated critiques and challenges is reviewed. Debates surrounding divergent definitions of development and key phrases such as 'Third World' are also analysed.

KEYWORDS:

NATURE AND HISTORY OF DEVELOPMENT; DEVELOPMENT DEFINITIONS AND DEBATES; GENDER; ENVIRONMENT; HUMAN RIGHTS; **HUMAN DEVELOPMENT**; MODERNISATION THEORY; **DEPENDENCY THEORY**; THIRD WORLD PERSPECTIVES; SUSTAINABLE DEVELOPMENT GOALS

INTRODUCTION

The half century between 1950 and 2000 has been characterised by many as the 'age of development', one, it is now argued, that has been superseded by the 'age of globalisation' and the era of sustainable development. In the aftermath of World War II, the re-building of Europe, the rise of the United States and the beginning of the process of decolonisation, international development became a dominant focus in international relations. This vision and agenda is perhaps best captured in the 1949 inaugural address of US President Harry S. Truman who proposed:

'We must embark on a bold new program for making the benefits of our scientific advances and industrial progress available for the improvement and growth of underdeveloped areas. The old imperialism - exploitation for foreign profit - has no place in our plans. What we envisage is a program of development based on the concept of democratic fair dealing ... More than half the people of the world are living in conditions approaching misery. Their food is inadequate. They are victims of disease. Their economic life is primitive and stagnant. Their poverty is a handicap and a threat both to them and to more prosperous areas. For the first time in history, humanity possesses the knowledge and the skill to relieve the suffering of these people.'

The decades that followed were characterised by the Cold War (with contrasting views of, and strategies for 'underdeveloped' countries); the establishment of the institutions and structures of the United Nations (especially those directly addressing development); widespread decolonisation; the eventual collapse of the Soviet Union and the opening up of Eastern Europe. While, in development terms, much was achieved in many developing countries (in health, literacy, basic needs and education), the fundamental divide and inequalities that characterise the world continued to grow and deepen.

In compiling the second edition of the Development Dictionary in 2010, editor Wolfgang Sachs insisted that today:

'The idea of development stands like a ruin in the intellectual landscape. Delusion and disappointment, failures and crimes, have been the steady companions of development and they tell a common story: it did not work. Moreover, the historical conditions which catapulted the idea into prominence have vanished; development has become outdated. But, above all, the hopes and desires which made the idea fly are now exhausted; development has grown obsolete. Nevertheless, the ruin stands there and still dominates the scenery like a landmark...'

Despite such dismissals, development remains a key frame of reference in international relations as well as in the popular imagination and it also forms a core element in the architecture of international cooperation. Despite the fact that 'pro-poor' development is regularly deemed to have failed (especially when viewed from the perspective of the poor) it continues to be financed, debated, measured, monitored and evaluated – development remains big business!

THREE KEY PERSPECTIVES

In the course of the past six decades, the idea of development has been expanded to encompass a great variety of perspectives and emphases, many of which are explored below but at this stage, three particular perspectives are worthy of note – the 'feminist'; the 'ecological' and the 'human rights'.

The feminist perspective has been outlined by many commentators, few more authoritatively than Gita Sen and Caren Grown in 1988:

'The perspective of poor and oppressed women provides a unique and powerful vantage point from which we can examine the effects of development programmes and

strategies ... if the goals of development include improved standards of living, removal of poverty, access to dignified employment, and reduction in societal inequality, then it is quite natural to start with women. They constitute the majority of the poor, the underemployed and the economically and socially disadvantaged in most societies. Furthermore, women suffer from additional burdens imposed by gender-based hierarchies and subordination.'

The environmental or ecological perspective has always paralleled the 'development story' but, in more recent decades it has become intrinsically central to it and vice versa. This view was elegantly outlined by Indian activist Vandana Shiva in 1989:

'Among the hidden costs (of development) are the new burdens created by ecological destruction, costs that are invariably heavier for women, both in the North and the South. It is hardly surprising, therefore, that as GNP rises, it does not necessarily mean that either wealth or welfare increase proportionately ... In actual fact, there is less water, less fertile soil, less genetic wealth as a result of the development process.'

Vandana Shiva (1989) Staying Alive: Development, Ecology and Women in Micheline R. Ishay, (ed., 1997) The Human Rights Reader, Routledge, London

In more recent years, the interface between human rights and human development has come more to the fore with significant implications for both. This perspective was coherently outlined by the UNDP Human Development Report for 2000:

'If human development focuses on the enhancement of the capabilities and freedoms that the members of a community enjoy, human rights represent the claims that individuals have on the conduct of individual and collective agents and on the design of social arrangements to facilitate or secure these capabilities and freedoms.'

One area in which there is almost unanimous agreement is that the definition of development is both controversial and contested – there is little agreement as to its precise definition and meaning with different groups emphasising different dimensions at different times. For those who argue that we now live in a 'post development age', it is time to abandon the very concept of development itself while for others in the era of the Sustainable Development Goals, it is far too soon to write its obituary.

The remainder of this chapter explores the debate.

EARLY IDEAS ABOUT DEVELOPMENT

Today, development is strongly associated with the idea of change but this has not always been so. The Ancient Greeks (from whom much of the West's thinking springs, especially from the philosophy of Aristotle) argued that all things have an essential and inherent nature and that life is a matter of cycles; all things that are born and grow will also fade and die, in a perpetual series of new beginnings followed by decline and decay. Arabic philosophers argued similarly. Gilbert Rist, in his influential History of Development (2008), argues that there are three important links or continuities between modern development thinking and historical philosophy:

– One, 'development' is seen as natural and necessary.
– Two, linking development with nature and the natural.
– Three, the links implied between science and myth (development as scientific progress but also as a religion).

However, with the rise of the Judaeo-Christian tradition, the idea of a God intervening in human history became crucial. This implied a couple of key ideas which are still with us, and which are still hotly debated.

- First, there is a universal history for all humankind *(is there?)*
- Second, history is a historical progression from creation to the end of time *(is it?)*
- Third, this is God's plan, unalterable by humans *(is this true?)*

This increasingly linear view of history (and of development) was strengthened further during the 17th and 18th centuries, particularly by the social evolutionism of the Enlightenment. In general, social evolutionism argued that the progress of civilisation is a 'one-way street' that all societies follow, from hunter gatherers to mid-nineteenth century England and Western Europe. Comparing societies with each other, scientists concluded that the march of civilisation could be divided into a series of sequential steps. The assumption that all human cultures develop along a single or unilinear path is illustrated, for example, by the ideas of American Anthropologist Lewis Henry Morgan who identified a series of steps from *'savagery and barbarism'* to *'civilisation'* with each society moving from step to step over time.

COLONIALISM AND DEVELOPMENT

The high point of colonisation occurred at the end of the 19th century spearheaded primarily by Britain, France and Germany with many different views and policies as regards the role and development of their colonies. While some liberal economists questioned the costs and the supposed benefits of having colonies, the armed forces, the merchants and the missionaries supported colonisation in their own interests.

From the beginning, colonisation was characterised by ambiguity - on the one hand, colonies were there to be exploited in the interests of Europe but, against this, colonisation was also seen to be a moral responsibility of Europe – the famous *'White Man's Burden'*. The colonisers offered a vision of worldwide 'civilisation' for all and argued that there

was common cause between coloniser and colonised. However, the reality of colonialism pivoted around resource, economic, political and military agendas while intellectual and popular commentators argued that the 'development' of a nation (especially 'undeveloped' nations) paralleled that of human life and was, thus, inevitable and a moral duty.

This remained the situation until the end of World War I in 1918 when Germany lost its colonies to Britain and France. In this context, the League of Nations was founded (the precursor to the United Nations) with security and the settlement of disputes by peaceful means as its primary goals (it also had a number of other development related goals). While the United States did not join the League, it was very influential in 'redefining and reshaping' colonialism especially in the creation of a 'mandate system' where some countries were deemed ready for independence; where others could achieve it in the future and where a third group were seen to have little prospect of independence. Article 22 of the founding articles of the League stated that in territories which ceased to be under the sovereignty of states, inhabited by peoples:

> *'...not yet able to stand by themselves under the strenuous conditions of the modern world', the tutelage of such peoples 'should be entrusted to advanced nations' and that the character of the mandate should differ 'according to the stage of the development of the people...'*

Thus, the concept of 'stages of development' was introduced, justifying a classification system with 'developed' nations at the top of the ladder. The language used also exhibited a strong humanitarian and religious tone with words such as *'civilisation'*, *'material and moral well-being'*, and *'social progress'*, *'sacred trust'* legitimising western intervention in other regions and countries.

Colonisation meant not only taking control of people and places but also of peoples' minds – in the West as much as elsewhere. It contributed significantly to the emergence of ways of thinking and a language about development which has lasted to the present time. It created the illusion of a world united and it also created the basis for the emergence of the Third World, although that term only emerged later (see below).

THE 'AGE OF DEVELOPMENT' BEGINS

The period following World War II heralded the modern age of development – one that had much in common with the past while also rejecting some of its key characteristics (e.g. its racial overtones and much of its social evolutionism) and creating much of the architecture of international development today. The politics and ideology of the world were fundamentally reshaped following 1945. The Allied Powers sought to ensure that many of the conditions which gave rise to WWII – mass unemployment, protectionist policies, competitive currency devaluations, collapse of commodity prices – would not recur.

Pre-eminent among the creations of the Allies were the International Bank for Reconstruction and Development (better known as the World Bank) and the International Monetary Fund (IMF), both located, tellingly, in New York, representing growing US hegemony internationally. The Bank and the Fund were to be specialised agencies within the United Nations (established in 1945), much like the Food and Agriculture Organisation (FAO) or the International Labour Organisation (ILO), located in Rome and Geneva respectively. The UN was to be the focal point for international economic management and the World Bank was set up to promote economic growth and development. At that stage, no distinction was made between these two closely related ideas.

By now, the idea of development was inextricably linked with economics, an economics that assumed economic growth was the fundamental necessity. Over time, the World Bank and the IMF became the dominant power brokers as regards development and, unlike the UN (which is run on a one-country, one-vote system), they were run on a one-dollar, one-vote system. In this way, the Bank and the Fund came to represent powerful financial interests and the development role of the UN was steadily transferred to them.

It was against this background that the idea of 'development' (and 'underdevelopment') came to be defined, most notably in the inaugural speech of President Truman in 1949 (referred to earlier). Truman's speech was important for a number of reasons - firstly, the adjective 'underdeveloped' appears for the first time (meaning economically 'backward') in an official document and subsequently the idea of 'underdevelopment' was introduced. These new words actually altered the way the world was seen. Development was now something one agent could do to another, whereas underdevelopment was apparently a 'natural' cause-less state. This obscured historical processes which created the conditions of development and underdevelopment, a view that was contested by many critics (for example, Guyanese historian and activist Walter Rodney in his influential book How Europe Underdeveloped Africa, 1972). The old dichotomy between coloniser and colonised was now replaced by that between 'developed and underdeveloped'. The latter group of countries could achieve the development status of the former through adopting a set of strategies and institutions characteristic of 'developed' states.

The key to prosperity and happiness for all would be achieved through increased production, measured by the new standard of Gross National Product (GNP). Later, broader and more 'sensitive' indices of development were created (see Chapter 1). The consequences for newly independent states were that they now had to follow the path of development mapped out for them by others – that of western capitalism or, alternatively, the communist Soviet Union. The 'age of development' created a situation where countries were no longer, in the words of Gilbert Rist '... *African, Latin American or Asian (not to speak of Bambera, Shona, Berber, Quechua, Aymara, Balinese or Mongol), they were now simply 'underdeveloped'.*

Predictably, given the nature and politics of the anti-colonial struggle in many parts of the world, this view of development and of recent world history was rejected as well as its constructions of 'development' and 'underdevelopment'.

DEVELOPMENT AS 'MODERNISATION'

With the rise of these new economic and political institutions and world order (post 1945 and especially in the context of the emergent 'Cold War' precisely at the time when the field of 'development' was taking shape), one of the most influential theories, claiming to provide a universal model of development applicable to all countries, was that of economist Walt Rostow in his 1960 Stages of Economic Growth, tellingly sub-titled A Non-Communist Manifesto. Rostow argued that all societies developed through a series of stages beginning with stage one (a traditional society), via stages two (preconditions for take-off – based on a reading of earlier European history), three (when societies integrated 'growth' as part of the habits and structures of that society), four ('the drive to maturity' when a society gears itself to 'efficient' modern production) to a final stage five (that of high mass consumption), when that society became 'developed'.

A central criticism of Rostow's theory was that it was based on the particular case of a limited number of Western economies and was not only inappropriate to other societies but was fundamentally inapplicable. It was also heavily criticised for failing to adequately integrate the realities of colonialism and imperialism, historical realities that not many states could emulate. A third criticism was that not all societies value the accumulation of material goods equally or indeed seek to establish an age of high mass consumption and yet these are deemed to be fundamental to development.

Nevertheless, Rostow was a product of his time. Ten years prior to his 'take-off' thesis the report prepared by the United Nations group of experts tasked with designing concrete policies and measures 'for the economic development of underdeveloped countries' stated:

> *'There is a sense in which rapid economic progress is impossible without painful adjustments. Ancient philosophies have to be scrapped; old social institutions have to disintegrate; bonds of cast, creed and race have to burst; and large numbers of persons who cannot keep up with progress have to have their expectations of a comfortable life frustrated. Very few communities are willing to pay the full price of economic progress.'*

United Nations, Department of Social and Economic Affairs 1951: 15

Rostow's theory was but one in a school of thought that viewed development as 'modernisation' in the mode and manner of western 'capitalist' societies. For example, US political scientist David Apter offered a political analysis linking democracy and good government with modernisation; while US psychologist David McClelland argued that modernisation is impossible in a society that does not value free enterprise and success; while Israeli sociologist Shmuel Eisenstadt argued that:

> *'Historically, modernisation is the process of change towards those types of social, economic, and political systems that have developed in Western Europe and North America from the seventeenth century to the nineteenth and have then spread to other European countries and in the nineteenth and twentieth centuries to the South American, Asian, and African continents.'*

S. Eisenstadt 1966, Modernisation, Protest and Change

Stages theory and modernisation theory were ultimately criticised for being theories about the 'westernisation' of the world rather than about development per se; for emphasising capitalism and western values over others and for the maintenance of western dominance worldwide. Logically and inevitably a range of counter-theories emerged, the most important of them being 'Dependency theory'.

DEVELOPMENT AND DEPENDENCY - THE THIRD WORLD CRITIQUE

The anti-colonialist and anti-imperialist movements that emerged worldwide post 1945 gave rise to many detailed critiques of western theories of growth, development and modernisation as being essentially about maintaining and strengthening western capitalist dominance. Forged in the furnace of political and armed struggle, they highlighted the violence and inequities that western development generated and imposed on others. They challenged the core idea that Third World countries could (or should) follow free market models as 'benign' or level playing fields in which developing countries could compete. They also highlighted the need for strong state intervention in support of development and were, in many fundamental ways, the intellectual and practical opposites of western modernisation theory. The intellectuals and activists who promoted these theories gradually came to focus on US policy and were routinely referred to as 'Third Worldists'.

Dependency Theory emerged from North American Marxists and Latin American intellectuals during the 1950s as a critique of modernisation – it represented a general school of thought followed by different intellectuals from a variety of disciplines and countries and was never set out as a coherent theory. They studied real history in concrete circumstances with countries being treated as part of an international structure and not as individual entities. They viewed colonialism and imperialism as processes in which 'things fall apart' (echoing Nigerian writer Chinua Achebe in his 1958 novel of the same name) and where development is not contrasted with tradition but rather 'underdevelopment' and, contrary to commentators such as Rostow, the expansion of western values

and institutions does not produce development but rather its opposite - underdevelopment. In the words of economist Andre Gunder Frank:

> *'...historical research demonstrates that contemporary underdevelopment is in large part the historical product of past and continuing economic and other relations between the satellite underdeveloped and the now developed metropolitan countries. Furthermore, these relations are an essential part of the capitalist system on a world scale as a whole.'*
>
> Andre Gunder Frank (1966) *The Development of Underdevelopment, New York, Monthly Review Press*

Dependency theorists also argued that the development of young or emerging economies required their withdrawal from the structure of exploitation that existed worldwide and in many cases the adoption of socialism rather than capitalism. Since capitalism was inextricably intertwined with colonialism and imperialism, then anti-colonialism needed to adopt socialism – this analysis was also fuelled significantly by the realities and ideologies of the Cold War.

As with modernisation theory, there were significant problems associated with dependency theory. The wealth of the developed countries was not solely due to colonial exploitation, but was also due to state regulation and the growth of domestic markets. Also, it did not pay sufficient attention to the cultural aspects of development or to the ecological consequences of treating industrialisation as necessary for collective well-being. In this way it did not offer an idea of development based on assumptions fundamentally different to those of modernisation.

But it became a strong component of a growing Third Worldist critique of western ideas and practices around the 'development idea' and it strengthened the view that underdevelopment was not a 'natural' state but could actually be created and, in the world of the 1960s and 70s, was being created by the West (for an excellent introduction to this literature and analysis, see Majid Rahnema and Victoria Bawtree eds. 1997, *The Post Development Reader*, London, Zed Press and Vijay Prashad 2012 *The Poorer Nations: A Possible History of the Global South*, Verso).

In the African context, Guyanese historian and activist Walter Rodney offered a scorching critique of colonialism and its impact on development in his How Europe Underdeveloped Africa (1972) in which he argued that European powers deliberately and systematically exploited and underdeveloped Africa and offered a new African insight into the issue. He wrote:

> *'African development is possible only on the basis of a radical break with the international capitalist system, which has been the principal agency of underdevelopment of Africa over the last five centuries.'*
>
> Walter Rodney (1983) How Europe Underdeveloped Africa (preface)

As a trained psychiatrist, the French philosopher and revolutionary Franz Fanon had taken a different view based on his own Algerian experience. The colonial state was an implant that imposed itself on the colonised society by restructuring social arrangements and reimaging the past to fit its own imperial agendas. Natives were actively alienated from their historical experiences and new social divisions were put in place. Moreover, Fanon believed that Africans should no longer be tempted by development by European design or as inspiration; his was a radical confrontation with the Western model of progress.

> *'THE BASIC CONFRONTATION WHICH SEEMED TO BE COLONIALISM VERSUS ANTI-COLONIALISM, INDEED CAPITALISM VERSUS SOCIALISM, IS ALREADY LOSING ITS IMPORTANCE. WHAT MATTERS TODAY, THE ISSUE WHICH BLOCKS THE HORIZON, IS THE NEED FOR A REDISTRIBUTION OF WEALTH. HUMANITY WILL HAVE TO ADDRESS THIS QUESTION, NO MATTER HOW DEVASTATING THE CONSEQUENCES MAY BE.'*
>
> Franz Fanon (1961) The Wretched of the Earth

'DEVELOPMENT' REDEFINED

The 1980s and 1990s witnessed the emergence of a strong challenge to the dominant economic models and analyses of development through what later became defined as the human development approach (known more popularly for its measurement index – the Human Development Index (HDI) and the annual Human Development Report). This approach is associated primarily with the United Nations Development Programme (UNDP) and the work of economists Mahbub Ul Haq and Amartya Sen. The first Human Development Report published in 1990 made explicit its approach and values base *'to shift the focus of development economics from national income accounting to people centred policies'* and its opening lines stated: *'People are the real wealth of a nation'* (United Nations Development Programme 1990); people were not simply the *'beneficiaries'* of economic and social progress in a society, but were active agents of development and change.

Within the then dominant economic model, characteristic of the vast majority of 'official' documents and policies whether from the World Bank, the IMF, the World Trade Organisation or many bi-lateral governmental aid organisations, the purpose of 'development' was to stimulate growth and from that 'growth' benefits would 'trickle down' to society. The primary purpose of the state should be to provide support and an *'enabling environment'* for that growth; other areas of focus - social, cultural or environmental issues - should be of only secondary importance. The economy, rather than human beings, occupied centre stage and while much (if not all) alternative academic and NGO analysis vehemently disagreed with this model, orthodox development theory and practice continued to promote it. In contrast, the approach advocated by the human development perspective fundamentally challenged this view and offered a much broader agenda - a comprehensive approach to all aspects of development, a set of policy priorities, tools of analysis and measurement and a conceptual framework.

The foundations of the human development approach were rooted in the approach of Indian economist Amartya Sen who, in 1989, defined human development as a process of enlarging people's *functionings and capabilities to function, the range of things that a person could do and be in her life'* later expressed in terms of expanding 'choices'. Sen went on to argue (in 1999) that key *freedoms are not only the primary ends of development; they are also among its principal means'*. Development should be seen as a process of expanding such freedoms. Development, he argued, requires the removal of poverty, tyranny, lack of economic opportunities, social deprivation, neglect of public services, and the machinery of repression and, additionally, *'the formation of values and the emergence and evolution of social ethics are also part of the process of development'*.

The concept of human development became far more complex, extensive and political/social than previous dominant models; development became about people being able to live in freedom and dignity; being able to exercise choice, pursue an engaged and creative life. Priorities in development thus came to focus on removing limitations such as illiteracy, ill-health, and lack of access to - and control over - resources, as well as increasing participation in the community, in decision-making

and in strengthening the ability to challenge social, cultural and political oppression. In 1995, the UNDP declared that *'one of the defining movements of the 20th century has been the relentless struggle for gender equality, led mostly by women, but supported by growing numbers of men. . . Moving toward gender equality is not a technocratic goal – it is a political process'*.

The era of the predominance of economic models of development had come to an end.

THE ERA OF DEVELOPMENT GOALS: FROM MDGS TO SDGS

Since 2000, much of the debate on development has been dominated by, initially, the Millennium Development Goals and, subsequently, the Sustainable Development Goals (see below). While neither amount to a theory of development, they both have adopted much from previous ideas and understandings. Progress in human development has been impressive, especially since 1990, and much of this has been attributed (not without disagreement) to the MDG agenda. While that agenda was framed to focus direct aid interventions on a range of human development indicators, it also recognised the broader international context of development. The MDGs have been both praised and criticised not simply for their content, choices, measurement and assessment but also as a broad framework for advancing human development in a world characterised by extreme and sustained inequality and climate change.

Criticisms have included the following:

- MDG impact has been highly uneven across and within geographical regions.
- MDG 'targeting' of the poor has been problematic in that the focus was primarily on those easier to identify and reach while those at the margins were neglected.

- The MDGs did not adequately count the costs of climate change adaptation or mitigation.
- Insufficient account was taken of population increase and of the impact of ongoing population momentum which continues to put extraordinary pressure on limited natural resources.
- The re-classification of almost three-quarters of the world's poor from low to middle income and the definition of poverty itself remain controversial.
- The MDGs have been criticised severely for changing measurement dates (backwards) in order to 'manage and achieve' targets.

Finally, the MDGs have been criticised by many for 'reducing' human development to a set of 'measurable' indicators which, inevitably ignore many others, especially those related to power and powerlessness. The SDGs follow on directly from the MDGs and while they 'inherit' much of that agenda and approach, they are far more sweeping in scope and objectives (17 goals and 169 targets – a source of criticism in itself). While the MDGs were formulated essentially behind closed doors by 'high level' delegates, this was not the case with the creation of the Sustainable Development Goals (SDGs). Civil society had unprecedented access to the negotiation rounds and were often able to have direct input. The MyWorld 2015 survey was filled in by 8.5 million people while 'on-the-ground' consultation work was also pursued in least developed countries in the largest public consultation exercise ever undertaken on priorities in international development.

The SDG agenda has been widely welcomed as offering an ambitious platform for advancing human development, yet it has been severely criticised for offering a model or framework for development which fails to address a number of key realities – realities that undermine much of its vision and ambition. In 2006, one of Africa's leading political economists, Samir Amin, described MDG-talk as:

'...intended to legitimize the policies and practices implemented by dominant capital and those who support it, i.e. in the first place the governments of the triad countries [US, EU and Japan], and secondarily governments in the South.'

As for cutting extreme poverty and hunger by half, Amin argued:

'This is nothing but an empty incantation as long as the policies that generate poverty are not analysed and denounced and alternatives proposed.'

This observation goes to the heart of the MDG (and by extension, the SDG) framework; from a development perspective, they offer remedial action without addressing the creation and re-creation of poverty and exclusion internationally. For some, (such as Patrick Bond, Director of the Centre for Civil Society at the University of KwaZulu-Natal, South Africa), the MDGs have reduced development to a technical obsession, a mechanical enterprise which 'tortures' the data to infer success.

For Amin and many others, the real goals operating within the MDG and SDG context are expanded privatisation of resources and services; increased private appropriation of agricultural land; maximum de-regulation of markets; the free flow of capital without hindrance (but not of people) and increased limitations on the role of the state in selected areas. Three particular 'development' critiques have been made of the SDGs.

Financing the goals is problematic at two levels; one, it remains voluntary at state level, is deemed insufficient to achieve stated objectives and relies heavily on private capital. Secondly, as noted also by Stefano Prato in the *2016 Spotlight on Sustainable Development* report by Social Watch (2016:122), the agenda places excessive emphasis on financial resources instead of on the removal of the structural barriers that damage and restrict many (poorer) countries; it ignores the 'financialisation' of the global economy and the need for systemic reform and it subjects the implementation of a global public agenda to the mechanisms and conditions of private investments and speculative markets.

For many critics the central problem rests with the ongoing belief in traditional economic growth-led models of development; as Gilbert Rist notes, infinite growth is impossible on a finite planet, yet, *'all the economic policies in operation preach the opposite. In a world that celebrates rationality, reason is giving way to faith'* (Rist, 2014).

A third critique echoes the observations of Patrick Bond, as noted above. With so many targets to be measured, data collection becomes paramount, so much so that many fear measurement will supersede delivery. One study by the Sustainable Development Solutions Network (a UN global initiative led by Jeffrey Sachs), estimates that it will cost US$1 billion per year for the next 15 years for 77 low-income countries to bring their statistical systems up to scratch to support and measure the SDGs.

ON THE DIFFICULTY OF 'DEFINITIONS' OF DEVELOPMENT

Attempting to provide a clear and comprehensive definition of development that might be agreeable to the majority of people worldwide is a well-nigh impossible task as different contexts; timeframes and circumstances as well as perceptions and aspirations inevitably vary hugely. For example, we could usefully consider how development might be conceived by a poor farmer in Zambia, a mother living in a slum in Sao Paulo, an environmentalist living in San Francisco or a chief executive of a transnational company based in London.

As Gilbert Rist points out, different understandings of development depend on how each individual (or group of individuals) picture the ideal conditions for social existence (as well as environmental existence). Rist argues that conventional thinking on development swings between two extremes:

- The expression of a general wish among all peoples to live and experience a better life (however defined).
- something which ignores the fact that the very different ways of achieving this general objective or vision would immediately encounter very different political, economic and environmental ways of achieving it.

The vast range of actions which are theoretically designed to achieve the greatest happiness for the largest number of people remain hotly contested.

The central issue is not to simply point out that one set of countries (labelled 'developed') have more of some things (schools, roads, average calorie consumption, computers, democracy, industrial employment, supermarkets etc.) and less of others (illiteracy, poverty, high infant and maternal deaths during pregnancy etc.) while others (labelled 'developing') have the reverse. What is crucially important to note is the processes that underpin and reproduce such contrast. Rist also makes the obvious comment that 'development' is not simply a priority for poorer countries but equally for richer countries.

Rist then proceeds to outline a number of key components of a definition of development which is broad enough to capture history and different systems and practices and to pose the question whether 'development' might be viewed as a part of modern religion:

> *'Development' consists of a set of practices, sometimes appearing to conflict with one another, which require - for the reproduction of society - the general transformation and destruction of the natural environment and of social relations. Its aim is to increase the production of commodities (goods and services) geared, by way of exchange, to effective demand'*

'Development' thus appears to be a belief and a series of practices which form a single whole in spite of contradictions between them.'

This discussion takes us some distance away from mechanical or simplistic definitions of development into the fields of not just economics and politics but also philosophy and history and even into the area of myth.

For Swedish economist Bjorn Hettne:

'Development is a contested concept, which implies that it has meant different things from one historical situation to another and from one actor to another.'

In his 2009 analysis Thinking About Development (London, Zed Press), he insists:

'A critical approach is also necessary because much harm has been done to people in the name of development. Development practice in the so-called developing countries is ultimately rooted in colonialism, and has therefore sometimes contained a good measure of paternalism, not to speak of arrogance and racism.' (2009:1)

Echoing much of the approach of Rist, Hettne extends the debate on development significantly beyond the search for a definition:

'Development thinking in fact constitutes an exceptionally rich tradition in social science, encompassing important theoretical debates on the dynamics of social change, as well as an ambition to represent a global experience of empirical conditions in different local corners of the world.'

He concluded in 1995:

'There can be no fixed and final definition of development; only suggestions of what it should imply in particular contexts.'

B. Hettne (1995) Development Theory and the Three Worlds, Essex, Longman

ON LANGUAGE AND LABELS

'Developing countries' is the name that experts use to designate countries trampled by someone else's development...'

This is the telling comment of 'development' critic and 'Third Worldist' Eduardo Galeano in his brilliantly challenging book *Upside Down: A Primer for the Looking Glass World*. In the book, he relentlessly attacks many 'western' constructions and understandings of the world and questions how we 'label' and describe that world. In this he enters the contested agenda of how the world is divided and how such divisions are 'named' and 'labelled'. As 2005 Nobel Prize winner for Literature, Harold Pinter has commented *Language... is a highly ambiguous business. So often, below the word spoken, is the thing known and unspoken'* and no-where is this more apparent than in the world of 'international development'.

It is a minefield of language in trying to describe both the diversity and the uniformity of those countries most frequently described as the 'developing world' – even the use of the word 'developing' is problematic. 'Developing' towards what and from what? If we can have a 'developing country' can we have an 'underdeveloping country' – a country going backwards in terms of human development? From the perspective and experience of the world's very poorest people, the term 'developing' could well be interpreted as a deliberate insult to their experience of life and a deliberate refusal to accurately describe their condition.

For decades there has been a vigorous political debate on how to describe the divisions that characterise the world today. Is it accurate to describe the 'West' as 'the developed world' (given the many characteristics of both underdevelopment and overdevelopment present) and the 'Rest' as the 'developing world' (given the historical sophistication and complexity of many of its 'societies' and economies)? At another level altogether, it is not possible to find a phrase that adequately encompasses the massive diversity that exists within both these worlds. Whatever phrases are chosen, it is clear that political choices and agendas cannot be avoided. Most recently, the World Bank has proposed abandoning the phrase 'developing world' in favour of a series of groupings based on income cut-off points, thus, once again, reinforcing the economic over the political.

In recent years, one of most vigorous debates, at least in the West, has been over the use of the phrase 'Third World' to describe the countries and agendas of Africa, Latin America and Asia collectively.

DEBATING 'DEVELOPMENT' AS FREEDOM TOWARDS DIGNITY

The persistence of underdevelopment in major regions of the world reiterates the lack of freedom, lack of dignity and respect. The term development has become far more seductive and politically sought after as a panacea for all the deprivations that plague the developing world. Development has highlighted the endemic contradictions of the plenty amidst the paradoxes of those who seek to survive. Development has become a contested terrain for engaging with diverse actors, institutions and structures. Development in other words, has really come to be understood as the management of uncertainty in a neoliberal world. *'Development implies security from famine, malnutrition, and unemployment as well as a social, economic and political uncertainty'* (Kumar, 2014: 77).

Development, therefore, despite its 'feel good' factor, suggests struggle and conflict over access to resources and increasing freedom of choice for the majority recognising the need to 'embed' development as a set of possibilities across geographically and spatially differentiated identities. Development has to be culturally grounded and placed in context for it to respect the dignity of life, where it is about sustaining communities rather than making them subservient to the dictates of global economic imperatives. What development means is a question, which has to be left to individual communities; this is the only way we can assure development becomes self-development thereby reinforcing the idea of development-by-people.

'Dignity' in the context of development today has become an accepted norm in decrying global poverty, inequality and under-development; goals of human dignity and social justice expand the very idea of development. The notion of dignity relates to ideas of gender equality, livelihood, freedom from exploitation and the security of human rights. Development with dignity implies the universal assertion of global ethics and justice for all. In Ecuador, for example, social activists have been crucial in institutionalising the principles of food sovereignty by successfully advocating for the concept's inclusion in the country's 2008 Constitution, known as Buen vivir or 'to live well', which seek to democratise access and control over resources like land, water, and seeds as introduced by *La Via Campesina,* the transnational movement of peasant organisations at the 1996 World Food Summit. A more people-centred approach can also be seen in recent discussions and arguments in developed and developing countries alike on 'fair wage' and 'decent work' (such as the Human Development Report: 2015: Work for Human Development) following the global economic recession in 2009.

As Japanese philosopher and peace activist Daisaku Ikeda noted in 2013:

> *'In order to create a society that upholds the dignity of life, a sense of irreplaceable value of each individual must be the foundation of the human bonds that sustain society' and indeed development.'*

Critics opposed to the use of the phrase describe it as pejorative (it places these countries 'third' in an international pecking order); negative (it fuels negative stereotypes and attitudes); outdated (in that the Second World – the Communist Bloc no longer exists) and inaccurate (it ignores the real achievements of such countries). As an alternative, such critics offer phrases such as Majority World and/or Global South. Clearly, given what has been said above, there is obviously no 'right' or 'wrong' phraseology but the debate is telling as regards the politics of the 'development/underdevelopment' debate today.

The phrase 'Third World' was introduced into the story of development by the French anti-colonialist writer and activist Albert Sauvy echoing the thinking and writing of many other earlier commentators such as Aimé Césaire (Martinique born poet and teacher), Ho Chi Minh (President and 'father' of modern Vietnam) and Franz Fanon who sought to highlight the common 'anti-colonialist' agenda of that world. Sauvy chose his phrase to echo the political struggles of French history where the monarchy had divided its servants into the First Estate (clergy), the Second Estate (aristocracy) and the Third Estate (the bourgeoisie). Sauvy emphasised the political nature of his categorisation by arguing that the: '... *ignored, exploited, scorned Third World, like the Third Estate, demands to become something as well*'.

The key point in Sauvy's analysis was that just as the Third Estate had been excluded from having a voice in the political life of France, so too had the Third World been similarly excluded. Sauvy was placing primary emphasis on the political agenda internationally. Jawaharlal Nehru (Prime Minister of India) echoed Sauvy's analysis in 1958 when he emphasised the need for countries outside the two dominant blocs of the capitalist and US-led West and the Communist, Soviet-led alliance to 'collect together' to oppose their plans for possession of the Third World. He argued that '...*it is right that countries of a like way of thinking should come together, should confer together, should jointly function in the United Nations or elsewhere*'.

The political and economic agendas of the Third World acting as a bloc of countries in opposition to the dominant blocs and interests was carried forward well into the 1990's by the Group of 77 or, the G-77. Established in 1964 by 77 developing countries the G77 (now made up of 134 countries - the original name has been kept because of its historic significance) is the largest intergovernmental organisation of developing states in the UN. It provides a platform for the countries of the developing world to state and promote their collective economic interests and enhance their

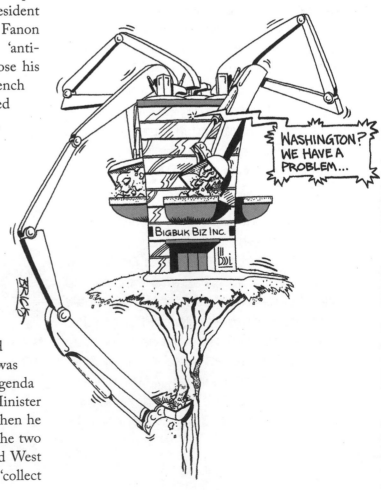

joint negotiating power in international meetings and agendas.

Proponents of the term 'Third World' continue to emphasise it as a 'political project' focused on *peace*, *bread* and *justice* in that the countries of that world remain largely excluded from international political and economic decision-making and that it is only in the last two decades that India and China (along with Brazil and post-Communist Russia) have become important and recognised political voices. (For more on this read Vijay Prashad's *The Poorer Nations: A Possible History of the Global South*, 2014).

Those who prefer to use the phrases Majority World or Global South argue that the terms are non-judgemental and 'neutral', arguments rejected by others. Critics of these categories argue that they:

- Are weak analytically and have little substance in describing the realities, histories and agendas of the countries included.
- Have the result of de-politicising a complex and rich agenda and reducing it to a dualism of simple majority and minority or to a geographical term Global South (but which must, of necessity, eliminate countries actually in the Global South).
- Ignore and even deny the history of the (unequal) relations between 'developed and developing countries'.
- Ignore the ongoing reality of the 'exclusion' of the poor from the key debates about the structure and functioning of the world today.

POST-DEVELOPMENT?

In the preface to the 2012 edition of *Encountering Development*, Colombian anthropologist Arturo Escobar reviews a number of the dominant themes and debates in development thinking in the past decade-and-a-half in a world he claims has changed immensely. He notes the role taken on by China, and to a lesser extent, India; the realignment of world politics post 9/11 (and the invasion of Iraq in 2003) and the end of the 'Washington Consensus' and the influence of neoliberalism on development. For him, the pre-eminent challenge is the global ecological crisis (which has also generated a 'global consciousness'). For Escobar, all of these (and additional other issues) have generated a profound critique of the concept of 'development' itself and of writing and research around development. Central to this challenge has been the suggestion of the 'overthrow' of development as the dominant story or central organising principle of life in Africa, Asia and Latin America. This view was captured by Gustavo Esteva (a strong critic of dominant development thinking, quoted by Escobar) as follows: '...*development failed as a socio-economic endeavour, but the development discourse still contaminates social reality.*'

Escobar (along with many others) argues that the 'industrial growth model' of development with its accompanying consumption patterns and its ideology of materialism is now under fundamental threat and is no longer sustainable. As a result, development thinking and practice is increasingly concerned with the debate on 'transition' – transition to a post-fossil fuel society based on ecological justice in addition to biological and cultural diversity. Central to the emergence of this 'transition' debate have been feminist, ecological and human development frameworks and, crucially for Escobar, indigenous organisations, especially in Latin America. A growing recognition of the 'rights of nature' has become increasingly important as outlined, for example by Uruguayan ecologist Eduardo Gudynas. For him, this new story of development marks a turning away from an anthropocentric view of modernity to one which recognises the relationship between humans and non-humans. For Escobar and many other commentators, this transition marks the end of globalisation – *'as we knew it'*.

DEVELOPMENT TOWARDS THE FUTURE: A CASE OF OLD WINE IN NEW BOTTLES?

To reimagine 'development' in the twenty-first century, especially in the wake of a weakening and an uncertain global economy, coupled with crisis of the three F's – *food*, *finance* and *fuel* – calls for a critical re-evaluation of priorities. Added to this is the issue of planetary limits imposed by climate change, sustainability and human security. Can 'development' today be advocated without imposing particular worldviews? How can issues of self-identity, individualism, and dissent square against rising inequalities - racial, financial, sexual and indeed geographical? The deepening of the economic divide between not just the traditional North versus the South but also within the North and the South are challenges, which have only intensified over time. This has challenged the very idea of capitalism and its competitive market-based frameworks and calls for a reassessment of what development means, or will mean, for the future.

Recent shifts in the development debate have been radical, from the increased focus on the under-developed South to the challenge of sustaining global development. The question is - has the 'South' become irrelevant because it is too complicated to be dealt with in one single story? The need to narrow the gap between the rich 'North' and the poor 'South' has been superseded by the demand of sustaining the global economy. Here, sustaining the global economy remains primarily focused on maintaining the lifestyles of the North. Managing

the uncertainties of the prosperous North is deemed to be more critical than securing the aspirations of the South through tackling embedded inequalities.

Three challenges present themselves in the context of dominant ideas of development. The rise and demise of the 'Asian Tigers', the ascendancy of India and China, the position of the BRICS and the gradual decline in all that is economic in the developed North once again questions the notion of linear stages of development. Secondly, in terms of the complexities of development in practice, there has been a shift in emphasis from models of standardised economic growth to ones that prioritise fiscal resilience, border security and private wealth creation. Development then is no longer about an idealistic universal or democratic outcome for all but rather about 'normalising' what have become persistent inequalities.

Lastly, the intersection of global challenges such as those of climate change, human geography, terrorism and extreme inequalities (both social and economic) have presented a real crisis in development outcomes in the immediate future. This crisis demands an approach that enhances interdependence between and within countries rather than remedial tinkering with the structural contradictions that persist between the rich and the poor.

The prognosis for development for the future is clear – economic growth under neoliberal states (and its championing institutions, such as the IMF) deepening inequality and an undermining of social and environmental sustainability. The morality of economic growth needs to be squared with reducing inequalities, vulnerability and environmental security.

READING

Maggie Black (2015) *The No-Nonsense International Development*, New Internationalist, Oxford

Wayne Ellwood (2015) *The No-Nonsense Globalisation*, New Internationalist, Oxford

Arturo Escobar (2012) *Encountering Development: The Making and Unmaking of the Third World*, Princeton and Oxford

Eduardo Galeano (2001) *Upside Down: A Primer for the Looking Glass World*, Picador, New York

M. Satish Kumar (2015) *'Thinking dignity' towards inclusive development*, Bulletin of the Institute of Oriental Philosophy, (31): 225-239; and (2014) *Challenges of a Development Idea Towards Sustainability*, Bulletin of The Institute of Oriental Philosophy, no.30

Vijay Prashad (2014) *The Poorer Nations: A Possible History of the Global South*, Verso, London, pp.1-3.

Gilbert Rist (2008) *The History of Development: from Western Origins to Global Faith*, Zed Press, London

Jeffrey Sachs (2008) *Common Wealth: Economics for a Crowded Planet,* Penguin, London

Wolfgang Sachs (2010) *The Development Dictionary,* Zed Press, London

Amartya Sen (1999) *Development as Freedom,* Oxford University Press

Vandana Shiva (2006) *Earth Democracy*, South End Press, Cambridge

UNDP (2010) *Human Development Report*, New York, Palgrave MacMillan (see chapters 1 and 2)

Social Watch (2016) *Spotlight on Sustainable Development*, Montevideo

MORE INFORMATION AND DEBATE

www.odi.org - Overseas Development Institute, UK

www.socialwatch.org - Uruguay-based international NGO network

www.hdr.undp.org/en - home of the Human Development Reports by UN Development Programme

www.worldwatch.org - Washington-based institute with focus on environment and development

www.theguardian.com/global-development - Guardian Newspaper UK section on development

www.data.worldbank.org - World Bank Open Data initiative (free access) collecting interactive global data sets from major UN international bodies and institutions

SUSTAINABLE DEVELOPMENT GOALS

The SDGs (formally known as Transforming our World: the 2030 Agenda for Sustainable Development) represents the latest framework for international development agreed in September 2015 by governments following a review of the Millennium Development Goals (MDGs) and their impact. The Goals are built around the '5 P's':

 People: 'We are determined to end poverty and hunger, in all their forms and dimensions, and to ensure that all human beings can fulfil their potential in dignity and equality and in a healthy environment.'

 Planet: 'We are determined to protect the planet from degradation, including through sustainable consumption and production, sustainably managing its natural resources and taking urgent action on climate change, so that it can support the needs of the present and future generations.'

 Prosperity: 'We are determined to ensure that all human beings can enjoy prosperous and fulfilling lives and that economic, social and technological progress occurs in harmony with nature.'

 Peace: 'We are determined to foster peaceful, just and inclusive societies which are free from fear and violence. There can be no sustainable development without peace and no peace without sustainable development.'

 Partnership: 'We are determined to mobilize the means required to implement this Agenda through a revitalised Global Partnership for Sustainable Development, based on a spirit of strengthened global solidarity, focussed in particular on the needs of the poorest and most vulnerable and with the participation of all countries, all stakeholders and all people.'

The 2030 Agenda is universal, not just because the SDGs are global in scope, but also because all countries have to do something to achieve them. No country can deem itself to be sustainably developed and having already done its part to meet the SDGs. The 2030 Agenda offers the opportunity to challenge the idea that development is a phenomenon that occurs only in countries of the global South while the North is already 'developed'. - Jens Martens (2016) in Spotlight on Sustainable Development report by Social Watch

MDG CHALLENGES FOR THE SDGS

- MDG impact was been highly uneven geographically
- MDG 'targeting' of the poor was problematic - the focus was primarily on the 'easy to access' leaving those at the margins neglected
- The MDGs did not adequately count the costs of climate change
- Insufficient account of population increase and its impact on limited natural resources
- The definition of poverty used was highly debated
- Re-classifying almost 75% of the world's poor from low to middle income remains controversial
- Strong criticism for changing measurement dates backwards to 'manage and achieve' targets
- Reducing human development to 'measurable' indicators ignored many significant issues, especially on power and powerlessness
- The MDGs significantly ignored the structural causes of poverty and left extreme inequality intact

DEBATING THE SDGS

The SDGs have been praised for:

- Consulting millions of people on their content (8.5 million plus)
- Involving civil society extensively
- Placing obligations on all states worldwide
- Recognising the central importance of climate change

The SDGs have been criticised for:

- Promoting expanded privatisation of resources and services
- Increasing private appropriation of agricultural land
- Advocating the maximum possible de-regulation with the free flow of unhindered capital but not people
- Arguing for increasing limitations (in selected areas) of the role of the state

3 KEY SDG CHALLENGES

Finance 'from billions to trillions': funding for the goals remains voluntary for states with too much reliance on the private sector and leaves damaging structural barriers intact

Inequality and growth-led development: the SDGs rely on increasing economic growth-led development in a world of diminishing resources and climate change

Data problems: data collection and availability (upon which measurement of progress depends) is hugely problematic and could undermine delivery; one estimate argues it will cost US$1 billion per year for 15 years to improve data systems for 77 low-income countries

Basically, the SDGs want to reduce inequality by ratcheting the poor up, but while leaving the wealth and power of the global 1 percent intact. They want the best of both worlds. They fail to accept that mass impoverishment is the product of extreme wealth accumulation and overconsumption by a few, which entails processes of enclosure, extraction, and exploitation along the way. You can't solve the problem of poverty without challenging the pathologies of accumulation. – Jason Hickel, anthropologist, London School of Economics 2015

'The challenges facing Joal demonstrates the complexity of the web woven between environmental, economic, political and social factors which make up the challenge of sustainable development.'

CHAPTER 3

SUSTAINABLE DEVELOPMENT
– ENOUGH FOR ALL, FOR EVER

ROLAND TORMEY

This chapter focuses on the idea of sustainable development and the many interconnections between environment and development. Different definitions of sustainable development are reviewed along with four 'frameworks' for approaching environment; diversity; the concepts of carrying capacity, ecosystem, ecological footprinting, feedback loops and environmental tipping points. The chapter includes case studies of over-fishing in West Africa and, in particular, Senegal; the Aral Sea and the disposal of 'old' computers. Finally, the chapter explores ecological footprinting.

KEYWORDS:

OVER-FISHING; SUSTAINABLE DEVELOPMENT; CARRYING CAPACITY; ECOSYSTEM; TIPPING POINTS; ARAL SEA; SENEGAL; BIODIVERSITY; ECOLOGICAL FOOTPRINTING; LIVING PLANET INDEX

INTRODUCTION

The town of Joal lies about 100 km south of Dakar, on Senegal's Atlantic coast. In a country of 14 million, the town is home to around 40,000 people, and its claim to fame is evident from the 1,500 colourful motorised canoes (called pirogues) that are strung along 16 kilometers of beach: Joal is Senegal's most significant fishing port and home to hundreds of small scale fishers.

Fishing is a huge industry in West Africa, where up to one-quarter of jobs are linked to the industry. Senegal is one of the world's poorest countries, with an annual Gross Domestic Product of only US$2,400 per person (compared to US$40,000 to US$50,000 dollars in the UK and Ireland respectively). Fish is also a major food in the region and it provides an estimated two-thirds of the animal protein eaten by people in the coastal states of West Africa. An estimated one million people in Senegal alone rely on the sea for their staple diets. According to a 2014 report of the African Progress Panel, any impact on fishing in the region would put the livelihoods and food security of millions of people in West Africa at risk.

But all is not well in Joal. Recent decades have seen the catch decline significantly. *'Catches are 75% down on 10 years ago,'* said Samb Ibrahim, manager of Joal's fishing port in an interview with The Guardian in 2014. *'In 2004 we landed 220,000 tonnes, now we catch only 120,000 tonnes per year. It's a very serious situation… At this rate, in 10 years' time there will be no fish left.'*

So what has happened to Joal's fish? According to local people, the problems began in the 1990s with the arrival of large foreign trawlers. A single large trawler is capable of catching 250 tonnes of fish in a single day – equivalent to what 50 pirogues might catch in a year. The trawlers operate away from the shoreline and are not visible from the coast, but their effects are seen in dwindling catches and spiraling local prices for fish. Trawlers from the European Union, China, Philippines, South Korea and Taiwan are operating in African waters. Some of these are operating under license from African states, but others (thought to be primarily from Russia and East Asia) appear to be engaging in illegal fishing. In West Africa as a whole, the estimated loss each year from illegal and 'misreported' fishing is something like US$1.3 billion. In Senegal alone in 2012 it was estimated to be as high as US$300 million. This is the equivalent of 2% of Senegal's GDP.

According to the African Progress Panel, the problem of overfishing in African waters is exacerbated by corruption at a national level. In Senegal corruption was suspected in the awarding of 11 special authorisations to large, foreign ships which allowed them to fish in sensitive areas. The problem is also made worse by the actions of western governments, who don't simply condone these practices but actually promote them. The European Union proposes to give about €6.5 billion (US$8.9 billion) in supports to the fisheries sector from 2014 to 2020, with some of this money going to support technological upgrades that will promote overfishing. Russia and Asian countries also provide supports to their fishing fleets. And at least some of the fish that is taken from West African waters finds its way into western supermarkets.

The overfishing problem in West Africa is just one part of a much wider problem of resource use. As long as there is enough fish left to breed, fish will continue to reproduce and grow and so people can continue to fish year after year. However, if people catch too much of a particular type of fish then there is not enough left to repopulate, and so fish numbers will decline rapidly. The United Nations Food and Agriculture Organisation (FAO) has estimated that at present almost 30% of fish stocks worldwide are being overfished in this manner.

The dwindling fish stocks of Joal and the impact upon people's living standards in the area and around the world is not a simple problem, but rather one which involves many elements:

- Fishing is a source of livelihood both for local artisanal fishers and for crews on industrial-scale trawlers. Restrictions on fishing will inevitably harm people's livelihoods and may lead to the decimation of local industries in waterside towns and cities. The Canadian ban on Cod fishing after the collapse of fish stocks in the 1990s, for example, led to the loss of an estimated 40,000 jobs and the decline of many towns in rural Canada. In Senegal there are an estimated 600,000 jobs dependent upon the fishing industry.

- This, in turn can lead to political pressure on countries to continue to support fishing industries that are contributing to overfishing. The collapse in the Canadian cod stocks was in part due to the overestimation of how much could be fished which in turn was partially the result of political pressure. The financial support for the fishing industry which is estimated as being of the order of US$27 billion annually is a further example of the effects of such pressures.

- The international regulation of fishing is weak and there is little appetite in some countries to improve such regulation.

- Poorer countries can find it hard to finance the surveillance that would be needed to ensure that illegal and underreported fishing was ended. Madagascar, for example, has only 3 small monitoring vessels, 8 speedboats, 18 inspectors and 22 observers to monitor fishing in its coastal zone.

- Poorer countries can also find it hard to minimise the impact of corruption on resource policies, as in the case of Senegal.

- Consumers are many steps removed from where the problem originates and so do not make the connection between what they buy and where it has come from. For example, it was reported in 2014 that prawns fed with fishmeal produced by slaves on Thai boats were being sold in the US, UK and France (in Walmart, Carrefour, Costco, and Tesco) without consumers having any idea that they were literally financing slavery.

The challenges facing Joal demonstrate the complexity of the web woven between environmental, economic, political and social factors which make up the challenge of sustainable development.

Figure 3.1: Global trends in the state of marine fish stocks, 1974-2011 (FAO, 2014)

Source: WWF Living Planet Report, 2014, page 80

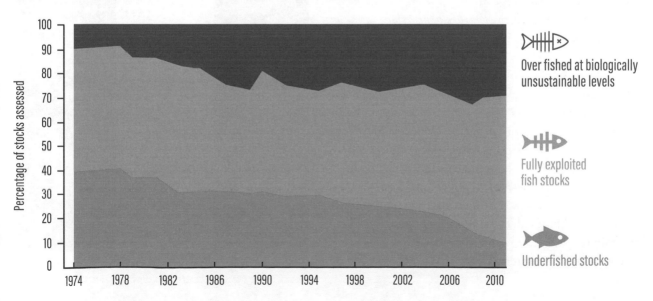

COMPETING DEFINITIONS OF SUSTAINABLE DEVELOPMENT

'The environment does not exist as a sphere separate from human actions, ambitions, and needs, and attempts to defend it in isolation from human concerns have given the very word "environment" a connotation of naivety in some political circles. The word "development" has also been narrowed by some into a very limited focus, along the lines of "what poor nations should do to become richer", and thus again is automatically dismissed by many in the international arena as being a concern of specialists...

But the "environment" is where we live; and "development" is what we all do in attempting to improve our lot within that abode. The two are inseparable.'

World Commission on Environment and Development (WCED)
Our Common Future (New York: Oxford University Press, 1987)

The concept of 'sustainable development' was introduced in the 1980s in order to reflect the idea that there is an inherent interrelationship between people and the planet. One widely cited early definition is that supplied by the World Commission on Environment and Development (WCED) in 1987: "*...to make development sustainable [means] to ensure that it meets the needs of the present without compromising the ability of future generations to meet their own needs*".

The WCED definition is vague, probably deliberately so, since it is easier to find political agreement on vague statements than on precise ones. And, although the concept of sustainable development gathered much political attention in the later years of the 20th century, the actual goals of sustainable development seemed to remain unclear. At the end of that century, a review of research studies by the US National Research Council's Board on Sustainable Development identified that much of the vagueness centered around three questions:

- What should be developed?
- What is to be sustained?
- Over what period?

They noted different answers to each of these questions were implicit in different definitions. For some, the answer to '*what should be developed?*' was 'the economy', for others it meant 'human well-being' and for others it meant 'democratic political and social participation and institutions' (these different emphases are explored in other chapters). In relation to the question as to '*what should be sustained?*' there were again different answers. For some, the focus was on sustaining the environment within which we live and which provides us with life support. The focus for this group was on protecting the aspects of the environment that humans need (such as air, water, energy resources and the living things that can provide us with food and medicines). For others, however, nature itself should be sustained (irrespective of whether or not it provides us with life support). Others also focused on sustaining cultures and societies that were threatened by 'westernisation'.

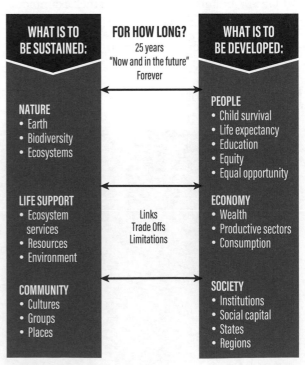

Source: US National Research Council Policy Division, Board on Sustainable Development *Our Common Journey: A Transition towards sustainability*. Washington DC: National Academy Press.

A further question that could be asked about sustainable development is *'How it is to be achieved?'* Here again, there were radically different views. For some, like the WCED, the solution would be in part based upon, economic growth, new technologies and smart management of the environment alongside market forces. Others, however, disagreed:

- Some, like the chemist James Lovelock, argued the Earth was self-regulating system and that the survival of life requires allowing the Earth and nature to self-regulate rather than requiring human management of 'the environment'. From this perspective, 'management of resources' is part of the problem, since it implies human interference in a self-regulating system. This idea is called the 'Gaia-hypothesis', named after the Greek goddess Gaia (despite the somewhat mystical name, Lovelock and others sought to support this idea using hard scientific evidence, although the evidence is regarded by some as being weak).

- A second strand of criticism focused on the idea that sustainable development could be achieved though large-scale interventions and policies. This perspective is often associated with the work of the British economist E.F. Schumacher who wrote a book called *Small is Beautiful: Economics as if People Mattered*, and who argued that part of the problem is that societies are driven by a demand for economic growth, which is to say for 'more stuff'. For him, sustainable development means accepting that we have 'enough'. Consequently, from this perspective, sustainable development would mean no economic growth. Others counter that economic growth is necessary to provide the resources to tackle poverty.

- A third criticism of the WCED approach focuses on the idea that environmental degradation and poverty are actually both created by the same global economic system, and are little more than the continuation of an economic system built during the colonial period. For this group, the scientific language of 'technological development' and 'resource management' is little more than an ideological justification for continued exploitation of nature and people. Authors associated with this perspective include the Indian writer Vandana Shiva.

'Sustainable development' is now a term which is increasingly regarded either as internally self-contradictory (an oxymoron) or, at best, plagued by ambiguous or distorted definitions. As a result, there are many constituencies which perceive the term 'sustainable development' as a vehicle to perpetuate many and varied corporate and institutional interests whilst giving the impression of adherence to, and observance of, environmentally-sound principles.'

Paul Johnston, Mark Everard, David Santillo and Karl-Henrik Robèrt. 2007. 'Reclaiming the Definition of Sustainability', *Environmental Science and Pollution Research International* 14(1): 60-66

'Sustainable development simultaneously reifies global capitalism as the liberating and protecting force that can ensure survival of the human race — this is the logic of the world it seeks to construct and impose. The Third World, still in need of development, now needs to be told how to develop sustainably. The consumer is still the king: nature is not so much understood as consumed, and the power dynamics in this new era of globalization and post-development remain unchanged"

Subhabrata Bobby Banerjee. 2003. 'Who Sustains Whose Development? Sustainable Development and the Reinvention of Nature' *Organization Studies* 24(1): 143-180

At its most fundamental then, sustainable development (like development) is a contested term. There are different political and ideological perspectives on what is the appropriate relationship between human wellbeing and the environment. These different positions are summarised in the table on the following page.

	GAIANISM	COMMUNALISM	ACCOMMODATION	INTERVENTION
Basic tenets	• The earth is a system, like a body, with the different parts being like different organs in the body. • The body of the earth is called Gaia, and we are all part of her. • Gaia and her parts (the animals and plants, rocks and soil) have rights that need to be protected in any 'development'.	• Global capitalism, international organisations like the WTO and World Bank and big scale business are destroying the earth. • Big technology, like nuclear power, is beyond people's control. • We need to move towards small-scale, self-reliant communities rather than big cities that do not produce what they consume. • We need to use renewable resources and 'appropriate technology' that people can understand and control.	• Humans have the right to exploit the earth's resources for their well-being. • The earth's resources are finite and must be properly managed. • We must carefully assess the potential dangers to the environment and their knock-on effects of humans. • We must manage human development to accommodate ourselves to environmental limits.	• The earth is robust and can survive human interventions. • When resources become scarce, the laws of supply and demand will make them expensive and will thereby reduce demand. • There will then be a market niche for businesses that will make a profit by developing new products that will fill any gaps. • Business will use these profits to fund research, which will find new ways of coping with such scarcity or other potential problems by developing new technologies when needed (such as using nuclear power to deal with a scarcity of fossil fuels). • There is, therefore no need for major social change, our current way of working will solve any problems.
Who tends to hold this view?	James Lovelock argued that we should regard the world 'as if' it were a single living organism, which he referred to as 'Gaia'. This position is often held by radical greens.	E F Schumacher published Small is Beautiful, promoting such small-scale, self-reliant community development in 1973. Radical socialists and environmentalists often hold this position.	This is, broadly speaking, the view of the Brundtland Commission report (WCED). Environmental scientists and liberal-socialist politicians often hold this view.	This view is often associated with business leaders, right-wing politicians and with some scientists and engineers.
How widespread is it?	0.1 – 3 percent of population in various opinion surveys.	5 – 10 percent in various opinion surveys.	55 – 70 per cent in various opinion surveys.	10 – 35 percent in various opinion surveys.
What are they likely to say?	The "entire range of living matter on Earth...could be regarded as a single living entity, capable of manipulating the Earth's atmosphere to suit its overall needs. This organism, of which human society is a part, but only one part, regulates her activities in a very complex and subtle way" (J Lovelock, 1979).	"Ever bigger machines, entailing ever bigger concentrations of economic power and exerting ever greater violence against the environment, do not represent progress: they are a denial of wisdom. Wisdom demands a new orientation of science and technology towards the organic, the gentle, the non-violent, the elegant and beautiful." (E F Schumacher, 1973).	"Human Beings are at the centre of concerns for sustainable development. They are entitled to a healthy and productive life in harmony with nature" (Principle 1 of the 'Rio Declaration of Environment and Development', 1992).	"It is time for the technical community to abandon its attempts to accommodate irreconcilable opponents [greens] and instead aim to re-establish the idea of scientific authority...[we] plead guilty with heads held high to the charge of having been trained to solve problems without imposing colossal social change". (M. Grimston, 1990 in the UK Atomic Energy Authority's Magazine Atom).

Source: Adapted and developed from T. O'Riordan (1989) 'The Challenge for Environmentalism' and from D. Pepper (1996) Modern Environmentalism: An Introduction

KEY CONCEPTS IN SUSTAINABLE DEVELOPMENT

CARRYING CAPACITY:

Imagine a group of hares living in a field and eating the grass in the field. The weather remains mild and so the grass grows back after being eaten and so the hares continue to have enough food. However, if new hares are born, then the increased population may eat the grass quicker than it can regrow. There are two possibilities for what happens next. One is that less grass will mean some hares will die of hunger and, as hare numbers decrease, more grass will grow again. The second is that the field will end up becoming bare and almost all the animals will die.

In this (very simplistic) example, the field has a maximum population size that it can sustain. This is called the field's *carrying capacity*, often defined as the maximal population size supported indefinitely by a given environment.

The idea of 'carrying capacity' implies that there are limits to growth, that is, a point at which the human population can no longer expand. Although the 'limit to growth' idea has been proposed since at least the eighteenth century, continued technological improvements in agriculture and food production have allowed the population on our planet to continue to grow.

In 1972 a report called *The Limits to Growth* was published, which used modern mathematical modelling techniques and factored in a range of different types of scenarios. The report argued that the use of resources, industrial output, population and pollution are growing at an ever increasing rate while the capacity of the earth to accommodate such growth is limited. They tested a range of different scenarios that factored in the development of new technologies to improve our adaptation to the earth's limits, but ultimately argued that, even allowing for new technologies, continued economic growth would lead to breaching the earth's limits and a consequent collapse. Although the *Limits to Growth* report was widely criticised for its methodology and its assumptions, it remained influential (as did the sequel reports, published 20 and 30 years after the original).

This idea led to the development of 'ecological footprints' as a measure of sustainable development (see page 66).

ECOSYSTEM:

The previous example described a single group of animals, relying on a single type of plant (grass) in a single space (the field). This is a very unrealistic description because the reality would be much more complex with numerous living organisms (including, for example, birds, insects, bacteria, as well as different types of grass and other plants) as well as the soil with its distinctive mineral composition. These different elements would, in fact, be interlinked. For example, some plants may be putting minerals into the soil, and others taking them out, some animals may be living off and breaking down the 'waste' products of other animals and plants and thereby ensuring that the whole field is not covered with animal waste, and so on. Rather than having just two species living in balance, any given area could have thousands of species each playing a role in shaping the environment within which they all live. One example of the complexity of such systems is the human intestine, which contains some 300 – 500 different types of bacteria which interact with each other and with their human 'host'. The number of bacteria cells in the human gut is ten times larger than the number of 'human' cells in a body!

These kind of systems in which a physical environment has a number of living organisms and in which they all function together as a unit, are called *ecosystems*.

The inter-reliance of different organisms and their physical environment in an ecosystem means that something which impacts one species in an ecosystem may have knock on effects on other species. A loss of honey bees (as was widely reported in the US and Europe in 2006 and following years) could lead to reduction in plant pollination, and to other impacts on farming. As one beekeeper memorably put it in a BBC interview in 2008: 'If there are no bees there will be no steak'.

One key element in balanced ecosystems is biodiversity, that is, the number of different species functioning within the ecosystem. Ecosystems that have greater diversity of species tend to show less overall variation in functioning over time. This is possibly because, if there are a number of species performing similar functions in an ecosystem, then the possibility of one of these species being resilient to any particular kind of shock to the system is higher than if only one species performs this function. This means the ecosystem as a whole can remain resilient to shocks (even if the numbers of a single species within it go up or down). If this theory is correct, a loss of biodiversity would mean ecosystems becoming less stable. Reduced biodiversity would make ecosystems more likely to collapse with catastrophic consequences for many species in it.

NEGATIVE FEEDBACK LOOPS:

In the original example above involving hares living in a field, the abundance of grass has an impact on a different part of the system: the population of hares. As the hare numbers increase, this, in turn has an impact back on the amount of grass in the field. This is called a negative feedback loop ('negative' because the feedback causes a change in the opposite direction, that is, an increase in hares causes a reaction which subsequently causes a decrease in hares, or a decrease in grass causes a change – death of hares – which in turn causes an increase in grass).

Feedback loops may also be economic. For example, an increased demand for carbon-based fuels like oil or gas may lead to an increase in their price, which in turn may lead to reduced demand for these fuels. As readily accessible oil becomes exhausted, oil extraction may become more expensive which may also drive price increases and development of alternatives.

The authors of the *Limits to Growth* report argued that the key to survival was having accurate feedback mechanisms that would enable impending trouble to be spotted and evasive action taken. Such mechanisms would tell us when we were approaching a critical point in resource use, in pollution or in global warming, for example. However, if feedback loops are to work to establish an equilibrium, then the feedback has to come early enough. If the feedback happens after we have already passed a key threshold in resource use, then we may go beyond it before we even know it is there (in the hare example above, if the hares eat the grass too quickly there may be no grass left by the time hares start to die and so the feedback will have come too late to bring the system back into equilibrium). In their sequel reports, the *Limits to Growth* authors suggest that we may already have passed some of these critical points.

WHAT ARE THE POSSIBLE SCENARIOS FOR GROWTH AND ITS LIMITS?

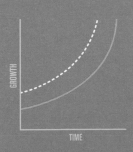

Where technology can enable the earth's carrying capacity to be increased along with resource use, industrial output, population and pollution, then the limits will never be reached and growth can continue indefinitely.

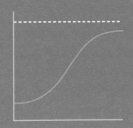

Where there is a limit to the extra carrying capacity that can be developed by technology, and where the feedback mechanisms that would alert people to such limits are quick, accurate and responded to by political leaders, then the limit will be approached but never breached.

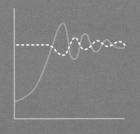

Where the feedback mechanism is delayed, inaccurate or ignored and where the earth can quickly recover from damage, then there will be a period of successive waves of growth and collapse, with economic activity eventually settling near the limits of growth.

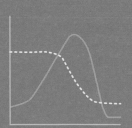

Where the feedback mechanism is delayed, inaccurate or ignored and where the earth cannot recover quickly from damage there will be a significant collapse in people's well being after growth is breached.

- - - - - - - -
Carrying capacity   Population & physical economy

TIPPING POINTS:

Feedback loops are not always negative: sometimes an increase in something can cause a change which in turn causes a further increase. For example, deforestation of a region can reduce rainfall, which can in turn increase the risk of fires which can lead to further deforestation. This is called a positive feedback loop ('positive' does not mean that the change is good, only that the change produces a reaction which gives rise to a further change in the same direction).

Positive feedback loops can mean the beginning of a spiral which leads to a radical and potentially irreversible change in an ecosystem. This is called a *tipping point*. Sometimes tipping points are only evident in retrospect. For example, a tipping point in the ecosystem of the North Sea was reached in the 1980s which led to reductions of certain species and the introduction of new species, however this tipping point was only identified a decade later when a range of different types of data was looked at together. We only know about the tipping point in the North Sea ecosystem because that ecosystem is heavily studied, and even in that case the tipping point was only identified ten years after it had passed. More generally, the fact that we have a limited understanding of the operation of many ecosystems means that making predictions as to tipping points can be quite difficult.

ENVIRONMENTAL TIPPING POINTS

THE MELTING OF SUMMERTIME SEA ICE IN THE ARCTIC, WHICH WILL AMPLIFY GLOBAL WARMING

A DECLINE IN SIZE OF GREENLAND'S ICE SHEET

THE WEST ANTARCTIC ICE SHEET SLIPPING INTO THE OCEAN

THE DRYING UP AND WITHERING OF BOREAL FORESTS

A DECREASE IN THE AMAZON RAINFOREST'S RAINFALL

AN INCREASE IN THE EL NIÑO EFFECT, CAUSING DROUGHT IN SOUTHEAST ASIA

A STRENGTHENING IN INDIA'S MONSOONS, AS WARMER AIR CARRIES MORE WATER

ANY SHIFT IN THE WEST AFRICAN MONSOON WILL IRREVERSIBLY DAMAGE THE SAHARA DESERT

A DISRUPTION OF THE GULF STREAM WILL LEAD TO A COOLER AND DRIER EUROPEAN CLIMATE

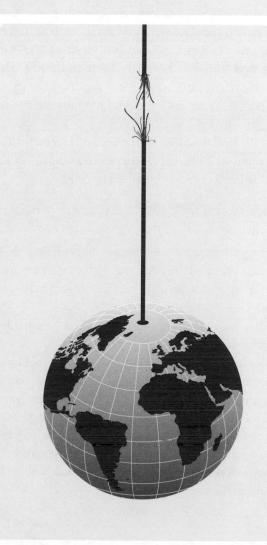

CASE STUDIES IN SUSTAINABLE DEVELOPMENT

WHERE DID THE ARAL SEA GO?

The Aral Sea is an inland body of water east of the Caspian Sea fed by the Amu Darya and Syr Darya rivers. It is shared between the countries of Kazakhstan and Uzbekistan. During the Soviet era (when both countries were part of the Soviet Union), the government used water from these rivers to irrigate the nearby lands in order to grow cotton and rice. This allowed the conversion of 7.9 million hectares of desert into fertile land, and allowed Soviet cotton production to grow from 2.2 million tons in 1940 to 9.1 million in 1980.

It also had the effect of reducing the flow of water into the Aral Sea dramatically. Overall, the volume of water in the Aral fell by 85% the sea level fell by 18 meters and the salinity (saltiness) of the Aral increased five-fold between 1960 and 2000. This had a catastrophic impact on the biodiversity of the region, by making the Aral too salty for its fish life. This had a knock-on affect on other species. Of 319 species of bird in the area in 1960 only 160 remained in 2000. Of 70 species of mammal in the area in 1960 only 32 remained in 2000.

Other impacts attributed to the damage to the Aral Sea include:

- Huge increases in disease including 30-40 fold increased in liver and kidney cancers, 60-fold increases in arthritic diseases and 30-fold increases in chronic bronchitis.
- Loss of the once substantial Aral Sea fishing industry.
- The increases to agricultural outputs achieved up to 1980 were not sustainable and cotton manufacture in the area is now at the same level it was at in 1960 when the large-scale irrigation programme began. It may be too late to reverse the damage to the Aral Sea and the costs of restoring the Aral may be too high to be undertaken.

Source: World Bank (2003) World Development Report 2003 and WWF (2004) Living Planet Report 2004

WHERE DO OLD COMPUTERS GO TO DIE?

The first modern mobile phone call took place in Finland in 1991, and within fifteen years there were 2 billion mobile phone users worldwide. In the same time period the number of internet servers grew from under 400,000 to almost 400 million. These two phenomena are seen as examples of "Moore's Law", which is that the processing power and storage capacity of information and communication technology (ICT) doubles roughly every eighteen months. One effect of this is that new technologies rapidly become obsolete and are quickly replaced. The average lifespan of a mobile phone, for example, has been estimated at between 17 and 21 months.

So what happens to old ICT?

In the 1970s and 1980s many western countries introduced laws on the management of dangerous waste products. One result of this increase in regulation was that it became easier and cheaper for western companies to ship hazardous waste to other countries where regulation was absent or weak and where the income derived from hosting such waste was welcomed. The problems which this generated were quickly seen and international agreements were put in place to regulate the situation.

Some regions (like the EU) also took action to try to ensure that electronic goods were effectively recycled locally (see the table below). Japan, Korea, Canada, Australia Switzerland, Norway, Belgium and Sweden have all been identified as having well-functioning systems for e-waste recycling. Still, it was estimated in 2013 that more than half of the e-waste collected for recycling in developed countries is still sent for processing or disposal to the developing world with China, India, Pakistan and Nigeria being the leading destinations.

Practices for treating this waste differ from location to location. One Nigerian study found that waste was typically disposed of in open dumps, in swamps or through backyard recycling which involved, for example, burning the insulating material off wires to recover copper. Piles of waste may also be burned it an attempt to get rid of plastics and reduce the volume of waste. This is generally carried out with little protective clothing or training and so hazardous fumes are inhaled.

Studies in the infamous Guiyu e-waste dump in China found high levels of carcinogens in local water and in the air. Higher than recommended levels of Cadmium, Copper, Nickel and Lead were also found in the land. Adult workers reported high levels of skin damage, headaches and gastro-intestinal disorders. Stillbirths were 4 times the level expected and 80% of children were found to have high blood lead levels.

Table: Some international sources of e-waste, its disposal, recovery, and dispersal: estimates for 2010

Country or region	From households	To landfills, incinerators, storage	Recovered domestically	Exported	Imported
USA	8.4	5.7	0.42	2.3	–
EU 25	8.9	1.4	5.9	1.6	–
Japan	4.0	0.6	2.8	0.59	–
China	5.7	4.1	4.2	–	2.6
India	0.66	0.95	0.68	–	0.97
West Africa	0.07	0.47	0.21	–	0.61

Amounts in millions of tonnes

Sources:

Suthipong Sthiannopkaoa and Ming Hung Wong. 2013. Handling e-waste in developed and developing countries: Initiatives, practices, and consequences, *Science of the Total Environment* 463/4: 1147-1153

Innocent Chidi Nnorom and Oladele Osibanjo. 2007. Electronic waste (e waste): Material flows and management practices in Nigeri, *Waste Management*, 28: 1472-1479

Estimates use assumptions based on data from previous years. Adapted from Zoeteman et at. (2010)

BIODIVERSITY

'The library of life is burning, and we don't even know the titles of the books'

- Gro Harlem Brundtland

Around 1.2 million species on planet earth have been identified and named, but the estimates published in the journal *Nature* in 2011 put the true number of species on the planet at about 8.7 million (this does not include very simple organisms such as bacteria). The World Conservation Union (IUCN) identifies that the records of extinctions over the past 100 years indicate that current extinction rates are 50 to 500 times higher than extinction rates in the fossil record. If 'possibly extinct' species are included this increases to 100 to 1,000 times natural extinction rates. They go on to note that this is *"an extremely conservative estimate"*, since it does not take account of undocumented extinctions.

The diversity of life on the planet is central to our well-being. Different plants and animals are often tangled together in an intricate and delicate balance which, if disturbed may have far-reaching consequences. When the Nile Perch was introduced into Lake Victoria in central Africa around 1970 to be used as a food source, for example, it turned out to be a voracious predator in its new environment. Since its introduction a number of other species of fish in Lake Victoria have become extinct or very rare. Plants, animals and microscopic organisms also often provide humans with a valuable source of medicines. Extracts from the rosy periwinkle plant of Madagascar, for example, form the basis for some of the most effective cancer treatment drugs, which can achieve a 90% remission rate against childhood leukemia. New important medicines will undoubtedly be based on new findings within our "library of life". Diversity of organisms can also provide important protection for food crops, which tend to be more vulnerable to disease when only a single sort of crop is planted. Some varieties of wild coffee, for example, may be immune to leaf rust, which afflicts many commercial coffee plant varieties. Diversity may also ensure that natural predators in the environment play a role in pest control.

Much of the diversity left on the planet is to be found in what are referred to as 'megadiverse', in fact, it is estimated that 60% to 70% of the world's biological diversity can be found in just 12 countries. Deforestation in tropical areas due to human activities is the major cause of species extinction.

The IUCN estimated in 2012 that:

- 13.3% of birds were threatened with extinction.
- 25% of mammals.
- 41% of amphibians.

The World Wide Fund for Nature (WWF) produces the 'Living Planet Index' as a measure of the state of the world's biodiversity. The index fell by about 50% between 1970 and 2010, indicating a huge decrease in measured diversity during that period with the number of wild animals set to fall by two-thirds (67%) by 2020. They note that, in the same period, the global Ecological Footprint grew from around 0.7 planets to 1.5 planets.

Sources: World Bank (1992) *World Development report 1992*, World Bank (2003) *World Development Report 2003*, WWF (2014) *Living Planet Report 2014 and Living Planet Report 2016*, IUCN (2004) *2004 and 2012 IUCN Red List of Threatened Species, A Global Species Assessment*, and Joy A. Palmer (1998) *Environmental Education in the 21st Century*

MEASURING SUSTAINABLE DEVELOPMENT

Earlier in this chapter the definition of 'sustainable development' was explored in terms of its *goals*. Another way of addressing this question is to ask how sustainable development is *measured*? You have seen in an earlier chapter, that the measurement of development is contested with some organisations preferring more economic measures (such as Gross Domestic Product per capita) and others preferring measures based on human well-being (such as the Human Development Index or the Gender Development Index). None of these measures include 'sustainability' elements and so while they may or may not measure whether a country is meeting "*the needs of the present*" they do not at all measure whether it does so, "*without compromising the ability of future generations to meet their own needs.*"

ECOLOGICAL FOOTPRINTS

One attempt to measure the sustainability of human development is the 'ecological footprint'. The concept of an ecological footprint is linked to the idea of 'carrying capacity', as described earlier. A first question is 'what is the carrying capacity of the planet?' This figure is not fixed: technological developments have meant that the same planet can now provide more resources than was the case in the past.

The WWF estimate that the capacity of the planet in 2010 was equivalent to 12 billion hectares, which must support all human life as well as those of the other approximately 8.7 million species on earth. Although the planet has not gotten any bigger, technological advances have meant that the carrying capacity of the planet is greater than in the past: they estimate that, using the same measures, the capacity of the planet in 1961 was only 10

Figure 3.2: Trends in total biocapacity, Ecological Footprint and world population from 1961 to 2010 (Global Footprint Network 2014)

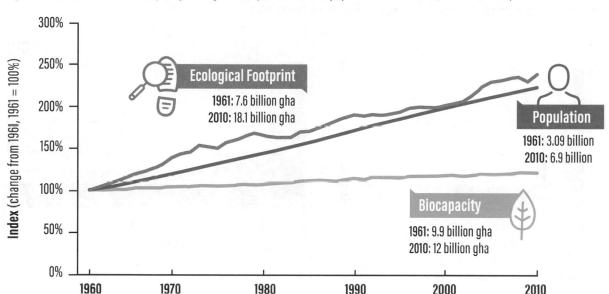

billion hectares. However, since the 1960s global population has also grown. And, while carrying capacity has increased by about 20%, the population has more than doubled (from about 3.1 billion, to about 6.9 billion).

Of course, whether the planet can support all of these people (as well as 8.7 million other species) and continue to regenerate itself, depends upon how much resources each person consumes. The ecological footprint seeks to measure the amount of space that would be necessary to give rise to:

- The food, timber and other resources people use.
- The energy that they consume.
- The space used for built-up land.

Added together this estimates how much ecological space humans take up on the planet – our 'footprint'. It is estimated that in 1961 the footprint of humans was about 7.8 billion hectares (out of 10 billion hectares then available). At that time, then, humans were living within the regenerative capacity of the planet. That situation changed, however, in the 1970s and by 2010 it was estimated that the 'footprint' of humans was 18.1 billion hectares, with

only 12 billion hectares available. In other words, we have been living beyond the carrying capacity of our planet for about 40 years. This implies the use of reserves which are not then fully renewed, leaving a permanently increasing problem.

Of course, not everyone on the planet has the same living conditions and has the same resource use. In Africa and Asia-Pacific regions, the 'ecological footprint' of the average person is still within sustainable limits. In the EU, however, the average person uses roughly two and one-half times more resources than is sustainable. In the US, the average person uses four times more resources than is sustainable. The ecological footprint therefore is not just a measure of human impact, but also of inequality (see pages 72-73).

IN AFRICA AND ASIA-PACIFIC REGIONS, THE 'ECOLOGICAL FOOTPRINT' OF THE AVERAGE PERSON IS STILL WITHIN SUSTAINABLE LIMITS. IN THE EU, HOWEVER, THE AVERAGE PERSON USES ROUGHLY TWO AND ONE-HALF TIMES MORE RESOURCES THAN IS SUSTAINABLE.

Figure 3.3: Change in the average Ecological Footprint per capita and in population for each geographic region in 1961 and 2010
The area of each bar represents the total Footprint for each region (Global Footprint Network 2014)

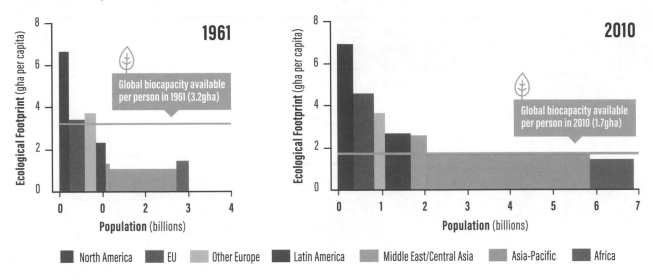

| North America | EU | Other Europe | Latin America | Middle East/Central Asia | Asia-Pacific | Africa |

LIVING PLANET INDEX

The importance of biodiversity from a sustainable development perspective have been highlighted a number of times in this chapter. One attempt to measure biodiversity in the planet is the 'Living Planet Index' (LPI), produced by the WWF.

One of the problems measuring biodiversity is that scientists have so far identified only a proportion of all species on the planet (the journal *Nature* estimated in 2011 that about 85% of species on the planet have yet to be discovered and identified). The Living Planet Index focuses on a subset of species that have been well defined and described: those with backbones (called vertebrates). This includes fish, amphibians, reptiles, birds and mammals. It does not, therefore, include the majority of animals on the planet (animals like beetles and other insects), nor does it include plants.

Figure 3.4: Living Planet Index shows a decline of 52% between 1980 and 2010 (WWF, ZSL, 2014)

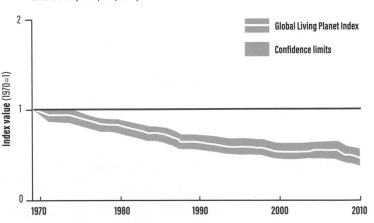

The Living Planet Index is based on measuring the population size of over 3,000 highly researched vertebrate species on land, freshwater and in the seas. Based upon this an overall index is calculated which can then be compared over the years to see if biodiversity is increasing or decreasing. Between 1970 and 2014, the LPI declined by 52%.

Source: WWF Living Planet Report, 2014, page 16

THE HAPPY PLANET INDEX

It was noted earlier than existing measures of 'development' (such as the Human Development Index or Gross Domestic Product per capita) do not include any measure of 'sustainability'. Both of the two measures discussed above (the Living Planet Index and the Ecological Footprint) arguably measure 'sustainability' but ignore 'development'.

The Happy Planet Index seeks to address this imbalance by looking both at measures of human wellbeing and balancing them with measures of environmental sustainability. Although the calculations involved are somewhat complex the basic concept of the Index is as follows:

Happy Planet Index =

$$\frac{Experienced\ well\ being \ \times\ Life\ expectancy \times Inequality\ of\ outcomes}{Ecological\ Footprint}$$

Data on well-being from an annual Gallup poll conducted in more than 150 countries is combined with data on life expectancy by the UN and compared with the country's ecological footprint based on data by the Global Footprint Network.

> *'Wealthy, western nations tend to score highly on life expectancy and wellbeing, but do not score highly on the Happy Planet Index overall, because of the environmental costs of how their economy is run.'*
>
> – The Happy Planet Index 2016 briefing paper

The Happy Planet Index is, in a sense, a measure of efficiency. The United States, for example, has a similar life expectancy and well-being scores to New Zealand and to Costa Rica, however it uses three times more ecological resources than Costa Rica and almost twice as much as New Zealand in order to achieve this goal. Hence, of the three, Costa Rica is most 'efficient' at 'producing happiness', New Zealand is middle ranked and the US is ranked

lowest of the three. In fact, the living planet index lists Costa Rica as the top performing country in on the "Happy Planet" measure for the third time.

A review of measures of sustainable development commissioned by the European Parliament in 2010 identified the following strengths and weaknesses with the Happy Planet Index:

Strengths

- It includes human and environmental factors.
- It measures important goals like happiness and life expectancy.
- It is easy to understand.
- The data is usually readily identifiable.

Weaknesses/Limitations

- Measuring happiness or life satisfaction is very subjective and may depend a lot on cultural norms.
- 'Happiness' is not easily affected by policy and so it may be unfair to judge a government based on the happiness of its people.
- The title of the index leads to misunderstandings and causes people to think it is a measure of happiness of people or countries when in fact it is intended as a measure of the planet's happiness (incorporating both the happiness of humans and the 'happiness' of the environment).

A further weakness not mentioned in this review is that the index contains no measure of political freedom meaning that non-democratic countries (like China) can readily appear as better performers than democratic countries (like the Netherlands, Denmark or Finland).

HPI Rank	Country	Region	Life Expectancy (years)	Well-being (0-10)	Inequality of outcomes	Ecological Footprint (gha/capita)		Happy Planet Index
1	Costa Rica	Americas	79.1	7.3	15%	2.8	=	44.7
2	Mexico	Americas	76.4	7.3	19%	2.9	=	40.7
8	Bangladesh	Asia Pacific	70.8	4.7	27%	0.7	=	38.4
12	Norway	Europe	81.3	7.7	7%	5.0	=	36.8
23	Brazil	Americas	73.9	6.9	22%	3.1	=	34.3
34	United Kingdom	Europe	80.4	6.9	9%	4.9	=	31.9
48	Ireland	Europe	80.5	7.0	8%	5.6	=	30.0
50	India	Asia Pacific	67.3	4.6	31%	1.2	=	29.2
72	China	Asia Pacific	75.4	5.1	17%	3.4	=	25.7
105	Australia	Asia Pacific	82.1	7.2	8%	9.3	=	21.2
108	United States of America	Americas	78.8	7.0	13%	8.2	=	20.7
111	Rwanda	sub-Saharan Africa	63.1	3.3	37%	0.9	=	19.6
128	South Africa	sub-Saharan Africa	56.3	5.1	33%	3.3	=	15.9
139	Luxembourg	Europe	81.1	7.0	7%	15.8	=	13.2
140	Chad	sub-Saharan Africa	50.8	4.0	51%	1.5	=	12.8

KEY FOR HPI COMPONENTS:
Average life expectancy:
75+ years = good

Average experienced
well-being: (0-10):
more than 6 = good

Inequality of outcomes:
less than 15% = good

Ecological Footprint (global
hectares per capita):
less than 1.73 (equal to the
world's biocapacity) = good

HPI Index data for selected
countries, source Happy Planet
Index report 2016:
http://happyplanetindex.org

IN NATURA...

READING

Wayne Ellwood (2013) *The No-Nonsense Guide to Degrowth and Sustainability*, New Internationalist, Oxford

D. Chivers (2011) *The No-Nonsense Guide to Climate Change*, New Internationalist, Oxford

Peter Singer (2002) *One World: the Ethics of Globalisation*, New Haven and London, Yale University Press

E. F. Schumacher (1973) *Small is Beautiful: Economics as if People Mattered*, Harper Perenniel (1989 edition), New York

Vandana Shiva (2005) *Earth Democracy: Justice, Sustainability, and Peace*, South End Press, New York

Social Watch (2016) *Spotlight on Sustainable Development*, Montevideo

UNDP (2007) *Human Development Report 2007/2008: Fighting climate change: Human solidarity in a divided world*, Basingstoke, Palgrave Macmillan

Worldwatch Institute (2011) Annual *State of the World Report*, Norton, New York and London

Living Planet Report (2014 and 2016) World Wildlife Foundation in association with the Zoological Society of London and the Global Footprint Network

MORE INFORMATION AND DEBATE

www.worldwatch.org – Worldwatch Institute in Washington

www.greenpeace.org – Greenpeace International site

www.ipcc.ch – home of the Intergovernmental Panel on Climate Change

www.guardian.co.uk/global-development – Guardian Newspaper UK section on development (includes a considerable amount of sustainable development)

www.unep.org – site of the United Nations Environment Programme

www.happyplanetindex.org – site of the New Economics Foundation (UK)

www.livingplanetindex.org – developed by the World Wildlife Foundation and the Zoological Society of London

OUR DEMAND FOR RENEWABLE ECOLOGICAL RESOURCES AND THE GOODS AND SERVICES THEY PROVIDE IS NOW EQUIVALENT TO MORE THAN 1.6 EARTHS

SINCE THE 1990S WE HAVE REACHED OVERSHOOT BY THE NINTH MONTH EVERY YEAR. WE DEMAND MORE RENEWABLE RESOURCES AND CO$_2$ SEQUESTRATION THAN THE PLANET CAN PROVIDE IN AN ENTIRE YEAR

ECOLOGICAL FOOTPRINT AND BIOCAPACITY

- The Ecological Footprint was developed to essentially measure human impact on the Earth's ecosystems. As outlined earlier in Chapter 3, the ecological footprint is related directly to the Earth's carrying capacity – its ability to support human life (and those of approximately 8.7 million other species)

- The Earth's carrying capacity is not fixed: technological developments have meant that the same planet can now provide more resources than was the case in the past. The World Wide Fund for Nature estimates that the capacity of the planet in 2010 was equivalent to 12 billion hectares (in 1961, it was estimated to be 8.7 million).

- However, since the 1960s global population has also grown as has overall consumption. While carrying capacity has increased by about 20%, population has more than doubled.

- It is estimated than in 1961 the 'footprint' of humans was about 7.8 billion hectares (of 10 the billion hectares then available); humans were then living within the regenerative capacity of the planet.

- However, in the 1970s, the situation changed completely– by 1980, it was estimated that the 'footprint' of humans was 12.3 billion hectares, with only 10.4 billion hectares available.

- In 2012, Global Ecological Footprint was 20.1 Billion Gha, or 2.8 Gha Per Capita. Earth's Total Biocapacity was 12.2 Billion Gha, or 1.7 Gha Per Capita.

 Ecological Footprint
the area of land and water it takes for a human population to generate the renewable resources it consumes and absorb the corresponding waste it generates

 Biocapacity
the capacity of the biosphere to regenerate and provide for life. It adds up the competing human demands, which include natural resources, waste absorption, water renewal, and productive areas dedicated to urban uses.

 A Global Hectare
a biologically productive hectare with world average productivity. Because each unit of space harbours a different portion of the global regenerative capacity, each unit is counted proportional to its global biocapacity share. For this reason, hectares are adjusted proportionally to their productivity and are expressed in global hectares.

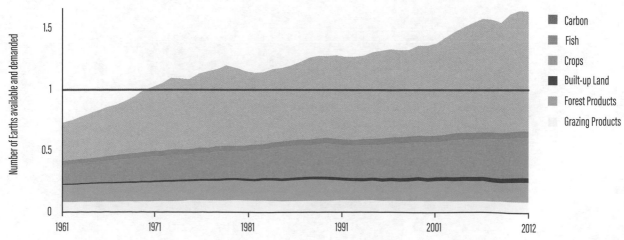

Legend:
- Carbon
- Fish
- Crops
- Built-up Land
- Forest Products
- Grazing Products

Y-axis: Number of Earths available and demanded

HOW MANY EARTHS DOES IT TAKE TO SUPPORT HUMANITY

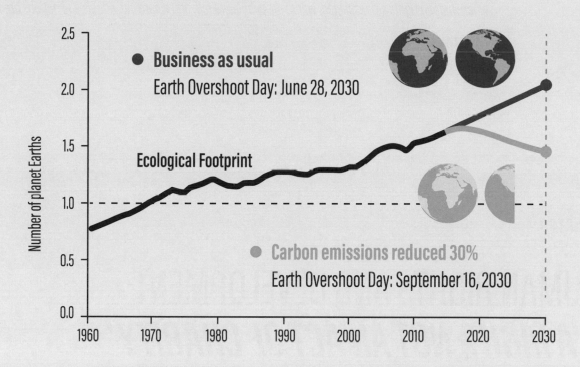

Business as usual
Earth Overshoot Day: June 28, 2030

Ecological Footprint

Carbon emissions reduced 30%
Earth Overshoot Day: September 16, 2030

Region	Population (millions)	Total Ecological Footprint Global Hectares Per Person in 2012	Biocapacity Deficit or Reserve	Number of Earths Required
World	7080	2.84	1.1	1.6
Africa	1035	1.4	0.2	0.8
Asia/Pacific	3880	2.3	1.4	1.3
EU 27	504	4.8	2.5	2.8
Latin America	605	2.8	2.5	1.6
Middle East/ Central Asia	396	2.9	2.0	1.7
North America	352	8.2	3.2	4.7
Other European	238	4.8	0.3	2.8
Low Income	836	1.0	0.1	0.6
Lower-Middle Income	2523	1.3	0.5	0.8
Upper-Middle income	2550	3.4	1.1	1.9
High Income	1100	6.2	3.0	3.6

Source: Global Footprint Network (2016) *National Footprint Accounts*
World Wildlife Fund (2014) *Living Planet Report* with the Zoological Society of London, Global Footprint Network and the Water Footprint Network

DEBATING ECOLOGICAL FOOTPRINTING

The idea of ecological footprinting has been the subject of argument and debate principally for its methods of measurement and the implications it has drawn from the results calculated. These debates aside (for a discussion visit www.footprintnetwork.org) the general outcomes from the reviewing the current footprints show that:

- most countries are in now significantly in ecological deficit, increasingly dependent on potentially unreliable trade in biocapacity;

- humanity is at or beyond global carrying capacity for key categories of consumption, particularly agriculture (factoring in soil loss and ecosystem degradation would reveal additional deficits);

- global carbon waste sinks are overflowing;

- the aggregate metabolism of the human economy exceeds the ecosystem's capacity to regenerate itself (and the gap is increasing)

'Peace, in the sense of the absence of war, is of little value to someone who is dying of hunger or cold. It will not remove the pain of torture inflicted on a prisoner of conscience. It does not comfort those who have lost their loved ones in floods caused by senseless deforestation in a neighbouring country. Peace can only last where human rights are respected, where the people are fed, and where individuals and nations are free'

DALAI LAMA

CHAPTER 4

HUMAN RIGHTS AND DEVELOPMENT - *'A RIGHT, NOT AN ACT OF CHARITY'*

OMAR GRECH

Having sketched the evolution of the concept of human rights and its emergence to the foreground of international politics post 1945, this chapter focuses primarily on the intrinsic relationship between development and human rights. It reviews the Universal Declaration of Human Rights and its associated Covenants; regional human rights institutions in Europe and Africa (and the debates surrounding each) and the 1986 Declaration on the Right to Development.

A number of current and contentious issues such as freedom of speech, human rights and security and migration are also explored.

KEYWORDS:

HUMAN RIGHTS; **PRINCIPLES**; FRAMEWORKS AND INSTRUMENTS; **UNIVERSAL**; INDIVISIBLE AND INALIENABLE; **CIVIL AND POLITICAL RIGHTS**; SOCIAL, ECONOMIC AND CULTURAL RIGHTS; **THE RIGHT TO DEVELOPMENT**; EUROPEAN CONVENTION ON HUMAN RIGHTS; **AFRICAN CHARTER ON HUMAN AND PEOPLES' RIGHTS**; SECURITY; **MIGRATION**; FREEDOM OF EXPRESSION

Photo: Elena Hermosa

INTRODUCTION

Human rights are a radical and revolutionary concept in a world dominated by states and intergovernmental institutions. The concept of human rights challenges the idea that rights can only be granted by the State or acquired by agreement; human rights are innate in every human person irrespective of the will of states or any contractual obligation. The language used in human rights treaties and declarations is that such rights are *inherent* in every individual by virtue of birth. Commenting on the United States Bill of Rights, US Supreme Court Judge, William J. Brennan noted in 1990:

> *'The Framers of the Bill of Rights did not purport to 'create' rights. Rather, they designed the Bill of Rights to prohibit our Government from infringing rights and liberties presumed to be pre-existing.'*

Such a perspective on rights has profound implications not just for rights per se but for a range of other fundamental issues – including development. In recent decades, the general debate on development has become increasingly influenced by the human rights 'conversation' as well as by human rights' principles, frameworks and instruments. This chapter focuses on human rights and on the ways in which human rights and development impact on each other. The major argument is that development issues need to be examined and analysed through a human rights' lens – implying that real human development is the platform upon which all may enjoy human rights and, in this sense, human rights and development are one and the same thing. A subsidiary argument offered is that a development perspective assists in achieving a more comprehensive understanding of human rights overall.

An understanding of human rights is crucial to a full 'reading' of development – something that is increasingly highlighted, especially in developing world commentary and analysis, with fundamental repercussions for international relations, aid and trade as well as humanitarian interventions. This chapter explores some of these key issues, in particular:

- how we understand and describe human rights.
- the evolution of human rights and the role of international law.
- the right to development.
- some debates and controversies surrounding human rights and the right to development.

DESCRIBING HUMAN RIGHTS

Although deceptively simple, defining human rights as *'the rights that every individual possesses simply by virtue of being a human being'* is revolutionary in its consequences especially in circumstances such as those of the developing world, where states like to present themselves as the source and origin of all rights and duties, including those related to development. Human rights challenge such assumptions by asserting that the human person is the source of rights independent of, and often in opposition to, state authority. American political scientist, Noam Chomsky comments:

> *'States are not moral agents, people are, and can impose moral standards on powerful institutions.'*

Source: The United States and the "Challenge of Relativity" in Tony Evans (ed. 1998) Human Rights Fifty Years On: A Reappraisal, Manchester University Press

If we examine the ways in which rights are acquired in domestic legal systems, it is indeed the State, through the laws which it enacts, that creates rights or allows rights to be created. The State creates rights through legislation: for instance the State may enact a law which grants children the right to inherit their parents' property. On the other hand, the State allows rights to be created when its laws enable individuals to sell or exchange rights. For example, contract law allows individuals to acquire rights over property through the consent of two or more individuals.

In recent decades, the UN has begun to emphasise three adjectives in describing human rights; human rights are said to be universal, indivisible and inalienable. The notion of universality of human rights was to the fore in the minds of the drafters of the Universal Declaration of Human Rights of 1948 as the title itself implies - the first paragraph of the Preamble makes an immediate reference to the *equal and inalienable rights of all members of the human family*. In the 1993 World Conference on Human Rights held in Vienna the ideas of indivisibility and interdependence of human rights were highlighted.

UNIVERSAL, INDIVISIBLE AND INALIENABLE

Universal - if human rights are rights human beings possess by virtue of being human, it follows that all humans possess them - there can be no distinction between human beings based on any criterion such as nationality, sex or sexual orientation, religion, culture etc. This is an important notion in the context of development and the right to development. It links all members of the human race in a chain of rights and responsibilities that have implications for law, justice and morality. Linked to universality is the notion of equality as emphasised in the Universal Declaration which in Article 1 states: *'All human beings are born free and equal in dignity and rights.'* Such ideas - universality, equality and a common humanity - lie at the heart of human rights. Concretely, this means that in the context of development the people of South Africa, India or Syria are entitled to the same enjoyment of human rights as people in Europe or the US.

Indivisible - the term human rights refers to a plurality of different rights - economic, civil, social, political and cultural. When we describe human rights as indivisible we mean that all of these various parts form one integral whole which may not be divided. Human rights can therefore be understood as a package which may not be divided into its various components for the purpose of picking and choosing some rights at the expense of others or for the purpose of giving importance to some rights while ignoring the rest.

Historically, and especially during the Cold War, the West tended to emphasise civil and political rights at the expense of economic and social rights whilst Communist states tended to reverse the emphasis - with very considerable implications for development.

Indivisibility is linked to the concept of interdependence - meaning that each right forming part of human rights is only fully enjoyed when the other rights are also being enjoyed. That is why we say that human rights are indivisible and interdependent; every right forming part of human rights is equally important, deserves equal protection and promotion and can only be truly enjoyed if all other rights are concurrently implemented.

Inalienable - is a legalistic word which simply means 'that which may not be given away'. To alienate means to sell or part with. If something is inalienable it means that it may not be sold or parted with in any other way. Hence when we describe human rights as inalienable we are saying that human rights may not be sold or renounced. This has practical implications for the protection of human rights - for example, if an individual is arrested by the police and is then forced to sign a document in which she/he accepts to be kept under arrest without trial indefinitely, that document would be invalid since no one may alienate or renounce her/his right not to be subject to arbitrary arrest.

THE STORY OF HUMAN RIGHTS

The history of human rights may be viewed from two perspectives. Firstly, there is the history of human rights themselves - lawyers and politicians sometimes like to think that the story of human rights started in 1945 with the establishment of the United Nations or in 1948 with the adoption of the Universal Declaration of Human Rights. However, according to the description of rights above, the history of human rights is essentially as long as that of humanity. The history of human rights is effectively the stories of the struggles to give legal definition and meaning to the value of human dignity on domestic and international levels. Thus, the history of human rights can be traced through the history of the values which underpin human rights such as freedom, justice and, above all, dignity.

Early philosophers and commentators on human rights' values included:

MO-ZI, CHINESE, 470BC-390BC

 Key idea - an individual owes respect to all other individuals and not only to family or clan but universally throughout the world

PLATO, GREEK, 427BC-347BC

 Key idea - the most important thing for a government to enforce is justice. Justice means doing what is right and fair

ARISTOTLE, GREEK, 384BC-322BC

 Key idea - if liberty and equality, as is thought by some, are chiefly to be found in democracy, they will be best attained when all persons alike share in the government to the utmost

CICERO, ROMAN, 106BC-43BC

 Key idea - justice consists in doing no injury to others and there is decency in giving them no offence

AL-FARABI, PERSIAN, 870-950

 Key idea - the perfect city is a society in which all individuals are endowed with rights and live in love and charity with their neighbours.

In addition, all major religions have had important and positive things to say about human dignity and therefore human rights. The following quote from Micheline Ishay highlights how religion has influenced the development of human rights, especially through a common emphasis on respect for fellow human beings.

> *'Despite many controversies regarding the origins of human rights, few would dispute that religious humanism, Stoicism, and natural rights theorists of antiquity influenced our secular modern understanding of rights...most religious texts, like the Bible, Buddhist texts, the New Testament and the Koran incorporate moral and humanistic principles, often phrased in terms of duties...The religious origins of universal ethics are greatly indebted to the Bible, whose teachings are shared by Jews, Christians and Muslims alike...The Ten Commandments represented a code of morality and mutual respect that had far-reaching influence on the Western world...Similar moral and humanistic principles can be found in Buddhism.'*

Micheline R. Ishay, (ed., 1997) The Human Rights Reader, Routledge, London

In this context, when we talk of respecting human rights we are essentially thinking about *justice*. A lack of human rights would mean an absence of justice. The genesis of human rights reflected this preoccupation with fairness and equality. The notion of natural law – people are born with rights, and their very existence presupposes the existence of such rights – was originally based upon the concept of natural justice.

Philosophers such as Rousseau and Hobbes, not satisfied with natural law, developed the idea of human rights as part of a social contract – people accept limitations on natural freedoms in exchange for social order and peace. Human rights were part of the *'state of humankind'*, created to ensure a peaceful and just existence that a *'state of nature'* could not. A human rights based approach to development, therefore, is one that is preoccupied with ensuring dignity, social justice and equality first and foremost.

It is important to recognise that human rights ideas did not suddenly emerge in 1945, while also acknowledging that the major developments in the adoption of legal measures, national or international, intended to promote and protect human rights, resulted from political crises, devastating wars or similarly challenging situations. This history of human rights therefore adheres to one of the laws of history outlined by the historian Arnold Toynbee who referred to the historical law of *'progress through crisis'*.

WORLD WAR II AND ITS AFTERMATH

The well-documented atrocities of the Second World War period forced the international community to reflect on necessary interventions to avoid such atrocities in the future with action being agreed on two fronts - human rights and human responsibilities. The values that were to lay the foundations for the human rights edifice constructed post-1945 had already been developed practically by the Allied Powers during World War II. In particular, President Franklin Roosevelt's 1941 enunciation of the Four Freedoms that ought to prevail globally was an important moment in shaping the post-war agenda. The freedoms outlined by President Roosevelt were:

- Freedom of speech and expression.
- Freedom of worship.
- Freedom from fear.
- Freedom from want.

The inclusion of the latter two freedoms was especially significant as they departed from the traditional American notion of civil and political freedoms to include conceptions of social, economic and human security, which are so fundamental to human development.

At the Nuremberg Tribunals of 1945-46, set up to try Nazi war criminals, a key principle was established; individuals have responsibilities and obligations under international law. Therefore, individuals who commit grave breaches of human rights are responsible under international law and are liable for punishment for such acts.

The human rights side of the coin was immediately evident in the Preamble to the Charter of the United Nations (1945) which points out that one of the aims of the UN is that of *encouraging respect for human rights and for fundamental freedoms*. The Charter as a whole contains numerous references to the term human rights but there is no definition or description of the term – the task of definition fell to the Commission on Human Rights established by the General Assembly of the UN and led to the formulation of the Universal Declaration of Human Rights, adopted on the 10th December 1948.

The Declaration is of particular interest in a number of respects:

- The Preamble describes the context, the values and the key ideas that underpin the document, in particular it refers to the *'inherent dignity'* of every individual and to *'inalienable rights'*.
- The Preamble also introduces the notion of gender equality by referring to the *'equal rights of men and women'*.
- It emphasises the equal importance of political and economic rights with phrases such as *'freedom of speech and belief and freedom from fear and want'*.

Unlike later human rights' documents and instruments, the Declaration brings together both civil and political rights (such as freedom of assembly, of expression and the right to life) as well as economic and social rights (such as the right to work and the right to education). Echoing Roosevelt's Four Freedoms, the Declaration in its Preamble envisages:

> *'the advent of a world in which human beings shall enjoy freedom of speech and belief and freedom from fear and want has been proclaimed the highest aspiration of the common people.'*

Following the adoption of the Declaration, the UN Commission on Human Rights started work on an International Covenant on Human Rights. This Covenant was intended to render the rights listed in the Declaration legally binding on states. The Covenant, unlike the Declaration, would impose direct legal obligations on states.

Originally, the Covenant was intended to be a single text, including both civil and political rights as well as economic and social rights - this would have continued the example set in the Declaration with a single document including all human rights. However, the work of the Commission fell victim to the political agendas of the Cold War. The Western bloc increasingly wanted to give preference to civil and political rights while the Communist bloc insisted on the primacy of economic, social and cultural rights. The notion of the indivisibility of human rights was challenged seriously and persistently.

These political rivalries and Cold War dynamics delayed the drafting of the Covenant and eventually a decision was taken to split the single text into two Covenants:

- the International Covenant on Civil and Political Rights (ICCPR).
- the International Covenant on Economic, Social and Cultural Rights (ICESCR).

These two Covenants were adopted in 1966, 18 years after the adoption of the Universal Declaration and only came into force in 1976, a further 10 years later. The United Nations has, over the past 50 years promoted the adoption of a number of treaties and conventions dealing with specific human rights' issues. This has been important because it has kept human rights on the agenda of the UN as well as providing legal protection for individuals suffering racial and gender discrimination, torture, as well as for specific categories, such as children.

A criticism of these Conventions is that the reporting mechanisms they utilise are weak and fail to ensure adequately the implementation of the rights contained in the various Conventions. For instance, none of the Conventions allow for an automatic right of individuals, whose convention rights have been breached, to bring a claim against the State before an international tribunal. Furthermore, the ICESCR acknowledges that the rights contained

THREE GENERATIONS OF RIGHTS?

Some commentators have classified human rights into *'three generations of rights'* reflecting the different historical periods in which these rights emerged:

- *First generation rights* - associated with civil and political rights (e.g. the right to freedom from arbitrary arrest, to freedom of assembly or freedom of conscience and expression).

- *Second generation rights* - those rights which guarantee the economic and social rights of individuals (e.g. the right to health, education, employment and housing).

- *Third generation rights* - these rights were not directly included in the Universal Declaration and are usually termed as Group or People's Rights (e.g. the right to self-determination, the right to development etc.,) and are rights which can only be fully achieved within the context of a community. Some commentators deny the status of human rights to this category, claiming that human rights are by definition only those rights pertaining to an individual.

There is now also talk of a Fourth Generation of Rights linked mostly to issues of Intergenerational Justice or the Rights of Future Generations.

therein should be realised 'progressively' and this has been used to justify failure to implement social and economic rights to any significant extent.

REGIONAL HUMAN RIGHTS MECHANISMS

Action to protect human rights can be taken at different levels - domestic (or national), regional and international – for example, regional mechanisms exist both in Europe (the European Convention on Human Rights) and in Africa (the African Charter on Human and People's Rights). These legal instruments are adopted by regional organisations such as the Council of Europe and the African Union while at the international level, it is usually the UN that drafts and adopts human rights treaties. The critics of such regional arrangements note:

- If human rights are universal should there not be also universal protection?
- Don't regional mechanisms reduce the

relevance of the international mechanisms supported by the UN?
- Isn't there a risk of increasing different interpretations of human rights by the different regional mechanisms?

Supporters of such mechanisms emphasise the positive aspects:

- It is easier to find agreement among a reduced number of states with common cultural/historical traditions.
- Decisions by regional bodies are more likely to be respected for the same reason.
- Regional bodies may have, as in the case of the European Court of Human Rights, powers which UN Treaty bodies simply do not have.

The UN was initially suspicious of regional mechanisms fearing they would reduce its own credibility but eventually the UN itself began to advocate the establishment of regional human rights instruments where none existed.

CIVIL AND POLITICAL RIGHTS WORLDWIDE

'Five years on from one of the most dynamic demonstrations of people power the world has ever seen, governments are using increasingly calculated means to crush dissent, not just in the Middle East, but globally. Particularly disconcerting is the ample evidence that repression has now become as sophisticated as it is brutal.' Amnesty International Annual Report 2016

GLOBAL FREEDOM: STATUS BY POPULATION

👤 TOTAL POPULATION: **7,315,804,000**

36%
40%
24%

FREE
PARTLY FREE
NOT FREE

GLOBAL FREEDOM: STATUS BY COUNTRY

🌐 TOTAL COUNTRIES: **195**

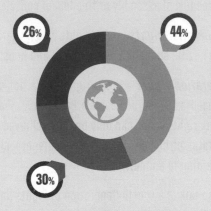

26%
44%
30%

The above data is based on the annual Freedom in the World Report produced by the independent US-based Freedom House using 25 indicators which essentially measure political rights and civil liberties (see: **www.freedomhouse.org/report/freedom-world-2016/methodology**)

GLOBAL FREEDOM: A DECADE OF DECLINE

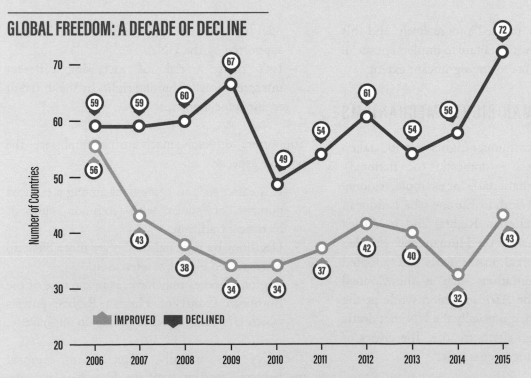

Number of Countries

70 —
60 —
50 —
40 —
30 —
20 —

59 59 60 67 49 54 61 54 58 72

56 43 38 34 34 37 42 40 32 43

▬ IMPROVED ▬ DECLINED

2006 2007 2008 2009 2010 2011 2012 2013 2014 2015

The recorded decline in global freedom in each of the past 10 years is the result of a number of factors including: ongoing political repression and human rights abuses in, for example China, Russia, Venezuela, Thailand, Ethiopia, Turkey and in the countries of the Gulf along with censorship and information control; widespread and ongoing corruption in, for example Nigeria, Brazil, and Moldova, as well as in entrenched authoritarian regimes and *'division and doubts about global leadership among democratic powers around the world, resulting in wavering support for democracy beyond their borders.'*

WORST OF THE WORST

 Only 18 of the world's 195 states and territories were known to carry out a death sentence in 2015. 102 have completely abolished the death penalty yet in 2015, an estimated 3,500-4,000 executions took place globally with the bulk of these in just 4 countries (China - by far the largest numbers - Iran, Saudi Arabia and the United States).

 According to Amnesty International, despite the existence of the 1987 the UN Convention Against Torture with 159 state signatories, torture still occurs in 141 countries - many of them actual signatories to that convention. 40% of people worldwide believe torture can be justified against suspected terrorists.

 The UN Working Group on Enforced Disappearances reported that in 2014, more than 43,000 cases of such disappearances involving 88 countries still remain to be 'clarified', many dating back decades (Iraq has the largest number with more than 16,400 along with Sri Lanka, Algeria, El Salvador, Guatemala and Peru).

 According to the World Health Organisation (2016), **recent figures** (80 countries) **indicate that about 1 in 3** (35%) **of women worldwide have experienced either physical and/or sexual intimate partner violence or non-partner sexual violence in their lifetime.**

 According to United Nations High Commisioner for Refugees (UNHCR), for the first time since 1945, the number of forcibly displaced people worldwide reached 50 million and is estimated to be almost 60 million which includes 15 million people deemed to be 'stateless' (Institute on Statelessness and Inclusion 2014).

 In 78 countries sexual acts between adults of the same sex are criminalised.

((•)) FREEDOM ON THE NET: GLOBAL POPULATION (BASED ON 88% OF THE WORLDS INTERNET USERS)

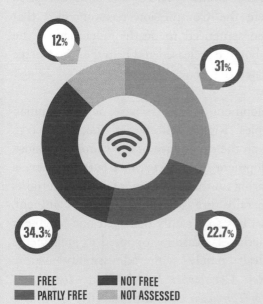

12%

31%

34.3%

22.7%

■ FREE
■ PARTLY FREE
■ NOT FREE
■ NOT ASSESSED

Most frequently censored topics: criticism of authorities, corruption, political opposition, satire, social commentary, blasphemy, mobilization for public causes and LGBT issues, ethnic and religious minorities and conflict.

The Freedom on the Net Report 2015 comments:

'Digital activism has been and remains a vital driver of change around the world, particularly in societies that lack political rights and press freedom. The greatest gains, however, have been made through legislative changes or judicial decisions, indicating that countries with meaningful political debates and independent judiciaries have a distinct advantage in safeguarding internet freedom over their more authoritarian counterparts.' (2015:13)

CASE STUDY:

THE AFRICAN CHARTER ON HUMAN AND PEOPLES' RIGHTS

The African Charter on Human and Peoples' Rights is one of the youngest and most challenging of human rights regional mechanisms; adopted in 1981 in Banjul (sometimes referred to as the Banjul Charter), it came into force in 1986. The title of the Charter immediately highlights its own particularities:

- It includes people's rights, such as the right to peace and security, as well as the people's right to development.

- It includes a list of the duties of individuals including the duty to preserve the harmonious development of the family, the duty to preserve and strengthen positive African cultural values as well as to pay taxes imposed by law in the interest of the society.

- The Preamble makes specific reference to African history - in particular colonialism - and emphasises the importance of the right to development.

- Unlike other regional human rights mechanisms, it includes economic and social rights including the right to health and to education.

These characteristics are considered as positive by some in that they produce a text that includes human rights from all generations of rights while acknowledging an African 'approach' making the Charter 'culturally sensitive'. Criticisms of the Charter have focused on the following:

- The references to certain specific duties owed by the individual to the State weakens human rights and are at any rate inappropriate in a human rights instrument.

- The rights guaranteed are subject to wider limitations than the limitations attached to the same or similar rights in the European or Inter-American regional instruments.

- The Charter provides a weak monitoring mechanism (the Commission), which has none of the judicial powers or the effectiveness of the European Court – however, since January 2004, there has been an African Court on Human and People's Rights but it is too early to assess its impact and, unlike the European Court, the African Court does not have jurisdiction to hear individual complaints against a State Party without the consent of the same State.

Unlike the European Convention, the African Charter's implementation and enforcement procedures are not well developed and the African Commission on Human and Peoples' Rights has limited enforcement powers. Nevertheless, the Commission has delivered important decisions, especially relating to the military government of Nigeria in the mid-1990s. In the *Civil Liberties Organisation v. Nigeria* case, the Commission found that Decrees issued by the military government suspending the Constitution and prohibiting Nigerian Courts from examining the validity of the Decrees were in breach of Article 7 of the African Charter (right to a fair trial). This decision was reiterated in *Constitutional Rights Project v. Nigeria* case where the Commission recommended that seven men sentenced to death under one of the Decrees should be released and held that the Decree itself violated the African Charter.

The development of the African Court on Human and Peoples' Rights will be of special interest. Drawing on the experience of the European Court, the development of the African Court may have a direct bearing on the development on human rights more generally throughout the African continent. The Court has so far only delivered one judgment on the merits of a case (as opposed to judgements which dealt purely with admissibility issues). In the *Rev. Christopher R. Mtikila v. The United Republic of Tanzania* case, a prospective candidate for elections claimed that Tanzania's Eighth and Eleventh Constitutional Amendment Act, which required any political candidate for president, parliament, or local government elections to be a member of, and sponsored by, a political party *'violated its citizens' rights of freedom of association, the right to participate in public/governmental affairs, and the right against discrimination.'* In its judgment the Court ruled that the constitutional provisions were incompatible with the provisions of the Charter and requested Tanzania to amend the constitution to allow independent candidates to run for election.

This serves to emphasise the point that the degree to which the Court will be successful will depend to some extent on whether State Parties allow individual petitions by aggrieved individuals. Tanzania is one of the few states in Africa to have done so. A campaign to lobby for the acceptance of the right to individual petition across the African continent would thus be a useful starting point.

THE DECLARATION ON THE RIGHT TO DEVELOPMENT

Agreed on the 4th December 1986, this Declaration essentially recognised development as a human right. It proclaims that every individual has a right to develop politically, economically and socially or, to put this in human rights terms, every individual has the right to all rights mentioned in the Universal Declaration and not simply to a selection of those rights depending on the whim of her/his state. The Declaration brings together, in concise form, the two Covenants. Its importance lies in the explicit statement that development of all human beings is a matter of right. Not merely of right but of human rights.

A Summary of the Declaration

The Declaration contains a Preamble and 10 articles which make explicit that there are rights and duties that operate at the individual, state and interstate level. Article 1 states that, the right to development is one which individuals and peoples should both enjoy and contribute towards. This Article also makes clear that development has economic, social, cultural and political dimensions.

Article 2 (2) makes an interesting point concerning the responsibility for implementing the right to development: *'All human beings have a responsibility for development, individually and collectively…'*

The subsequent Articles also focus on the primary responsibility of States to:

- Formulate appropriate national and international development policies.
- Create national and international conditions favourable to development.
- Cooperate with each other in ensuring development and eliminating obstacles to development.
- Take all steps to eliminate massive violations of human rights.
- Cooperate with each other to promote all human rights for everyone without distinction.
- Promote international peace and security and achieve disarmament.
- Take all necessary measures to ensure the right to development and ensure equality of opportunity in access to education, health, food, housing etc.
- Encourage popular participation in every sphere of activity.

The Declaration attempts to bring together the individual, the community in which she/he lives and the international system. All these actors have a role to play in ensuring the implementation of the right to development – in this context the debate on the right to development has highlighted a key aspect of modern thinking and practice on development – the fundamental importance and role of civil society. Development is no longer the preserve of the state but also includes all types of civil society organisations.

HUMAN RIGHTS AND DEVELOPMENT

In 2000, the United Nations Development Programme (UNDP) Human Development Report focused upon human rights and development. Its conclusions were resoundingly clear: human rights are not some form of 'reward' of development – they are critical to achieving it. The report draws a parallel between human rights and development: they both seek to ensure the freedom, well-being and dignity of all people everywhere.

When human rights and development progress together, they reinforce one another. As the report concludes, *'human development is essential for realising human rights, and human rights are essential for full human development'.*

Human rights add value to the development agenda by:

- Drawing attention to accountability for providing all people with rights.
- Providing a moral legitimacy to development.
- Shifting priority onto the most deprived and excluded societal groups.
- Directing attention towards the need for information and the creation of a political voice for all people.

In turn, human development is an asset to human rights through:

- Creating a dynamic, long-term perspective on the fulfilment of rights.
- Focusing attention on the socio-economic context required for human rights to be realised, as well as on the contexts in which human rights are threatened.
- Providing a systematic assessment of the economic and institutional constraints to the realisation of rights.

The report has a number of suggestions in the quest to achieve global human development and ensure that the human rights of all individuals are respected;

- **Legislation is not a sufficient safeguard** - every country must strengthen its social arrangements for securing human freedoms. Laws alone do not guarantee human rights: they require adequate institutions to implement legislation, as well as a backing culture of norms and ethics that reinforces, rather than threatens, the legal structure.

- The fulfilment of all human rights requires **democracy** that is inclusive, with a separation of powers and public accountability. Elections are not enough.

- The **eradication of poverty** is not just a challenge to development: it is also a central goal of human rights fulfilment.

- **Accountability should not be limited to states**, but also extend to non-state actors. Furthermore, state accountability does not end at their borders. In an integrated world, human rights must be accompanied by global justice.

- **Information and statistics** are powerful tools for creating a culture of accountability and realising human rights. Spreading correct information can prevent myth-making and mobilise changes in policy and behaviour.

- Achieving universal human rights will require **action and commitment from all societal groups** – from government, to NGOs, media, the business communities and other opinion leaders.

- **Stronger international action is needed**: development cooperation must be rights-based and free of conditionality and existing human rights legislation and mechanisms must be strengthened.

For more see: UN Office of the High Commissioner for Human Rights (2016) *Frequently asked Questions on the Right to Development,* Fact Sheet 37

DEVELOPMENT - BETWEEN PEOPLE'S RIGHTS AND INDIVIDUAL RIGHTS

The right to development within the African Charter, which was referred to earlier, is considered to be a 'people's right' rather than an individual right. One may argue that development (together with the right of self-determination) has been a catalyst in introducing the notion of people's rights into human rights language – such rights might be described as those rights persons enjoy as members of their community rather than on a purely individual level.

Development thus provides new perspectives on how human rights work in, and relate to, the state, the community and the individual. Development operates at all of these levels and therefore is a link between them all. The human rights of an individual 'live' in a community that, in its turn, is rooted in a state.

This debate is also relevant within the context of the right to development itself. Some lawyers have argued that the 'beneficiary' of the right to development is the community and not individuals. It may be suggested that the question of who is the beneficiary of the right is wrongly framed. Suggesting a contradiction between the individual and the community in respect of the enjoyment of the right to development presupposes that development is a finite quantity. A more appropriate proposition could revolve around how we are to ensure development of the individual, the community and the state together. The development of each of these is interdependent and interconnected.

Finally, development brings to human rights a more balanced perspective to how human rights function i.e. that rights are not enjoyed by individuals in a vacuum, but within the fabric of society.

A RIGHTS-BASED APPROACH TO DEVELOPMENT

'The satisfaction of the needs of a people should be perceived as a right and not as an act of charity. It is a right which should be made effective by norms and institutions.'

The quotation above from Algerian international lawyer and former President of the International Court of Justice, Mohammed Bedjaoui, stresses what might be considered the most crucial contribution of human rights to development i.e. the move from considering development as a morally desirable objective to considering development as a right belonging to every person.

To those brought up in the West, contributing money to charity is a widespread and mostly unquestioned activity; images of the starving African child present impulses of moral or religious responsibility. We should do *'good'* and thus give of our plenty to those who happen to be *'less fortunate than ourselves'*. There are few suggestions that the starving child has a right to eat or drink, s/he is merely unlucky. The underlying assumption is that we are the active ones, the ones who are central or of most importance – there is little suggestion of an issue of law or rights.

Human rights challenge such assumptions and ask us to look at the image in a different frame, a legal one - the child is having her/his rights violated and, legally, when a right is being violated the corollary is that someone is responsible for that breach and the image now becomes much more demanding and potentially dangerous. The viewer of the photo changes from a potential saviour (by virtue of their good deeds) to a potential rights violator.

A rights framework approaches development in a more rigorous fashion posing a set of difficult questions:

- What is the legal basis of the right to development?
- Who is/are the beneficiary/ies of the right?
- Who is responsible for ensuring that the persons owning the right actually enjoy it?
- How is the right implemented?
- What happens if the right is not implemented?

'For too long the development debate has ignored the fact that poverty tends to be characterised not only by material insufficiency but also by denial of rights. What is needed is a rights-based approach to development. Ensuring essential political, economic and social entitlements and human dignity for all people provides the rationale for policy. These are not a luxury affordable only to the rich and powerful but an indispensable component of national development efforts.'

UN Commission for Social Development, 36th session, 1998

The practical consequences of the existence of the right to development are of utmost importance as they present the greatest challenge to the right itself. Critics of the right to development argue that no such right exists because its content and consequences have not been clarified. As Mohammed Bedjaoui states:

'It is clear, however, that a right which is not opposable by the possessor of the right against the person from whom the right is due is not a right in the full legal sense. This constitutes the challenge which the right to development throws down to contemporary international law...'

The future of the right to development relies, to a considerable extent, on whether and how the challenge presented by Bedjaoui is met. What international norms should be in place stating the exact content of the right to development? What

international institutions should be established monitoring the implementation of the right? What sanction should be imposed on those responsible for breaches of the right?

These questions apply equally to other human rights that are, as yet, not adequately implemented. Issues of implementation present core difficulties for international law in general and human rights in particular.

SOME CURRENT DEBATES ON HUMAN RIGHTS

'Norms, especially global norms, are exceedingly fragile things... As more players conform to a norm, it gets stronger. In the same way, as more players flout it, disregard it or loudly attack it, it begins to lose that ever so subtle effect on the mind that is the basis of its power. When a norm is flouted and consequences do not follow, the norm begins to die.'

Sina Odugbemi, World Bank 2015

SECURITY AND HUMAN RIGHTS

Ever since the September 11th attacks of 2001 security considerations have impacted significantly on the practice of both human rights and human development throughout the world. Governments have always used the threat of terror or disorder to limit human rights within their jurisdictions. The use of special legislation to combat states of emergency whether real or (wilfully) imagined is of ancient origin and historically states and empires have suspended the liberties of their citizens or subjects whenever they felt it necessary (or convenient) to do so, citing reasons of security and stability.

In recent times the prioritising of security over freedom became a key human rights concern in the context of the response to the 2001 attacks on New York and Washington DC. In the USA and the

UK, the immediate reaction to the attacks was the enactment of legislation giving wide powers to the state to address terrorist activities and organisations. These Acts (the PATRIOT ACT in the USA and the Anti-Terrorism, Crime and Security Act in the UK) involved the suspension of a number of human rights provisions related (mainly) to arbitrary detention as well as fair trial provisions. In the case of the UK legislation, one of the sections was found to be in breach of the European Convention on Human Rights by the House of Lords in 2004.

In the wake of the 'Arab Spring' and the spread of popular movements across the Arab World and elsewhere and as a direct response to recent Isis-inspired terrorist attacks in various parts of the world, there has been a re-ignition of the debate as to how states should balance security considerations and human rights obligations and agendas under domestic, regional and international law. International human rights law accepts that in times of emergency states may legitimately derogate from their human rights obligations. The International Covenant on Civil and Political Rights (ICCPR) provides in Article 4 that in *time of public emergency which threatens the life of the nation and the existence of which is officially proclaimed* states may derogate from their obligations under the Covenant but only *'to the extent strictly required by the exigencies of the situation, provided that such measures are not inconsistent with their other obligations under international law and do not involve discrimination solely on the ground of race, colour, sex, language, religion or social origin'.*

Derogation is not permissible with respect to certain specified rights such as the right to life, freedom from torture (and other inhumane and degrading treatment) and freedom of thought, conscience and religion. It should be noted that the wording is carefully chosen in this context. In order to derogate from their human rights obligations, states have to prove that such a derogation is strictly required by the situation.

IN THE WAKE OF THE 'ARAB SPRING' AND THE SPREAD OF POPULAR MOVEMENTS ACROSS THE ARAB WORLD AND ELSEWHERE AND AS A DIRECT RESPONSE TO RECENT ISIS-INSPIRED TERRORIST ATTACKS IN VARIOUS PARTS OF THE WORLD, THERE HAS BEEN A RE-IGNITION OF THE DEBATE AS TO HOW STATES SHOULD BALANCE SECURITY CONSIDERATIONS AND HUMAN RIGHTS OBLIGATIONS AND AGENDAS UNDER DOMESTIC, REGIONAL AND INTERNATIONAL LAW.

The history of all derogations from the ICCPR, from European and American Conventions highlight the fact that a variety of states internationally seek such derogations including, for example Peru, the UK, Israel, Algeria, Chile, Russia, Nicaragua, Turkey etc.

The reality is that most (but not all) human rights are not absolute. Rights such as freedom of expression and assembly have always been subject to limitations. It is also well established in international human rights law that certain rights may be suspended in times of emergency. This does not mean that rights may be arbitrarily curtailed on the basis of legislative or bureaucratic discretion. The manner in which restrictions are to be determined and imposed and the criteria which apply to the formulation of restrictions are crucial.

To be meaningful, human rights cannot be subject to the whims and fancies of the legislative, the executive branches of government or majoritarian dictates swayed by gusts of public passion. This is especially the case in the wake of terrorist atrocities that create a climate suitable to the restriction of human rights. In these circumstances it is extremely easy for governments to fan the flames of public indignation in order to erode human rights by imposing restrictions which transform human rights into ordinary statutory rights that governments are free to confer or withdraw at their pleasure.

There is no question that terrorism is in itself an abuse of human rights and that acts of terror can constitute crimes against humanity. It is equally clear that governments do have a duty to prevent terrorist acts. However, anti-terrorist legislation would be counterproductive if, in itself, it breaches fundamental human rights. Legislation claiming to protect citizens cannot blatantly breach their rights. Striking the right balance between the interests of human security and human rights is critical. This is where a truly independent and impartial judiciary plays a crucial role in ensuring that the legislative and executive branches of government do not tilt the balance unduly in favour of security at the expense of human rights.

In conclusion, it is evident that at a time when international, regional and domestic agendas are dominated by the threat of terrorism, security has become the prevailing paradigm, pushing human rights (and, by implication human development) to a subsidiary role. Within such a context, there are two important aspects that need to be emphasised:

1. Human rights legislation needs to be carefully constructed and formulated to ensure that limitations to rights and derogations from rights (where applicable) are narrowly defined; and

2. Domestic, regional and (if available) international courts need to be in the vanguard in ascertaining that governments apply any limitations and derogations in a reasonable and judicious manner.

In the context of development today, critics of the focus on security argue that the balance has swung away from human development (and human security, broadly defined) towards a far narrower and traditional definition of security thereby undermining key aspects of 'universalist'

human rights understandings and practices in recent decades. Critics also argue that development (including aid and humanitarian intervention agendas) is now being absorbed in narrowly defined security concerns. Aid, human rights and development NGOs argue that the threat of terrorism has given states the opportunity to effectively undermine human rights; not only has the practice of detention without trial reappeared in countries such as the US and Britain, many members of the global *'coalition of the willing'* have passed new national security laws which have used terrorism as a pretext for repressing legitimate internal opposition in states as varied India, China, Thailand, Pakistan, Nepal, Zimbabwe, Bangladesh, Afghanistan, South Africa, Nigeria, Uganda, Kenya and Tanzania *(on this debate, see Christian Aid 2004, The Politics of Poverty: Aid in the New Cold War and British Overseas NGOs for Development (BOND) 2003, Global Security and Development).*

FREEDOM OF EXPRESSION

As discussed in chapter 10 one of the consequences of the failure to place issues such as migration squarely in a human rights framework (in particular its human development components) has been increasingly xenophobic and anti-immigrant sentiments being expressed in social as well as traditional media worldwide. This raises the question as to whether the right to freedom of expression is being used to undermine the dignity and rights of migrants and the extent to which freedom of expression should be controlled and restrained. This is a frequently asked question in the field of human rights and often also in relation to development and the developing world.

Freedom of expression, unlike freedom from torture or slavery, is not an absolute right. Human rights law acknowledges this clearly. The International Covenant on Civil and Political Rights (ICCPR) stipulates that there may be restrictions to freedom of expression since this right 'carries with it special duties and responsibilities' as long as such restrictions are laid down by law and are intended to protect the rights and reputations of others or *'for the protection of national security or of public order, or of public health or morals'*. Moreover, the ICCPR also imposes a specific obligation on State Parties to prohibit by law any propaganda for war or any *'advocacy of national, racial or religious hatred that constitutes incitement to discrimination, hostility or violence.'*

There then seems to be consensus that freedom of expression is not an absolute right but that consensus, however, almost immediately dissolves when an attempt is made to delineate exactly the extent of such limitations. This is also evident if one looks at the regional human rights mechanisms which utilise different wording in determining this right. The African Charter simply states: *'Every individual shall have the right to express and disseminate his opinions within the law'*. This wording seems to provide very wide latitude to states in determining the extent of freedom of expression people enjoy. The provision seems to imply that laws may limit the right at the discretion of the legislative branch of government.

The American Convention also establishes the right to freedom of expression but the exercise of the right may be 'subject to subsequent imposition of liability, which shall be expressly established by law to the extent necessary to ensure:

a. respect for the rights or reputations of others; or

b. the protection of national security, public order, or public health or morals.'

FREEDOM OF EXPRESSION, UNLIKE FREEDOM FROM TORTURE OR SLAVERY, IS NOT AN ABSOLUTE RIGHT. HUMAN RIGHTS LAW ACKNOWLEDGES THIS CLEARLY.

This formulation seems to support the view that everyone is entitled to express themselves in whatever way they deem fit, in understanding that, in exercising this right, the rights or reputation of others are not infringed upon or national security etc. impinged upon, which might be subject to ex-post facto punishment. Furthermore, following the same vein of the ICCPR the American Convention obliges States to render illegal *'any propaganda for war and any advocacy of national, racial, or religious hatred that constitute incitements to lawless violence or to any other similar action against any person or group of persons on any grounds including those of race, colour, religion, language, or national origin'*.

Finally, the European Convention on Human Rights provides for freedom of expression but then states that since it carries with it duties and responsibilities this right *'may be subject to such formalities, conditions, restrictions or penalties as are prescribed by law and are necessary in a democratic society, in the interests of national security, territorial integrity or public safety, for the prevention of disorder or crime, for the protection of health or morals, for the protection of the reputation or rights of others, for preventing the disclosure of information received in confidence, or for maintaining the authority and impartiality of the judiciary'*.

What is most interesting in the formulation adopted in the European Convention is the double test that any restriction to the right to freedom of expression needs to surpass if it is to be valid. Any restriction must not only be established by law for one of the reasons listed (protection of health or morals etc.) but, very significantly, it must be necessary in a democratic society. This latter test allows the European Court to act as a guarantor that the right balance between freedom of expression and the restrictions thereon is struck by all State Parties.

These divergent formulations of the limitations that are attached to freedom of expression are a clear indication of the different views that exist with respect to this right. Nevertheless, it seems clear that the right cannot be regarded as absolute. In particular, using freedom of expression to incite hatred towards groups or individuals cannot be tolerated. In this setting it is also useful to recall that inciting genocide is not only a crime in terms of most domestic jurisdictions but also a crime under international law. Thus, one can conclude that there are some situations in which it is clearly appropriate to restrict freedom of expression. At the same time, it is also clear that restricting freedom of expression is a favourite tool of oppressive regimes. The Committee to Protect Journalists every year lists the number of journalists arrested by states and its annual report evidences the risks faced by journalists in countries which wish to restrict access to information for political ends. In 2014, 221 journalists were arrested worldwide. This same NGO compiles a list of the 10 most censored countries which in 2015 was topped by Eritrea, North Korea and Saudi Arabia. This illustrates the extent to which oppressive regimes use censorship to protect themselves.

If freedom of expression is to have any meaning it must extend beyond expressions of comfortable platitudes or innocuous banalities. In one of its judgments the European Court of Human Rights famously remarked that this freedom should be *applicable not only to 'information' or 'ideas' that are favourably received or regarded as inoffensive or as a matter of indifference, but also to those that offend, shock or disturb the State or any sector of the population'*. On the one hand the right must be limited in certain cases for the protection of the rights of others and for similar purposes but such restrictions if interpreted widely may defeat the object of the right itself. Once again the difficulties inherent in configuring the exact scope of this right lead to the conclusion that a truly independent and impartial judiciary is an indispensable guarantor for this right.

—ÊLES ME DISSERAM,
QUE QUERIAM O DIÁLOGO
MAS NÃO DISSERAM
ONDE !

(translation: "They said they wanted to dialogue, but didn't say where!")

READING

Mary Ann Glendon (2001) *A World Made New: Eleanor Roosevelt and the Universal Declaration of Human Rights*, Random House, New York

Thomas Pogge (2008) *World Poverty and Human Rights*, Polity Press, New York

Omar Grech (2007) *A Human Rights Perspective on Development*, Bray, 80:20 Educating and Acting for a Better World, Bray, Ireland

Olivia Ball and Paul Gready (2006) *The No-Nonsense Guide to Human Rights*, New Internationalist, Oxford

Micheline R. Ishay, (ed.,1997) *The Human Rights Reader*, Routledge, London

Samantha Power (2002) *A Problem from Hell: America and the Age of Genocide*, Basic Books, New York

Geoffrey Robertson (1999) *Crimes Against Humanity: The Struggle for Global Justice,* Allen Lane, London

Philippe Sands (2016) *East West Street: On the Origins of Genocide and Crimes Against Humanity*, Weidenfeld and Nicolson, London

MORE INFORMATION AND DEBATE

www.amnesty.org – popular human rights movement NGO Amnesty International

www.hrw.org – regional monitoring and research NGO Human Rights Watch;

www.african-court.org – African Court on Human and Peoples' Rights

www.euromedrights.org – news, research and advocacy from network of more than 80 human rights organisations, institutions and individuals based in 30 countries in the Euro-Mediterranean region

www.frontlinedefenders.org – case studies and resources protecting human rights defenders at risk

www.ohchr.org – Office of the UN High Commissioner for Human Rights (access to all human rights instruments, human rights committee reports per country and resources archive with training, learning and research resources)

https://youtu.be/Vd7P6bUKAWs – Talal Asad (2009) Reflections on the Origins of Human Rights lecture at the Berkley Center for Religion, Peace, and World Affairs

www.un.org/womenwatch – UN Inter-Agency Network on Women and Gender Equality

'If we are to make poverty eradication a real possibility, if not within our own lifetimes, at least within those of our children or our grandchildren, there seems little choice but to move beyond limited "add-on" solutions such as aid and debt relief to reassess fundamentally our whole approach to development and to the global economy, and to make such changes as may be required to make it fit for purpose.'

ECONOMIST DAVID WOODWARD

CHAPTER 5

JUSTICE AND DEVELOPMENT - 'AN ILLUSION OF INNOCENCE...?'

COLM REGAN

This chapter sketches out many of the key dimensions of the justice perspective on development and underdevelopment. Having posed the question as to whether poverty in the world today is a matter of duty or charity, the chapter surveys the arguments and debates offered by philosophers and activists concerning *'our place in the world'.* Case studies explore the issues of climate injustice, the 'global commons', the nature of 'radical inequality', and the idea of a 'global resource dividend'. The parameters of different conceptions of justice are also explored.

KEYWORDS:

POSITIVE AND NEGATIVE DUTIES; POVERTY AND HUMAN RIGHTS; CLIMATE INJUSTICE; WELFARISM; CULPABILITY; RECTIFICATORY, DISTRIBUTIVE AND REGULATIVE JUSTICE; THE GLOBAL COMMONS; GLOBAL RESOURCE DIVIDEND

How do you see and understand these facts – inevitable or not; avoidable or a 'natural part' of the order of things or the result of human action and/or inaction?

TODAY, MORE THAN **1 BILLION PEOPLE** LIVE IN EXTREME POVERTY (ON LESS THAN US$1.25 PER DAY); AN ESTIMATED **2 BILLION PEOPLE** LIVE ON LESS THAN US$2 PER DAY IN 2015 AND **A STAGGERING 84%** OF THE WORLD'S PEOPLE HAVE INCOMES OF LESS THAN US$20 PER DAY

Is there a relationship between the wealth and welfare of some and the poverty and ill-fare of others and, if yes, what is that relationship?

THE AVERAGE LIFE EXPECTANCY FOR A JAPANESE PERSON WAS **80 YEARS** (2010-2015) WHILE THAT FOR SOMEONE FROM SIERRA LEONE WAS JUST **45**

Is the co-existence of the (over)development of one part of the world alongside the underdevelopment of other parts side by side and in full public view a matter of concern? Why?

THE WEALTH OF THE RICHEST 62 PEOPLE HAS **RISEN BY 44%** IN THE FIVE YEARS SINCE 2010 - THAT'S AN INCREASE OF MORE THAN HALF A TRILLION DOLLARS (US$542BN); MEANWHILE, THE WEALTH OF THE BOTTOM HALF FELL BY JUST OVER A TRILLION DOLLARS IN THE SAME PERIOD - **A DROP OF 41%**

Are these matters simply a question of providing assistance and support to those in need, or one of challenging a system that produces such extremes? Are they a matter of charity and welfare, or one of justice and injustice?

IN 2015, THE MATERNAL MORTALITY RATIO IN DEVELOPING COUNTRIES WAS **239 PER 100,000 LIVE BIRTHS;** IN DEVELOPED COUNTRIES, IT WAS **12**

- *What are our duties with respect to issues such as this; are we, in any way obliged to respond and to what extent?*
- *Where should our response begin…and end?*

INTRODUCTION

Questions such as those on the page opposite have long underpinned and challenged discussion of development and aid and allied areas for many decades. While many of the dominant debates appear to be essentially technical (e.g. how can we improve current international development models and initiatives; in what ways are international economic relations fair or unfair; how to manage climate change? etc.), underpinning them is a set of ethical, philosophical and political questions that go right to the heart of today's world. How do we understand why the world is so unequal; how did (does) this state of affairs happen; how do we fit in and what are our duties (if any) to those in desperate need, or to future generations? Is there a direct connection between wealth and poverty, or between the current dominant model of growth and climate injustice?

In recent years, these and similar questions have been the focus of vigorous debate and disagreement among analysts, commentators and activists, and the debates have raised very fundamental and uncomfortable questions about our place in the world – especially for those of us living in the 'West' or those elsewhere in the world living an affluent lifestyle. Why is it that, while many millions of people continue to suffer from the most extreme forms of poverty, hunger, ill-health and exclusion, the more affluent members of the world's population (wherever located, including in the 'emerging economies' of the developing world) allow it to continue and why do we apparently do so little to eradicate it? Faced with world hunger and inequality, do we have a moral duty to respond or is it a matter of personal choice and preference? In what ways are we implicated in the current order of things? What begins as a discussion on how to assist those in need is rapidly transformed into a far more challenging, complex and disturbing debate.

EXPLORING HUMAN SUFFERING AND DUTY IN THE WORLD

Australian philosopher and activist Peter Singer has been pre-eminent in addressing many of these questions and concludes that we do indeed have a 'duty' to respond to human suffering in the world for a number of reasons:

- One, such suffering is evil.
- Two, people 'must' respond to relieve suffering whenever they are in a position to do so and not to do so is morally wrong.
- Three, affluence places very considerable moral demands on the affluent to continue to respond up to the point where they would sacrifice something of equal moral importance if they were to give more.

Arguing that the world requires (and possesses the possibility for) a *new ethics* to match an ever-increasing interconnectedness associated with globalisation, Singer goes even further insisting that we are obliged to give as much as we can spare without damaging our own health, our children's education or whatever else is deemed to be *'morally important'*:

> *'... going out to nice restaurants, buying new clothes because the old ones are no longer stylish, vacationing at beach resorts - so much of our income is spent on things not essential to the preservation of our lives and health. Donated to one of a number of charitable agencies, that money could mean the difference between life and death for children in need.'*

Singer insists that our obligations are not limited to those people in need in our own area or community, those that we, in some way *'know'* (our *'immediate circle of concern'*) but extend equally to those we do not know and those whom we will never meet and who exist thousands of miles away; his essential focus is on those living in absolute and avoidable poverty:

'In the present situation we have duties to foreigners that override duties to our fellow citizens. For even if inequality is often negative, the state of absolute poverty that has already been described is a state of poverty that is not relative to someone else's wealth. Reducing the number of human beings living in absolute poverty is surely a more urgent priority than reducing the relative poverty caused by some people living in palaces while others live in houses that are merely adequate.'

He argues that because the cost of eliminating extreme hunger and poverty is very small in the grand scheme of things and makes up such a small percentage of our overall income and wealth, that there is no moral *'get out'* clause that we can appeal to. Equally, he argues that in recent times, we cannot claim ignorance of the plight of others (modern communications has ended that argument) and, as distinct from the past, we now have the mechanisms and structures in place to deliver assistance via an extensive network of official and voluntary aid and development agencies. Singer, echoing the work of Amartya Sen and others, argues that affluent individuals should donate a minimum of 1% of their income to the elimination of absolute poverty – not to do so is *'morally wrong'*:

'Those who do not meet this standard should be seen as failing to meet their fair share of global responsibility and, therefore, as doing something that is morally wrong ... There is something to be said for seeing a 1 percent donation of annual income to overcome world poverty

as the minimum, (in practice, Singer argues for a much higher level of giving than this), *that one must do to lead a morally decent life. To give that amount requires no moral heroics. To fail to give it shows indifference to the indefinite continuation of dire poverty and avoidable poverty-related deaths'*

Peter Singer (2002) One World: the Ethics of Globalisation, New Haven and London, Yale University Press: 194

For philosophers such as Singer and others (including Peter Unger who challenges 'our illusion of innocence', Gareth Cullity who insists that we have both individual and collective responsibilities, or A C Grayling who challenges the 'deification' of success as measured by the 'wattage' of our lifestyle), the fundamental argument is that if it is within our power to prevent something bad or evil from happening, at little cost to ourselves, then we have a moral obligation to do it. According to these commentators, international issues such as poverty, hunger and aid fall into this framework and arguments about who is ultimately responsible for such situations, or those about the effectiveness of aid or the realities of international and local corruption do not, in any way, diminish our obligations. Ultimately, they insist, that it is immoral and unjust to allow world poverty and hunger to continue to exist alongside immense and extensive global affluence that is capable of ending such immense human suffering.

For Amartya Sen, our obligations to uphold justice and challenge injustice arise from our innate (and intuitive) human capacity to reason and our sense of what is *'reasonable'* in any given situation. He insists that we have a duty to act *'reasonably'* and our obligations go way beyond those immediately close neighbours to embrace people throughout the world as, in the twenty-first century, we have few *'non-neighbours'* left, our obligations in justice are now clearly global.

> *'We could have been creatures incapable of sympathy, unmoved by the pain and humiliation of others, uncaring of freedom, and – no less significant – unable to reason, argue, disagree and concur. The strong presence of these features in human lives does not tell us a great deal about what particular theory of justice should be chosen, but it does indicate that the general pursuit of justice might be hard to eradicate in human society, even though we can go about that pursuit in different ways.'*
>
> Amartya Sen (2009) The Idea of Justice: 414-415

For these commentators, the challenge of underdevelopment and its most significant human consequences should not be the focus of a *'welfarist'* approach, one that places the primary emphasis on providing *'assistance'* to the poor and hungry (an approach characterised by Paulo Freire as *'assistencialism'*) but rather should be driven by a relentless pursuit of justice and the rejection of all forms of injustice. As argued by Sen, even if we cannot achieve a state of an absolutely *'just society'* (however defined), we are still obliged to create as just a situation as is reasonably possible in any given circumstance.

Characteristic of this approach is also the view, championed by Thomas Pogge, that we have two sets of duties – positive and negative. While there is considerable debate about the scale of individual and collective positive duties (to act positively to reduce human suffering), there is almost unanimous agreement that we have negative duties (the principle of, at least, *'doing no harm'*). While we continue to argue about the scale and nature of our duties in the world, we do not have the *'right'* to continue to act unjustly and that the current world order is profoundly unjust to the very significant advantage of the affluent (the minority) and the disadvantage of the poor (the majority).

A key argument in discussions of our moral duties and obligations in the world revolves around whether they are primarily individual or primarily collective, and around the scale and degree of moral responsibility affluence places on individuals as well as on society.

Singer places primary emphasis on the duty of the individual and argues for what is described as the *'extreme demand'* approach – every individual is morally obliged to respond to the maximum extent regardless of whether others do likewise – each case of need must be judged on its own merits. This approach is described as *'iterative'*. On the other hand, Cullity prefers an *'aggregative'* approach – where the moral demands of affluence are essentially collective (this does not, however, absolve individual obligation) where the demands on the individual, while still significant, are more moderate, and where the demands on society as a whole are greater. Globally, justice and injustice need to be approached collectively. Cullity has also criticised Singer for placing too high a level of demand on affluent individuals, arguing that there are justifiable limits for restricting individual contributions (although he agrees such limits are infinitely greater than what is the current norm, he accepts that there exist *'moral requirements of great self-sacrifice'*).

...EVEN IF WE CANNOT ACHIEVE A STATE OF AN ABSOLUTELY 'JUST SOCIETY' (HOWEVER DEFINED), WE ARE STILL OBLIGED TO CREATE AS JUST A SITUATION AS IS REASONABLY POSSIBLE IN ANY GIVEN CIRCUMSTANCE.

For those who critically engage with the arguments and analysis of philosophers (and activists) such as Singer, Sen, Cullity and Pogge, there are a number of significant issues to be addressed. These include (but are by no means limited to) the following:

- On what basis should the *'culpability'* or otherwise of the world's affluent citizens be calculated – on the basis of past wrongs from which they have benefitted (slavery, colonial plunder, resource pillaging etc.); participation in the current unjust world economic structures (cheap products, resource use, environmental damage etc.) or simply shared characteristics, such as membership of the human species? How should we assess the degree and nature of culpability and the corresponding duties?

- Which causal factors should be given most weight in our assessment and what are the implications of this – are they individual, collective, institutional?

- How do their analyses relate to the *'rights and responsibilities'* associated with other, more *'minimalist'* views of duty and rights in the world? Are some *'individual rights'* to be *'overruled'* by other duties - private property vs. collective need, individual rights vs. environmental duty?

- The *'solutions'* offered by, for example, Singer and Pogge are simplistic (Singer's emphasis on the value and impact of charities and aid organisations or Pogge's Global Resource Dividend - see below) and unworkable.

- They are *'extreme'* in the duties they place on ordinary citizens who, themselves, are *'victims'* (albeit at an entirely different level) of the international political and financial system.

Note: for an excellent introduction to some of these debates, see Alison Jaggar (ed., 2010) Thomas Pogge and His Critics, Cambridge, Polity Press and the Ethics and International Affairs Journal, 19.1 (Spring 2005).

DUTY AND RESPONSIBILITY IN THE WORLD
– KEY DEBATING POINTS

ARGUMENT	RESPONSE
We cannot be held accountable for what happened in the past through slavery, colonial plunder etc.; what happened in the past cannot be undone	*If this is true, then we have no right to the benefits of the past and must make recompense. We do have responsibility for what happens now*
If we listened to philosophers such as Peter Singer and Thomas Pogge and acted on their suggestions, western economies would be weakened and undermined and this would have negative consequences for everyone including the world's poor	*The current western model of development is based on harming others, especially the poor in the Third World and this is unacceptable – we do not have the right to harm others. Anyway, western development is unsustainable in the longer term and has to change*
The emphasis on charity and on giving is discredited because aid no longer works, even if once it did	*Even if aid doesn't work, we have obligations to help others and we recognise this intuitively in very many ways. Our duty is to ensure that aid does work, much more effectively than is the case today*
If I take my duties seriously and act on them and others do not, then it will have no impact and, anyway, I cannot change the system	*There are duties that can only be realised collectively e.g. climate justice but this does not absolve us from our own individual duties – to say that it does is merely a self-serving excuse*
Who should decide what is morally correct in today's world where there are no agreed international moral codes? So long as I do not deliberately harm someone else, I have done my duty	*We all accept a variety of internationally recognised codes of different types around genocide, murder, airline travel, dumping at sea etc., we need these for our own protection as much as for that of others. All major world religions and philosophies accept we have duties to others – even those we may not know*
I have rights and responsibilities, especially to my own family, my community and my country – they come first	*Agreed but duties do not cease at the end of the street or at our borders, otherwise our own well-being would be compromised*

DEBATING THE LINKS BETWEEN (IN)JUSTICE AND (UNDER)DEVELOPMENT

In his analysis of the moral demands of affluence in the world, Australian philosopher Garrett Cullity identifies three key approaches to justice and to our collective responsibilities – a rectificatory approach, a distributive approach and a regulative approach, all of which have significant implications for current approaches to development (and underdevelopment).

- **Rectificatory justice**: we are collectively responsible for assisting the world's poor because we are collectively responsible for creating and sustaining their poverty. This gives the poor at least a moral claim on us – the rich. The challenge is to identify and act upon what we ought to do collectively to rectify the injustice. Individually, the challenge is to identify what each person ought to contribute as a *'fair share'*, regardless of what others might do (or not do). Challenges to such an approach include the following: since most people are neither colonialists nor international financiers, in what ways are we collectively responsible; is responsibility divisible so that shares can be divided individually; can shares of responsibility be discharged individually, independently of others; what if others are not discharging their responsibilities etc.? Cullity argues that nothing in these criticisms undermine the principle of individual responsibility.

- **Distributive justice**: this approach argues that it is simply a matter of fact that the world's resources are inequitably distributed, rather than offering an explanation as to how that distribution came about. The reality of sustained and extensive inequality in the distribution of resources implies a duty to change the situation. Therefore, it is morally wrong for the affluent across the world not to discharge a fair share of this collective duty. Challenges to this view again include the debate as to what is an appropriate individual share of responsibility and how to

discharge it; how are priorities decided and by whom; is my share diminished by others not doing their fair share etc.? And, again, Cullity argues that these questions do not undermine the fundamental one regarding our responsibilities in today's world.

- **Regulative justice**: this perspective essentially objects to the rules that currently govern international trade and financial accountability; it objects to the rules themselves, rather than the unequal distributions that result from their application. There is compelling and documented evidence that such rules unjustly enforce the poverty of others to the advantage of the affluent and that, therefore, we are collectively responsible for reforming them; and, again, each individual has a role to play in such reform. Many of the same challenges described above apply to this approach also.

As noted earlier, Cullity places primary emphasis on our collective responsibilities rather than simply on our individual responsibilities. The collective or aggregative approach does not undermine individual accountability but it does insist that there are reasonable (and morally defensible) limits to what can be expected of the individual. However, the current situation worldwide does require that we change '... *our practice, in a demanding direction.'* Any justice-based perspective insists that *'we combine a proper recognition of the desperate needs of other people with a full engagement with the goods that provide us with our own interests'*. He challenges the *'comfortable vindication of moral 'common sense' as revealed in the practical attitudes of most affluent people'* and concludes: *'We are left with a serious practical challenge; but not, I think, one that is beyond us.'*

The remainder of this chapter explores further some of the implications of the arguments above through a set of four 'case studies':

- Current global social and political priorities.
- The debate on climate injustice.
- The debate on the *'Global Commons'*.
- The idea of a *'Global Resource Dividend'*.

CONTRASTING SOCIAL AND POLITICAL PRIORITIES

US$ 16.5 billion

The combined yearly cost of scaling up health investments to ensure the continued reduction of child mortality rates in the coming decade plus the annual cost of supplying access to clean water and basic sanitation for all in the developing world as against the current annual global spend on perfume.

Sources: WHO Commission on Macroeconomics and Health 2002, World Bank 2015, World Health Organisation 2015, Global Industry Analysts Report 2013

US$ 28 billion

US$ 50 billion

The annual illicit financial outflows from Africa by governments and multinational companies as against the cost of achieving zero hunger by 2030.

Sources: Global Financial Integrity 2015, FAO 2015

 US$ 267 billion per year

US$ 2.0 billion

US$ 750 million

The cost of each US Stealth Bomber in 2013 (as of 2015, the US is planning to build another 100) as against the estimated cost of saving the lives of the 289,000 women who died in 2013 from complications during pregnancy, childbirth or immediately following it – nearly all of these deaths occur in developing countries.

Sources: World Bank 2011 and UNICEF 20143

US$ 1 trillion

Annual outflow of illicit resources from developing countries

US$ 1.7 trillion

World military spending, 2014

US$ 4-6 trillion

Estimated 'real' cost to US taxpayers of the wars in Iraq and Afghanistan

US$ 12-13 trillion

IMF 2009 lower estimate of the cost of bank bailouts following the financial chaos of the previous two years

Sources: Global Financial Integrity Report 2015, Stockholm International Peace Research Institute 2015, Harvard economist Linda Bilmes, 2013)

'WORST AND FIRST' - THE DEBATE ON CLIMATE INJUSTICE

'In recent years we have become more aware that we cannot have life to the full on a plundered, polluted and ailing planet. While climate change is a technical, scientific and economic issue, it is also a moral one. The core of the moral issue is that actions which we take today can undermine the well-being of millions of people now, especially the poor, and condemn further generations to live in an inhospitable world.'

The Cry of the Earth (2014) A Call to Action for Climate Justice Pastoral Reflection on Climate Change from the Irish Catholic Bishops' Conference

Many of the key justice dimensions of the climate change discussion echo and extend broader debates on structural inequalities in international economics and politics, emphasising the core message that climate change is occurring in a world that is already highly unequal and unjust and, therefore accentuates and deepens that injustice. In a context of deep and enduring inequality, the impacts of climate change are highly differentiated. Reflecting the analysis and commentary of writers and researchers since the 1950s and especially since the emergence of the field of environmental ethics in the 1970s, activists such as Mary Robinson, Vandana Shiva and Bill McKibben highlight the differential 'vulnerabilities' of diverse groups through the lens of climate justice and injustice. Most recently, the issue was commented on extensively by Pope Francis in his 2015 encyclical Laudato Si: on care for our common home.

The nature and consequences of climate injustice were explored in detail in a 2007 work by J. Timmins Roberts and Bradley Parks who argue that *'...rich nations pay for climate change with dollars and poor nations pay with their lives...'* and that as a result of existing structural inequalities internationally, developing countries experience 'first' the 'worst' of climate change. This is as a result of an embedded 'triple inequality' of vulnerability (the unequal distribution of impacts), responsibility (the unequal responsibility for accelerating climate change) and

mitigation (unequal costs of adaptation). Their focus on the justice dimensions emphasises the core role of socio-economic and political realities (as against bio-physical processes) in shaping vulnerability to climate change and capacity to respond effectively.

'...rich nations pay for climate change with dollars and poor nations pay with their lives...'

The authors, along with a host of other analysts and organisations (including the Intergovernmental Panel on Climate Change (IPCC), the UN Rapporteur of Food Security, the UNDP, the EU and a wide range of international development and human rights NGOs), have highlighted the particular climate change vulnerability of the poor. Such vulnerabilities are both direct and indirect and include growing food insecurity and the breakdown of food systems; increased risk of drought, soil erosion and depletion; increasing risk of loss of rural livelihoods and income due to insufficient access to drinking and irrigation water; loss of marine and coastal ecosystems, biodiversity and ecosystem goods (upon which poor people particularly rely) with accompanying health, security and land tenure risks.

Climate change compounds, and is compounded by, widespread and deeply embedded poverty. It is the poor and the poorest countries with the least resources and the least capacity to adapt, who remain the most vulnerable and, in a travesty of any concept of justice, the least culpable in terms of its causes and who are likely to bear the greatest burden of climate change in terms of loss of life and relative effect on the economy and society. (on this see IPCC 2001 and OECD 2003)

Through exploring over 4000 extreme weather events between 1980 and 2002, Roberts and Parks argue that poor, rural dwellers in poor countries consistently suffer death, homelessness, and displacement from climate-related disasters, in orders of greater magnitude ranging from 10 to 100 times that of wealthier countries. This, they argue is due to the historical and contemporary processes through which inequality and injustice was/is generated and maintained.

The issue of responsibility for climate change is analysed by Roberts and Parks through using the four most common ways of assessing responsibility for carbon emissions - total CO_2 emissions, carbon intensity per unit of GDP, CO_2 emissions per capita, and cumulative emissions per capita between 1950 and 1999. Not surprisingly, GDP per capita and size of the economy were the strongest predictors for emissions; countries with high shares of total exports in manufacturing were also high emitters of carbon.

While it is clear that responsibility for climate change falls on a great many shoulders - from individuals through the daily choices we all make, to emitting industries, to nations – but given entrenched inequality, some are more responsible than others. An important 2013 study by Richard Heede of the Climate Accountability Institute showed that 63% of all industrial carbon dioxide and methane released to the atmosphere (in the period 1854 to 2010) can be traced to fossil fuel and cement production by just 90 entities from investor-owned companies, such as Chevron and Exxon-Mobil to state-run companies, such as Gazprom and Saudi Aramco and to government-run industries, such as in the former Soviet Union and China (for its coal production). Research by universities in the UK and New Zealand in 2014 highlighted that the USA has the highest cumulative cost of carbon emissions during the period 1902 - 2009, contributing between 24%-27% of the cumulative global cost, followed by the EU with 17%-19%. Today, China is the biggest source of carbon dioxide, but the cumulative costs of its emissions still lag behind with 10-12%.

Evidence from studies such as these illustrate that the main reason for a warming climate is the historical greenhouse gas emissions of developed countries; between 41% and 47% of the costs are due to the cumulative emissions of carbon dioxide from the USA and the EU alone - the emissions of the big four major contributors account for 57%-59% of total costs, leaving over 40% to the 'rest of the world' with the developing world and its poorest people trailing very far behind. And, as argued in 1991 by Anil Agarwal and Sunita Narain (in exploring the concept of environmental colonialism), the 'survival emissions' of the poor are fundamentally different than the 'luxury emissions' of the world's rich. In a similar vein, geographer James Samson and his colleagues developed, in 2011, the Climate Demography Vulnerability Index (CDVI) which highlighted the reality that the countries that have contributed the least to carbon dioxide emissions are the same regions that will be most affected by the impacts of climate change. Globally, the research noted that highly vulnerable regions included central South America, the Middle East and both eastern and southern Africa while less vulnerable regions were largely in the northern part of the Northern Hemisphere.

EVIDENCE FROM STUDIES SUCH AS THESE ILLUSTRATE THAT THE MAIN REASON FOR A WARMING CLIMATE IS THE HISTORICAL GREENHOUSE GAS EMISSIONS OF DEVELOPED COUNTRIES; BETWEEN 41% AND 47% OF THE COSTS ARE DUE TO THE CUMULATIVE EMISSIONS OF CARBON DIOXIDE FROM THE USA AND THE EU ALONE - THE EMISSIONS OF THE BIG FOUR MAJOR CONTRIBUTORS ACCOUNT FOR 57% - 59% OF TOTAL COSTS, LEAVING OVER 40% TO THE 'REST OF THE WORLD' WITH THE 'DEVELOPING WORLD' AND ITS POOREST PEOPLE TRAILING VERY FAR BEHIND.

A linked dimension in the justice debate on climate change in recent years is that of 'unequal ecological exchange and ecological debt' where industrialised countries have re-located carbon-intensive activities 'offshore' and are subsequently importing carbon intensive products; for example, imports to the European Union are predominantly materials-intensive while exports are significantly less so but yet of much higher value in monetary terms. The EU's trade regime which penalises developing country economic diversification reinforces this injustice and contributes to such ecological debt. A linked injustice is that measuring the carbon intensity of domestic production ignores the carbon components embedded in international trade flows; an issue that needs to be fully taken into account in international negotiations.

A third strand in the debate is that of climate change and intergenerational justice, a principle central to the simple maxim outlined historically by philosopher John Locke and more recently by John Rawls, Edith Brown Weiss and Mary Robinson (amongst many others) that we have ties to, and therefore, duties towards future generations, particularly as regards the resources of the planet. These duties are based on three basic axioms outlined succinctly by Ronald M Green in 1977:

- We are bound by ties of justice to real future persons.
- The lives of future persons ought ideally to be better than our own and certainly no worse.
- Sacrifices on behalf of the future must be distributed equitably in the present, with special regard for those presently least advantaged.

For more on this, see Chapter 9

DEBATING THE 'GLOBAL COMMONS'

Philosopher Peter Singer provides an additional illustration of a justice perspective in the context of waste and sustainable development issues with a case study of what he terms the *'global sink'*. He begins his discussion in the following way:

> *'Imagine that we live in a village in which everyone puts their waste down a giant sink. No one quite knows what happens to the wastes after they go down the sink, since they disappear and have no adverse impact on anyone, no one worries about it. Some people consume a lot, while others with more limited means, have barely any, but the capacity of the sink seems so limitless that no one worries about the difference. As long as that situation continues, it is reasonable to believe that, in putting waste down the sink, we are leaving 'enough and as good' for others, because no matter how much we put down the sink, others can also put as much as they want, without the sink overflowing.'*

The phrase *'enough and as good'* is derived from the arguments of John Locke made in 1690 in his justification for the existence of private property. Locke argued that the earth and all its contents *'belong to mankind in common'* and that the use of such *'commons'* for private gain is acceptable so long as there is *'enough and as good'* left in common for others. Singer draws on Locke to argue that the sink analogy is relevant if its capacity is, or appears to be, limitless so that everyone can put in as much waste as desired so long as this does not hinder others' capacity to do likewise.

However, Singer argues that if the capacity of the sink is reduced or is found not to be limitless the argument is seen to be fallacious. There are common consequences if the sink's capacity is fully used up – smells arise, local water holes (where children may swim) become unusable and many begin to fear that if the use of the sink is not reduced, the village water supplies may become contaminated. If we continue to dump waste in the sink we no longer leave *'enough and as good'* for others and hence *'our right* to unchecked waste disposal becomes questionable' as other's right to use the sink is reduced or eliminated if we wish to avoid the unwanted results. This he describes as the 'tragedy of the commons' in that the sink needs to be used equitably but how should this be realised?

This challenge raises fundamental questions of distributive justice. Singer draws a parallel between such a local sink and the global atmosphere where its capacity to absorb our gases without harmful consequences has been, at best, severely restricted and that the benefits and goods generated by the 'global sink' have been so unevenly distributed internationally.

Focusing on US in this instance, Singer goes further:

> 'The average American, by driving a car, eating a diet rich in the products of industrialised farming, keeping cool in summer and warm in winter, and consuming products at hitherto unknown rates, uses more than fifteen times as much of the global atmospheric sink as the average Indian. Thus, Americans, along with Australians, Canadians, and to a lesser degree Europeans, effectively deprive those living in poor countries of the opportunity to develop along the lines that the rich ones themselves have taken. If the poor were to behave as the rich now do, global warming would accelerate and almost certainly bring widespread catastrophe.'

He argues that since the wealth of the industrialised world is inextricably linked to the extensive use of carbon fuels, it is a small step to conclude that the present global distribution of wealth is the result of the wrongful expropriation by a small fraction of the world's population of a resource that belongs to all human beings 'in common'. Furthermore, if we ask when the level of greenhouse gases contributed by each individual in the developing world will equal those currently contributed by each individual in the developed world, this will only occur towards the end of this century – so, the argument is simple if,

as far as the atmosphere is concerned, the developed world 'broke it' then the onus is on those nations to 'fix it' – the polluter pays principle (this issue is explored further in chapter 9).

For Singer, there are fundamental justice issues implicated in current debates about the global atmosphere and the many technical and political objections and reservations about proposals for change do not alter the fundamental moral issues involved. Echoing the research and work of many scientists as well as philosophers, the solution favoured by Singer is based upon a combination of an equal *per capita* entitlement share to future global sink capacity tied to current UN population projections and a system of global emissions' trading (where countries can buy or sell shares internationally). There are, however, many ongoing debates and disagreements regarding such solutions.

Whatever the objections to suggested solutions there might be, for Singer there is no ethical basis for the present distribution of the atmosphere's capacity to absorb greenhouse gases without drastic climate change. His views are echoed by many, including Brazilian Christovam Buarque who strongly linked economic development, social need and environment debates in 1993:

> 'We stand at a crossroads; either we blunder on in a doomed search for a brand of development geared to universal consumption and technology, building up a system of social partition on a global scale; or else we branch off onto fresh ground by accepting the challenge to build a new order in which the economic system is governed by ethical principles; a framework in which respect for nature and abolition of human want would be key social objectives to be pursued and accomplished.'

Note: for a more extended discussion of the issues, see Peter Singer (2002) One World: the Ethics of Globalisation, New Haven and London, Yale University Press; Cristovam Buarque (1993, 2012 updated) The End of Economics?: Ethics and the Disorder of Progress, London, Zed Press and George Monbiot (2006) Heat: How to Stop the Planet from Burning, London, Penguin.

THE GLOBAL RESOURCE DIVIDEND

German philosopher and co-founder of Academics Stand Against Poverty, Thomas Pogge argues in *World Poverty and Human Rights* (2nd edition, 2008) that one of the greatest challenges to any morally sensitive person today is the extent of global poverty; he argues that there are two ways of understanding how such poverty is a major moral challenge:

- One, we may be failing to fulfil our positive duty to help others in acute distress.

- Two, we may be failing to fulfil the stricter negative duty not to uphold, contribute to, or profit from the unjust impoverishment of others.

He argues that some people believe that the existence of '*radical inequality*' in the world is a sufficient condition to violate our negative duties to others. He summarises five key conditions that define radical inequality:

- The worse-off are very badly off in absolute terms.

- They are also very badly off in relative terms – very much worse off than many others.

- The inequality is impervious: it is difficult or impossible for the worse-off substantially to improve their lot; and most of the better-off never experience life at the bottom for even a few months and have no vivid idea of what it is like to live in that way.

- The inequality is pervasive: it concerns not merely some aspects of life, such as the climate or access to natural beauty or high culture, but most aspects or all.

- The inequality is avoidable: the better-off can improve the circumstances of the worse-off without becoming badly-off themselves.

These conditions alone are, he argues, insufficient to prove a violation of negative duties in the context of global poverty today and adds a further five conditions:

- There is a shared institutional order that is shaped by the better-off and imposed on the worse-off.

- This institutional order is implicated in the reproduction of radical inequality in that there is a feasible institutional alternative under which severe and extensive poverty would not persist.

- The radical inequality cannot be traced to extra-social factors (such as genetic handicaps or natural disasters) which, as such, affect different human beings differentially.

- The better-off enjoy significant advantages in the use of a single natural resource base from whose benefits the worse-off are largely and, without compensation, excluded.

- The social starting positions of the worse-off and the better-off have emerged from a single historical process that was pervaded by massive, grievous wrongs.

These conditions lead Pogge to argue that:

> '*... the existing radical inequality is unjust, that coercively upholding it violates a negative duty, and that we have a moral reason to eradicate world poverty.*'

This analysis leads Pogge to make a 'modest' proposal for reform in the shape of a Global Resources Dividend (GRD) through which '*... those who make more extensive use of our planet's resources should compensate those who, involuntarily, use very little.*' He proposes a modest GRD of approximately US$300 billion which could radically alter the situation of approximately 2,533 million people experiencing severe poverty while only amounting to half the defence budget of the US alone; half the 'peace dividend' of the high income countries in 2007 as a result of the ending of the Cold War and about one-seventh of the market value of current oil production. This GRD is modest and could be developed further depending on agreed objectives and timeframes. He concludes '*It is clearly possible – without major changes to our global economic order – to eradicate world hunger within a few years by raising a sufficient revenue stream from a limited number of resources and pollutants.*'

Thomas Pogge (2008) World Poverty and Human Rights, 204 -212

FOOD: providing the additional calories needed by the 13% of the world's hungry people would require just **1% of the current global food supply**

FOOD WASTE: each year the average consumer in Europe and North America throws away 95–115kg of edible food while food wasted by consumers in industrialised countries each year (222m tons) is almost as high as the **total net food production of sub-Saharan Africa** (230m tons)

INCOME: Ending income poverty for the 21% of the world's people who live on less than US$1.25 a day would require just **0.2% of global income**

'...the biggest source of planetary-boundary stress today is excessive resource consumption by roughly the wealthiest 10 per cent of the world's population, and the production patterns of the companies producing the goods and services that they buy...'

INCOME: 57% of global income is in the hands of just **10% of people**

CARBON: about 50% of global carbon emissions are generated by just **11% of people**

NITROGEN: 33% of the world's sustainable nitrogen budget is used to produce meat for people in the EU – **just 7% of the world's population**

ENERGY: bringing electricity to the 19% of the world's population who currently lack it could be achieved with less than a **1% increase in global CO_2 emissions**

For more, see Kate Raworth (2012) A Safe and Just Space for Humanity: can we live within the doughnut? Oxfam Discussion Paper

READING

Julian Baggini (2014) The Virtues of the Table: how to eat and think, London, Granta

Garrett Cullity (2004) The Moral Demands of Affluence, Oxford, Oxford University Press

Alex Evans, (2011). Resource scarcity, fair shares and development. WWF-UK / Oxfam Discussion Paper

Thomas Pogge (2008 2nd ed.) World Poverty and Human Rights, New York, Polity Press

Michael Sandel (2009) Justice: What's the Right Thing to Do? London, Allen Lane

Amartya Sen (2009) The Idea of Justice, London, Allen Lane

Peter Singer (1993) A Companion to Ethics, London, Blackwell

Joseph Stiglitz (2012) The Price of Inequality, London, Penguin

Peter Unger (1996) Living High and Letting Die: Our Illusion of Innocence, Oxford, Oxford University Press

MORE INFORMATION AND DEBATE

www.oxfam.org/en – information and campaigns on economic issues

www.tradejusticemovement.org.uk – UK based focus on trade issues by 60 member organisations

academicsstand.org – international organisation focused on using scholarship to influence policy and public attitudes to poverty

www.cesj.org – Washington-based, non-profit Center for Economic and Social Justice

www.worldjusticeproject.org – independent law focused site highlighting the Rule of Law Index

www.ethicalconsumer.org – UK-based ethical consumption information and debates

'...without the promotion of people-centred development none of our key objectives can be met - not peace, not human rights, not environmental protection, not reduced population growth, not social integration'

UNDP HUMAN DEVELOPMENT REPORT 1994

CHAPTER 6

DEVELOPMENT AND POLITICS – TWO SIDES OF THE SAME COIN?

TONI PYKE

Despite persistent talk of progress, a majority of the world's population remain locked in poverty. Inequality continues to increase and progress in human development is undermined by conflict and 'bad' governance. Human rights are consistently abused, with women and young people particularly at risk, while the 'bulging' youth demographic in developing countries is claimed to threaten social cohesion. Yet the poor respond with resourcefulness, harnessing their individual and collective skills and knowledge to survive the constant shocks.

KEYWORDS:

AGENCY; CIVIL SOCIETY; CONFLICT; HUMAN DEVELOPMENT; HUMAN RIGHTS; POLITICS OF DEVELOPMENT; POVERTY AND INEQUALITY; 'UNFREEDOMS'; SOCIAL MOVEMENTS; SOCIAL ACTION; 'WEAPONS OF THE WEAK'; YOUTH BULGE

Photo: Doctorho

INTRODUCTION

For many decades the majority of South Africans were embroiled in a struggle against an oppressive and tyrannical internal structure, which affected every facet of the lives of the black majority population. The structure became legally established in 1948 under the label 'apartheid', and ensured white supremacy up until the first democratic elections took place in 1994. Prior to this, all rights and freedoms agreed elsewhere under the UN Declaration of Human Rights (1948) were aggressively denied to anyone of non-white origin. For many, inside and outside South Africa, apartheid appeared to be untouchable and yet, through largely peaceful opposition and campaigning nationally and internationally, it was resolutely defeated.

For five decades the African National Congress (ANC) was a non-violent movement engaged in peaceful opposition to the daily violent repressions of apartheid. However, with the intensification of brutality and oppression on 'black', 'coloured' and 'Indian' populations and in the context of events such as the Sharpeville massacre in 1960, the ANC was forced into responsive military action through the formation of a military wing, Umkhonto We Sizwe – 'MK' (the Spear of the Nation). While violence dominated accounts of resistance to escalating levels of government repression, South Africans continued to engage in widespread non-violence.

For South Africa, the transition from apartheid to democracy has been widely described (despite intense phases of internal violence) as a 'peaceful' process; the 'road to freedom' was ultimately achieved through non-violent means. Literally, tens of thousands of small, medium and large 'actions' at every level locally, nationally and internationally shaped that journey. South Africans were not simply apartheid's victims – they were also its opposition and its alternative – a political reality echoed in much analysis of the role of 'the poor' in development today.

WITHOUT THE FULL PARTICIPATION OF AN ACTIVE CIVIL SOCIETY, DEVELOPMENT THAT IS SUSTAINABLE AND EQUITABLE IS UNLIKELY AND CITIZENS ARE FORCED TO SEEK ALTERNATIVE WAYS AND MEASURES IN ORDER TO SURVIVE AND TO MAKE THEIR VOICES HEARD.

This chapter explores the politics of human development in the contemporary world as it impacts most acutely on the lives of women and young people. Despite the progress and improvements noted in previous chapters, the daily realities for the majority are significantly shaped by ongoing poverty and widening inequality, conflict and 'bad' governance. As also noted by many UNDP Human Development Reports, these realities threaten to undermine human development. Yet, despite this, the poor continue to survive by accessing individual and collective ability and knowledge ('agency') in various ways. While change is notoriously slow (and routinely 'invisible'), the example of South Africa (and countless many others throughout history) shows that change is not just possible but normal and inevitable. Through focusing on the issue of rising global unemployment later in the chapter, key aspects of the politics of human development are highlighted.

DEVELOPMENT AND POLITICS: TWO SIDES OF THE SAME COIN?

Human development, according to Wangari Maathai in her 2009 book *The Challenge for Africa*, should not be viewed as restricted to 'the acquisition of material things'. Although basic needs are critical, its definition should also consider *'achieving a quality of life that is sustainable, and of allowing the expression of the full range of creativity and humanity.'* One way of achieving such a goal is through good governance, where democracy is defined as much wider than simply the electoral vote. It is a concept that incorporates and empowers government and non-governmental institutions, civil society and the individual. It normally does this through the protection of basic human freedoms and human rights for all members of a society regardless of their class, gender and racial/ethnic identity. Maathai illustrated this through the image of the 'African Stool' (see pages 56-7):

> 'The African Stool is made out of a single block of wood, each leg, or pillar, is reinforced by the other and formed from the same grain...[t]he first leg represents democratic space, where rights - whether human, women's, children's, or environmental - are respected. The second leg symbolises the sustainable and accountable management of natural resources both for those living today and for those in the future, in a manner that is just and fair, including for people on the margins of society. The third leg stands for what I term 'cultures of peace.' These take the form of fairness, respect, compassion, forgiveness, recompense, and justice.'

Within a functioning democracy, where all three legs are supportive of the seat, citizens feel secure and have the capacity to contribute towards their own development. An effective democracy is one where individuals are able to enjoy their human rights and fundamental freedoms. However, with 'bad governance' the stool becomes destabilised and is no longer able to support the seat. In an African context this has often been experienced through, for example, autocracy, dictatorship and one-party systems which routinely deny the voice of citizens, threaten peace and increase the likelihood of conflict. Without the full participation of an active civil society, development that is sustainable and equitable is unlikely and citizens are forced to seek alternative ways and measures in order to survive and to make their voices heard.

'Politics,' in development terms can be defined as collective or public action and can include democracy, electoral politics, revolutionary struggle, local resistance and peaceful movements. It is about *power and power relationships* at various levels, relationships that often compete, may collaborate, are routinely combative or may dominate different rights, agendas and groups – or indeed may be any combination of these. As the many examples of social change throughout history have shown, people are both resilient and resourceful and such power relations continue to be challenged, confronted and routinely reconstructed.

There are countless historical examples throughout the world that testify to the individual and group struggles that strive for development and change. Civil society is a space that is not just about organisational responses to injustice, but a mobilisation of individuals who come together as activists to collectively and actively seek change. This is not just experienced through public demonstrations, but also for example, through legal means, through supporting particular 'causes' and more recently, through the internet. The *2015 Civicus State of Civil Society Report* documents countless examples of 'on-line activism' throughout the world by international 'bloggers' such as Raif Badawi from Saudi Arabia, the many secular bloggers in Bangladesh and China, all who dedicate their skills and energy (and sometimes their freedom) to raising awareness of injustice.

Popular historical examples of progressive social movements have included the women's suffragette movement formed in the early 1900s to speak out against the exclusion of women in politics, which later evolved into the feminist movement; the Anti-Apartheid and Black Consciousness Movements in South Africa along with the Civil Rights Movement in the US; the Gay Rights Movement; the Indigenous People's Movement; Slum Dwellers' organisations, anti-colonial movements, etc. Individuals have also been instrumental in movements or in activating change, such as Nelson Mandela, Mahatma Gandhi, Kwame Nkrumah, Martin Luther King, Malala Yousafzai and the many, many unnamed others who contributed and have often given their lives in the struggle for political, social and economic justice. All of this attests to the fact that people (especially the poor, excluded and oppressed) are not simply victims but are simultaneously also agents for change in their own lives, those of the communities and countries.

THE POOR AS *ACTIVE AGENTS OF CHANGE*

The poor are often popularly perceived in terms of victimhood and powerlessness, not least amongst themselves. Yet, as Jeffrey Sachs argues in his 2005 book, *The End of Poverty* the poor are victims of circumstances. They are not poor because they are 'lazy' or solely due to corrupt governments, rather, their capacity to react is negatively impacted by many structural factors that are beyond their control such as global world trade, trade barriers, climate

THE POOR, FINANCE AND 'SURVIVAL'

What are frequently referred to as the 'survival strategies' of the poor are not limited to conflict or outright opposition – they are often interwoven in the everyday lives of individuals and communities. The reality of the 2 billion people throughout the world living on US$2 or less a day is not a new phenomenon. Even this dollar figure is an average, since few people actually receive this amount daily. Much of the inflow of money into poor households is unpredictable and inconsistent. Yet despite this, the poor engage in resourceful 'survival strategies'. They employ a sophisticated 'portfolio' of creativity to ensure their survival. As noted by Abhijit Banerjee and Esther Duflo in *Poor Economics* (2011):

> *'Precisely because they have so little, we often find them putting much careful thought into their choices: They have to be sophisticated economists just to survive.'*

Many studies over the years have challenged the popular image of the poor as simply victims of, for example, moneylenders who charge extortionate interest rates or as individuals and families lacking the skills to manage finances and match them with current and/or potential future needs. A detailed study carried out between 1999 and 2005 on 250 families living in urban and rural Bangladesh, India and South Africa revealed an intricate and sophisticated series of financial 'survival' strategies amongst the poor. The study

conducted by Daryl Collins and others, titled *Portfolios of the Poor: How the World's Poor Live on $2 a Day*, published in 2009, revealed that poor people spend a significant amount of time managing their money and use a wide range of financial instruments for a variety of ends. The study also revealed that what may appear to 'outsiders' as less than optimal ('inefficient') decisions often makes considerable sense when reviewed more closely and in context.

Finance is critically important in the lives of the poor – for health and education needs, for funerals and weddings, for land purchases or for starting a business – needs that require a significant level of planning and maintenance. To manage such 'risks' and needs, poor households use savings and borrowings simultaneously, routinely mixing informal (often interest free loans from friends and family), wage advances and arrears of rent alongside semi-formal loans (usually microfinance) and, sometimes, even established banks. What the study revealed is appropriate and sustainable financial planning and management where cash flow is what actually matters and not the actual balance-sheet. One of the key outcomes from the study (and from other studies and practical experiences such as the Grameen Bank) is the recognition that the 'poor' are indeed 'bankable' and if appropriately supported, are agents for change.

shocks, water shortages, illness and disease, bad governance, conflict, etc. Within these limitations, the poor continue to be disempowered by repressive and often violent leadership, ongoing state neglect or localised violence, in particular that against women and girls (see for example the 2016 UNDP Human Development Report).

Despite political and socio-economic deprivations and uncertainties, the poor have the capacity to positively impact on their own lives regardless of the situation they may find themselves in. In the absence of the protection of human rights within a context of poverty and rising inequality, human beings continue individually and collectively to avail of diverse resources to make necessary life choices.

> 'THE POOR ARE POPULARLY PERCEIVED IN TERMS OF VICTIMHOOD AND POWERLESSNESS, NOT LEAST AMONGST THEMSELVES... AS THEY CONTINUE TO BE DISEMPOWERED BY REPRESSIVE AND INCREASINGLY VIOLENT LEADERSHIP, STATE NEGLECT OR LOCALISED VIOLENCE SUCH AS GENDER BASED VIOLENCE, IN PARTICULAR VIOLENCE AGAINST WOMEN AND GIRLS'

The concept of 'agency' has become synonymous with human development and the politics of development. For a simple definition political scientist Patrick Chabal (in his 2009 book *The Politics of Suffering and Smiling*), explains that 'agency' is popularly interpreted as *'directed, meaningful, intentional and self-reflective social action'* and, as the development economist Amartya Sen adds, individuals with agency are *'active agents of change'* (see his Development as Freedom, 1999). The word 'active' is important because it defines the critical factor where agency through action leads to effecting change. For Sen, understanding people as 'agents' rather than 'motionless patients' is critical

to understanding their role as change-makers. Therefore, agency is about knowing that we have choices and that we have the capacity to consciously respond to those choices.

Sen also argues that it is critical to acknowledge that individuals have agency and are responsible in making their own behavioural choices by choosing to act or not to act in a particular situation. For Sen, 'individual agency' is key to addressing global poverty and inequality (or as he terms them 'deprivations'), that are seen as obstacles to obtaining the social, political and economic opportunities available to all. This was acknowledged in a later expanded definition of agency that incorporated democracy, the market and human rights.

> '...UNDERSTANDING PEOPLE AS 'AGENTS' RATHER THAN 'MOTIONLESS PATIENTS' IS CRITICAL TO UNDERSTANDING THEIR ROLE AS CHANGE-MAKERS...'

THE 'WEAPONS OF THE WEAK'

Political scientist and anthropologist James C. Scott in his 1985 book the *Weapons of the Weak: Everyday Forms of Peasant Resistance*, highlighted that oppression and resistance can fluctuate so by focusing on the visible, larger historic events such as organised rebellions or collective action we tend to overlook the smaller, yet still powerful forms of creative 'every day resistance'. For example, local level peaceful responses to state oppression have included the use of art and graffiti in war zones to challenge armed groups or demand peace, such as in Northern Ireland, Syria and Egypt.

Other demonstrations of the 'invisible power' of the poor have included ridicule and sabotage, tax evasion, false compliance, robbery, feigned ignorance, etc., or work-to-rule or working slowly or without interest. As a practical example, during

CHANGE:
EVENTS, IDEAS, INGREDIENTS

SYSTEMS

SYSTEMS:
are complex; no simple cause and effect; our change models often simplistic; leads to failure and missed opportunities

CHANGE:
normally slow and steady; often affected by sudden events; advance planning not always possible; need for diverse systems of change

POWER is central;
resistance is normal; institutions, ideas and interests often oppose change; broad range of allies are important; avoid working only with *'people like us'*

SOCIAL CHANGE:
has deep roots; shifts in social ideas and behaviour promote change; issue-based campaigns propel change

INSTITUTIONS

INTERNATIONAL CORPORATIONS:
drive change; NGOs often confront them or cooperate with them: activists use law, campaigning, lobbying and public shaming to promote change

POLITICAL PARTIES, MEDIA, AND **SOCIAL ACCOUNTABILITY INITIATIVES**
play a key role

INSTITUTIONS:
appear permanent but the status quo far less fixed than appears; to survive institutions adapt and change

INTERNATIONAL SYSTEMS: a critical
role: shapes ideas and change: many key human challenges require collective rather than individual action alone: building effective alliances is crucial

STATES: drive change; are not
static; conflicts, bargaining and power changes affects them

LAW: is important for change and constantly changes
itself: courts, police, customary and international law: often promotes human rights and challenges privilege and discrimination

ACTIVISIM

LEADERSHIP:
is everywhere: especially among the world's poor; reinforces identity and cohesion: mobilises collective effort: offers inspiration and motivation: is often shaped by travel, struggle and conflict: faith-based leadership often pivotal

PROTEST MOVEMENTS:
have been important historically: day-to-day campaigns of local groups e.g. trade unions, coops, consumer groups promote change: can limit excessive power

ADVOCACY:
historically important (e.g. anti-slavery): can produce striking results

ACTIVISM:
popular movements can help create public commitment: citizen action on many levels propels change: faith groups, neighbourhood associations, producer organisations, trade unions etc. affect change: they nourish vital trust and co-operation

CRITICAL JUNCTURES:
opportunities and crises influence change: can highlight system failure and the need for change

CIVIC COALITIONS:
promote change worldwide: tactics include boycotts, mass protests, blockades, strikes, civil disobedience

This infographic is inspired by the ideas and arguments in Duncan Green's book *How Change Happens* published by Oxford University Press 2016.

apartheid ANC political prisoners held in maximum security prisons with severely restricted rights were able to engage in peaceful opposition to prison living conditions. A famous example was Nelson Mandela's demand for long trousers for black prisoners, who were negatively regarded as 'boys' and therefore devalued and forced to wear short trousers. Even within destabilised political conditions or in conflict environments where life options are severely limited, individuals and communities have a portfolio of opportunities for 'social navigation' through what Scott calls the 'weapons of the weak.' For example, civilian populations may passively resist the presence of armed forces or militia, or they may openly confront them. They may choose to collaborate with them in order to negotiate their security or access to resources for their livelihoods.

'...BY FOCUSING ON THE VISIBLE, LARGER HISTORIC 'EVENTS' SUCH AS ORGANISED REBELLIONS OR COLLECTIVE ACTION WE TEND TO OVERLOOK THE SMALLER, YET STILL POWERFUL FORMS OF CREATIVE 'EVERY DAY RESISTANCE'

Within an African context the rise of civil society that challenged the power of the state was widely viewed as a progressive development and a key driver of change. An awareness of local resistance activities revealed the agency of individuals and communities in surviving the everyday struggles that they encountered in their lives. Within international human development policy this promoted a shift from the more 'paternalistic' responses to development (such as the hugely damaging Structural Adjustment period of the 1980s) to supporting civil society and local level activities in the 1990s.

However, in the contemporary political and economic climate, the realities faced by the poor are often hampered by their limited capacity to voice and take action on, for example, restrictions of their political freedoms. The 2015 CIVICUS *The State of Civil Society Report* recorded (page 5) that intimidation of 'civic freedoms' was experienced in 96 countries worldwide:

> *'If you take these countries' populations into account, this means that 67 years after the Universal Declaration of Human Rights guaranteed our freedoms of expression, peaceful assembly and association, 6 out of 7 humans live in countries where these freedoms were under threat. And even the most mature democracies are not exempt. In the United States, there were heavy-handed responses to protest, environmental groups in Australia and Canada have come under attack from their governments, and, as I write, friends in Indian civil society are trying to resist a cynical raft of measures to shut them up and shut them down.'*

The Action Aid Annual Report 2015 also finds that the poor are impacted not only by their poverty, but also through the continuing oppressive political and socio-economic conditions that continue to oppress them alongside a reducing 'space' for civil society with ongoing violation of women's rights and increasing religious fundamentalism, which make claiming human rights all the more difficult. A good example of this is the rise in homophobia hampering the contemporary LGBT (lesbian, gay, bisexual, and transgender) movement, where in some countries being gay has been criminalised and is punishable by death.

The environmental movement is routinely impeded by the increasing frequency of attacks on human rights defenders and environmental activists throughout the world. In 2015 alone, more than three people per week were killed in defending their land, forests and rivers against extractive destructive industries (see the 2016 Global Witness Report *On Dangerous Ground*). Global unemployment, coupled with a 'youth bulge' is hampering the effective participation of youth in development activities and has been linked to local and international conflict situations that threaten to reverse past development efforts. A recent publication entitled *World Protests 2006-2013* (by Columbia University, New York and the Friedrich-Ebert-Stiftung) examined the occurrence of strikes, demonstrations, rallies, riots, road blockages, occupations and other protest actions across 90 countries worldwide. Between 2006 and 2013 some 70 events were associated with global demands. Nine out of ten of these were directed at national governments and focused around four categories:

- *Economic (in)justice* – austerity measures, unemployment, poverty, taxes and inequality.
- *Opposing political systems* – protesting corruption, demanding democracy, justice and transparency.
- *Global (in)justice* – specifically targeting the IMF and other global financial institutions such as the World Bank, etc., trade agreements or to protect the environment.
- *Seeking or defending human rights* – ethnic/ indigenous/racial rights; right to the Commons (digital, land, cultural, atmospheric); labour rights; women's rights; right to freedom of assembly/speech/press; religious issues; LGBT rights; immigrants' rights; prisoners' rights.

In terms of having their voices heard, about four in ten protests were considered as having achieved some level of the demands sought.

EMPLOYMENT, DEVELOPMENT AND AGENCY

The 2015 UNDP Human Development Report focused on the issues of global unemployment and the intrinsic link between employment, development and agency. The International Labour Organisation (ILO) in its 2016 World Employment and Social Outlook report *Transforming Jobs to End Poverty* found that globally there are an estimated 197.1 million people without work; a figure that is expected to rise by 2.3 million in 2016 and an

additional 1.1 million in 2017. While job prospects improved in 2015, in some developed economies such as the United States and some Central and Northern European countries (excluding southern Europe which experienced negative growth rates), the realities of unemployment have impacted most severely on emerging and developing countries.

The ILO report found that:

- Rising unemployment rates had worsened in Latin America, some Asian countries (especially China) and some oil exporting countries in the Arab States.

- In addition to the scarcity of employment opportunities, labour markets have experienced negative wage rate growth and increasing wage inequality, which is linked to 'vulnerable' employment (low-paying jobs, unsatisfactory job quality, along with difficult and dangerous working conditions, unregulated and irregular work, wage inequality and heightened susceptibility of worker's rights). There are 1.5 billion people throughout the world estimated to be in conditions of vulnerable employment – more than half of this number are concentrated in South Asia (74%) and sub-Saharan Africa (70%), affecting 3 out of every 4 workers and a disproportion of these are women and youth.

- At the end of this decade it is expected that one out of every 14 workers will continue to live in extreme poverty conditions, with some 839 million workers in developing countries trapped in the US$2 or less a day poverty threshold, unable to pull themselves and their families out of poverty.

- While structural underemployment and working poverty (where individuals live on less than US$1.90 a day) has decreased over the past 20 years, it continues to affect an estimated 327 million (2015) workers throughout the world. This number increases to 967 million if the 'near poor' are included (those living between US$1.90 and US$5 a day in Purchasing Power Parity (PPP) terms).

- Although poverty is overwhelmingly concentrated in developing regions, there is evidence to suggest that working poverty is also on the rise in Europe.

WOMEN, POVERTY AND AGENCY

Poverty cuts across all genders, race, age, ethnicity and geography. Throughout the world and especially in developing world regions, women and girls are particularly vulnerable. Having work and earning an income is considered critical to individual agency, reducing poverty, and contributing to human development (see the UNDP Human Development Report 2015). Women and girls are amongst the most vulnerable to unemployment where globally just 47% of working aged women were employed as compared to 72% of men. Socio-economic and cultural issues, along with women's associated care roles in the home negatively impacts on their capacity to participate in the workforce. Women work longer hours and earn less than men primarily because of their employment options - they are limited to low-paid sectors, concentrated in the areas of healthcare, care work and education.

Women have unequal access to credit, land or bank accounts and women are most vulnerable in contexts of violence and conflict. The 2015 UNDP Human Development Report finds that the number of women who experience violence throughout all stages of their life is comparable to the total population of sub-Saharan Africa and nearly three times the population of the United States.

Throughout history women have been central in shaping change within societies yet they have traditionally been viewed as passive and without agency. The focus of international human development policy and practice has been traditionally on women's well-being (or 'ill-being' as Amartya Sen adds), and which responded to women's perceived victim status through a 'welfare' approach. This, of necessity, remains an important focus due to the ongoing deprivations and human rights abuses that women uniquely experience throughout the world. However, to focus on women without attention to their agency, ignores the underlying causes of their deprivations and impacts negatively on the lives of everyone around them. This view has begun to change internationally and women are now considered as active agents of change not only in their own lives and the lives of others around them but also as part of broader movements for social change.

COUNTRIES WHERE WOMEN EARN LESS THAN 50% OF MEN'S INCOME

Source: UNDP Human Development Report 2015

| 48% | 46% | 45% | 43% | 43% | 39% | 36% | 30% |
| Benin | Bangladesh | Sierra Leone | Equatorial Guinea | Togo | Eritrea | Cape Verde | Yemen |

As Sen has noted, women are '... *dynamic promoters of social transformations that can alter the lives of both women and men'*.

While women such as Mary Woolstonecraft, Emily Pankhurst, Susan B. Anthony, Rosa Parks, Eleanor Roosevelt, Wangari Maathai and Malala Yousafzai have made it into the history books for their tireless pioneering of human rights and in particular the rights of women, it is women all over the world at all levels of society that challenge oppression in their daily lives.

YOUTH, POVERTY AND AGENCY

Young people in developing countries are increasingly vulnerable to what is often termed 'working poverty'; they are amongst the poorest and neglected populations and most at risk of unemployment. According to the ILO (2011), they account for 23.5% of the total working poor and in some countries unemployment rates are claimed to be twice the rate of the general workforce. For example:

- During the period 2000-2015 Bosnia Herzegovina recorded its youth unemployment rate at a staggering 57.5%, Greece at 53.9%, Libya 48.9% and Spain 53.9%.

- South Africa has the highest rates of youth unemployment on the continent of Africa at 50.1%.

- North Africa claims the highest regional youth unemployment in the world, where 30.5% of youth have no work.

- Being out of work for long periods results in youth being 'stuck' in long term unemployment as experienced by youth in the EU where more than 1 in 3 have been looking for work for 12 months or more.

- There are some 43% cent of the global youth labour force either unemployed, or working but living in poverty.

In recent years the concept of a 'youth bulge' has been used to describe a country that experiences a reduction in its infant mortality rate alongside a continuing high fertility rate that results in a significant section of a country's population comprised of children and young people. Each year, there are an estimated 121 million young people throughout the world who will reach their 16th birthday. Of these, 89% are located within the developing world. In countries considered 'fragile' (as defined by the World Bank) such as Burundi, Afghanistan, Syria, Central African Republic, Chad etc., nearly three-quarters of the population are under 30 years of age, a phenomenon which is expected to continue into the future.

The highest growth rates have been recorded in Africa where around 40% of the population is under 15 years and nearly 70% are under the age of 30 years. Within a decade, 15-29 year olds are expected to comprise 28% of the continent's population. By 2050, the United Nations (2011) predicts that in sub-Saharan Africa in particular, young people will constitute a quarter of its population.

All things being equal, a youth bulge should be an economic advantage. In situations where young people are provided with the right conditions and a country is economically viable and educationally stable, young people would be a beneficial boost to an economy – the 'demographic dividend'. A country's dependency ratio would decline as young people would enter the jobs market and become productive agents within their societies. The level of average income per capita should also increase.

However, this would require full employment and the majority of young people are job seekers who are increasingly unable to find work. This situation is expected to worsen in the future as 1.1 billion additional prospective employees are projected by 2020 (from 2012).

- Within five years there will be an estimated additional 213 million new labour market entrants of which 200 million are predicted to be from developing countries - all looking for work.

- Many young people have to forego their educational opportunities, unable to afford school fees and spending much of their time looking for work. In Colombia, for example, 60% of the young working poor had not completed their primary education compared with the 20% who lived just above the US$2 a day poverty line. In the Philippines, 35% of poor working youth had not received a basic education, compared with only 6% of the non-poor youth population (based on 2003 data for both countries). In sub-Saharan Africa, three in five young workers do not have the level of education expected to make them productive on the job.

- Poor young people remain trapped in low-productivity, low-paying jobs, many of which are 'high risk'.

- This cycle of poverty is perpetuated from generation to generation as the children of the youth of today, through economic necessity, will be expected to also work from an early age.

THE MUNDURUKU PEOPLE, BRAZIL AND THE SÃO LUIZ DE TAPAJÓS DAM

In a historic victory, one of Brazil's largest indigenous groups has managed to suspend construction of a mega-dam that threatened to submerge their home. The Brazilian indigenous agency FUNAI finally demarcated the territory of the Munduruku people, providing the legal basis to suspend construction of the São Luiz de Tapajós dam.

These 700 square miles of land – known as Sawre Muybu – are now legally recognized as the traditional territory of the Munduruku and protected under the Brazilian constitution, which grants indigenous people the right to free, prior and informed consent, before the government can use their land.

The Munduruku have been fighting for this right since 1975, standing up to a government more interested in questionably "green" energy and expansion than in protecting indigenous communities. In 2013, FUNAI conducted research confirming the status of Sawre Muybu as Munduruku territory, but failed to publish it due to government pressure. In response the Munduruku began the process of "auto-demarcating" their land, setting up signs and trenches to mark off their territory. They organised meetings, wrote letters, built alliances and staged occupations. Over the years they refined their strategy and took lessons from the fight against the Belo Monte mega-dam, which also wiped out species and displaced thousands of indigenous people.

Women played an important role in this struggle, as they often do in movements for land rights and against resource extraction. In 2015, Maria Leusa Kaba travelled to Paris for the 2015 United Nations Climate Change Conference to receive the UN Equator Prize for the Munduruku's campaign to self-demarcate their land.

'We, the Munduruku people are going in the reverse direction the Europeans went 500 years ago, to tell the world that we will resist until the last man the construction of hydroelectric dams on the Tapajós River,' Kaba said.

Adapted from Feministing.com

CIVIL SOCIETY AND AGENCY IN HONG KONG

'Pain is temporary. We are fighting for a permanent democracy'

In Hong Kong, a key demand of the pro-democracy movement in 2014 was that the election of the Special Administrative Region's next Chief Executive in 2017 be held under universal franchise. China's proposal was that candidates would be selected and vetted by a nominating committee. Protests quickly outgrew their initial intention ... what started out as Occupy Central (a district in Hong Kong) spilled into three sites, under the banner of the Umbrella Movement. Umbrellas became the visual symbol of the movement, starting out as practical protection against tear gas, and then finding form in sculptures and additional protest art. As in previous protests, online tools were used to plan protest and communicate messages; this helped protests to spread, with an estimated 100,000 eventually involved.

Another characteristic of the Hong Kong protests, which they share with other recent movements, is that demands and responses were multiple and complex, and resist easy analysis. Underneath the umbrella, there was considerable diversity, in both tactics and goals. The movement remained loose, encompassing different students' groups, but also other movements and opposition parties.

Ultimately, the protests can be seen as having petered out for a variety of reasons (although an umbrella protest in early 2015 brought many back on the street while leaders of the movement were elected to the legislative Council in September 2016). However, while the protesters may not have achieved all of their aims, part of the value of protests is in connecting previously disconnected people and increasing their awareness of and commitment to action. Most protestors did not belong to any organised group, becoming involved as individuals, and many were young (over three quarters of protestors were aged between 18 and 39, and 37% were under 24). Many were new to any kind of protest movement and, as in many other situations, women played a strong role in the protests. The strength of the protest can be seen in the birth of the 'umbrella generation' who have been brought out of relatively affluent individual isolation into collective action.

Adapted from Civicus *State of Civil Society 2015*, pp. 36 - 38

DEMOGRAPHICS, POVERTY AND SOCIAL UNREST

The ILO in its Social Unrest Index (2013) clearly linked the global levels of social unrest to the crisis of unemployment and to poor quality and poorly paid jobs, in particular among youth. The report also found that income inequality will continue to widen in the future as the richest 10% are set to earn between 30%-40% of total income, compared with the poorest 10% who are expected to earn between 2%-7% of total income. Such continuing and worsening trends, warns the ILO, are anticipated to lead to heightened social unrest throughout the world in particular in regions where there is a youth bulge and where youth unemployment is highest or expected to rise.

... INCOME INEQUALITY WILL CONTINUE TO WIDEN IN THE FUTURE AS THE RICHEST 10% ARE SET TO EARN BETWEEN 30%-40% OF TOTAL INCOME, COMPARED WITH THE POOREST 10% WHO ARE EXPECTED TO EARN BETWEEN 2%-7% OF TOTAL INCOME...

Professor Paul Collier (reporting on the Economic Causes of Civil Conflict and their Implications for Policy in 2006) found that the reality of large masses of frustrated youth who are unable to find work or earn an adequate income is an explosive context in terms of social and political instability. Throughout the world young people have expressed their agency through public demonstrations and protests since 2010, some of which have seen political regime changes across many parts of Europe, the Middle East and North Africa. Additionally, research by economist Rasmus Heltberg and others (*Living through Crisis: How the Food, Fuel and Financial Shocks Affect the Poor*, World Bank 2012), found that 'income shock' is associated with increased incidences of crime and theft which have been recorded as 'coping strategies' for individuals and families in Bangladesh, Cambodia, the Central African Republic, Kenya, Mongolia, the Philippines, Thailand, Ukraine, Vietnam and Zambia as well as in Dominica.

The World Bank 2011 *World Development Report: Conflict, Security and Development* showed that some 40% of those who join rebel movements claim to be motivated by a lack of employment opportunities. The opportunity costs along with the minimal recruitment costs of enticing young people into opposition contexts increases this risk; young people are more likely to initiate and participate in anti-government protests. The current political instability in the Arab world (as experienced through the revolutions in the Arab Spring and the fall of dictatorships in Libya and Egypt and anti-government protests in other parts of the continent) were spearheaded by youth who challenged the stereotype of Africans as passive agents under state repression.

Young men are particularly exposed to the opportunities and motives for political violence. The 2011 World Bank Report finds that young males are the main perpetrators of violence and the largest number of victims in contexts of violent conflict, as well as outside civil war contexts in countries with high levels of violent crime and social unrest.

In the South African context for example the youth bulge, alongside poverty and increasing unemployment is seen to negatively impact on peace, security and stability. This recently exploded through the many 'service delivery protests,' the 'Rhodes Must Fall' and 'Zuma Must Fall' campaigns to oppose poverty, corruption and state neglect, which resulted in fatal violence. The campaigns and movements were rooted in social, political and economic injustices where demonstrators saw no other way to effectively air their grievances and communicate with local and/ or national governments. Localised rioting and protest demonstrations accounted for 82% of all conflict events in South Africa during the period

January 2013 to December 2014. In 2011, Greece, followed by Spain three years later, experienced some of the worst rioting in Europe for many years in response to the political and economic crisis while the uprisings in the Arab Spring that began in December 2010 continue.

CONCLUSION

History is abundant with examples of marginalised, poor and excluded groups and individuals finding their voice and exercising a wide range of creative and resourceful actions that challenge the notion of them as simply passive or just the victims of other's agendas or power. Education, a job, access to credit, membership of social, political or religious groups, health opportunities or participation in a local development or community project frequently acts as a catalyst for change and further opportunity. In the face of considerable adversity, the poor continue to utilise a huge array of strategies and tools which often ensure not just survival but also ongoing resilience and even power. Women farmers in sub-Saharan Africa, indigenous groups in Latin America, urban slum dwellers and small scale entrepreneurs across many of the poorest regions of Asia, self-help education and health groups, women's and mothers' groups, youth organisations and church congregations continue to highlight human creativity and resilience, often against very significant odds.

However, the reality of rising global unemployment, vulnerable employment, poverty and inequality alongside the persistent denial of women's rights and a bulging youth demographic circumscribe and restrict that creativity and resilience. For example, higher unemployment rates for young people (in particular young males) in so many developing countries is popularly linked to escalating social and civil unrest often reversing international and local development efforts.

The 'political space' available for the poor and marginalised to express their concerns and alternatives is frequently restricted and controlled. Such realities continue to impact on the agency of the poor and marginalised constraining their voice, actions and impact. Despite this, their voice continues to be heard and their actions and responses continue to impact significantly on human development.

(For more on change, see chapter 15)

I bring you a veritable kaleidoscope of diversity, pluralism, differences and multifarious multicultures!*

* TERMS AND CONDITIONS APPLY.

READING

ActionAid (2015) *Annual Report 2015* and *Annual Report 2016*, Johannesburg

Abhijit, V. and Ester Duflo (2011) *Poor Economics*, Penguin, London

Patrick Chabal (2010) *The Politics of Suffering and Smiling*, Zed, London

Civicus (2015) *State of Civil Society Report*, Johannesburg

Daryl Collins and others (2009) *Portfolios of the Poor: How the World's Poor Live on $2 a   Day*, Princeton University Press, New Jersey

Duncan Green (2016) *How Change Happens*, Oxford University Press, Oxford

Wangari Maathai (2009) *The Challenge for Africa*, Arrow Books, London

Jeffrey Sachs (2005) *The End of Poverty*, Penguin Books, London

Amartya Sen (1999) *Development as Freedom*, Oxford University Press, Oxford

Social Watch (2014) *Annual Report: Means and Ends,* Montevideo, Uruguay

UNDP (2015) *Human Development Report: Rethinking Work for Human Development,* New York

MORE INFORMATION AND DEBATE

www.civicus.org – international alliance of civil society organisations, UK, US, South Africa, Switzerland

www.euromedrights.org – news, research and advocacy from network of more than 80 human rights organisations, institutions and individuals based in 30 countries in the Euro-Mediterranean

www.hdr.undp.org – flagship thematic annual UN Human Development Reports

www.odi.org – independent research and think tank, UK

www.socialwatch.org – international network of citizens organisations, Montevideo, Uruguay

www.unwomen.org – UN structure for gender equality and the empowerment of women

'The reality is that Africa is being drained of resources by the rest of the world. It is losing far more each year than it is receiving.'

HONEST ACCOUNTS? THE TRUE STORY OF AFRICA'S BILLION DOLLAR LOSSES, 2014

CHAPTER 7

'...THE MOST DEVASTATING ECONOMIC ISSUE IMPACTING THE GLOBAL SOUTH' – FROM THE POOR TO THE RICH

BERTRAND BORG AND COLM REGAN

This chapter examines many of the realities of the international system of finance, debt and economics and their implications for human development, especially in poorer countries. It directly focuses on key issues such as financial transfers (legal and illegal), tax havens, illegal economic activity and the brain drain which fuel and support the current international economic system to the significant advantage of rich countries and the disadvantage of the poor.

KEYWORDS:

FINANCIAL FLOWS FROM POOR TO RICH; DEBT REPAYMENTS; ILLEGAL ECONOMIC ACTIVITY; ILLICIT FINANCIAL TRANSFERS; TAX HAVENS AND THE BRAIN DRAIN

INTRODUCTION

One of the great communications success stories of the 20th century has been the selling of the 'giving us' and the 'taking them' perspective with regard to the relationship between the developed and developing world. The dominant popular view, reinforced by official and voluntary stories and reports, is that the relationship is essentially benevolent with 'us' (the West) doing as much as we reasonably can to assist 'them' (the poor of the world) – this view has almost become an axiomatic truth that is incontestable.

The ongoing focus on aid, the key debates around, for example the Millennium Development Goals (and now the Sustainable Development Goals) tend to reinforce this world view. The reality is, not surprisingly almost the total opposite, the poor of the world continue to support and 'develop' the rich of the world through an international political, economic and financial system that hugely reinforces and re-creates inequality within and across countries.

The 2015 UN World Economic Situation and Prospects Report neatly summarises a key element of the current situation as regards (official) financial flows:

> 'A net transfer of financial resources of approximately $970.7 billion from developing to developed countries is estimated in 2014... This negative net transfer of financial resources for most developing and emerging economies has continued for almost 20 years, with the exception of the least developed countries (LDCs), which continue to receive net positive transfers.' (2015:64)

In addition to this figure, non-governmental organisation Global Financial Integrity in its 2015 report has estimated that US$1.1 trillion (the highest amount to date) was transferred from developing countries in illicit financial flows in 2013 alone (and a total of some US$7.8 trillion between 2004 and 2013). In acknowledging such realities, the UN noted (in 2014) that such resources 'could be invested domestically to achieve greater economic, social and environmental outcomes'. In effect, resources that are urgently needed to fund basic human development in poorer countries are being used to fund development in richer countries.

In summarising the implications of the international economic and financial system for sustainable human development (especially of the poorest), the UN also comments that 'current financing and investment patterns are inadequate in achieving significant sustainable development...that private capital flows... are volatile and insufficient... that official aid flows and concessional lending 'remain deficient'. In addition, efforts to raise public resources via taxation are undermined by 'financial engineering, tax loopholes and accounting practices' and that regulation of the international financial sector continues to 'lag behind' the reality of global economic and financial structures.

This chapter describes and explores key aspects of these realities and how the international system of trade, finance, debt and economics make a mockery of international commitments to sustainable human development. The diagram opposite illustrates clearly the overall flow from poorer countries while the case study of Africa and the international economic and financial system illustrates vividly the realities as distinct from the rhetoric of the world 'market'.

> 'The reality is that Africa is being drained of resources by the rest of the world. It is losing far more each year than it is receiving. While $134 billion flows into the continent each year, predominantly in the form of loans, foreign investment and aid; $192 billion is taken out, mainly in profits made by foreign companies, tax dodging and the costs of adapting to climate change. The result is that Africa suffers a net loss of $58 billion a year. As such, the idea that we are aiding Africa is flawed; it is Africa that is aiding the rest of the world.'

Continued on p. 133

QUESTION: HOW MUCH MONEY WAS TRANSFERRED FROM RICH COUNTRIES TO POOR COUNTRIES BETWEEN 1998 AND 2015?

ANSWER: MINUS $9,715 BILLION

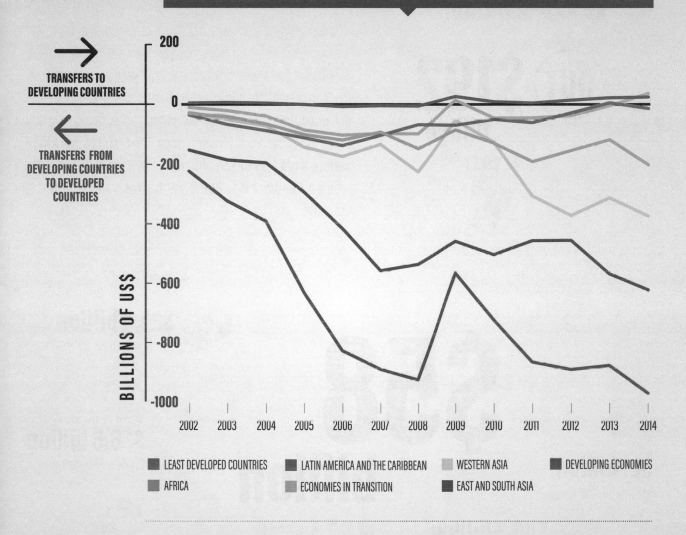

→ **TRANSFERS TO DEVELOPING COUNTRIES**

← **TRANSFERS FROM DEVELOPING COUNTRIES TO DEVELOPED COUNTRIES**

BILLIONS OF US$

200 — 0 — -200 — -400 — -600 — -800 — -1000

2002 2003 2004 2005 2006 2007 2008 2009 2010 2011 2012 2013 2014

■ LEAST DEVELOPED COUNTRIES   ■ LATIN AMERICA AND THE CARIBBEAN   ■ WESTERN ASIA   ■ DEVELOPING ECONOMIES

■ AFRICA   ■ ECONOMIES IN TRANSITION   ■ EAST AND SOUTH ASIA

Note: the above figure is an estimate of net financial transfers which includes items such as overseas aid, foreign direct investment, remittances etc.

*For more see Report of the Secretary-General (2016) International Financial System and Development, United Nations A/71/312

In presenting the figures upon which the above diagram is based (on pages 82 and 83 of the 2016 World Economic Situation and Prospects Report), and as commented on by the UN Secretary-General in his 2016 report*, the UN continues to use the heading **'Net transfers of financial resources to developing economies and economies in transition, 2003-2015'** thereby maintaining the fiction of resource transfers to the poor when, in fact the opposite is the case.

The reality is that in the period of the much publicised Millennium Development Goals (2000-2015) the net transfer of financial resources from poorer countries to richer countries amounted to an estimated US$9,300 billion.

Sources: UN/DESA, based on International Monetary Fund World Economic Outlook Database, October 2014 and World Bank, Migration and Remittances database

IN → **$134** billion

OUT ← **$192** billion

AFRICA AND THE INTERNATIONAL ECONOMIC SYSTEM - WHO'S AIDING WHO?

'The reality is that Africa is being drained of resources by the rest of the world. It is losing far more each year than it is receiving. While $134 billion flows into the continent each year, predominantly in the form of loans, foreign investment and aid; $192 billion is taken out, mainly in profits made by foreign companies, tax dodging and the costs of adapting to climate change. **The result is that Africa suffers a net loss of $58 billion a year.** As such, the idea that we are aiding Africa is flawed; it is Africa that is aiding the rest of the world.'

$58 billion Net Loss each year ↓

$25.4 billion in loans to other governments

$36.6 billion Climate Change Costs

$3 billion in outward remittances

$17 billion in illegal logging

$1.3 billion in illegal fishing

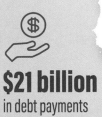
$21 billion in debt payments

$46.3 billion in profits made by multinational companies

$35.3 billion in tax evasion and other illicit financial outflows

$6 billion the 'Brain Drain'

Source: Honest Accounts? The true story of Africa's billion dollar losses, 2014

This was one of the key conclusions of a 2014 research study *Honest Accounts? The True Story of Africa's Billion Dollar Losses* published by 13 UK non-governmental organisations which explored the annual 'balance sheet' of financial resource flows in and out of Africa (excluding North Africa) in recent years. In noting that there were a number of outflows that they had been unable to calculate, the authors concluded that the figure of US$192 billion was likely to be an underestimate; they also made no attempt to quantify historic costs and noted that not all inflows are automatically benefitting Africans or that all outflows are automatically negative.

When these financial outflows and costs are compared with inflows into Africa, the result is a net annual loss of US$58.2 billion equivalent to over one and half times the amount of additional monies needed to deliver affordable health care to everyone in the world. This reality means African citizens are losing almost six and a half times what their countries receive in aid each year, or for every £100 given in aid, £640 is given back. The report also highlighted the fact that if the rest of the world continued to raid Africa at the same rate, US$580 billion would be taken from African people over the next ten years.

AVERAGE ANNUAL FINANCIAL INFLOWS TO AFRICA

Item	Reference Year (2012 unless otherwise stated)	Amount in US$ billions
Official Aid from OECD sources	OECD (Average for 2009-11)	29.1
Official Aid from non-OECD sources	OECD Development Assistance Committee Report 2013 (Figures for 2011)	0.4
Net Private Grants	OECD (Average for 2009-11)	9.9
Loans to Governments	World Bank, World Development Indicators database 2014	23.4
Loans to the Private Sector (FDI and non-FDI)	World Bank, World Development Indicators database 2014	8.3
Portfolio Equity	World Bank, World Development Indicators database 2014	16.2
Net FDI Equity	UNCTAD, World Investment Report 2014	23.2
Inward Remittances	World Bank, Migration and Remittances Factbook 2011	18.9
Debt Payments Received	World Bank, World Development Indicators database 2014	4.3
Total		**133.7**

AVERAGE ANNUAL FINANCIAL OUTFLOWS FROM AFRICA

Item	Reference Year (2012 unless otherwise stated)	Amount in US$ billions
Debt Repayments	World Bank, World Development Indicators database 2014	21.0
Increase in International Reserve Holdings	World Bank, World Development Indicators database 2014	25.4
Multinational Company Profits	World Bank, World Development Indicators database 2014	46.3
Illicit Financial Outflows	African Development Bank and Global Financial Integrity, Illicit Financial Flows and the Problem of Net Resource Transfers from Africa, 2013	35.3
Outward Remittances	World Bank, Migration and Remittances, Factbook 2011	3.0
The Brain Drain	Various WHO, OECD and individual research 2006 - 2013	6.0
Illegal logging	Africa Progress Panel, 2014	17.0
Illegal Fishing	Africa Progress Panel, 2014 and Global Witness 2014	1.7
Climate Change Adaptation Costs	UNEP 2013, African Development Bank, 2014 and Pan African Climate Justice Alliance, 2009	10.6
Climate Change Mitigation Costs	UNEP 2013, African Development Bank, 2014 and Pan African Climate Justice Alliance, 2009	26.0
Total		**191.9**

The authors (Sharples, Jones and Martin) comment that while the (UK) public perceive the causes of poverty to be essentially internal to poor countries, the reality is somewhat different:

'Africa is not poor; but a combination of inequitable policies, huge disparities in power and criminal activities perpetrated and sustained by wealthy elites both inside and outside the continent are keeping its people in poverty.'

In a similar vein, research on illicit financial transfers from Africa by Washington-based non-profit organisation, Global Financial Integrity, and the African Development Bank concluded that for the period 1980-2009, Africa was a net creditor to the world. When adjusted for inflation net recorded resource transfers outwards amounted to an estimated lowest figure of US$597 billion to a highest of US$1.4 trillion over the period:

'While there were brief periods in the early 1980s and the 1990s, when Africa received small net resource transfers from the rest of the world, the continent has been a net provider of resources to the world...'

African Development Bank and Global Financial Integrity (2013) Illicit Financial Flows and the Problem of Net Resource Transfers from Africa: 1980-2009:1

This research indicated that if the focus is on recorded transfers (excluding illicit outflows) net inflows to Africa were recorded over the period 1980-1999 followed by a sharp reversal to net outflows in the period 2000-2009. This change from net inflows to net outflows was mainly due to outflows associated with reserve accumulation, reflecting African countries' desire to self-insure against financial crisis. Outflows from Africa in the past decade were not evenly distributed - they were largely driven by outflows from North Africa; West and Central Africa experienced considerable outflows related primarily to repayment of loans

and trade credits, rather than reserve accumulation. However, much-faster growing illicit financial flows (IFFs) remained the main driving force behind the net drain of resources from Africa in the period 1980-2009 with illicit outflows from sub-Saharan Africa, especially from West and Central Africa dominating.

Such illicit outflows from sub-Saharan Africa outstripped those from North Africa while in real terms, three African regions - West and Central Africa (US$494 billion – 37%), North Africa (US$415.6 billion – 31%) and Southern Africa (US$370 billion – 27%) accounted for 95% of total illicit outflows from Africa over the 30-year period. Such illicit outflows were dominated by Nigeria, Egypt, South Africa, the Republic of Congo, Cote d'Ivoire, Algeria, Libya, Mauritius and Angola. While debates continue as to the measurement and scale of such illicit outflows, there is little disagreement on the overall significant negative impact in human development terms.

Commenting on the challenge of illicit financial transfers from Africa, former South African president Thabo Mbeki (Chair of the African Union's high-level panel on illicit financial flows) indicated in 2015 that:

'The information available to us has convinced our panel that large commercial corporations are by far the biggest culprits of illicit outflows, followed by organised crime. We are also convinced that corrupt practices in Africa are facilitating these outflows, apart from and in addition to, the related problem of weak governance capacity.'

INTERNATIONAL FINANCIAL RESERVES

International reserves are a country's external assets - all government and central banks need reserves in foreign currencies, to support the purchase of imports and to pay foreign debts if their own export revenues decline. These reserves are built up by lending to those governments whose currencies are used in international trade – in effect this means loans to the US, to various European governments, Japan and the UK. In return the 'loaning' government gets a bond indicating the debt; such bonds are tradeable internationally. The reserves of developing countries increased rapidly after the financial crises of the 1990s as governments sought to increase financial stability after these shocks; this pattern has asserted itself again following the western banking crisis of 2007/8. The International Monetary Fund (IMF) has also linked its loans to increased foreign reserves by applicant countries. In this way, developing countries have become net lenders on a significant scale to developed countries.

While organisations, such as the IMF have encouraged the build-up of such reserves, other organisations such as the OECD and the World Bank, have highlighted their negative implications - by investing heavily in foreign reserves, a country invests less in its own economy – often spending significantly less on education, healthcare or key infrastructure – all vital to longer-term human development. The growth in international reserves has increased competition to lend to Northern governments with the result that interest rates paid by developed countries for such loans are reduced. Additionally, lending is mediated by private banks which means that loaning governments often have little control on how the money is invested. Developing countries normally have to pay a much higher interest rate on the borrowing they undertake as against what they loan for obtaining reserves – this means yet further disadvantage and consequent financial losses each year.

ILLICIT FINANCIAL TRANSFERS

Illicit financial flows (money that is illegally earned, transferred or spent) are now recognised by a politically and institutionally diverse range of organisations as a large and growing obstacle to human development and democracy worldwide, with particularly devastating consequences for the world's poorest. Historically, NGOs have spearheaded research and advocacy on the issue but now, its dimensions and consequences are so great that International organisations such as the World Bank, the IMF, the UN Economic Commission for Africa, UNDP, the OECD and the Africa Progress Panel etc. and international non-governmental organisations such as Global Financial Integrity (GFI), Transparency International and the Tax Justice Network have catalogued what Raymond Baker, President of GFI, described in 2013 as *'the most devastating economic issue impacting the Global South.'*

Recent research and analysis has highlighted the negative consequences of illicit financial transfers – they dwarf official aid and foreign direct investment (thereby negating much of their impact); they fuel corruption internationally, undermine democracy and human rights and divert (for personal and shareholder benefit) vast amounts of resources that, in justice, should be used in the struggle against poverty and its consequences. Commentators also draw attention to the reality that while much of the debate and discussion on the issue tends to focus (necessarily) on the unethical, criminal, corrupt and regulatory dimensions of such flows, there is also a pressing need to focus on the structural and systematic dimensions of these transfers.

ILLICIT FINANCIAL FLOWS FROM DEVELOPING COUNTRIES, BY REGION, 2004-2012 (selected years in billions of nominal U.S. dollars)

	2004	2010	2013	Total 2004-2013
sub-Saharan Africa	32.5	78	67.5	675
Asia	174.6	381.7	482	3,048.3
Developing Europe	107.3	221.8	250.4	1,998.9
Middle East & North Africa + Asia Pacific	29.9	53	70.3	556.5
Western Hemisphere	120.9	172.0	212.8	1,569.3
All developing countries	465.3	906.6	1,090.1	7,847.9

The 2015 report by Global Financial Integrity highlights a total developing world loss of a staggering US$7.8 trillion between 2004 and 2013 in illicit outflows (an increase of 8.6% for the period). Following a brief slowdown during the financial crisis of 2007/2008, outflows once again rose reaching an all-time high of US$1090.1 billion in 2013. In contrast, the cumulative total of official development assistance (ODA) to the developing countries in this period was just US$1,245.5 billion and in 2013 ODA to these countries stood at US$134.8 billion according to the OECD. The clear implication of this equation is that for every US$1 granted in development aid to developing countries in 2013, over US$8 'leaked out' in illicit transfers. This reality makes a mockery of the intent and possible impact of official aid itself let alone the rhetoric most frequently associated with such aid.

The real tragedy associated with such mathematics is the impact that such a haemorrhage of resources could have had on addressing urgent basic human

ILLICIT TRANSFERS AND AID COMPARED

US$ 7,847 billion ▸ **US$ 1,245 billion**

- the illicit transfer of finances from developing countries 2004-2014

- the total volume of official aid to developing countries 2004 – 2014

US$ 1,090 billion ▸ **US$ 135 billion**

- the illicit tranfers in just one year, 2013

- the total volume of aid in just one year 2013

▶ The **real tragedy** associated with such mathematics is the impact that such a haemorrhage of resources could have had on addressing urgent basic human need and the potential it could have unlocked if used in the service of human development.

need and the potential it could have unlocked if used in the service of human development.

The GFI report for 2014 also reviewed illicit outflows against foreign direct investment (FDI - investment from one country into another normally by private companies rather than governments) in the period from 2003 to 2012. While FDI was significantly larger than ODA at US$5.7 trillion over the period, it still amounted to less than illicit outflows. When combined together, both FDI and ODA are slightly less than illicit outflows at US$6.5 trillion.

There are many channels through which money can be moved illicitly - these include over-invoicing or under-pricing trade deals, transfer pricing and using offshore financial and banking centres and tax havens. The vast majority of illicit financial flows – 77.8% in the period reviewed by GFI were due to trade-misinvoicing (the deliberate misreporting of the value of a commercial transaction on an invoice submitted to customs) while much of the remainder is due to illicit 'hot money' outflows. Transfer pricing occurs when multinational companies allocate profits to different parts of the same company operating in different countries with different company tax regimes with the aim of reducing the overall tax bill; today, about 60% of global trade is conducted within multinational corporations.

Asia is the region of the developing world with the greatest volume of illicit flows amounting to 40.3% of the 2003-2012 total followed by Developing Europe at 21%, the Western Hemisphere at 19.9%, the Middle East and North Africa at 10.8% and sub-Saharan Africa at 8%. Asia's regional total is essentially fuelled by the People's Republic of China (the leading source of illicit financial flows from developing countries for nine of the ten years studied by GFI) while Developing Europe's large share is primarily due to the Russian Federation (the number two country for nine of the ten years studied). The top five exporters of illicit capital over the past ten years on average are: China, Russia, Mexico, India, and Malaysia.

According to estimates by GFI corrupt activities such as bribery and embezzlement constitute only about 3% of illicit outflows with criminal activities such as drug trafficking and smuggling make up 30% to 35% and commercial transactions by multinational companies amounting to 60% to 65%. Contrary to popular belief, argues GFI's President, Professor Baker, money stolen by corrupt governments is insignificant compared to the other forms of illicit outflow.

'By exploiting weaknesses in investment contracts and loopholes in valuation, pricing and taxation regimes, corporations are able to use all sorts of devices to minimize their tax exposure and illicitly move capital out of the region to preferred "tax haven" jurisdictions. These illicit flows rob poor countries of greatly-needed public revenue that could be mobilized and invested to fight poverty, build infrastructure, improve livelihoods and finance development.'

Briggs Bomba of Trust Africa, 2014

ILLEGAL ECONOMIC ACTIVITY

Aside altogether from legal and illegal financial transfers, a third key element in the draining of wealth from the poor is that of illegal economic activity itself. By design and by definition, it is very difficult to fully capture the scale and value of illicit economic activity internationally – it is constantly 'on the move' and changing its boundaries and behaviours and has in recent decades, according to many commentators, 'crossed' over into the apparently 'legal'. On the following pages we have included a summary of the main categories of illegal economic activity plus an estimate of their 'value' (and its source) and a brief summary of some of its impact on developing countries.

IT IS ESTIMATED THAT IN THE PERIOD 1988 – 2000, SUCH ACTIVITIES MEASURED AS A PERCENTAGE OF GDP AMOUNTED TO AN ESTIMATED 35-44% IN DEVELOPING COUNTRIES, 21-30% IN COUNTRIES IN TRANSITION AND 14-16% IN OECD COUNTRIES.

Area of illegal activity	Value (est.) $US	Impact on the developing world
Illicit Oil Trade	Average yearly value 2003-2010: US$10.8 billion (United Nations 2012)	Promotes criminal networks, undermines government, promotes corruption, conflict, arms purchases; the illicit oil trade is both a product and a perpetuator of underdevelopment
Illicit Fish Trade	US$4.9 to US$11.3 billion each year (Panda 2013)	Developing countries are most at risk from illegal fishing, with total estimated catches in West Africa being 40% higher than reported; a significant link between the high levels of illegal fishing and poor governance; targets countries which rely most heavily on their fishing industries; fish accounts for 'a fifth of protein nutrition in developing countries' and 'exports of fish from developing countries … are worth more than exports of many other agricultural commodities combined'. Insufficient law enforcement and patrolling and, as a result, they are deliberately targeted.
Illicit Timber Trade	US$10 billion annually (World Bank)	Limited benefit to the poor at the hands of powerful international interests, environmental, economic, social and political impacts 'illegal forest activity represents between 5% - 10% of global industrial production'; environmental damage costs governments billions of dollars in lost revenue, promotes corruption, undermines the rule of law and funds armed conflict; actively undermines development; theft of a vital resource, loss of revenue; often promotes slavery, Illegal logging accounts for 50% - 90% of all forestry activities in key producer tropical forests, such as those of the Amazon Basin, Central Africa and Southeast Asia, and 15-30% of all wood traded globally.
Illicit Trade of Art and Cultural Property	US$4 to US$5 billion (Interpol 2014)	Loss of cultural property and loss of tourism revenue.
Illicit Gold Trade	US$2.3 billion (conservative) (Enough Project 2013)	Loss of income and resources; conflict and violence, corruption and undermining of law.

Drug Trafficking	<US$320 billion (UNODC 2005)	Approx. 15% of profits remain in developing countries while an estimated 60% of opiates are consumed there; profits are routinely used to fund other illegal activity; it criminalises the state itself through corruption, damages the rule of law (e.g. profits funding elections) and can even lead to 'state capture'.
Human Trafficking	Economic exploitation US$3.8 billion; sexual exploitation US$27.8 billion Total est. US$31.6 billion	Should be differentiated from smuggling; a conservative estimate of 2.5 million people are trafficked annually; 50% of the profits go to sources in the developed world yet only 11% of the traffic; 89% of those trafficked are destined for developing countries; has significant economic, health, health, family and human rights impact.
Illicit Wildlife Trade	US$10-25 billion (World Wildlife Fund 2010)	Tigers, elephants and rhinos (e.g. rhino poaching in South Africa up by a staggering 7,700% between 2007 and 2013). Increase in activity threatens conservation already achieved; loss of tourism revenue; bribery, damage to rule of law, weakening of the state; spread of disease (75% of emerging diseases arise through animals); fuels instability and promotes conflict when used to fund militias.
Counterfeiting	US$250 billion (OECD 2009)	Expected to reach $US 1.7 trillion by 2015 (International Chamber of Commerce) = 2% of the world's total current economic output e.g. currency counterfeiting; loss of tax revenue; abuse of workers including children (this also happens in legal activity); makes available dangerous goods (e.g. drugs); promotes criminal gangs, undermines law, promotes bribery and instability.
Illicit Trade in Human Organs	US$600 million and US$1.2 billion per year (WHO 2009)	It is banned in all countries except Iran; serious health risks; donors paid little with huge profits to the middlemen; generally promotes criminal interests for those profiting from poverty and state weakness, perpetuates health and other inequalities.
Illicit Trade in Small Arms and Weapons	US$1-3 billion per year (UN Office for Disarmament Affairs 2015)	Demand located almost exclusively in developing countries; weapons used 'to kill, maim, rape, and forcibly displace', insecurity and instability, undermines law and the state, promotes bribery; damages economic development.
Illicit Trade in Diamonds and Coloured Gemstones	Diamonds US$860 million - US$1.4 billion: coloured gemstones around US$400 million (Brilliant Earth 2013)	'20% of worldwide trade in rough diamonds is illicit in nature'; promotion of conflict diamonds; instability, violence, rape and war; corruption, and arms trading.

Sources:

Brilliant Earth www.brilliantearth.com/conflict-free-diamonds/

Jeremy Haken (2011) Transnational Crime In The developing world, Global Financial Integrity

International Organisation for Standardisation www.iso.org

Lippert and Walker, The Underground Economy: Global Evidence of its Size and Impact. Vancouver, B.C., The Frazer Institute, 1997

New Internationalist www.newint.org/issues/2014/05/01/

Schneider and Enste (2002) Hiding in the Shadows, International Monetary Fund

The Enough Project www.enoughproject.org

UN Office on Drugs and Crime www.unodc.org/toc/en/crimes/organized-crime.html

World Wildlife www.worldwildlife.org/threats/illegal-wildlife-trade

World Wildlife Fund wwf.panda.org/about_our_earth/deforestation

DEBT – AN ONGOING BURDEN

More than a decade after the cancellation of billions of dollars of debt, developing countries owe US$4 trillion - the amount of money owed by developing countries (including the 'Big 20' of China, Turkey, Vietnam, Indonesia, India etc.) keeps rising. In 2005 they owed around US$2.4 trillion. By 2013, eight years later, they owed more than double that - US$5.5 trillion. The good news is that the amount owed by the poorest of the poor – the countries the World Bank classifies as 'low income' – is not rising as quickly. In 2005 these countries owed a total of US$117 billion; by 2013 that had risen to US$147 billion.

It should also be noted that many poor countries in Asia and Latin America (for example, Jamaica and El Salvador) did not have their debts written off because their income per capita was too high to meet the IMF and World Bank criteria. Others, such as Bangladesh, did not qualify for cancellation because their debts were seen as sustainable.

What else can we establish about this debt? We know that African countries spend around US$21 billion every year paying back debts. We know that the nature of debt has changed significantly over the past 15 years – while developing countries are still borrowing money from richer ones, and taking out loans with multinational institutions like the IMF, nowadays it is private capital from commercial banks, private investors or the issuing of bonds, that is dominant. In 2005, debt to public entities (i.e. countries or institutions like the IMF) was double that owed to private ones. By 2013, that gap had been practically erased. This represents a huge, unprecedented surge in private borrowing. And it was private debt, remember, that led to the global financial crisis – from the sub-prime mortgages that brought Lehmann Brothers crashing down, to Irish banks' dud loans, all the way to Greece's billion-dollar debts to French banks. But in the case of richer countries, these gross debt figures are routinely balanced by debts owed to them by other countries.

On the one hand, countries like private loans because they are usually unconditional: the IMF will usually make a loan contingent on the borrower making certain policy changes, something that has caused plenty of tension, and sometimes tragedy, in the past. But private loans come with significant risks, too. For one thing, they come with higher interest rates. In 2013, with interest rates at historic lows, loans from governments and international institutions had an average interest rate of 1.5%, compared to 3.2% for private loans.

Private borrowing frequently attracts vulture fund investors - investors in a fund that buys the distressed debt of countries or companies at a cheap price and then often sues them for the entire value of that debt; the term arises from their resemblance to vultures circling a dying creature. Assuming private debt also leaves countries at the mercy of investors' whims, and those whims can shift very quickly. According to research by Eurodad in 2013, Ghanaian bonds, for example, yielded 8% in 2008 but surged to a massive 20% just one year later, before plunging to 5% in 2010. The fact that developing countries continue to borrow is not a good sign - countries only tend to borrow when they cannot raise money in other ways.

We also know that, for the most part, developing countries have been doing a reasonable job of growing their economies. Between 2005 and 2013 – a period that includes the global financial crisis that

PRIVATE BORROWING FREQUENTLY ATTRACTS VULTURE FUND INVESTORS - INVESTORS IN A FUND THAT BUYS THE DISTRESSED DEBT OF COUNTRIES OR COMPANIES AT A CHEAP PRICE AND THEN OFTEN SUES THEM FOR THE ENTIRE VALUE OF THAT DEBT

caused so many economies to shrink, rather than grow – the combined Gross National Income of all developing countries grew from US$8.7 trillion to US$23.8 trillion. That's almost a tripling in size in less than a decade. Even the very poorest did pretty well, with combined GNI more than doubling from US$228 billion to US$547 billion. Perhaps the most worrying thing of all is that we simply don't know just how much private debt low income countries have assumed. Given that even the world's most advanced financial systems were taken by surprise when the financial crisis hit, is it any surprise that the poorest countries on Earth lack reliable data?

What all this borrowing will mean to African countries in the longer term is unclear; developing countries currently get more money in loans than they pay out in repayments. But this is an unsustainable situation – at some point, the bubble will burst. Countries unable to pay back their debts are usually put through the same steps. They are promised additional emergency loans, on the condition they enact economic reforms in line with neoliberal tenets – cut spending, privatise industries, deregulate sectors. The loans are then used to pay off creditors, with the revenue saved from spending cuts used to pay back the emergency loans.

This process results in two key problems. Firstly, it leaves debtors caught in a debt trap. Taking on new debts to pay old ones is a trap individuals have fallen prey to for thousands of years, and the result is much the same when scaled up to nations. The fiscal restraints imposed on nations as a condition of these loans have invariably caused debtor nations significant strain. The social impact – high unemployment, reduced public services, de-investment in crucial sectors – is undeniable, while the economics remain highly contested. This cycle also creates a moral hazard for creditor countries, making their loans practically risk-free. The bailouts drawn up by the IMF end up being bailouts for the creditors and, as a result, creditors have no necessity to implement good governance reforms in international loans.

THE BRAIN DRAIN

The debate on the overall impact of the 'brain drain' has continued for decades and is equally relevant for richer and poorer countries although its impact differs widely. Two very contrasting views of the challenge highlight the diverse experiences of different countries as well as both sides of the basic debate around the issue. Speaking in 2010, Indian Prime Minister Manhoman Singh commented:

'...Today we in India are experiencing the benefits of the reverse flow of income, investment and expertise from the global Indian diaspora. The problem of 'brain drain' has been converted happily into the opportunity of 'brain gain'.

By way of contrast the Governor of the Bank for Fiji, J. Y. Kubuabola commented in 2003:

'...our limited capacity to handle this task (of implementing tax avoidance practices) is exacerbated by the continued loss of our skilled and trained human resources to other countries. The direct and indirect cost of this brain drain is enormous to our small island economy.'

According to the United Nations and the OECD in 2013, more than 230 million people were living outside their countries of birth with an additional 700 million migrating internally within their countries. Between 1960 and 2010, the global migrant stock increased from 74 to 188 million, only slightly faster than world population growth, so that the share of the world's population who are international migrants only increased from 2.7 to 2.8% (UNDP, 2009). However, what has characterised the migrant flow internationally has been the increased flow from less developed to more developed countries. The number of individuals migrating from South to North increased from 14 million in 1960 to 60 million in 2000; at the same time, the percentage of migrants with third level education qualifications increased significantly (by as much as 400% according to some researchers). The increasing amount of South-North migration coupled with the increasing skill level of those migrating (with the exception of sub-Saharan Africa) means that the brain drain is increasing in absolute terms.

Globally, the rate of brain drain varies widely across countries; the average developing country has an estimated 7.3% of its third level educated population working in higher-income countries, with this proportion varying from 5.4% or below in developing countries with populations of 40 million or more to 13% in sub-Saharan Africa and 45% in small developing island nations. Sending-country population size is a key factor regarding the impact of the brain drain – countries with smaller populations generally have higher levels of brain drain. Small island states are the most affected as are countries with conflict and political instability and with low levels of 'human capital' (the talent, skills and capabilities of its people). While skill levels amongst migrants are similar for males and females internationally, this translates into higher brain drain rates for women given that home-country education rates for women lag behind those for men in many developing countries.

There are large differences in the regional distributions of the brain drain and their dynamics; for example the largest numbers of educated migrants come from Europe and South and East Asia. The highest migration rates, in terms of the proportion of the total educated force, are from Africa, the Caribbean and Central America. Some of the numbers are truly staggering, especially for small and isolated countries. For example, many Central American and island nations in the Caribbean had more than 50% of their university-educated graduates living abroad in 2000. Although the share of skilled workers in the total labour force in sub-Saharan Africa is only 4%, these workers comprise more than 40% of all migrants with the result that close to 20% of all skilled workers have

emigrated out of sub-Saharan African countries, excluding South Africa.

The situation in Asia is slightly different. Skilled workers account for nearly 50% of all migrants. However, because the overall migration rate is much lower for a variety of reasons, only 6% of all educated workers have migrated abroad. Another, often forgotten reality is that a large number of educated citizens from OECD countries are also migrants. For instance, millions of people from EU countries live abroad, mostly within other EU countries.

Overall, the evidence indicates that the brain drain from developing countries is routinely a subsidy to richer countries and that there are many more losers than winners among developing countries. The costs of the brain drain are essentially threefold:

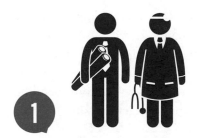

Skilled workers and professionals cost money to educate. Kenya spends over US$40,000 on each medical student within the country, and yet in 2006 there were 167 Kenyan-born and trained doctors working in OECD countries. Researchers from the World Health Organisation and Kenyatta University have illustrated the cumulative cost of losing doctors to the West and highlighted that for every doctor that emigrates, Kenya loses over US$500,000 - or US$87 million in total for those 167 doctors.

One in every six highly educated people from Cameroon emigrate to OECD countries. Ghana has a similar rate to a small island state like Ireland. Being both a small island *and* poor is the brain drain double impact: in Mauritius, 41% of highly educated people move to OECD countries; in Haiti 74% while in Guyana, an incredible 93% of highly educated people relocate to wealthier countries (International Organisation for Migration (IOM), 2010/11).

2

When skilled workers emigrate, they leave gaps in the workforce that must somehow be filled.

The UNDP estimated in 2007 that, in order to fill the human resource gap created by brain drain, *Africa employs up to 150,000 expatriate professionals at a cost of US$4 billion a year*. The situation in Sierra Leone is hugely indicative; in 2010, the country had 136 doctors and 1,017 nurses (one doctor for every 45,000 people); in 2014 Sierra Leone's health system was deemed by the World Health Organisation *'very weak'* – one of the world's weakest – while that of the UK was deemed by the Commonwealth Fund one of the strongest. In mid-2014, 27 doctors and 103 nurses trained in Sierra Leone were working in the UK.

While it is not possible to quantify the losses to Sierra Leone in terms of the value of their care or in lives that could have been saved, the financial subsidy to the UK health sector has been estimated by Health Poverty Action at about GBP£22 million. In 2015, some 26% of doctors in the UK received their primary training outside of Europe. The top non-EU countries providing doctors to the UK are India, Pakistan, South Africa, Nigeria, Egypt, Sri Lanka, Iraq and Sudan.

A 2013 study published by the WHO reported that 83 countries have a lack of basic healthcare workers, and that things are not getting any better. Of the 47 countries in sub-Saharan Africa, 11 have no medical schools, and a further 24 have just one each ('A Universal Truth: No Health Without a Workforce, WHO 2013). Congo famously had less than 20 university graduates when Belgium granted it independence in 1960, and more than 50 years later, it and its neighbours continue to lack the human intellectual capital necessary to propel development.

3

The human development cost – while it is clear that there are considerable human development benefits from the brain drain, there are also significant costs at household level (e.g. in terms of health, gender and emotional well-being) as well as at community and national level (e.g. labour shortages, the emergence of a 'culture of migration' and potential increases in inequality). When a doctor or nurse emigrates from Kenya to the EU, the most devastating cost is not financial, it is medical. When an engineer leaves Namibia to work in the USA, it is Namibian technical expertise that pays the biggest price.

It is commonplace to argue that the remittances sent back home by migrants will have a significant impact even beyond those in direct receipt of such remittances; this often leads commentators to argue for 'remittance-led growth'.

The sheer size of remittances sent home by developing country expats is staggering: US$439 billion in 2015 alone (World Bank 2016), a figure far higher than official aid and even foreign direct investment in developing countries. In some nations, remittances are the single most important source of national income: a quarter of Tonga's GDP and an even more staggering 49% of Tajikistan's, for instance, come from remittances (*Migration and Remittances: Developments and Outlook*, World Bank 2015). Various studies have confirmed that recipient households benefit from remittance money, and use it to provide for basic needs or improved housing. Other studies have found evidence that in some countries, children from families receiving remittance money tend to stay in school longer than those with no remittance income.

But despite this positive impact at household level, the evidence seems to indicate that remittances play no role in stimulating economic development at a national level. Some countries which receive large amounts of remittances have performed well economically (China, India) while others have done poorly (Philippines, Ecuador), and studies tracking remittances and economic development have found no causal link. (*Remittances: Myths, Rhetoric and Realities*, IOM 2006). The UNDP has itself cautioned against banking on the idea of remittance-led development, writing in its 2009 Human Development Report that:

> *'In general, 'remittance-led development' would not appear to be a robust growth strategy. Like flows of foreign aid, remittances alone cannot remove the structural constraints to economic growth, social change and better governance that characterize many countries with low levels of human development.' (2009:79)*

OFFSHORE TAX SHELTERS

'The very existence of the global offshore industry and the tax free status of the enormous sums invested by their wealthy clients is predicated on secrecy : that is what this industry supplies as it competes for, conceals and manages private capital from all over the planet from any and all sources, no questions asked.

We are up against one of society's most well entrenched interest groups. After all, there's no interest group more rich and powerful than the rich and powerful who are the ultimate subject of our research.'

J.S.Henry (2012) The Price of Offshore revisited, Tax Justice Network

According to the research report *Going Offshore* by Mathieu Vervynck and published by the European Network on Debt and Development in 2014 the bulk of illicit money today is channelled through international tax havens highlighting such 'secrecy jurisdictions' where millions of disguised corporations and shell companies (companies existing on paper only) flourish and where anonymous trust accounts and fake charitable foundations specialise in money laundering and trade over-invoicing and under-pricing.

The point was reinforced by Kofi Annan in the introduction to the *Africa Progress Report* for 2013 (p.7):

> *'It is unconscionable that some companies, often supported by dishonest officials, are using unethical tax avoidance, transfer pricing and anonymous company ownership to maximize their profits while millions of Africans go without adequate nutrition, health and education...'*

The report also observes that the problem is not simply caused by the behaviour and actions of immensely rich individuals but is also systemic because *'tax evasion, illicit transfers of wealth and unfair pricing practices are sustained through global trading and financial systems'.*

Developing countries are, according to a recent IMF working paper, locked in a 'partial race to the bottom' over tax incentives arguing that large numbers of investors can obtain hugely 'generous' incentives in developing countries amounting to, on average, a near zero tax rate down from 5% in 1996. The most significant competition between countries was in Asia, where the effective rate of tax had fallen from 10% in 1996 to a negative rate by 2006.

According to research by NGO Action Aid in 2013, a similar pattern exists across sub-Saharan Africa where the majority of countries offer tax holidays to investors, in addition to other benefits; tax free zones which barely existed in 1980, are now used by half the region. Making matters worse for badly needed public finances in African countries, the tax giveaway has been accompanied by a reduction in statutory corporation tax rates: between 1980 and 2005, the average rate in sub-Saharan Africa declined from 40% to 33%, a huge reduction in real terms.

The report argues that where figures are available (obtaining comprehensive information is extremely difficult as details are routinely secretive) *'they demonstrate the scale of the incentive epidemic'.* For example, in 2008/9 the Kenyan government gave away US$123 million in generalised investment promotion incentives, US$68 million through special economic zones, and US$120 million in incentives for exporters (Action Aid 2013:6). Research by the same NGO in 2011 highlighted Rwandan government data which showed that losses from tax incentives equalled 25% of its potential tax revenue – over US$234 million. In 2013, the Malawi Economic Justice Network estimated the tax lost through exemptions from 2008 -12 at over US$300 million almost exactly the same amount as the corporate income tax raised during that period (Action Aid 2013:7).

Based on a sample of 16 developing countries, of varying sizes, per capita incomes and regions, the Action Aid report estimated that over US$138 billion is likely given away by governments every year, just in statutory corporate income tax exemptions (not taking discretionary exemptions into account). The report stressed the consequences from such tax exemptions:

- The estimated US$138 billion 'lost' to human development amounted to enough to put every primary-school-aged child in school, meet all the health-related Millennium Development Goals and invest in the agricultural programmes needed to end hunger.

- Cancelling even one incentive scheme could make a big difference - in Zambia, the revenue 'lost' in a single year from just one company, Zambia Sugar, through tax breaks, could likely cover half the entire cost of the nutrition interventions needed to tackle the country's child malnourishment.

- In Tanzania, the US$10 million 'lost' to the Pan Africa Energy Company annually could pay for the education of 175,000 girls.

The scale of the problem of tax havens was outlined in a Tax Justice Network study *(The Price of Offshore Revisited)* undertaken in 2012: the study suggested that:

- At least US$21 to US$32 trillion of global private financial wealth (a conservative estimate) has been invested almost tax free across the world – this amount is constantly expanding (this just represents financial wealth and does not include assets).

- Since the 1970s (routinely with either eager or aggressive support from the private banking sector), it appears that rich elites in some 139 countries (World Bank and IMF data) accumulated between US$7.3 to US$9.3 trillions of unrecorded offshore wealth by 2010.

- The debt of these 139 countries amounted in 2010 to US$4.08 trillion yet once we subtract these countries' foreign reserves (invested in developed country securities), the aggregate net external debt amounted to **minus** US$2.8 trillion.

- So, as a result of the offshore system, these supposedly 'indebted' countries (this includes all key developing countries) were not debtors at all – they were lenders to the extent of a possible US$10.1 – US$13.1 trillion.

- Such levels of offshore earnings threaten to overtake illicit outflows and foreign direct investment and they certainly swamp official aid levels.

An updated analysis of the impact of tax havens by University of California economist Gabriel Zucman in 2015 - The Hidden Wealth of Nations: The Scourge of Tax Havens – has suggested that some 8% of individual financial wealth is now 'offshore' and rapidly growing and which represents a tax loss of at least US$190 billion.

Following the consequences of the 2008 financial crisis and its impact in developed countries, the G8 leaders agreed to introduce, for the first time, rules to fight tax evasion which require multinationals to disclose the taxes they pay in countries in which they operate. The G8 agreed a 10-point statement calling for an overhaul of corporate transparency rules urging the international sharing of tax information, to invest in capacity to fight tax evasion and called on extractive industry companies to report payments to all governments, which should make them public. A 'scorecard' on the implementation of the Loch Erne declaration was published by 4 NGOs – the Financial Transparency Coalition, Christian Aid, Global Witness and Action Aid - in 2014 concluded:

'Sadly, the verdict is that while there has been some progress in some countries and in some areas, there is still a long way to go. What is especially concerning is how slow the progress has been for developing countries, whose citizens suffer the most from illicit financial flows.'

 A **2007 JOINT REPORT** BY THE WORLD BANK AND UN OFFICE ON DRUGS AND CRIME ESTIMATED THAT EVERY **US$100 MILLION** RETURNED TO A DEVELOPING COUNTRY COULD BE USED FOR:

 UP TO **10 MILLION** INSECTICIDE-TREATED BED NETS

 UP TO **100 MILLION** ACT TREATMENTS FOR MALARIA

 FIRST-PHASE HIV AND AIDS TREATMENT FOR **600,000** PEOPLE FOR ONE YEAR

 250,000 HOUSEHOLD WATER CONNECTIONS

 240 KM OF TWO-LANE PAVED ROADS

READING

Wayne Ellwood (2015) *NoNonsense* Globalization: *Buying and Selling the World*, New Internationalist, Oxford

Bertrand Borg, Dylan Creane and Colm Regan (2009) *5:50:500 or how the world rewards the rich at the expense of the poor and where we fit in!*, 80:20 Educating and Acting for a Better World, Bray

Peter Stalker (2009) *NoNonsense Guide to Global Finance*, New Internationalist, London

Natalie Sharples, Tim Jones and Catherine Martin (2014) *Honest Accounts? The true story of Africa's billion dollar losses,* a coalition of NGOs, London

Dev Kar and Joseph Spanjers (2015*) Illicit Financial Flows from Developing Countries: 2004-2013*, Global Financial Integrity, Washington

Jeremy Haken (2011) *Transnational Crime in the Developing World,* Global Financial Integrity, Washington

Mathieu Vervynckt (2014) *Going Offshore*: *How development finance institutions support companies using the world's most secretive financial centres*, European Network on Debt and Development, Brussels

UN (2016) *World Economic Situation and Prospects,* New York

MORE INFORMATION AND DEBATE

www.afrodad.org – the African Forum and Network on Debt and Development

www.taxjustice.net – Tax Justice Network website

www.gfintegrity.org – the US based Centre for International Policy

www.debtireland.org – Irish Debt and Development Coalition

www.eurodad.org – European Network on Debt and Development

www.oxfam.org/en/campaigns/trade – Oxfam website related to trade issues

www.unctad.org – *UN Conference on Trade and Development website*

www.odi.org.uk – the Overseas Development Institute, UK

'Women should be able to enjoy all the human rights that are enshrined in international law, on equal footing with men. Yet, unequal power relations between women and men, deep rooted discrimination result in women's continued subordination, depriving women of their human rights. This underlying inequality comes into play at every turn of a woman's life, creating multiple barriers that women must confront on a daily basis.

Today, simply being born female can still mean automatic and systematic disadvantage: Women and girls are still fighting for the most basic control over their own bodies and their own lives and government actions have fallen short of the mark'

AMNESTY INTERNATIONAL 2013

CHAPTER 8

'...AS IF HER WHOLE SELF BELONGS IN THAT MARK...' - WOMEN, DEVELOPMENT AND (DIS)EMPOWERMENT

CIARA REGAN

Using a number of case studies and stories, this chapter catalogues the significant progress achieved in recent decades as regards key elements of women's well-being and human rights. It details progress in the areas of education, health, political participation and economics and outlines its benefits not just for women but for society as a whole.

The chapter poses the question as to whether this progress has been sufficient or comprehensive enough. This chapter questions recent progress against the backdrop of the broader agenda of the Beijing Platform for Action of 1995. The ongoing issues of violence against women and women in conflict situations are also explored.

KEYWORDS:

MULTIPLE AND COMPOUND DISCRIMINATION; WOMEN'S RIGHTS; PROGRESS; HEALTH; EDUCATION; ECONOMICS; THE MDGS AND WOMEN'S RIGHTS; POLITICAL PARTICIPATION; VIOLENCE AGAINST WOMEN; WOMEN IN CONFLICT SITUATIONS; BEIJING PLATFORM FOR ACTION

'HERE'S A STORY'

'Here's a story from my childhood. When I was in primary school in Nsukka, a university town in south-eastern Nigeria, my teacher said at the beginning of term that she would give the class a test and whoever got the highest score would be the class monitor. Class monitor was a big deal. If you were class monitor, you would write down the names of the noise-makers each day, which was heady enough power on its own, but my teacher would also give you a cane to hold in your hand while you walked around and patrolled the class for noise-makers. Of course, you were not allowed to actually use the cane. But it was an exciting prospect for the nine-year old like me. I very much wanted to be class monitor. And I got the highest score on the test.

Then, to my surprise, my teacher said the monitor had to be a boy. She had forgotten to make that clear earlier; she had assumed it was obvious. A boy had the second-highest score on the test. And he would be monitor.

What was even more interesting is that this boy was a sweet, gentle soul who had no interest in patrolling the class with a stick. While I was full of ambition to do so.

But I was female and he was male and he became class monitor.

I have never forgotten that incident.

If we do something over and over again, it becomes normal. If we see the same thing over and over again, it becomes normal. If only boys are made the class monitor, then at some point we will all think, even if unconsciously, that the monitor has to be a boy. If we keep seeing only men at the heads of corporations, it starts to seem 'natural' that only men should be heads of corporations.'

Chimamanda Ngozi Adiche, 2014

ANALYSING A STORY

'Women's equal right to development has been called a universal good. However, the realization of their right to development is beset by challenges rooted in the inequalities that pervade their lives. For women, the right to development does not simply require consideration of how income poverty, understood as lack of money and resources, influences their ability to enjoy their human rights; human poverty, in the sense of women's lack of voice and participation in decision-making within their families and societies, also impacts upon their lives and further reinforces their powerlessness.'

Fareda Banda: Women, Human Rights and Development, 2013

INTRODUCTION

In the context of research in Zambia on HIV and AIDS in 2010, Godfrey Malembeka (former prisoner and now Director of NGO Prisons Care and Counselling Association) managed to capture in a single quote the essence of the many ongoing discriminations faced by women in the Zambian prison system:

'Women are in effect serving three sentences: as their husbands have divorced them; because they are worried about their babies because they cannot feed them or take care of them properly; and then the years that they are actually serving.'

Although Malembeka's statement was specific to a particular context, it directly echoes what UNIFEM referred to in 2002 as the *'multiple and compounded discrimination'* faced by women internationally and, most especially in the developing world. Looking back to the 4th World Conference on Women in Beijing in 1995, there is without doubt much to celebrate, women's human development worldwide has improved and improved significantly. Gender equality is now (at least rhetorically) on the political agenda as evidenced in the MDG and now the SDG agendas and in numerous UN resolutions on Women, Peace, Security and Development. Worldwide, countries have expanded women's legal rights and entitlements and there is now in place a well-developed international system for measuring progress and analysing obstacles and resistances.

Yet, the years since Beijing have been equally marked by deep frustration – frustration at continuing widespread violations of some of the most basic of women's and girls' human rights; at growing and substantive inequality as regards economic choices, political participation; at the levels of violence towards women and at widespread discrimination. Despite international rhetoric, women, in effect remain a footnote in development with devastating consequences for themselves, their families, communities and societies. Their subordinate status continues to inhibit and undermine progress in human development, reinforce inequality and deepens the threat posed by climate change. There has been widespread failure (perhaps even refusal) to recognise the structural causes of gender inequality or to acknowledge the impact of current economic policies and practices in generating such injustices. And, there has been a re-emergence of some traditional prejudices and practices that threaten the very basis of progress to date.

This chapter is based on a proposition; the current focus on identifying, measuring and reporting on incremental improvements in key aspects of women's lives (e.g. health, education, political representation etc.) is both welcome and necessary but remains insufficient and by some distance. It presents an ongoing context that the rights and fundamental freedoms of half the world's population are becoming 'operationalised' in a set of selected, obviously important, but yet limited dimensions. Imagine, if you will, the argument and debate if international bodies were receiving ongoing reports on the same basis on men's development (and imagine the commentary if it were predominantly women doing the reporting!).

After many decades (centuries?) of engaging the debate on gender equality, this represents a potential and significant regression politically. Unless the fundamental prejudices, practices and policies that sustain discrimination are directly challenged, progress achieved to date on women's health, education etc., will remain fragile and at risk of reversal, in particular instances. The view, described by Kaye McInturff of the Canadian Center for Policy Alternatives as the *'…we are here for women rhetoric that is actually quite disempowering'* needs to be challenged (Socialwatch Annual Report 2014:22).

WOMEN: A HUMAN DEVELOPMENT PRIORITY?

To take it in its most basic form, Indian economist Amartya Sen's vision of development is a process of ever expanding freedoms equally for all. It is logical, that if we were to follow Sen's line of reasoning on development as freedom, then equality for women in the development process is of paramount and fundamental importance and yet, despite progress, the realisation of this equality remains a distant dream (see below). So, just as development should mean less poverty and hunger, better direct access to basic needs and growing access to participation in those policies and practices designed to ensure these, it should then certainly mean less 'gaps' in all aspects of life for men, women, boys and girls. Equality for women should be and needs to be relentlessly pursued as an intrinsic part of development, rather than an optional or secondary outcome of current development end-goals or priorities. Once again, the Sustainable Development Goals agenda adopted in 2015 has been forced to 'single out' the role of women in development despite decades of argument and debate – it seems that while we make (instrumental) progress, we continue to fail on many of the basics. As argued by Irish President Michael D. Higgins at the Humanitarian Summit in Istanbul in 2016:

'A healthy society is, by definition, unachievable if it is based on the marginalisation of women and girls'

The history of the struggle for gender equality has consistently demonstrated that empowering women effectively will benefit the process of human development itself, the economy and the broader society at every possible level – it is a 'yeast' for human well-being. This is true universally and particularly so in the developing world. In all parts of the world, women fulfil many traditionally defined roles such as mothers and carers, support workers and, especially since the impact of HIV and AIDS, as heads of household, yet the literature on development continues to lament the lack of effective recognition of these roles.

In more recent decades, the role of women in politics, community mobilisation, human rights activism and economic leadership has gradually been more fully recognised and analysed, especially as regards understanding the obstacles women face in realising such roles. There is now widespread agreement (at least theoretically) that the desired economic, social and political progress can only be achieved if countries invest heavily in their women through, for example, greater access to education and healthcare opportunities, a greater power in all types of decision-making and more extended access to resources of all types. However, it will also require confronting and dismantling traditional prejudices, fears and practices that fuel systematic discrimination across all societies.

In relation to the realities of prioritising women's development in human development, a number of simple examples emphasise its key importance:

- **Poverty reduction:** currently women account for 6 of every 10 poorest people worldwide; improved access to resources (physical, financial, support, legal etc.) will directly increase household incomes. For example, the UN Food and Agriculture Organisation argues that by ensuring women have increased access to human capital, credit, land and fertiliser, total agricultural production could increase by between 6-20% in sub-Saharan Africa alone because of the central role of women in agriculture and food production.

- **Improved education and health:** according to the World Resources Institute's EarthTrends, from 1975 to 1995, gains in women's education in 63 different countries contributed significantly to a reduction in malnutrition and, as catalogued by the World Health Organisation, significant improvement in family basic health. Sustained access to increased educational opportunities for women also has a direct (positive) impact on HIV infection rates.

- **The economic dimension** is captured by Linda K Fuller, in her book *African Women's Unique Vulnerabilities to HIV and AIDS* (2008):

  'In the fields, in the home, and in the marketplaces throughout Africa, women workers reign. Although 'household activities' are not calculated into the national income, we all know how invaluable their work, while sometimes invisible and nearly always undercompensated, can be'

In some parts of the world, 80% of basic food is produced by women. In doing this, women contribute to national agricultural output, general environmental maintenance and most importantly, food security for their families. They achieve this despite the unequal access to land, machinery, fertilisers etc. The data on page 157 highlights many of the economic realities of gender, the progress made in a number of areas and the challenges and resistances still encountered.

While women now comprise 40% of the global workforce, they remain significantly over-represented in poorly paid employment (and therefore lower incomes) and in vulnerable sectors; they continue to experience lack of access to credit, land and asset ownership etc. Some 60% or more, of female workers in developing countries are in informal employment (outside of agriculture). In sub-Saharan Africa alone, 84% of female, non-agricultural workers are informally employed (for more see the Human Development Report 2015).

This is neither fair nor, for the World Bank, is it smart economics. The lack of investment in women limits economic development, slows down poverty reduction and sustainable growth. Researchers also note that while gender equality can have a catalytic effect on achieving economic sustainability, dominant patterns of economic growth are all too often premised on reinforcing gender inequalities, such as those displayed in wage gaps, discriminatory norms, values and institutions. (World Bank, *Gender, Equality and Development Report 2012*)

According to UN Women, when women have a greater voice and participate more fully in governance and administration, public resources are more likely to be allocated towards investments in human development priorities including child health and nutrition. International frameworks and instruments for the realisation of women's rights are premised on the belief (borne out by the evidence) that equal participation is central to policy making (UN *Women Progress of the World's Women 2015-2016*). The collective agency of women has the potential to transform society through directly challenging norms, policies, institutions and laws.

Despite this, women remain massively underrepresented at all levels within politics, across private corporations and within civil society; only 19% of parliamentarians worldwide are women and, as the evidence presented on page 157 the pattern is similar in law and in business.

At a more fundamental level, Susan Markham of USAID noted in a 2015 interview:

'...women are not only impacted by certain issues like education and health...they can have a valuable insight as to how to address them. When women are empowered they can often lead the way in managing the impacts of climate change and disasters. When they play an active role in civil society and politics, governments tend to be more responsive, transparent and democratic. Countries that invest in girl's education have lower maternal mortality deaths, lower HIV and AIDS prevalence and better child nutrition.'

As demonstrated definitively over the past three decades, the benefits of empowering women are by no means exclusive to women alone; they permeate across society as a whole through the empowerment of a key catalytic group of leaders. The empowerment of women, the realisation of their rights, their dignity and their capabilities is a central necessity for the realisation of everything from access to education, food and health security to the environment, conflict resolution, democracy and good governance.

Despite such social benefits, an underlying theme and value in the discussion and debates of the past three decades (and beyond) has been the insistence that women have the right to live with dignity and freedom from want and fear. Recognising and working to realise this fundamental principle is a moral, ethical imperative – a point which is too often lost in debates around women's importance in relation to development (for more, see Social Watch Annual Report 2014 *Means and Ends*).

GLOBAL PROGRESS ON LEGAL REFORM

There has been significant progress on legal reform in favour of women's rights in the past thirty years. Globally, 139 constitutions include guarantees of gender equality, 125 countries outlaw domestic violence, at least 117 countries have equal pay laws, 173 guarantee paid maternity leave, and 117 outlaw sexual harassment in the workplace. Women have equal rights to own property in 115 countries and in 93 have equal inheritance rights.

173 countries guarantee paid maternity leave

139 constitutions guarantee gender equality

125 countries outlaw domestic violence

117 countries outlaw sexual harassment

117 countries have equal pay laws

115 countries guarantee women's equal property rights

Source: UN Women, Progress of the World's Women 2012: 24

SEEING THE LIGHT AND NOT THE DARKNESS – THE IMPORTANCE OF EDUCATION

Yeshi was born in rural Oromia, Ethiopia. She was married and divorced before she was 18, and has spent her adult life struggling to raise three children as a single mother with meagre earnings. When she looks back on her life, she believes that most of the struggles she has faced are the result of a lack of education.

> *'When I was a child I always wanted to go to school. I actually went very briefly, but my parents took me out so I could look after the animals. I remember asking if I could go to school and them saying to me, 'Come on, a girl who is sent to school will just have a baby and nothing else.' That was the attitude in those days, that if you send a girl to school the only thing she'll do is have a child with a boy there, without even getting married in the traditional way. So I didn't go, and then I got married at 13.*

> *I think if I'd been educated and my husband had been educated, we'd both have made better decisions. We didn't know how to manage anything, from our marriage to our property to anything.'*

> *After I divorced I moved to this place. I was new here and I knew no one. Life was so hard, I seriously wanted to commit suicide. I think God intervened because we were OK. But at the time I just kept thinking that if I'd only been educated, I would have known how to struggle and how to survive.'*

Yet Yeshi did survive, and has been determined to make sure her children do not face the same struggles she endured. Despite her low income, she successfully sent both her sons through school and is adamant her daughter Firegenet will receive an education too.

> *'I don't want my daughter to be like me. If you are educated you will have knowledge, and you will choose what's best for you. It is more important than money. I know that a person who is educated sees the light, not the darkness.'*

To make sure Firegenet can go to school, Yeshi has done whatever she could to earn money - selling food in people's homes and at the local market to make ends meet.

Through the assistance of some local and international organisations, Firegenet was helped with her immediate schooling costs and Yeshi joined a community self-help and savings group to help finance her daughter's education in the long term.

> *'I am still in the savings group. We meet every Sunday afternoon to talk about saving money and how to change our daughter's lives as well as our own. My children always say to me, 'You're not educated but you educated us.'*

And through her daughter's education, she feels she is growing in knowledge and confidence herself. Firegenet has helped her mother learn to sign her name – a new skill that Yeshi performs with careful precision every time, as if her whole self belongs in that mark. Proud of her signature, she explains why it means so much, pointing out that education is a matter of identity and not just jobs and money:

> *'I know that many girls will leave school and not become doctors. They might just stay in rural, farming areas. But their education is still important. At least they have knowledge. At least they're not going to use their fingers to sign. Because do you know, it is such a shame to use your finger for a signature? I normally have to use my finger but with Firegenet I am teaching myself to write my initials. If you're educated, at least you can sign your name.'*

WOMEN AND THE MDGS?

Did the MDGs renege on the promise of the Beijing Platform for Action (BFPA)?

According to many commentators such as Peggy Antrobus (*Gender and Development* 2007:95), *'...the Beijing Platform for Action remains the most important basic text. Structured around 12 Priority Areas of Concern, its theoretical framework is consistent and much more comprehensive. It addresses gender issues from within a theoretical framework of social reproduction, which relates to the realities of women's lives and the ways in which women organise, and considers each of the Priority Areas in relation to women's equality and empowerment.'*

By contrast: *'For women, the MDGs have inadequate targets and indicators. The indicators used are restricted to quantifiable indicators, when much of what is most important – such as women's equality and empowerment – is not easily quantifiable. In addition, it omits important goals and targets, such as the elimination of violence against women and sexual and reproductive rights.'*

Taking the MDGs and the Beijing Platform in their most basic form, it could be argued that the MDGs did not necessarily 'renege' on the priorities but, rather did not take their nuances into account when building the framework for measuring progress – in effect they became too 'instrumentalised' particularly as regards the politics of the issue and the challenge of discrimination.

Did the MDG agenda substantially move on the status of women? Are we making real progress or just getting distracted by measurement?

There have been quantifiable changes to the status of women, based on the MDG report for 2015 yet, according to the same report (page 7): *'...women continue to face discrimination in access to work, economic assets and participation in private and public decision making. Women are also more likely to live in poverty than men... Women remain at a disadvantage in the labour market... Despite continuous progress, today the world still has far to go towards equal gender representation in private and public decision making.'*

It is arguable whether the quantifiable progress that has been made can be equated to 'real' progress or not, that relates directly to context. Take, for example, the fact that many more girls are now in school compared to 15 years ago: this is most certainly significant progress. However, the enduring progress would be seen in how many girls actually remain in school when faced with challenges such as early marriage, menstruation (e.g. in Sierra Leone, according to girleffect.org, more than one in five girls miss school due to lack of access to sanitary pads or tampons) or cost issues especially when measured against girl's 'household' chores. There is also the ongoing issue of family and community discrimination in favour of boy's over girl's education. Most important of all, is whether or not the quality of the education they are receiving will empower them enough to better their own circumstance.

Will the reported successes of the MDGs change or challenge the structural discrimination women face? Will the quantifiable changes measured by the MDGs lead on to more fundamental change?

Is the Sustainable Development Goal framework better?

Yet again, each goal is being treated as a separate issue, which tends to ignore the way in which they are interconnected. It could be (and has been) argued that the SDGs (like the MDGs) cannot and will not be realised without the achievement of women's equality and empowerment. However, within SDG 5, the targets are much more comprehensive covering issues such as discrimination, decision-making, gendered division of labour, policy, issues directly relating to women's bodies and sexuality. These targets are much closer to the priorities outlined in Beijing, so they appear to have the potential to make greater progress happen for women.

Does the 'frame-working' of women's rights avoid core issues such as powerlessness?

Evidence (from the 2015 MDG report) would suggest that, while such frameworks don't actively avoid these core issues, they very clearly do not address them adequately. As a general comment on the MDGs, the report makes it clear that *'despite many successes, the poorest and the most vulnerable are being left behind',* of which women would be in the majority.

As stated in the *Beijing Declaration and Platform for Action Turns 20 Report,* published in 2015, which they refer to as a 'wake up call',

'...twenty years on, it is a hard truth that many of the same barriers and constraints that were recognised by the Beijing signatories are still in force globally. There are bright highlights where progress has been made. But no country has achieved gender equality' (2015:6).

(Source: The Beijing Platform for Action Turns 20 Summary Report 2015)

WOMEN'S RIGHTS; REAL PROGRESS BUT...

Selected Issues	Positive Trends	Existing Realities
Health	Life expectancy has risen over the last 20 years for both men and women; average life expectancy of women has increased from 64 in 1990 to 72 in 2015. Globally, the number of maternal mortality deaths in 2013 amounted to 289,000 – down by 45% from 1990: the global MMR in 2013 was 210 maternal deaths per 100,000 live births down from 380 in 1990. In 2014, 83% of pregnant women in developing regions had at least one antenatal care visit, an improvement of 19% since 1990. By 2015, some 119 countries had passed laws on domestic violence, 125 had laws on sexual harassment and 52 had laws on marital rape. Record numbers of women in developing countries now use family planning (especially in poorer regions) suggesting that projections for global population growth could be reduced by as much as 1 billion by 2030. In 2015, an estimated 64% of women (aged 15-49) married or living with a partner were using modern or traditional family planning (as against 36% in 1970).	Progress is uneven regionally and locally; in sub-Saharan Africa, only half of pregnant women receive adequate care during childbirth; only 52% of pregnant women had the recommended minimum of 4 antenatal care visits. Health conditions related to pregnancy and childbirth, combined with HIV and AIDS, are the leading cause of death among young women aged 15 to 29 in developing regions, mainly in sub-Saharan Africa. In 29 countries in Africa and the Middle East, more than 125 million girls and women alive today have been subjected to female genital mutilation. In 2015, 22% of African and 10% of Asian and Latin America/ Caribbean women had 'unmet' contraceptive needs with significant variations by country (a total of 225 million have 'unmet' needs particularly in Africa – 24% of women).
Literacy & Education	In 1990, 44% of the world's illiterate were women; by 2012, this had reduced to 30%. Globally, primary school enrolment is almost universal with the exception of sub-Saharan Africa (where 75% of girls and 81% of boys are enrolled) and Oceania (86% of girls and 91% of boys).	About 58 million children remain out of (primary) school and more than 50% are girls (sub-Saharan Africa and Southern Asia have the highest 'out of school' rates). An estimated 781 million people aged 15 and over remain illiterate and nearly two thirds are women (this proportion has remained unchanged for 20 years).
Political, Legal and Economic Representation	Women's representation at lower or single houses of parliament has increased from 12% in 1997 to 22% in 2015; the number of female Heads of State or Government has increased from 12% in 1995 to 19% in 2015. Women's representation among cabinet ministers increased from 6% in 1994 to 18% in 2015.	Women are outnumbered by men among judges and magistrates in about half of the countries with data and at higher levels in the judiciary, women's representation declines drastically. The media remains a male-dominated industry often reinforcing stereotypes. Less than 4% of CEOs of corporations are women and the gender composition of executive boards of private companies remains hugely unequal.
Economics	Women now make up 40% of the global workforce; there has been a general increase in participation for women in the older age groups. Over half of countries now offer at least 14 weeks' maternity leave and the proportion has increased in the last 20 years. The number of countries with unequal property and inheritance rights for women and men has declined overall in recent decades.	Only 50% of women of working age are in the labour force, compared to 77% of men; the gap remains especially large in Northern Africa, Western Asia and Southern Asia; occupational segregation of women and men continues to be deeply embedded in all regions. Women spend, on average, 3 hours more per day than men on unpaid work in developing countries and 2 hours more per day than men in developed countries. In nearly a third of developing countries, laws do not guarantee the same inheritance rights for women and men, and in an additional half of countries discriminatory customary practices against women persist.

Sources: UNDESA (2015) *World's Women: Trends and Statistics*; *Trends in Maternal Mortality:1990 to 2013* (2014) Estimates by WHO, UNICEF, UNFPA, The World Bank and the United Nations Population Division; World Economic Forum (2015) *The Global Gender Gap Report 2015*; UNFPA *2015 State of World Population*; World Bank (2016) *The Little Data Book on Gender*

$95 billion Per Year
the cost of the **gender gap** in sub-Saharan Africa

> *'Deeply-rooted structural obstacles such as unequal distribution of resources, power and wealth, combined with social institutions and norms that sustain inequality are holding African women, and the rest of the continent, back.'*

According to the *Africa Human Development Report 2016*, gender inequality is costing sub-Saharan Africa on average US$95 billion a year equivalent to 6% the region's GDP. The UNDP report analyses the political, economic and social 'drivers' that hamper African women's advancement and makes a series of proposals to close the gap including addressing the contradictions between the law and everyday practices; challenging harmful social behaviour and tackling institutional discrimination in addition to promoting women's economic, social and political participation.

As noted by UNDP Africa Director Abdoulaye Mar Dieye: *'With existing gender disparities, achieving the Sustainable Development Goals and Africa's Agenda 2063 would remain an aspiration, and not a reality.'*

KEY POINTS

- The report estimates that a 1% increase in gender inequality reduces a country's human development index by 0.75%.

- While the continent is rapidly closing the gender gap in primary education enrolment, African women achieve only 87% of the human development outcomes of men, driven mainly by lower levels of female secondary attainment, lower female labour force participation and high maternal mortality.

- While 61% of African women are working they still face economic exclusion as their jobs are underpaid and undervalued, and are mostly in the informal sector.

- African women hold 66% of all jobs in the non-agricultural informal sector but only make 70 cents for each dollar made by men.

- Only between 7% and 30% of all private firms have a female manager.

- Social norms and behaviour remain a clear obstacle for African women, limiting the time women can spend in education and paid work, and access to economic and financial assets. For example, African women still carry out 71% of water collecting amounting to some 40 billion hours a year, and are less likely to have bank accounts and to access credit.

- African women's health is also severely affected by harmful practices such as under-age marriage and sexual and physical violence, and high maternal mortality - the most at-risk women being those of childbearing age.

GENDER BASED VIOLENCE

'Violence against women and girls is a problem of pandemic proportions. At least one out of every three women around the world has been beaten, coerced into sex, or otherwise abused in her lifetime with the abuser usually someone known to her.'

UN Secretary General Kofi Annan 2006

Violence against women does not discriminate; it knows no social, economic or national boundaries and it permeates each and every level of society. The UN Family Planning Agency has described it as the most pervasive human rights abuse in the world and yet, it is often the least recognised. It is an affront to women's health, dignity, security and autonomy and yet, it is routinely shrouded in and perpetuated by a culture of silence. Current data suggest that an estimated 1 in 3 women worldwide will experience physical and/or sexual violence by an intimate partner or sexual violence by a non-partner in their lifetime (*The World's Women 2015: Trends and Statistics,* UNSTATS and World Health Organisation 2016, Fact Sheet 239).

Intimate partner violence is the most common form; 2 out of 3 victims of intimate partner or family related homicides are women. In 1993, the UN General Assembly Declaration on the Elimination of Violence Against Women provided a framework for action on the pandemic but yet, more than 20 years later:

- I in 3 women still experience physical or sexual violence, mostly by an intimate partner.

- In 2012, a study conducted in New Delhi found that 92% of women reported having experienced some form of sexual violence in public spaces in their lifetime, and 88% of women reported having experienced some form of verbal sexual harassment (including unwelcome comments of a sexual nature, whistling, leering or making obscene gestures) in their lifetime.

- At least 200 million women and girls alive today have undergone female genital mutilation/cutting in 30 countries, according to new estimates published on the United Nations' International Day of Zero Tolerance for Female Genital Mutilation in 2016. In most of these countries, the majority of girls were cut before age 5 (see page 162).

- Around 120 million girls worldwide (slightly more than 1 in 10) have experienced forced intercourse or other forced sexual acts at some point in their lives. By far the most common perpetrators of sexual violence against girls are current or former husbands, partners or boyfriends.

- Adult women account for almost half of all human trafficking victims detected globally. Women and girls together account for about 70% with girls representing 2 out of every 3 child trafficking victims.

- 1 in 10 women in the European Union report having experienced cyber-harassment since the age of 15 (including having received unwanted, offensive sexually explicit emails or SMS messages, or offensive, inappropriate advances on social networking sites). The risk is highest among young women between 18 and 29 years of age.

- An estimated 246 million girls and boys experience school-related violence every year and 1 in 4 girls say that they never feel comfortable using school latrines, according to a survey on youth conducted across four regions (Facts and Figures. Ending Violence against Women, UNWomen 2016). The extent and forms of school-related violence that girls and boys experience differ, but evidence suggests that girls are at greater risk of sexual violence, harassment and exploitation. In addition to the resulting adverse psychological, sexual and reproductive health consequences, school-related gender-based violence is a major obstacle to universal schooling and the right to education for girls.

- Evidence suggests that certain characteristics of women, such as sexual orientation, disability status or ethnicity, and some contextual factors, such as humanitarian crises, including conflict and post-conflict situations, may increase women's vulnerability to violence.

WOMEN, CONFLICT AND DISPLACEMENT

'More than 100 million people are in need of humanitarian assistance – more than at any time since the end of the Second World War. Among those displaced by conflict or uprooted by disaster are tens of millions of women and adolescent girls.'

'A crisis can heighten women's and girls' risks and vulnerabilities to HIV infection, unintended and unwanted pregnancy, maternal death, gender based violence, child marriage, rape and trafficking'

UNFPA State of World Population 2015

Not since the Second World War has there been so many people displaced by a crisis as now; over 200 million people are affected by disasters of one kind or another. The United Nations Population Fund estimates that as a direct result of conflict and displacement, a refugee today will spend an average of 20 years away from their home. Currently, a higher number of countries are seen to be fragile than in recent years, leaving them vulnerable to conflict or to the effects of a natural disaster (fragile states are routinely defined as those trapped in, or emerging from cycles of violence with high poverty levels, poor governance and a very weak economy). There are a number of factors which leave populations vulnerable; poverty (lack of provisions and services, adequate housing and living conditions), geography or location (some countries are geographically more vulnerable to natural disasters), climate change (leading to an increase in natural or human created disasters).

Although there are important differences among women and young people in any given crisis, compounding these general factors are a few overarching components that contribute to a heightened risk for women and girls. These factors include gender inequality and discrimination, which not only continue during humanitarian crises but more often than not actually increase. From the outset, women and girls have unequal access to almost every aspect of life: income, land, education, health services, a political voice, equal protection under the law and a realisation of their human rights. In a setting of conflict or displacement, women's vulnerability is further compounded by the extreme financial hardship which may stem from such a situation, potentially leading to transactional sex and trafficking (see, for example UNHCR (2015) *Women on the Run* and UNHCR (2016) *Forced Displacement in 2015*).

Another contributing factor is the breakdown or disruption of critical sexual and reproductive health infrastructure and services occur in crisis settings and the difficulty in accessing these services, where they still exist, as a result of chaos or insecurity. According to the UNFPA, a lack of basic access to reproductive health services makes delivering a baby in a setting of conflict potentially deadly – particularly so for young girls.

'It is a plain and simple truth that disasters reinforce, perpetuate and increase gender inequality, making bad situations worse for women.'

Margareta Wahlstrom, Special Representative of the Secretary General for Disaster Risk Reduction

NOT SINCE THE SECOND WORLD WAR HAS THERE BEEN SO MANY PEOPLE DISPLACED BY A CRISIS AS NOW; OVER 200 MILLION PEOPLE ARE AFFECTED BY DISASTERS OF ONE KIND OR ANOTHER.

SETTINGS OF CONFLICT, DISPLACEMENT AND NATURAL DISASTERS ACCOUNT FOR **53% OF UNDER-FIVE DEATHS, THREE IN FIVE PREVENTABLE MATERNAL DEATHS AND 45% OF NEO-NATAL DEATHS**

WOMEN ARE **14 TIMES MORE LIKELY** TO DIE IN A CRISIS THAN MEN

IN COLUMBIA ALONE, MATERNAL DEATHS ARE ALMOST **EIGHT TIMES HIGHER** IN COMMUNITIES WHERE ARMED GROUPS ARE PRESENT

IN SYRIA, SKILLED BIRTH ATTENDANTS ASSISTED IN AS MUCH AS **96% OF DELIVERIES**. NOW, ACCESS TO ANTENATAL CARE, SAFE DELIVERY SERVICES AND EMERGENCY OBSTETRICS HAS BECOME EXTREMELY LIMITED, AND SOME AREAS, INCLUDING PARTS OF HOMS, HAVE NO REPRODUCTIVE SERVICES AT ALL

IN VANUATU, WHICH HAS ALREADY HIGH RATES OF GENDER-BASED VIOLENCE, A COUNSELLING CENTRE RECORDED A **300% INCREASE IN REFERRALS** FOLLOWING CYCLONES VANIA AND ATU IN 2011

INCREASED GENDER-BASED VIOLENCE WAS ALSO REPORTED FOLLOWING THE BLACK SUNDAY BUSHFIRES IN AUSTRALIA IN 2009, THE CHRISTCHURCH EARTHQUAKE IN 2011, HURRICANE KATRINA IN THE US IN 2005, THE INDIAN OCEAN TSUNAMI IN 2004 AND IN JAPAN FOLLOWING THE EARTHQUAKE IN 2011

WOMEN AND THE WORLD'S HUMANITARIAN CRISES

- Of the more than 125 million people in need of humanitarian assistance worldwide, over 75% of these are women and children.

- In 2015, 61% of maternal deaths occurred in 35 countries experiencing emergency situations. Their average maternal mortality ratio was on a par with England between the years 1800 and 1850.

- Approximately four times as many women as men died in the 2004 tsunami in Aceh, Indonesia.

- Of the 10 countries with the highest rate of child marriage, 9 are fragile states.

- 90% of early first births occur among child brides – and complications during childbirth is the second-leading cause of death among adolescent girls worldwide. This risk is compounded in crisis settings.

- Globally, at least 35% of women have suffered from gender-based violence. While data is limited, anecdotal reports from around the world – from Ecuador to Yemen – show that prevalence sharply increases during emergencies.

- Sexual violence against women is often deployed as a systemic tool of war. To date, at least 200,000 women have been sexually assaulted during the ongoing conflict in the Democratic Republic of the Congo.

- In disasters and humanitarian emergencies, women are more likely than men to suffer from food insecurity. Even though women produce more than half of the world's food, they comprise 70% of the world's hungry.

- Today, more than half of refugee women and girls live in cities, not in refugee camps.

- The average time of displacement among the world's 60 million refugees, half of which are women and girls, has now reached 30 years.

Source: UNFPA 2016 10 things you should know about women & the world's humanitarian crises
- See more at: www.unfpa.org/news

FEMALE GENITAL MUTILATION/CUTTING

Female Genital Mutilation or Cutting (FGM/C) is the partial or total removal of the female external genitalia or other deliberate injury to the female genital organs for cultural or other non-medical reasons. New figures from 2016 estimate that at least 200 million girls and women alive today have undergone this ritual cutting – with as much as half of them living in only three countries (Egypt, Ethiopia and Indonesia). The exact number of women and girls who have undergone FGM/C remains unknown. Somalia has the highest prevalence of FGM/C with as much as 98% of the female population between the ages of 15-49 having been cut (UNICEF 2016).

The procedure has been known to have been performed on infants, women who are about to be married and in some cases women who have just given birth. In most of the countries, the majority of girls were cut before age 5. In Yemen, for example, 85% of girls are cut within their first week of life. It is usually performed by a traditional midwife or barber, most often without anaesthetic, using scissors, razor blades or broken glass. It is a hugely traumatic experience, both physically and psychologically. More often than not, FGM/C leads to ulceration of the genitals, blood poisoning, infertility, obstructed labour, haemorrhaging and in some cases even death.

According to UNICEF, there has been an overall decline in the prevalence of FGM/C in the last three decades. Yet, not all countries have made progress and the pace of the decline has been uneven. UNICEF also argues that current progress is insufficient to keep up with increasing population growth. If the current trends continue, the number of girls and women undergoing FGM/C will actually rise significantly over the next 15 years. (Female Genital Mutilation/Cutting: A Global Concern, UNICEF 2016)

> No ethical defence can be made for preserving a cultural practice that damages women's health and interferes with their sexuality.
>
> Nahld Toubia MD (a physician from Sudan and a clinical professor in the Central for Sexual Pleasure and Health's Population and Family Department)

> 'There are 3 million girls a year at risk of being cut. This means that in 2015, more than 540,000 girls are at risk of being cut by health personnel, who in turn are probably earning an income from practicing FGC. That's the sort of fact that really keeps me awake at night.'
>
> Julia Lalla-Maharajh Founder and Chief Executive of the Orchid Project in Huffington Post 2015

CONCLUSION

> 'The stakes are high. It is impossible to eradicate poverty, build resilient health systems and take care of the planet if women are not healthy, thriving members of society...Advancing the health and rights of women is the right - and smart - thing to do for any nation to remain or emerge as a leader on the global stage'
>
> Katja Iversen, NGO Women Deliver in June 2015 article, the Guardian newspaper

One of the enduring critiques of the MDG agenda especially as regards women's rights (and when compared to the 1995 Beijing Platform for Action) is that they did not go far enough; the agenda settled for easy and communicable issues of focus. The majority of the more difficult, more controversial issues such as violence against women and girls and the impact of macro-economic policies were side-lined. One of the main issues has been that gender inequality has been seen as women's work; yet, as this chapter has illustrated, gender inequality is, first and foremost, an issue for all of society – it is a human rights issue which must permeate all dimensions of human development. Its centrality is crucial.

Achieving gender equality will never be easy as it will fundamentally challenge long-established norms and practices as well as deeply entrenched attitudes. And it is urgent; pressing issues such as extreme inequality, climate change and regressive attitudes and practices will never be tackled if women are not to the forefront. According to the World Economic Forum, all of the world's regions – from North America to sub-Saharan Africa – now have wider health gaps than a decade ago. This is simply not acceptable; time and time over, research has highlighted that when women have equal rights and can lead healthy lives with real participation and ownership of the agenda, not only individuals but whole communities and nations prosper.

> 'All of us, women and men, must do better'
>
> Chimamanda Ngozi Adiche

DISTANCE FROM GENDER PARITY BY REGION

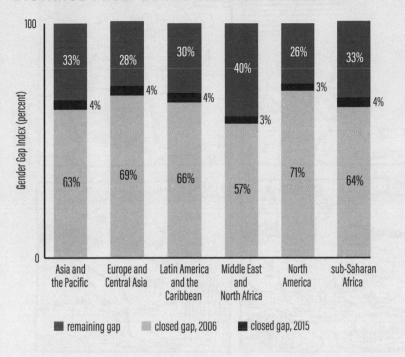

Gender Gap Index (percent)

Region	remaining gap	closed gap, 2006	closed gap, 2015
Asia and the Pacific	33%	63%	4%
Europe and Central Asia	28%	69%	4%
Latin America and the Caribbean	30%	66%	4%
Middle East and North Africa	40%	57%	3%
North America	26%	71%	3%
sub-Saharan Africa	33%	64%	4%

■ remaining gap   ■ closed gap, 2006   ■ closed gap, 2015

THE GENDER GAP BY CATEGORY

 EDUCATIONAL ATTAINMENT: 25 countries have fully closed the education gap. Angola, Yemen, Guinea, Benin and Chad hold the last five spots in this category with Benin and Chad having closed less than 70% of the education gender gap. In total, there are 21 countries where women still have less than 90% of the education outcomes that men have and 35 countries remain below the world average (weighted by population).

 HEALTH AND SURVIVAL: 40 countries have now fully closed their gap on the Health and Survival. Mali, Albania, India, Armenia and China are the lowest-ranked countries, and no country currently has a gap bigger than 90% - only 9 countries are below the world average (weighted by population).

 ECONOMIC PARTICIPATION AND OPPORTUNITY: 14 countries, including 4 from sub-Saharan Africa and 5 from Europe and Central Asia, have closed more than 80% of this gap. Norway, Barbados, Burundi, Sweden and Iceland occupy the top 5 positions; 16 countries have closed less than 50% of the gap including 11 from the Middle East and North Africa region. Iran, Jordan, Pakistan, Syria and Yemen hold the last 5 positions while 31 countries are below the world average (weighted by population).

 POLITICAL EMPOWERMENT: only Iceland and Finland have closed more than 60% of this gender gap while 39 countries have closed less than 10%. Yemen, Kuwait, Oman, Lebanon, Qatar, and Brunei Darussalam have the lowest rankings having closed less than 3% of the political gender gap. 101 countries are below world average (weighted by population) and Brunei Darussalam still has a score of zero with no representation of women.

'NO COUNTRY IN THE WORLD HAS FULLY CLOSED THE GENDER GAP, BUT FOUR OUT OF THE FIVE NORDIC COUNTRIES AND IRELAND HAVE CLOSED MORE THAN 80% OF IT...'

THE GENDER GAP ANALYSED

Over the past 10 years, the World Economic Forum has published a gender gap report ranking 109 countries on the basis of four key indices – economic participation and opportunity; educational attainment; health and survival and political empowerment.

Selected rankings for 2015 include:

1. Iceland
2. Norway
3. Finland
4. Sweden
5. Ireland

---

12. Nicaragua
17. South Africa
18. United Kingdom
27. Mozambique
28. United States
36. Australia
37. Austria
64. Bangladesh
85. Brazil
101. Japan
108. India
134. Saudi Arabia

---

141. Iran, Islamic Republic
142. Chad
143. Syria
144. Pakistan
145. Yemen

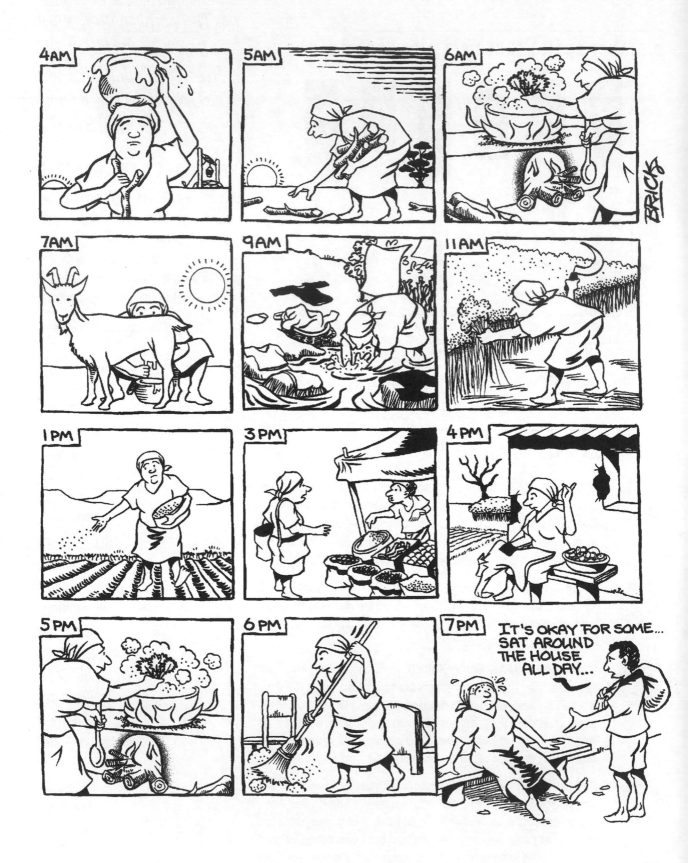

READING

Chimamanda Ngozi Adichie (2014) *We should all be feminists*, Fourth Estate, London

Nikki van der Gaag (2008) *The No-Nonsense Guide to Women's Rights*, New Internationalist, Oxford

Socialwatch (2014) *Report 2014: Means and Ends: A Global Progress Report on Poverty Eradication and Gender Justice*, Montevideo

IINFPA (2015) *State of the World's Population: Shelter from the Storm*, New York

UNICEF (2016) *Female Genital Mutilation/Cutting: A Global Concern*, New York

UN Women (2015) *The Beijing Platform for Action Turns 20*, New York

UN (2015) *The Millennium Development Goals Report 2015*, New York

World Economic Forum (2015) *The Global Gender Gap Report 2015*, Cologne

MORE INFORMATION AND DEBATE

www.amnestyusa.org/our-work/issues/women-s-rights – Amnesty International USA

www.hrw.org/topic/womens-rights – NGO Human Rights Watch research focus on women

www.pambazuka.org – pan-African website of the African NGO network Fahamu with articles, radio documentaries and more on women's rights

www.sustainabledevelopment.un.org/sdgs – official SDG information and debate

www.ohchr.org – country reports, NGO submissions and committee observations on women's rights issues under UN human rights treaty body Committee on the Elimination of Discrimination against Women (CEDAW)

www.unwomen.org – UN women's agency and development site

www.hdr.undp.org – annual flagship thematic UN Human Development Report which includes Gender Inequality Index (GII) which measures 155 countries for gender gaps in major areas of human development

'Climate change is the defining human development issue of our generation. All development is ultimately about expanding human potential and enlarging human freedom. It is about people developing the capabilities that empower them to make choices and to lead lives that they value. Climate change threatens to erode human freedoms and limit choice. It calls into question the Enlightenment principle that human progress will make the future look better than the past.

The early warning signs are already visible...'

HUMAN DEVELOPMENT REPORT 2007-2008: FIGHTING CLIMATE CHANGE – HUMAN SOLIDARITY IN A CHANGING WORLD

CHAPTER 9

CLIMATE CHANGE AND DEVELOPMENT – *'...RICH NATIONS PAY FOR CLIMATE CHANGE WITH DOLLARS AND POOR NATIONS PAY WITH THEIR LIVES...'*

TONY DALY, LORNA GOLD AND JERRY MAC EVILLY

This chapter introduces the links between climate change and development; it reviews the science behind climate change, the arguments and evidence of the Intergovernmental Panel on Climate Change and the scientific evidence for global warming and a planetary 'carbon budget'. It then explores its impact on human development as well as the debates on climate justice and equity. This chapter includes an overview of the Paris Agreement and the arguments around it, particularly from a developing world perspective. The nature of action on climate change at both official and non-official levels is also examined.

KEYWORDS:

ADAPTATION; CLIMATE CHANGE; CLIMATE JUSTICE; CLIMATE SHOCKS; GREENHOUSE GAS EMISSIONS; INTERGOVERNMENTAL PANEL ON CLIMATE CHANGE; MITIGATION; POVERTY; NATURAL DISASTERS; PARIS AGREEMENT; SUSTAINABLE DEVELOPMENT GOALS; WATER

INTRODUCTION

Climate change is a fundamental threat to poverty eradication and human development, as average global temperatures are now estimated to be at 1°C above pre-industrial levels and the poorest people in developing countries are already experiencing devastation from climate change impacts. Because of this, action to tackle climate change may no longer be limited simply to questions of energy and environmental management has now become a key issue in international development. Not only does climate change affect development outcomes, but the need to respond to climate change increasingly shapes development choices.

Twenty years of faltering diplomacy at the United Nations seeking to secure agreements on mitigating the impacts of climate change and reducing Greenhouse Gas (GHG) emissions, has highlighted a two-pronged challenge. One, the need to improve human development for all, especially the poorest while, two, adapting to a rise in extreme weather events and rapidly moving towards a low carbon world.

Over the past decade the World Economic Forum (comprising over 1,000 of the world's top corporations and business interests) in its annual World Risk Report has identified challenges related to environment, climate change and sustainability as among the world's most immediate and pressing risks. In its 2016 Report, the Forum identified environmental challenges as four of the top ten risks in terms of likelihood and as number one in terms of anticipated impact. The view of the Forum is matched in a very different arena by that of the insurance industry across the developed world which has seen climate related claims increase very significantly in recent years to the point where some companies in, for example, Florida in the US, are refusing to provide insurance in areas 'at risk'.

Major insurance company *Allianz* has predicted a 35%+ increase in losses from 'extreme events' within a decade. In this context, the industry often portrays itself as 'being on the frontline' of climate change.

Currently, the impact of climate change is deeply unjust and tackling it poses fundamental questions of equity and justice. While the 'developed' world is responsible for the bulk of historic global emissions, vulnerable communities are disproportionately affected, not only because they are often more exposed and vulnerable but also because they have fewer resources and supports. In its 2016 *Shock Waves* report the World Bank notes:

> *'The poor live in uncertainty, just one natural disaster away from losing everything they have. We need good, climate-informed development to reduce the impacts of climate change on the poor. This means, in part, providing poor people with social safety nets and universal health care. These efforts will need to be coupled with targeted climate resilience measures, such as the introduction of heat resistant crops and disaster preparedness systems... without this type of development, climate change could force more than 100 million people into extreme poverty by 2030.'*
>
> World Bank (2016) Shock Waves: Managing the Impacts of Climate Change on Poverty: xi

While the risks from climate change and environmental damage are primarily measured in economic terms in the developed world, elsewhere among the world's poorest, the impact on those on the frontline is measured starkly in terms of human rights negatively impacted, lives severely damaged, and resources denied.

In this context, delivering on the aspirations of a more sustainable, fairer and peaceful world has never been more challenging and more necessary. In essence, a new approach is needed across rich and poor countries that mainstreams climate change into development strategies and planning at national and local level.

This chapter explores the issue of climate change and its impact on human development; it reviews some of the main debates (and disagreements); it explores some of the key data and argument on the issue of 'responsibility'. As was highlighted earlier in chapter 5, the concept of climate justice (and injustice) remains central to the debate and is briefly explored.

Finally, the chapter identifies a series of actions already underway and which need broader recognition and adoption in order to respond effectively to climate change.

CLIMATE CHANGE IMPACTS TODAY

- The 2015 Human Development Report estimates that climate change could expose 250 million people to greater water stress in Africa and, in some countries drought could halve the yields from rainfed agriculture by 2020, noting that *'since 2008 an estimated one person every second has been displaced by a disaster, with 19.3 million people forced to flee their homes in 2014 alone.'*

- The 2015 United Nations review on Small Island Developing Nations reports that *'high sea levels and swells have already resulted in the displacement of people in a number of small island developing states including Kiribati, Solomon Islands, the Marshall Islands, and the Federated States of Micronesia'* (2015:33).

- Monsoons displaced 14 million people in India, seven million in Bangladesh and three million in China (with the second highest death toll since records began), according to the 2007 Human Development Report on climate change.

- Lack of access to water is also linked to increasing poverty and vulnerability: almost one-fifth of the world's population (about 1.2 billion people) live in areas where water is physically scarce. One quarter of the global population live in developing countries that face water shortages due to weak governance and human capacities, and a lack of infrastructure to transport water from rivers and aquifers.

While the debates on climate change now take centre-stage internationally, the movement for positive change grows in tandem. Global emissions of carbon dioxide increased 50% between 1990 and 2013. Many international bodies, corporations, communities, civil society organisations and individuals have embraced the need for change in our growth and consumption models and patterns. One example illustrates the point - the fossil fuel divestment campaign emerged in the US in 2010 but spread quickly across the continents. The Fossil Free campaign reports institutions committing to divestment, which include Glasgow and Oxford Universities in the UK, Stanford and Georgetown Universities in the US, the Norwegian State Pension Fund, the California State Pension Fund, the British Medical Association, the World Council of Churches, local councils and over 50 cities across Europe, North America, Australia and New Zealand.

As of August 2016 more than 500 institutions globally have committed to divesting fossil fuel investments within 5 years – totalling an asset base of US$3.4 trillion.

AN ERA OF UNPRECEDENTED WARMING

Increases in global temperature trends between 2001 and 2015 have not only indicated a pattern of gradual and incremental change but also one of significant upheaval carrying profound social and environmental implications. The debate is not simply limited to variations in temperature and recorded changes in our weather; it is about present and future human well-being and our capacity to provide secure and sustainable lives for all, particularly for the poorest and most vulnerable.

Analysing and interpreting how the Earth's climate is being disturbed is an essential part of this process. It is only through evidence-based assessment that we can establish the nature, scale and likely impact of climate change, what its drivers are and what further potential impacts are likely. In summary, analysis by the main scientific organisations, such as the Intergovernmental Panel on Climate Change (IPCC), continues to indicate that 'change' to the Earth's climate does not amount to a *benign natural variation*. On the contrary, we are faced with an unprecedented warming of the planet that is human-made, is hugely damaging and is projected to get substantially worse. This analysis has profound implications for international development.

The opportunity to drive dramatic climate action based on equity and justice is still possible but requires immediate and sustained action at all levels of society, particularly in developed countries. The science suggests that the next 10–15 years are critical if the most dangerous and irreversible effects of climate change are to be avoided.

INTERGOVERNMENTAL PANEL ON CLIMATE CHANGE (IPCC)

The IPCC (established in 1988) is an international body of scientists tasked by governments to independently analyse evidence related to climate change. Their periodic assessments are systematically reviewed and provide the dominant scientific basis for actions on climate change.

For a number of decades, there was much contested and often distorted debate as to whether or not climate change was taking place, whether this change was human induced, and whether the potential impacts were underestimated or exaggerated. Controversy routinely appeared, especially in popular broadcast, print and online media where discussions of the credentials, analysis and conclusions of the IPCC descended into 'climate change denial', a rejection of the scientific evidence and the risks of climate change and a fundamentalist belief that technology would resolve the issue. Many counterclaims have stemmed from groups and industries that would stand to lose out financially from changes to the *status quo*.

While some uncertainties are inherent to climate science, the evidence for human-induced climate change is resounding. There exists a very high degree of consensus as to the realities of climate change, its broad dimensions and impacts, notwithstanding continuing research into its timeframe and severity of its effects. A 2013 research study by John Cook and others which examined 4,000+ academic papers over a 20-year period found that 97.1% agreed that climate change is anthropocentric – caused by human activity (Environmental Letters, Vol.8:2).

The authors concluded: '*...our findings prove that there is a strong scientific agreement about the cause of climate change, despite public perceptions to the contrary*'.

While it is entirely possible that detrimental impacts may not be quite as devastating as projected in certain regions, British sociologist Anthony Giddens highlights, in his 2011 book *The Politics of Climate Change*, that uncertainty related to future projections cuts both ways, the dangerous consequences of climate change may be substantially worse than expected and such a risk must equally be closely assessed.

'Climate change is real. There will always be uncertainty in understanding a system as complex as the world's climate. However, there is now strong evidence that significant global warming is occurring. The evidence comes from direct measurements of rising surface air temperatures and subsurface ocean temperatures and from phenomena such as increases in average global sea levels, retreating glaciers, and changes to many physical and biological systems. It is likely that most of the warming in recent decades can be attributed to human activities.'

INTERNATIONAL SCIENCE ACADEMIES: JOINT STATEMENT 2005

RISING TEMPERATURES AND GLOBAL WARMING

Building on earlier analyses, the IPCC has concluded that warming *'…of the climate system is unequivocal, and since the 1950s, many of the observed changes are unprecedented over decades to millennia. The atmosphere and ocean have warmed, the amounts of snow and ice have diminished, and sea level has risen.'* Importantly, the IPCC has further clarified that it is 'extremely likely' (with a 95-100% degree of certainty) that human activity has caused most of the increase in global temperatures since the middle of the 20th century.

The most important and damaging human activity has been the release of increasing amounts of greenhouse gases, such as carbon dioxide, methane and nitrous oxide. The IPCC has noted that the concentrations of these gases are now at levels that are unparalleled in at least 800,000 years. In the atmosphere, these gases prevent energy and heat from escaping the Earth and their increasing release is intensifying this process, thus warming the Earth's climate.

These increases in greenhouse gas emissions are largely the result of intensive fossil fuel combustion and industrial processes in the energy industry (electricity and heat production, fuel extraction etc.), transport and agriculture sectors. Developed countries are principally responsible for these processes, driven largely by 150 years of economic and population growth.

THE CASE OF 2 DEGREES

The graph on the following page shows the projected changes in global temperature published by the IPCC in its report *Climate Change 2014 Impacts, Adaptation, and Vulnerability: Summary for Policy Makers.* The blue line shows a limited increase which would require serious action right now by governments to drastically reduce emissions and the red line shows a catastrophic increase of more than 4°C if a 'business as usual' approach continues with emissions increasing into the future.

The IPCC's most recent assessment in 2014 confirms that these emissions are continuing to rise – and at a higher rate with the result that global temperatures are likely to increase significantly by the end of the century. Taken globally, 2015 was the first year that average temperatures were 1°C above pre-industrial levels. A 1°C overall increase may seem quite low: however, as an average over the surface of an entire planet, it is remarkably high and is resulting in range of severe weather events and other environmental impacts. 2015 was the hottest year ever recorded with 2016 projected to be even hotter; 15 of the 16 warmest years have occurred since 2001.

Taking into account the current trajectory, governments have focused on how to limit global warming to a 2°C increase above pre-industrial levels in order to prevent the worst effects of climate change. This level is now being reached rapidly and even such a level involves unacceptable impacts for billions of people, as illustrated below (see Climate Change and Human Development). If the objective is to keep overall increases below 2°C, it is possible to release only a finite amount of harmful greenhouse gases into the atmosphere - an amount termed the 'global carbon budget'. Since carbon dioxide is the most important greenhouse gas in terms of volume, it is used as a standard measurement when assessing emissions. The idea of 'CO_2 equivalent' is therefore used to refer to the amount of CO_2 emissions that would be involved to produce the same quantity as all the greenhouse gases combined.

THE GLOBAL CARBON BUDGET

Significantly, in its 2014 synthesis report the IPCC put forward different scenarios on the global carbon budget related to a 2°C limit. In order to achieve a 'strong likelihood' (i.e. 66% chance) of staying below the 2°C threshold, the IPCC concluded that a cumulative carbon budget stretching from the 19th to the end of 21st century of less than 2,900 gigatonnes must be respected. However, the majority of this budget has already been consumed and from 2011 to end of the century, a budget of only 1000 gigatonnes remains for the period. Naturally, this budget has been further reduced since 2011 as emissions continue to rise.

On current production and consumption trends, the IPCC (2015) expects this carbon budget will be consumed in the next 10 - 20 years. While the science of climate change has progressed and the 2°C threshold features in international climate agreements, a global carbon budget does not form part of such obligations. Although low-carbon and de-carbonising commitments are increasingly being made by political leaders, the majority of developed countries have not put in place national carbon budgets and have not put forward climate policies in line with a 2°C pathway. Given this failure, and ongoing increases in emissions, many regard the 2°C limit as already extremely difficult to achieve without radical political, behavioural and technological change.

The Case of 2 Degrees

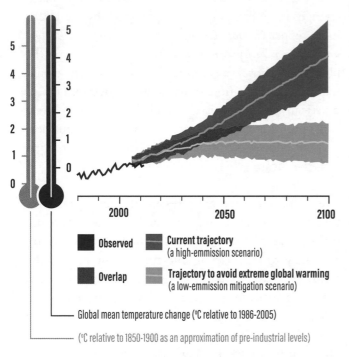

Observed

Overlap

Current trajectory (a high-emmission scenario)

Trajectory to avoid extreme global warming (a low-emmission mitigation scenario)

Global mean temperature change (°C relative to 1986-2005)

(°C relative to 1850-1900 as an approximation of pre-industrial levels)

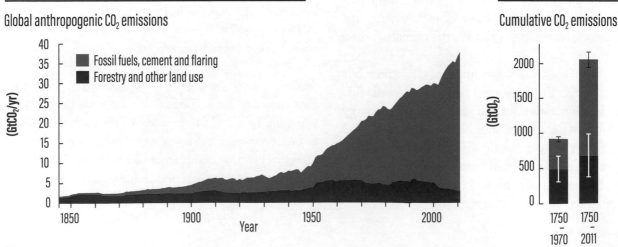

Global anthropogenic CO_2 emissions

Fossil fuels, cement and flaring
Forestry and other land use

($GtCO_2$/yr)

Cumulative CO_2 emissions

($GtCO_2$)

1750
–
1970

1750
–
2011

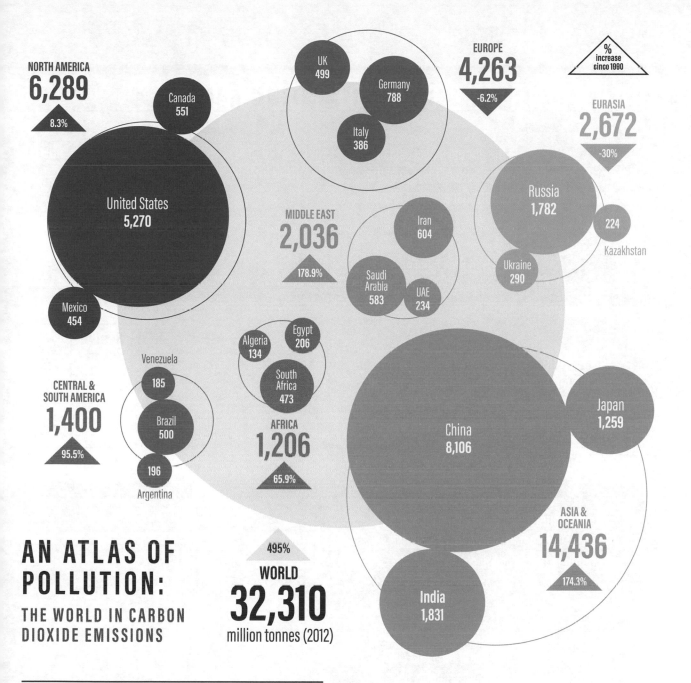

NORTH AMERICA
6,289
8.3%

- Canada 551
- United States 5,270
- Mexico 454

EUROPE
4,263
-6.2%

- UK 499
- Germany 788
- Italy 386

% increase cinco 1990

EURASIA
2,672
-30%

- Russia 1,782
- Kazakhstan 224
- Ukraine 290

MIDDLE EAST
2,036
178.9%

- Iran 604
- Saudi Arabia 583
- UAE 234

CENTRAL & SOUTH AMERICA
1,400
95.5%

- Venezuela 185
- Brazil 500
- Argentina 196

AFRICA
1,206
65.9%

- Algeria 134
- Egypt 206
- South Africa 473

ASIA & OCEANIA
14,436
174.3%

- China 8,106
- Japan 1,259
- India 1,831

AN ATLAS OF POLLUTION:
THE WORLD IN CARBON DIOXIDE EMISSIONS

495%
WORLD
32,310
million tonnes (2012)

Top 5 carbon emissions per capita in developed and developing countries

DEVELOPED COUNTRIES, 2014

Country/ Region	Per capita carbon emissions in metric tons per person	Total of global emissions (%)
USA	17.4	15.5%
EU 28	6.6	9.3%
Russia	11.1	4.4%
Canada	15.7	3.4%
Japan	9.7	3.4%
Global	4.9	100%

DEVELOPING COUNTRIES, 2014

Country/ Region	Per capita carbon emissions in metric tons per person	Emissions Total (%)
China	7.1	27%
India	2.0	7.23%
Indonesia	2.5	1.78%
Iran	7.9	1.72%
Saudi Arabia	19.5	1.68%
Global	4.9	100%

Source and Notes: this latest data from the US Energy Information Administration highlights a unique picture of economic growth and decline. China has sped ahead of the US, as highlighted by this map, which resizes each country according to CO2 emissions. For the first time, world emissions have gone down significantly in 2014 (but not everywhere) and the debate continues as to whether this trend will be ongoing.

COUNTING THE COST OF POLLUTION

US$5.11 TRILLION – the annual global cost of premature deaths due to air pollution (the size of the gross domestic product of India, Canada, and Mexico combined)

US$225 BILLION - cost to the global economy in lost work days due to premature deaths (cost of treating illness not included)

87% of the world's people lived in areas that exceeded the Air Quality Guideline of the World Health Organisation. In low- and middle-income countries 90% of populations were exposed to dangerous levels of ambient air pollution

1 in 60 children under age 5 in lower-income countries are more than 60 times as likely to die from exposure to air pollution as children in high-income countries

8% – 10% GDP in 2013 – China lost nearly 10% of its GDP through economic costs of indoor and outdoor pollution; India 7.69% and Sri Lanka and Cambodia roughly 8%

Sources: figures based on 2013 data in The Cost of Air Pollution by World Bank and Institute for Health Metrics and Evaluation University of Washington, 2016.

1 IN EVERY 10 DEATHS ATTRIBUTABLE TO HOUSEHOLD AND AIR POLLUTION IN 2012

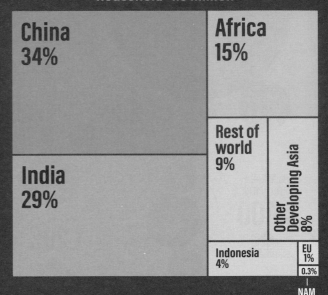

Household 4.3 million

- China 34%
- India 29%
- Africa 15%
- Rest of world 9%
- Other Developing Asia 8%
- Indonesia 4%
- EU 1%
- 0.3% NAM

Outdoor: 3.0 million

- China 35%
- India 21%
- Rest of world 16%
- Africa 10%
- Other Developing Asia 9%
- Russia 5%
- INDO 2%
- NAM 2%
- EU 1%

Notes: EU = European Union, NAM = North America, INDO = Indonesia.

Sources: WHO (2016); IEA analysis; International Energy Agency (2016) Energy and Air: World Energy Outlook Special Report

DEBATING EQUITY

A commitment to sharing the responsibility of reducing emissions equitably and fairly is at the heart of the international debate on climate change. Equity and justice have been central to the international negotiations on climate change, firstly as the impacts are adversely affecting those who have contributed the least to global emissions and, secondly, as measures to cut emissions need to be fair if they are to be accepted.

In this way, climate change raises more than technical and environmental questions – it poses fundamental questions of justice and injustice. Clearly, however, not all countries have contributed equally to the building up of GHG emissions and, obviously, not all countries have the same resources to support the transition to a low carbon sustainable economy. This issue is at the very core of the debate around international climate negotiations; how should responsibility and ability to reduce emissions be shared across developing and developed countries.

The main intergovernmental response to climate change began with the United Nations Framework Convention on Climate Change (UNFCCC) which entered into force in 1994. In negotiations, the issue of equity is linked directly to the legal principle of 'common but differentiated responsibilities and respective capabilities'. This principle acknowledges that while climate action is a common duty, all countries have not contributed to climate change to the same extent. Therefore, the responsibility of countries to take action should be differentiated. The UNFCCC explicitly distinguishes between developed and developing countries with the former required to take the lead in reducing emissions. The Kyoto Protocol signed in 1997 followed this approach and specific emission reduction commitments were given only to developed countries.

While this approach was accepted in principle, its practical implementation became a major source of outright disagreement between developing and developed countries. The USA failed to ratify the Kyoto Protocol arguing that the required emissions reductions would hamper economic growth. Many developed countries have continued to question further and greater climate commitments when developing countries with growing middle-income economies and sizeable emissions (e.g. China) were not required to take action to reduce emissions despite their growing capability. In response, developing countries have pointed not only to historical responsibility for climate change but also to the range of financial and technological resources available to developed countries and the high costs that are associated with ensuring a sustainable development pathway for many developing countries.

The latest international climate agreement under the UNFCCC signed in Paris in 2015 marks a break with this debate in that it applies to all countries (for more on the Paris Agreement see page 180). Countries have also agreed to take action on the basis of equity and according to a revised principle of *'common but differentiated responsibilities and respective capabilities, in the light of different national circumstances'*. In line with this revised principle, stringent commitments to reduce emissions and increase resilience now also apply to developing countries and the binary divide between 'rich' and 'poor' countries has been removed.

CLIMATE CHANGE AND HUMAN DEVELOPMENT

While climate change may seem a distant concern to many in the rich world, poor people in developing countries are already being impacted:

'Today, we are witnessing at first-hand what could be the onset of major human development reversal in our lifetime. Across developing countries, millions of the world's poorest people are already being forced to cope with the impacts of climate change. These impacts do not register as apocalyptic events in the full glare of world media attention. They go unnoticed in financial markets and in the measurement of world gross domestic product (GDP). But increased exposure to drought, to more intense storms, to floods and environmental stress is holding back the efforts of the world's poor to build a better life for themselves and their children.'

This was one of the key conclusions of the UN's 2007-2008 Human Development Report which argued that the decade following presented a narrowing window of opportunity to address the issue; with this decade now almost passed, the situation continues to deteriorate with the world's poor bearing the brunt of the impact. A 2015 report, *From Decisions to Actions*, by the UN Conference on Trade and Development (UNCTAD), summarised the challenge succinctly: *'Being vulnerable implies being less capable to deal with sudden changes, crises and shocks. One of the great injustices in our world is that those that are poor are more often the most vulnerable – both in terms of people and nations. As such, they tend to carry the brunt of the cost of economic, social and environmental crises. For some crises, as in the case of climate change, this may even boil down to a question of life or death. This is not only questionable from a moral perspective, it is also directly incompatible with the ambitions of eradicating poverty and achieving the sustainable development goals.'*

In a 2014 study of five countries (the Philippines, Honduras, Kenya, Malawi and Ethiopia), the Irish international development NGO Trócaire catalogued the impact of climate change on developing countries: *'In all of the countries, increases in temperature both during the day and at night are clearly observable. Longer dry seasons and hotter days, leading to greater evaporation losses leads to serious risk of droughts. When rain does fall, it falls more intensely than before, leading to greater risk of floods, damage to crops and risks to human health through water- and vector-borne diseases. As the ocean warms, tropical storms are expected to get stronger. This is a huge concern in those countries already massively affected by tropical storms. In 2013, super typhoon Haiyan killed over 6,000 people in the Philippines and displaced millions more. In the last century, six of the twelve strongest hurricanes in the world impacted Honduras, including Hurricane Mitch which killed 10,000 people in 1998.'* (Feeling the Heat, 2014: iii).

Extending the analysis above, the Trócaire study highlighted six key areas of immediate and future concern.

- **Agricultural production and food security**: while demand for food rises, crops are failing in many developing countries due to climate variability and drought, thus increasing food insecurity locally and regionally. These risks are exacerbated by low levels of investment in small scale farming, low access to technology, reliance on rain-fed agriculture, and high levels of pre-existing food poverty.

- **Water stress and scarcity:** hotter days and a longer dry season mean less rain to feed water sources, greater losses from evaporation and, in many water stressed countries less drinking water, less water to grow crops, and less water to power electricity. When rain does fall, it will often fall more heavily, and when this happens, less of it soaks into the ground where it's most useful for crops – instead, it runs off quickly and may cause flooding. Heavier rainfall also leads to increased sediments and pollutants in fresh water bodies. This is particularly harmful where people do not have access to safe water.

- **Health Risks:** the World Health Organisation predicts 250,000 additional deaths per year globally from 2030: 38,000 due to heat exposure in elderly people, 48,000 due to diarrhoea, 60,000 due to malaria, and 95,000 due to childhood under-nutrition. Climate change has also been linked to increased epidemics in several countries; rising temperatures linked with outbreaks of dengue fever and an increase in malaria in already affected areas and in additional high-altitude areas.

- **Gender:** climate change impacts women more severely as they continue to experience significant powerlessness and discrimination e.g. while women make up half the agricultural workforce in least developed countries, they own just 10% to 20% of land. Access to water has important gender dimensions, with young girls in particular being more vulnerable to water availability and competition.

- **Migration:** increased natural disasters, rising sea levels and prolonged droughts all resulted in increased displacement and migration; typhoon Haiyan forced some 4 million people in the Philippines to leave their homes, approximately 400,000 of whom are still in evacuation centres. In Ethiopia and Kenya, droughts have contributed to increased rural-urban migration, increasing urban vulnerability.

- **Economic Impact:** in Honduras for example, hurricanes caused direct and indirect damages of over US$5 billion in the 20th century, equivalent to 95% of Honduras' GDP in 1998. In the Philippines, the cost of adaptation for agriculture and coastal zones is expected to be about US$5 billion per year by 2020 on average. In Kenya, net economic costs of climate change, including health burdens, energy demand and infrastructure could be equivalent to almost 3% of GDP each year by 2030.

While each of these individual risks and trends pose fundamental threats to human development, when combined together and situated in the context of extreme inequality and marginalisation, they have the clear potential not only to slow human progress but to significantly reverse it. The wider social, economic, political, cultural and ecological processes that mould human development multiply vulnerabilities, overwhelmingly so for the world's poor.

The World Bank *Shock Waves* report notes that due to the impacts of ongoing increases in emissions: '…*between now and 2030 climate policies can do little to alter the amount of volume and impact of global warming: the only realistic option being to reduce vulnerability through targeted adaptation investments and improved socioeconomic conditions. Such a strategy implies higher incomes, lower levels of poverty and reduced inequality – elements at the core of any definition of human development*'.

CLIMATE JUSTICE

All the evidence and the accompanying debates make one point crystal clear - climate change is not just an environmental issue, with very serious environmental impacts, but a phenomenon which affects all aspects of human life. Climate justice is the term routinely used to describe the ethical and political dimensions of climate change. It refers to the fact that climate change is an issue with far reaching implications in terms of human rights, equality and social justice. As a phenomenon it is happening within a historical context where different parts of the world bear differing levels of historic responsibility. From an ethical standpoint, climate justice draws attention to a number of important factors which are often lost when climate change is thought of solely as an environmental issue.

A justice perspective draws attention to a fundamental injustice underpinning climate change; those who have caused the problem, for the greater part, are also those who have benefited most from economic development. This is due to the interconnection between the economic model on which globalisation is based, an increasing reliance on fossil fuels and industrialised agriculture and the impacts these have on the planet's climate systems. Since the start of the industrial revolution, a model of economic development has evolved which is based on an unsustainable approach to production and consumption and is hugely reliant on the burning of fossil fuels. The true social and environmental costs of this model have never been accounted.

'To conclude that there is a necessary trade-off between economic progress and environmental integrity would however be wrong. Rather, this dilemma reflects the narrow framing of economic goals and policies and the overarching priority given to GDP growth in almost all countries. As a consequence, the economy has been managed as if it were largely delinked from its social and environmental contexts.'

Thomas Tanner and Leo Horn-Phathanothai (2014)

Those who have done least to cause the problem, in particular the world's poorest, have benefitted least from economic development to date. Future generations which naturally have not contributed to this crisis also stand to lose the most. The distribution of responsibility and 'blame', therefore, is uneven. A 2015 Oxfam briefing demonstrates that the wealthiest 10% of the world's population are responsible for over 50% of global emissions while the poorest 3.5 billion account for just a tenth, as the graph below demonstrates. In line with the polluter pays principle, the responsibility for the problem lies primarily with those who have caused the problem, and therefore the wealthiest populations and nations.

Climate justice draws attention to the current and future effects of climate change which are highly uneven, as is the capacity to deal with them. The first communities to feel the adverse effects of changing weather patterns associated with climate change have been those living in tropical and sub-tropical regions, as well as

Percentage of CO_2 emissions by world population

Source: Oxfam 2015 World's richest 10% produce half of carbon emissions while poorest 3.5 billion account for just a tenth

Richest 10% responsible for almost half of total lifestyle consumption emissions

World population arranged by income (deciles)

Richest 10% — 49%
19%
11%
7%
4%
3%
2.5%
Poorest 50% — 2%
1.5%
1%

Poorest 50% responsible for only around 10% of total lifestyle consumption emissions those living in small island states, particularly in the South Pacific. This particular geographical pattern compounds already existing vulnerabilities, such as widespread rural poverty, meaning that the poorest communities have felt the effects first and worst (see Chapter 5). These communities, moreover, due to their pre-existing vulnerabilities, are least prepared to respond to the new challenges presented by a changing climate; they often lack the knowledge, technologies, and the resources to adapt their livelihoods in a timely and appropriate manner.

In direct contrast, the majority of the wealthiest populations, due to geography and also the ready availability of public resources to address weather related emergencies, have been largely sheltered from many of the most serious impacts of climate change. The urbanised populations of North America, Western Europe and Australia have until relatively recently been able to develop coping strategies without any serious questioning of the unsustainable production and consumption patterns which underpin climate change. This situation is now changing as the early impacts of climate change are generating serious effects across developed countries.

Additionally, climate justice draws attention to the fact that in tackling climate change through mitigation and adaptation measures (see page 180), issues of equality, human rights and social justice need to be integrated. It is possible for responses to climate change to deepen pre-existing inequalities and undermine human rights through so-called 'false solutions', which attempt to preserve high-consumption lifestyles whilst reducing the direct climate impacts.

One example of such a damaging solution is the set of policy approaches to support a shift to the use of bio-fuels in cars. Rather than focusing on reducing car usage, making engines more efficient and supporting the development of electric vehicles, the decision to facilitate big agricultural companies in the use of crop-based bio-fuels through policy incentives and public subsidies has had serious impacts on the livelihoods of the poorest people as biofuel production is outsourced to developing countries. Producing one litre of biofuels requires 2,500 litres of water. The indirect land use change in the Polochic Valley region of Guatemala, for example, resulted in the forced eviction of over 800 small-scale farming families and large swathes of land and water being taken up to produce biofuels instead of food by 2011. The International Institute for Sustainable Development found that the EU spent €9.3 billion to €10.7 billion subsidising biofuels in the same year. By 2013, more than 60 developing countries had put in place their own subsidies and policy mandates for biofuel production and consumption. Former UN special rapporteur on the right to food, Jean Ziegler, referred to this practice in a scathing critique in The Guardian in 2013 as '*a crime against humanity*.'

It is not commonly known that the industrial food system, and in particular meat and dairy production, is one of the key drivers of climate change: agriculture accounts for almost a quarter of greenhouse gas emissions globally. Certain approaches commonly referred to as 'climate smart Agriculture' regularly promoted by large agri-businesses often facilitate a business-as-usual approach focusing on ever greater food production but facilitating increases in harmful emissions, as well as unsustainable chemical and energy intensive models of agriculture.

OFFICIAL ACTION ON CLIMATE CHANGE

Official responses to the escalating threat of climate change focus on two key strategies – **mitigation** (responses employed to reduce emissions being released into the atmosphere, e.g. decommissioning coal burning power plants) and **adaptation** (reducing vulnerability to climate change impacts e.g. improving flood defences); policies which support both strategies are underpinned by national and international law. Given the need for collective action and negotiation internationally, action on climate change has had a long and contentious history.

The main intergovernmental response to climate change began with the 1994 United Nations Framework Convention on Climate Change (UNFCCC) the central goal of which was to put in place a legal roadmap upon which states could initiate steps to stabilise greenhouse gases and prevent further negative human interference. A supplementary agreement stemming from the UNFCCC was signed in Kyoto, Japan in 1997 and committed developed countries to achieve specific emissions reductions up to 2020. This agreement, known as the Kyoto Protocol, came into effect in 2005. Since 1995, government representatives have negotiated at a series of annual meetings under the UNFCCC known as Conferences of the Parties (COPs).

These negotiations have focused on putting in place further agreements related to mitigation, adaptation, finance and technology based on a new long-term framework for cooperative action. However, negotiations have suffered many setbacks and almost collapsed in 2009 in Copenhagen due to disputes over transparency, process and greater mitigation commitments, leaving a legacy of mistrust and tension. Despite this, a new Agreement was reached in Paris in December 2015 which will enter into force in 2020 and which represented a breakthrough in approach and cooperation internationally. Having been adopted unanimously, the Agreement is the first truly global climate deal that will shape climate action over the coming decades. Its core legal obligations are mainly procedural, putting in place a new legally-binding framework for reviewing and reporting on mitigation, adaptation and finance to achieve long-term goals.

The international agreement signed in October 2016 to phase out use of hydrofluorocarbons (HFCs), mostly produced by air conditioners which don't harm the ozone layer but act as a greenhouse gas, is another important step taken in limiting the warming of the planet which will, for now, be reflected by countries that can afford updating refrigeration and coolant technology changes.

As has been widely noted, while climate change is now much higher up the agenda, many countries, both developing and developed, continue to simplistically regard climate action as a brake or limit on their economic growth, rather than an essential response that presents both immediate benefits and opportunities.

The primary concern is that early and concrete action in developed countries continues to be delayed and this impacts on justice, equality, food, jobs, and human rights.

Adaptation to the adverse effects of climate change is vital in order to respond to the impacts of climate change already underway while, at the same time preparing for future impacts. Even where GHG emissions are reduced in the near future, harmful emissions already released will continue to have a warming effect on the Earth's climate. Adaptation actions enhance the resilience of vulnerable communities and regions, thereby reducing potential damage.

For many of the world's poorest and most vulnerable countries, their climate change priority is adaptation and managing the impacts of climate change which are urgent and immediate. Climate financing has, however, mainly supported **mitigation** efforts and it is questionable that the Paris Agreement will release the required level of new and additional monies for adaptation.

However, the costs of adaptation for developing countries by 2030 (setting aside developed economies) are likely to be two-to-three times higher than current global public finance for adaptation and potentially four-to-five times higher by 2050. Previous global estimates of the costs of adaptation have been placed at between US$70 billion and US$100 billion a year for the period 2010-2050. The UN Environment Programme (UNEP) in its 2016 Adaptation Finance Gap Report, estimated that the costs of adaptation could range from US$140 billion to US$300 billion by 2030, and between US$280 billion and US$500 billion by 2050.

THERE IS NO PLAN B: THE PARIS AGREEMENT ON CLIMATE CHANGE

The Agreement (and a set of accompanying decisions) was unanimously accepted by 195 nations in Paris in December 2015 and is therefore the first truly global climate deal that will substantially shape climate action, cooperation and support over the coming decades.

The importance of the Paris Agreement was highlighted on the opening day by the presence of 150 presidents and prime ministers, the largest ever single-day gathering of heads of state. Unlike many previous UNFCCC conferences, the negotiations in Paris were significantly free of the kind of 'procedural wrangles' characteristic of previous negotiating summits. While many of the operational details of the new framework were left to future summits, and the fact that the Agreement will only take effect once enough countries have formally ratified it, the Agreement itself was hailed as 'historical'.

While the Paris Agreement represents a political breakthrough for increased international cooperation in responding to climate change, regrettably much remains unclear in terms of the implementation and interpretation of its many provisions and commitments.

A summary of the main issues is provided below:

- Importantly, the Paris Agreement is the first multilateral climate agreement to note the importance of climate justice, a just transition, and human rights when taking action to address climate change. These are not, however, set out as binding obligations. In order for the Agreement to be a success, safeguards must be put in place to ensure that climate actions are taken in a manner that protects local communities and fully integrates human rights' protections.

- The wording of the long-term goal – that countries must aim to peak global emissions as soon as possible and achieve a 'balance' between emissions and removals - leaves plenty of room for interpretation; the strengthened commitment to limit the global temperature rise to 'well-below' 2°C while pursuing efforts to 1.5°C is extremely ambitious. However, it remains highly uncertain that this commitment will be met with correspondingly ambitious policies by governments to immediately and drastically reduce emissions.

- The Agreement does not specifically refer to fossil fuels, aviation and shipping sectors or to a damaging global food system and does not stipulate specific mitigation actions that are necessary across energy, transport and agriculture.

- Emission levels associated with a 2°C pathway are based on large volumes of emissions being removed from the atmosphere later this century. Assuming such 'future' removals of emissions risks delaying clear mitigation action now, and potentially locking in even higher levels of warming now. It is also based on the assumed use of 'geo-engineering' (e.g. huge increases in plantations with trees and crops grown specifically to take in CO_2). However, this extent of crops would require the use of vast amounts of arable land, potentially undermining food security and land rights.

- The Paris Agreement, unlike previous international climate agreements under the UNFCCC, is based on a 'bottom-up' approach to allow for countries to individually determine their 'contribution' to addressing GHG emissions. This has resulted in highly unequal levels of commitment; the UN has already reviewed the pledged mitigation actions (known as Intended Nationally Determined Contributions) and noted that they will not be sufficient to deliver the 'well below 2°C' target let alone the 1.5°C objective and would likely mean a 3°C increase in temperatures. Civil society organisations have analysed these pledges and concluded that those from the EU countries and the USA both represent approximately a fifth of their respective efforts needed to keep the 2°C target within reach. By contrast, the majority of developing countries have made mitigation pledges that exceed or broadly meet their 'fair share'.

- In response, other commentators have emphasised the positives of the Agreement, noting that it formalises a specific procedure for all countries to submit new improved pledges to reduce emissions and to collectively assess implementation every 5 years. However, there remains considerable concern that short-term political and economic priorities, not to mention powerful high-carbon interests, will undermine these new procedures.

- There are also new common transparency rules and reporting obligations which will require all countries to measure, report and verify their emissions and policies under a common framework.

- Since developing countries contributed the least to the problem and have the fewest resources equity demands that developed countries help finance action in developing countries; the former countries have committed to deliver US$100 billion annually for climate finance by 2020 and to build on this level by 2025. The Agreement also re-commits developed countries to continue to take the lead in providing financial support to developing countries.

At the heart of the debate is the view that the Agreement will not result in sufficient action this decade and will not ensure the steep emission reductions necessary to achieve the 2°C goal. As stated by the Global Justice Now network:

> *'It's outrageous that the deal that's on the table is being spun as a success when it undermines the rights of the world's most vulnerable communities and had almost nothing binding to ensure a safe and livable climate for future generations.' (BBC December 13th, 2015)*

The key question is whether the Agreement's central elements will be acted upon and work for the benefit of vulnerable communities in the short, medium and long-term (see, for example, issues raised prior to the Agreement in *The People's Test on Climate* drawn up by civil society organisations in 2015). Despite the date by which these details will begin to be negotiated being brought forward from 2020 (as originally anticipated in Paris) to early November 2016 (the result of the key threshold of 55 countries representing 55% of global emissions agreeing), the primary concern is that early and concrete action in developed countries continues to be delayed and that impacts on justice, equality, food, jobs, and human rights continue to be ignored. We are left with a lasting legal framework which facilitates the injustice of climate change.

TACKLING CLIMATE CHANGE: THREE VIEWPOINTS

The types of responses and changes that follow from the Paris Agreement which would achieve the necessary reduction in global GHG emissions imply unprecedented and urgent transformations, not just of economies but also generally accepted 'ways of life' particularly as regards consumption and economic growth. Broadly speaking, three viewpoints are presented below.

VIEWPOINT 1: MITIGATION: MOVING TOWARDS LOW CARBON ECONOMIES

The mitigation challenge has been interpreted by some as merely an additional cost or a burden rather than as fundamental to sustainable development. It has been noted that a single focus on mitigation fails to address the inherent negative environmental impacts of development based primarily on economic growth. Additionally, commentators such as Michael Sandel caution against leaving the challenge of climate change to market-based mitigation tools such as carbon trading:

> *Letting rich countries buy their way out of meaningful changes in their own wasteful habits reinforces a bad attitude - that nature is a dumping ground for those who can afford it. Economists often assume that solving global warming is simply a matter of designing the right incentive structure and getting countries to sign on. But this misses a crucial point: norms matter. Global action on climate change may require that we find our way to a new environmental ethic, a new set of attitudes toward the natural world we share. Whatever its efficiency, a global market in the right to pollute may make it harder to cultivate the habits of restraint and shared sacrifice that a responsible environmental ethic requires.*

> Michael Sandel (2012) *What Money Can't Buy: The Moral Limits of Markets, p.76*

As summarised in IPCC (2014), there are clear limits to what current low-levels of mitigation can achieve, and these limits will be increasingly confronted by climate change realities: '*Without additional mitigation efforts beyond those in place today, and even with adaptation, warming by the end of the 21st century will lead to high to very high risk of severe, widespread and irreversible impacts globally.*'

VIEWPOINT 2: A QUESTION OF GROWTH?

A transfer of technology and knowledge is required in order to minimise adverse climate impacts, such as coastal area engineering, early warning systems and to exploit beneficial opportunities such as clean energy (renewable sources such as wind, sun and hydropower) and agroecology (sustainable soil and water management practices, resource conservation and socioeconomic factors). However, a very large adaptation burden remains and the communities least equipped to bear this burden will face the greatest impacts. Writing in the Guardian newspaper in July 2016, anthropologist Jason Hickel argued that when it comes to climate change, the problem is not just the type of energy we are using, it is also what we are doing with it:

> *What would we do with 100% clean energy? Exactly what we are doing with fossil fuels: raze more forests, build more meat farms, expand industrial agriculture, produce more cement, and fill more landfill sites, all of which will pump deadly amounts of greenhouse gas into the air. We will do these things because our economic system demands endless compound growth, and for some reason we have not thought to question this.'*

Following the arguments of many other commentators over the past 4-5 decades, Hickel and many other development and climate experts argue that we need to abandon GDP growth as our primary measure of progress, and that we need to do this immediately. Despite the diplomatic achievements of the Paris Agreement, Naomi Klein believes that transnational civil disobedience and grassroots activism (also known as 'Blockadia' – see case study in chapter 15), managed de-growth, the blocking of new free trade deals, rebuilding and reviving local economies or '*reclaiming our democracies from corrosive corporate influence*' is the only tangible action left if human well-being and sustainability are the objectives.

VIEWPOINT 3: CHANGING THE ECONOMIC SYSTEM TO SHRINK THE PLANET'S ECOLOGICAL FOOTPRINT

Many are extremely critical of the 30 years of delayed international action to cut GHG emissions at conferences. This critique as outlined by journalist and social activist Naomi Klein argues that UNFCCC 'COP' summits '*started to seem less like a forum for serious negotiation than a very costly and high-carbon group therapy session*' where poorer nations outlined their experiences and concerns regarding climate impacts, while the richer nations '*stare at their shoes*'.

In her 2014 book, *This Changes Everything: Capitalism vs the Climate*, Klein argues that no gradual, incremental options are available to us anymore; slow behavioural change is not an option. Instead, 'managed de-growth' is the only rational avenue for action rather than pursing a corporate-led '*greenwashing*' of the nature's commons. Echoing the arguments of Indian biologist and activist Vandana Shiva, she argues (2014:21): '*The bottom line is that our economic system and our planetary system are now at war*. Or, more accurately, our economy is at war with many forms of life on earth, including human life. What the climate needs to avoid collapse is a contraction in humanity's use of resources; what our economic model demands to avoid collapse is unfettered expansion. *Only one of these sets of rules can be changed, and it's not the laws of nature.*'

Greenhouse gas emissions by economic sectors

Source: IPCC AR 5 (2014). Note: AFOLU stands for Agriculture, Forestry, and Other Land Use

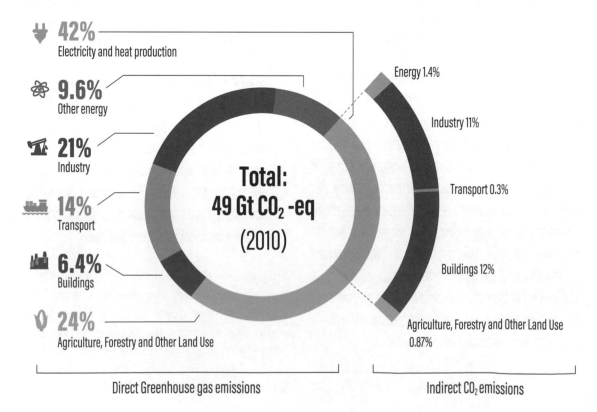

42% Electricity and heat production

9.6% Other energy

21% Industry

14% Transport

6.4% Buildings

24% Agriculture, Forestry and Other Land Use

Total: 49 Gt CO_2-eq (2010)

Energy 1.4%

Industry 11%

Transport 0.3%

Buildings 12%

Agriculture, Forestry and Other Land Use 0.87%

Direct Greenhouse gas emissions

Indirect CO_2 emissions

53:1

CLIMATE CHANGE BY THE NUMBERS

$5.3 TRILLION — The International Monetary Fund estimated that global direct and indirect subsidies to the fossil fuel industry in 2015 was US$5,300 billion.

$140 BILLION — In 2016, the UN Environment Programme estimated the costs of adaptation between US$140 billion - US$300 billion by 2030 and between US$280 billion - US$500 billion by 2050.

$135 BILLION — US$135 billion - Subsidies to aid the deployment of renewable energy technologies were US$112 billion in 2014, with another US$23 billion spent on supporting biofuels (International Energy Agency, 2016)

$100 BILLION — These figures contrast starkly with the 2015 Paris Agreement, which commits governments to provide US$100 billion a year and by 2025 to set a new goal 'from a floor of US$100 billion'.

53 — **Subsidies to the fossil fuel industry amounts to 53 times the Paris monies allocated to poorer nations.**

Sources: The hidden agenda: how veiled techno-utopias shore up the Paris Agreement by Kevin Anderson (2015); Graphic adapted from UNEP The Adaptation Finance Gap Report 2016. United Nations Environment Programme (UNEP), Nairobi, Kenya

CLIMATE ACTION AND SUSTAINABLE DEVELOPMENT

It is widely accepted that meeting the long-term goals specified in the Paris Agreement will require a fundamental transformation of how we all travel, produce and consume with major implications for the energy, transport and agriculture sectors. As part of the goals agreed through the UN's 2030 Agenda for Sustainable Development in 2015, governments also expressed their commitment to take urgent action on climate change and its impacts.

As growing evidence presented in *Living Planet Report 2016* by WWF suggests, the Earth has already exceeded the Planetary Boundary for climate change and is approaching several thresholds in the global land and ocean environment (see tipping points on page 65 and page 190 on our oceans), an idea that illustrates the risks of human interference with the earth system. The loss of Arctic summer sea ice is almost a certainty within a few decades unless strong mitigation action is taken soon.

Climate responses cannot, however, be divorced from wider development concerns: the model of development which allowed wealthy countries to industrialise, and on which the current global economy is built, is dependent on fossil fuels, driven by the exploitation of natural resources and an unfair food system. Clearly, this model of development is unsustainable and the shocking impacts and environmental costs cannot be dismissed.

Some argue that developing countries should be exempted from mitigation commitments and allowed to develop and achieve economic growth as countries in the Global North have done. However, the size of the challenge and the increasing level of emissions from developing countries means that the responses of developed countries alone will not be enough. As detailed by the Mary Robinson Foundation for Climate Justice, a low-carbon sustainable transition is as necessary in the poorest countries as in developed economies.

The human rights costs are also considerable; London-based NGO, Global Witness, observed that more than three people per week were killed in 2015 defending their land, forests and rivers against destructive industries:

> *'As demand for products like timber, minerals and palm oil continues, governments, companies and criminal gangs are exploiting land with little regard for the people who live on it. Increasingly, communities that take a stand are finding themselves in the firing line of companies' private security, state forces and a thriving market for contract killers.'*

The worst hit countries were Brazil (50 killings), the Philippines (33) and Colombia (26). Conflicts over mining were the number one cause of killings with agribusiness, hydroelectric dams and logging also key drivers of violence: almost 40% of victims were from indigenous groups.

In China, public concern over environmental protection and threats to public health, such as air pollution, polluted underground water in cities and rivers, have been rising steadily since failure of the COP 15 Copenhagen talks. As reported in the New Internationalist in November 2015:

> *'Chen Jiping, formerly of the Chinese Communist Party's committee of political and legislative affairs, said in 2013 that the country sees an estimated 30,000 to 50,000 'mass incidents' (i.e. protests) every year, of which the 'major reason' is the environment.'*

A failure to ensure sustainable development for poor countries based on low-emissions would mean 'locking-in' fossil fuel-based infrastructure that may be cheaper in the short-term but highly-polluting and economically unsustainable in the long-term. It would also mean excluding developing countries from the benefits of a low-carbon transition and reduced emissions, such as energy security, reduced air pollution, improved health, better nutrition and improved land rights.

READING

Thomas Tanner and Leo Horn-Phathanothai (2014) *Climate Change and Development*, Routledge, UK

Trócaire (2014) *Feeling the Heat: How climate change is driving extreme weather in the developing world*, Maynooth, Ireland

Vandana Shiva (2005) *Earth Democracy: Justice, Sustainability, and Peace*, South End Press, New York

Wayne Ellwood (2014) *The No-Nonsense Guide to Degrowth and Sustainability*, New Internationalist, Oxford, UK

WWF and Zoological Society of London (2016) *Living Planet Report: risk and resilience in a new era,* WWF International, Switzerland (the Living Planet Report series is published every two years)

MORE INFORMATION AND DEBATE

www.climasphere.org for reporting on news and key debates

www.carbonbrief.org UK-based website covering the latest developments in climate science, climate policy and energy policy

gofossilfree.org on the global campaign on divesting from fossil fuels and www.350.org for the global climate movement

www.ipcc.ch Intergovernmental Panel on Climate Change (IPCC). Prepares comprehensive Assessment Reports about the state of scientific, technical and socio-economic knowledge on climate change, its causes, potential impacts and response strategies.

newsroom.unfccc.int UN Framework Convention on Climate Change updates, news and Paris Agreement updates

www.twn.my Third World Network (Malaysia) – platform for NGOs on social economic and environmental issues pertaining to the Global South; policy, research and perspectives

www.guardian.co.uk/global-development Guardian Newspaper (UK) section on development (includes a considerable amount of sustainable development)

www.unep.org - site of the United Nations Environment Programme

OUR OCEAN **UNDER PRESSURE**

'For centuries, people have regarded the ocean as an inexhaustible source of food and a convenient dumping ground, too vast to be affected by anything we do. But in the space of just a few decades, it has become increasingly clear that the ocean has limits and that in many important parts of our seas the sustainability thresholds have been well and truly breached. The data presented in *The Living Blue Planet Report* gives us a snapshot of an ocean in trouble: populations of marine species have fallen dramatically and vast areas of vital habitats have been degraded and destroyed, with implications that we are only just beginning to comprehend.

+2 billion

The global population is expected to grow by another 2 billion to reach 9.6 billion people by 2050 – with a concentration in coastal urban areas.

300%

Ship traffic has quadrupled over the past two decades with the largest growth in the Indian Ocean and the Western Pacific Seas.

US$14-35 billion

Subsidies that encourage overfishing, mostly in developed countries, are worth an estimated US$14-35 billion – even though the global fishing fleet is 2-3 times larger than the ocean can sustainably support .

50% destroyed

Half the world's corals and a third of all seagrasses have been lost.

3-5°C ocean warming by 2100

At current rates of temperature rise, coral reefs will disappear by 2050.

Driving all these trends are human actions: from overfishing and extractive industries, to coastal development and pollution, to the greenhouse gas emissions causing ocean acidification and sea temperature rise. These pressures have a cumulative impact: for example, an ecosystem degraded by pollution and fragmented by development is likely to be slower to recover from the effects of overfishing and less resilient to the impacts of climate change.'

LIVING BLUE PLANET REPORT, 2015

80% of all tourism is based near the sea.

x2

Average per capita fish consumption globally increased from 9.2kg in the 1960s to 19.2kg in 2012.

A moderate-sized cruise ship on a one week voyage generates:

795,000 litres of sewage, 3.8 million litres of grey water, 500 litres of hazardous waste, 95,000 litres of oily bilge water, 8 tonnes of garbage.

Based on 2,200 passengers and 800 crew

x3-5

Deforestation of the planet's mangroves is exceeding average global forest loss by a rate of three to five times.

1/3

More than a third of oil and gas comes from offshore sources, and growing demand is fuelling interest in deep-sea deposits.

29%

of global fish stocks are over exploited.

8 millon tonnes

of plastic waste is dumped in the ocean each year – or **15 large garbage bags** for every metre of coastline. That number is set to double by 2025.

Source and references: 'Our ocean under pressure' based on p.24-25 of the Living Blue Planet Report: Species, habitats and human well-being (2015) by WWF and Zoological Society of London, London and Switzerland

CHAPTER 10

MIGRATION AND DEVELOPMENT

AMAL DE CHICKERA, PHIL GLENDENNING, PAUL POWER AND COLM REGAN

Having reviewed the data on migration internationally, this chapter explores the evidence and debate about the impact of migration on sending and recipient countries. It summarises some of the legal principles relating to the treatment of migrants and refugees. The chapter includes case studies of Australia's immigration policy and practice, the issue of statelessness in the world and the growing reality of climate refugees.

KEYWORDS:

MIGRATION FACTS AND FIGURES; SURVIVAL MIGRATION; MIGRATION DEBATES; THE IMPACT OF MIGRATION; HOST COUNTRIES; AUSTRALIAN POLICY; ABORIGINAL PEOPLE; CLIMATE REFUGEES; LEGAL INSTRUMENTS; STATELESSNESS

INTRODUCTION

When it comes to the debate on migration and development, there are two diametrically opposed perspectives – one, rooted in data, documentation, analysis and a human rights perspective; the other in popular myth, half-truths and rhetoric. The former is the perspective of many (but by no means all) migration researchers and academics, policy analysts and civil society groups; the latter is routinely that of many politicians, many media outlets, some (usually right and far right) political groupings and much 'public discussion'. The former sees migration as a universal, normal and positive reality with significant pluses for international development; the other sees it as a negative trend, one that threatens economic and political stability and established 'ways of life'. The former is rooted in an understanding of the realities of all historical migration worldwide while the other routinely decries *'their'* migration while studiously ignoring *'ours'*. The former recognises the inherent dignity, human rights and equality of all migrants, while the latter categorises migrants as 'good' and 'bad' and cherry picks the rights it would afford them.

The popular wisdom underlying much discussion is that war and poverty are the root causes of mass migration (especially from and within Africa today); popular images of conflict and destruction, poverty and, more recently, environmental degradation reinforce this view. However, the reality is more complex with what has been described as 'survival migration' better characterising current trends; from a human development and human rights perspective it is not simply those fleeing war and persecution who have the right to a better life for themselves and their families. It also includes those who experience structural discrimination which can manifest itself in extreme cases as direct persecution but most often in subtle discrimination e.g. the denial of opportunity etc.

In his report to the UN General Assembly in July 2013, the UN Secretary General summarised the current context succinctly:

'Migration continues to increase in scope, complexity and impact. Demographic transition, economic growth and the recent financial crisis are reshaping the face of migration. At the heart of this phenomenon are human beings in search of decent work and a better or safer life. Across the globe, millions are able to move, live and work in safety and dignity. Yet others are compelled to move owing to poverty, violence and conflict, or environmental changes, and many face exploitation, abuse and other human rights violations along the way'

This chapter presents an overview of international migration facts and figures, their characteristics and regional dimensions in addition to exploring some of the key debates and disagreements around the issue today, particularly that on whether migration has a positive or negative impact on host countries. The historical and current situation in Australia is analysed particularly in the context of that country's history and its relationship to Aboriginal People. The legal principles relating to the topic are also briefly summarised and, finally, the chapter introduces and explores the growing challenge of statelessness.

MIGRATION AND DEVELOPMENT - THE NUMBERS

There are considerable differences between countries in the way in which migration figures are defined and collected; there are also considerable differences between the definitions of regions around which data is organised by UNDP, the World Bank and the UN Department of Economic and Social Affairs (UNDESA). Taking this into account, it is estimated that more than 230 million people were living outside their countries of birth or nationality in 2013 with an additional 700 million migrating internally within their countries (World Migration in Figures UNDESA and OECD).

Current research and analysis has suggested that in the coming decades, demographic changes, increasing globalisation in a context of growing international inequality and climate change will significantly increase migration pressures within and across borders, at least in the short to medium term (see, for example the 2009 Human Development Report and the World Migration Reports for 2010 and 2013 and the Migration Policy Institute). Migration is set to remain a key driver of and challenge for human development and human rights in the coming decades.

Of today's 232 million international migrants, 59% currently live in regions of the developed world; between 2000 and 2013, the estimated number of such migrants increased by 32 million and by 2013 made up nearly 11% of total population (up from 9% in 2000). In the same period the migrant population living and originating in developing world regions increased by almost 23 million and made up about 2.5% of total population although these figures are very likely an underestimate (World Migration Report 2013, UNHCR Global Trends: Forced Displacement in 2015).

232 MILLION MIGRANTS WORLDWIDE

Of the estimated **232 million migrants worldwide**, some 10-15% are *'unauthorised'* or *'irregular'*

86% HOSTED BY DEVELOPED COUNTRIES

In 2015, developing countries hosted **86% of the World's refugees** (13.9 million) while the Least Developed Countries provided asylum to 4.2 million refugees or 26% of total

82.3 MILLION SOUTH-SOUTH

81.9 MILLION SOUTH-NORTH

South-South migration is now as common as South-North migration - in 2013, about **82.3 million international migrants** who were born in the South were residing in the South, which is slightly higher than the 81.9 million international migrants originating in the South and living in the North

72 MILLION HOSTED BY EUROPE

Europe and Asia combined host nearly two-thirds of all international migrants worldwide with Europe remaining the most popular destination with **72 million migrants in 2013**, compared to 71 million in Asia.

136 MILLION HOSTED BY DEVELOPED COUNTRIES

Developed countries host an estimated **136 million international migrants,** compared to 96 million in developing countries. Most international migrants are of working age (20 to 64 years) and account for 74% of the total. Globally, women account for 48% of all international migrants.

10 COUNTRIES

International migration remains highly concentrated - in 2013, **half of all international migrants lived in 10 countries** with the US hosting the largest number

Asians living outside of their home regions form the largest global migrant group with those from **Latin America** and the **Caribbean** representing the second largest

Overall, **22% of movement** represents 'North to North' migration; **5%** is North to South; **33%** is South to South migration and **40%** is South to North

A GLANCE AT THE '4 MIGRATION PATHWAYS' 2013

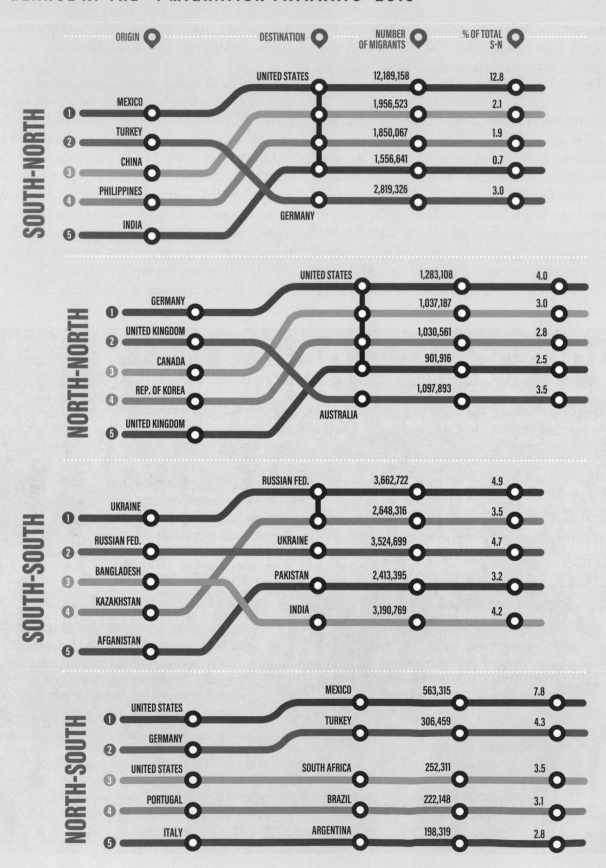

ORIGIN	DESTINATION	NUMBER OF MIGRANTS	% OF TOTAL S-N

SOUTH-NORTH

1. MEXICO → UNITED STATES — 12,189,158 — 12.8
2. TURKEY → — 1,956,523 — 2.1
3. CHINA → — 1,850,067 — 1.9
4. PHILIPPINES → — 1,556,641 — 0.7
5. INDIA → GERMANY — 2,819,326 — 3.0

NORTH-NORTH

1. GERMANY → UNITED STATES — 1,283,108 — 4.0
2. UNITED KINGDOM → — 1,037,187 — 3.0
3. CANADA → — 1,030,561 — 2.8
4. REP. OF KOREA → — 901,916 — 2.5
5. UNITED KINGDOM → AUSTRALIA — 1,097,893 — 3.5

SOUTH-SOUTH

1. UKRAINE → RUSSIAN FED. — 3,662,722 — 4.9
2. RUSSIAN FED. → UKRAINE — 2,648,316 — 3.5
3. BANGLADESH → UKRAINE — 3,524,699 — 4.7
4. KAZAKHSTAN → PAKISTAN — 2,413,395 — 3.2
5. AFGANISTAN → INDIA — 3,190,769 — 4.2

NORTH-SOUTH

1. UNITED STATES → MEXICO — 563,315 — 7.8
2. GERMANY → TURKEY — 306,459 — 4.3
3. UNITED STATES → SOUTH AFRICA — 252,311 — 3.5
4. PORTUGAL → BRAZIL — 222,148 — 3.1
5. ITALY → ARGENTINA — 198,319 — 2.8

Top 10 Migrant Recipient Countries 1960 – 2015:
International migrant Population (millions) and Percentage Migrant Share of Total Population

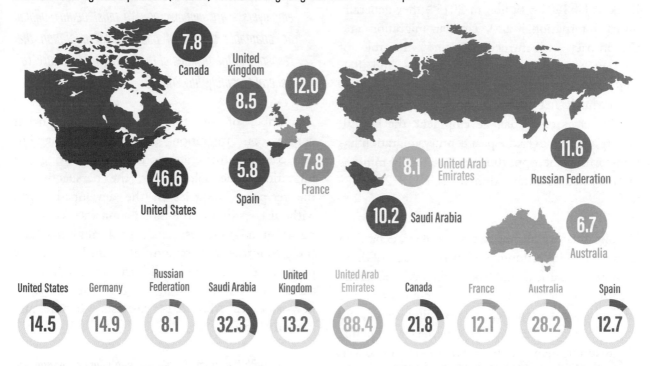

7.8 Canada

12.0 United Kingdom

8.5

11.6 Russian Federation

5.8 Spain

7.8 France

8.1 United Arab Emirates

46.6 United States

10.2 Saudi Arabia

6.7 Australia

United States	Germany	Russian Federation	Saudi Arabia	United Kingdom	United Arab Emirates	Canada	France	Australia	Spain
14.5	14.9	8.1	32.3	13.2	88.4	21.8	12.1	28.2	12.7

Source: International Organisation for Migration (2013 and 2015) World Migration Report

DEBATING MIGRATION ISSUES INTERNATIONALLY

There are very few areas in international development research and policy where there is almost total agreement among informed commentators and analysts yet, surprisingly migration is one of them. The consensus was reflected in the UNDP Human Development Report 2009 which argued that:

'...research has found that while migration can, in certain circumstances, have negative effects on locally-born workers with comparable skills, the body of evidence suggests that these effects are generally small and may, in some contexts, be entirely absent... this report argues that migrants boost economic output, at little or no cost to locals...' (UNDP 2009:3).

This view was echoed by the World Bank in its Migration and Policy Brief 20, 2014 which noted

that: '...International migration boosts world incomes. By allowing workers to move to where they are more productive, migration results in an increase in aggregate output and income...'

This view is shared widely by researchers and research institutes (such as the UK Overseas Development Institute and the American Academy of Political and Social Science), by international organisations directly engaged with development (such as the OECD, 2012 and the UN Conference on Sustainable Development) and by civil society organisations (such as the International Council of Voluntary Agencies). Their analyses have highlighted that while there may be limited and, usually short-term negative impacts from migration in both recipient and sending countries the overall impact is positive at a variety of levels.

These include the role of migrant remittances in international development (estimated by the World Bank at US$581.6 billion in 2015 - they generally dwarf international aid), circular migration and the impact of returned migrants, the role of migrant networks in recipient countries and their contribution to economic development locally (they are normally net contributors to the host society) etc. In terms of human development, the UNDP has argued that over the past century, migration has transformed the opportunities of literally millions of poor people internationally (UNDP 2009:28-33).

Despite this overall positive assessment, debate on migration today is dominated by the impact of those economic, political and social failures and crises affecting developed countries (economic downturn, unemployment, prejudice and xenophobia etc.), and is most frequently viewed through the lens of public discussion in such countries rather than those faced by countries in the developing world. For example, migration to Europe and Australia is currently the subject of increasingly restrictive legislation – a reality that stands in stark contrast to the dominant economic theories and business arguments in support of the increased liberalisation of markets, trade and other economic flows. While private capital increases its global mobility and moves with increased ease across national and international borders and as barriers to trade continue to be reduced, labour mobility remains constrained by restrictive policies and procedures. This contrast highlights the unequal character of the globalisation process dominant today, a process with profound implications for migration and migrants.

The human rights dimension to the debate was also highlighted by the UN Secretary General:

'Too few channels exist for legal migration. The human rights of migrants, therefore, are compromised. Millions travel, live and work outside the protection of laws.

As a result, those who exploit migrants - smugglers and traffickers, unscrupulous recruiters and corrupt employers - are empowered. We must begin building an adaptable system of international migration that responds to the realities of the twenty-first century. (UN General Assembly, July 2013:2).

A number of key themes characterise current debates on migration and development but one core argument stands out - addressing the migration issue solely from the perspective of the recipient countries in the developed world without considering the broad contexts, needs and rights of migrants especially poor migrants (and their countries and regions of origin), is neither practical nor just and will certainly not achieve stated objectives. Commenting in the Guardian newspaper in May 2014, analysts Glennie and Turton observe:

'...as with the drugs debate, as with climate change and energy consumption, as with cheap clothes, so with immigration: the way rich country policies affect others far away should be taken into account more fully as those policies are devised and implemented.'

Similarly, in 2010 the World Bank noted:

'The negative portrayal of migration can foster policies that seek to reduce and control its incidence and do little to address the needs of those who migrate, when migration may be the only option for those affected by climate hazards. Indeed, policies designed to restrict migration rarely succeed, are often self-defeating, and increase the costs to migrants and to communities of origin and destination.'

Additional themes and debates include, migrant remittances and aid; changing international demographics and their implications for migration; the impact of the 'brain drain' on migrant donor countries (and recent proposals to compensate them); future international strategies for managing migration and the tensions between individual country perceptions and realities; 'environmental migration' and the need for internationally co-ordinated policy and action. Labour rights and protection for migrants (particularly migrant workers in the Middle East), the growing criminalisation of irregular migration and immigration detention practices (which have become increasingly privatised) also feature strongly. A final theme of increasing importance is the diverse and often contradictory public perceptions and attitudes towards migrants and its influence on policy.

CASE STUDY:

FIRST AND LAST: UNFINISHED BUSINESS IN AUSTRALIA

Former Australian Prime Minister Paul Keating in a now famous 1993 speech in Redfern in Sydney when referring to the survivors of the Aboriginal Australia's 'Stolen Generations' and upon the harm which this policy inflicted said '...*we did these things (taking children away) because we could not imagine what it would be like if they were done to us*'. Later, in 2007, Prime Minister Kevin Rudd offered a formal apology to those Stolen Generations on behalf of the nation.

While these events represented an important symbolic start to 'undoing' those parts of the past that could be undone, much of the substantive agenda remains unfulfilled. Many commentators in Australia's current policy and practice with regard to migration draw direct parallels with the treatment of the nation's First People and now, with its latest or 'Last' peoples in terms of the harm it is doing not only to those people but also to Australia itself today and in the longer term.

The second verse of the Australian national anthem declares: *"For those who've come across the seas we've boundless plains to share"*. However, those who come across the seas to seek asylum in today's Australia are not welcomed onto the boundless plains. Instead they face mandatory, indefinite detention on Manus Island in Papua New Guinea, or on Nauru, or being sent back to where they came from.

This is a practice described by Amnesty International as a fundamental human rights abuse. It is in breach of the Refugee Convention, Australia's domestic legal obligations, and the Supreme Court of Papua New Guinea has found the operation of Manus to be unconstitutional under the law of PNG, and hence illegal.

Since 2001, successive Governments have made it clear: boat people are not welcome in Australia. And yet, with the exception of Australia's Aboriginal and Torres Strait Islander people, all other Australians or their ancestors came from somewhere else, and most of them came by boat. History throws up some strange ironies indeed. When the British arrived in 1788, Australia was home to over 300 Aboriginal nations, those who had lived there for over 50,000 years; they had sophisticated systems of communication, language, law, culture and spirituality. The British however reported to London that the continent was *terra nullius*, - no-one's land. In fact, there were between 800,000 and 1 million people in Australia in 1788. By 1900 that number had fallen to just 100,000 (through a process which Australia's 1997 landmark report into the *Stolen Generations*, stated met the international definition of genocide).

The *White Australia* policy was the first law passed in the first Australian Parliament in 1901. Australia was to be was a land for white people. Aboriginal people did not count, and were not even included in the census until 1967, and did not receive their full citizenship rights until 1992 when *terra nullius* was over-turned by the High Court, and their native title rights to land were restored. Today, 670,000 Indigenous people make up 3% of the Australian population; they are the custodians of one the world's oldest living cultures. However, discrimination and dispossession continues: Aboriginal and Torres Strait Islander children are 24 more times likely to be in prison, and incarceration of Indigenous adults occurs at a rate 14 times above the mainstream. Life expectancy for Aboriginal Australians is still 17 years less than the general population.

Such statistics represent one key strand of the 'unfinished business' of Australian history – a history that remains unreconciled, and one that was characterised by widespread cruelty and harshness, often invisible to the 97% of the Australian society that is non-Indigenous.

The recent changes to Australia's refugee and asylum seeker policies, have been largely a political response to an increase in the number of asylum seekers arriving in Australia by boat (51,637 arrivals in the five years to December 2013) and a consequent increase in deaths at sea between Indonesia and Australia (at least 862 deaths recorded in the same period). Both of Australia's major political parties have attempted to address this issue through deterrence-based policies which block access to protection in Australia and impose penalties on people who arrive by boat.

Australia detains people seeking asylum and acknowledged refugees, who have arrived by boat, on Nauru and on Manus in Papua New Guinea with no plan for the future and no access to services (including legal services). This policy costs Australia about $430,000 per person per year for the 1600 people in detention on Nauru and Manus (as of June 2016). Australia also spent a further $56 million in a deal for re-settlement from Nauru to Cambodia. Four people took up the option, none remain in Cambodia.

The Government states that their policies have stopped the boats and the drownings at sea. However, the UNHCR reported in 2014 that 53,000 people seeking asylum embarked on dangerous sea journeys in the region to Australia's north indicating that boats have not been stopped but simply deflected. The exact numbers of boats currently attempting to arrive in Australia is unclear as the Government has a policy of secrecy with regard to *on-water matters*. These boats are not allowed to reach Australia's shores. They are intercepted by the Australian Navy with people seeking asylum having brief assessments on board. Then, they are either turned back to the boat's place of origin, or are taken to Nauru or Manus. All are denied entry to Australia.

The consequences of current policy for those returned can be extremely harsh and even brutal (e.g. arrest and imprisonment in Sri Lanka and Vietnam, according to Reuters in May 2016) while a number of Afghan returnees have been tortured. These are clear cases of *refoulement* (or returning people to danger and persecution) which is prohibited under the Refugee Convention and Australian domestic law. However, without a Bill of Rights in Australia, the only redress is to challenge these decisions through the courts which is difficult, costly and time-consuming. In recent years, there have been upwards of 2,000 children in detention, including unaccompanied minors but, to its credit, in early 2016 the Government released all children held on-shore in Australian detention centres, but there are children still being held in detention on Nauru.

These hardline aspects of Australia's policy were condemned by over 60 nations at the UN Human Rights Council Universal Periodic Review of Australia in Geneva in 2015. In particular, the practice of pushing back boats, *refoulement,* mandatory and indefinite detention, the detention of children, and off-shore processing were condemned. The offshore camps were heavily criticized for numerous human rights abuses, including sexual assaults, and ongoing reports of violence against refugees in Nauru. There have been cases of preventable deaths, suicides, self-immolations and a murder on Manus Island. In addition, in 2015 two-year prison sentences were legislated by the Government for any government staff member or contractor, including health, education and child welfare professionals, who speak out about these human rights abuses in immigration detention.

A negative portrayal of boat arrivals in the public discussion has also accompanied the harsh policies: comments like *'there might be terrorists on the boats'*, or they are all *'queue jumpers'* fly in the face of the evidence. Not one boat arrival has been found to be a terrorist, and given that only 1% of the 60 million people in the world seeking protection actually get re-settled, it is more accurate to state that there is no effective queue, just tickets in an impossible lottery. Additionally, as argued by the Minister for Immigration in the 2016 election campaign, refugees are presented as costing the economy and that they were *'innumerate and illiterate, even in their own languages let alone English, they take Australian jobs and they lurk around on unemployment queues'.* It is hard to see how they could take jobs and be unemployed at the same time!

Contrary to the popular argument offered, the evidence (from a 2011 study by Professor H. Graeme for the Department of Immigration and Citizenship) suggests that within a decade of their arrival *former boat people had a lower unemployment rate and relied less heavily on social assistance than the general population; one in five had started their own*

business.' In general, *'as time passes the workforce participation level of humanitarian entrants converges towards the Australian average, and in the second generation there is an increase in the labour force participation rate and a decrease in the unemployment rate'.* This echoes the findings of international research; see, for example the Human Development Report 2009 published by UNDP and Migration and Development Brief 20 as published by the World Bank in 2014.

Ultimately, there will need to come a time when Australia (and other countries) deals with its history, learns from it and puts it right. For much of that history Aboriginal people have been largely invisible to the mainstream, or have been presented through a prism of deficit or disorder, as problems to be solved, with their humanity consequently undermined and denied. Those arriving today by boat to seek asylum are similarly treated - placed in remote detention centres, identified by number not name and with their humanity similarly denied. Treating the 'other' with cruelty becomes possible when the 'other' is not seen 'as human as us', or not seen at all.

The current policy is almost as if those coming to the island continent by sea hold up a mirror to non-Indigenous Australians in which they can see their ancestors, if not themselves, undertaking the very same journey. The past and recurrent treatment of Aboriginal Australians and now asylum seekers and migrants continues an historical wrong; a history based on original and continuing dispossession (including those of dignity and rights) – a wrong which Australian historian Henry Reynolds has entitled *'This Whispering in Our Hearts'* (published as a book of the same name in 1998) and a wrong which will need to be put right.

CLIMATE CHANGE AND 'CLIMATE REFUGEES'

The global rise of the 'environmental migrant' (a term first coined by Lester Brown) looms large – according to the International Organisation for Migration by 2008 some 20 million people had been displaced by extreme weather events, compared to 4.6 million internally displaced by conflict and violence over the same period. Research indicates that gradual changes in the environment tend to have an even greater impact on migration than extreme events. Gradual changes, such as desertification, coastal and soil erosion, tend to be less dramatic and therefore attract less attention than natural disasters. However, such changes tend to affect a larger number of people and will continue to do so in the long term. For example, during the period 1979-2008, 718 million people were affected by storms compared to 1.6 billion people affected by droughts.

Researchers Frank Laczko and Christine Aghazarm of the International Organisation for Migration have estimated that by 2050, between 25 million to 1 billion people may migrate or be displaced due to environmental degradation and climate change. Additionally, 1.3 million square kilometres is likely to become flooded; developing countries are likely to bear the brunt of such events with as much as 98% of all human casualties from extreme weather events and with South and East Asia, Africa and small island states becoming the most severely affected (for more on this, see World Risks Report 2015).

Some implications of these trends were outlined in 2005 by Walter Kälin (retired Professor of Public Law at the University of Bern and Representative of the UN Secretary General on the Human Rights of Internally Displaced Persons) in the Forced Migration review (see also http://phys.org).

'We know that since 2008 around 22 million people per year have been forced to flee at least temporarily as a result of sudden weather events such as storms or floods. What we do not know is how many of them seek refuge abroad. Similarly, the number of persons who come to us as a result of creeping environmental changes such as droughts or rising sea levels is also unknown. No one is going to cite a drought as grounds for asylum, because the law as its stands grants protection only for those fleeing from war or political persecution.

'Instead of climate refugees, we speak of disaster-displaced persons...The term 'disaster' takes into account the human factor... the number of disaster-displaced persons will certainly rise, especially if we do nothing, but exact forecasts are difficult. The reasons for population movements vary widely, and climate change as such does not lead directly to sustained migration. The deciding issue is how vulnerable people are, how sensitive they are to climate change and how well they adapt to it... the more vulnerable people are, the more likely they are to leave.

'...So migration itself must become a means of adaptation. We need legal opportunities for migration. In the longer term, as sea levels rise, the only options open to the inhabitants of low-lying Pacific islands will be permanent emigration or relocation. Australia is already granting such people temporary work permits, so that their families can use the money to deal more effectively with the consequences of climate change. So migration can also adopt a circular pattern... When people migrate for a limited period of time to escape the effects of a disaster such as a storm, flood or drought, we describe that as circular migration. It might be a matter of months or years. Appropriate programmes must be set up for this purpose, as well as for people who have to leave their homeland permanently.

REFUGEES AND MIGRANTS: A SUMMARY OF SOME INTERNATIONAL LEGAL PRINCIPLES

Convention Relating to the Status of Refugees (1951) and the Protocol Relating to the Status of Refugees (1967)

Defines a refugee as any person who:

> 'owing to well-founded fear of being persecuted for reasons of race, religion, nationality, membership of a particular social group or political opinion, is outside the country of his nationality and is unable or, owing to such fear, is unwilling to avail himself of the protection of that country; or who, not having a nationality and being outside the country of his former habitual residence as a result of such events, is unable or, owing to such fear, is unwilling to return to it.

The Convention states that the 'refoulement' (the expulsion of those who have the right to be recognised as refugees) is illegal under international law and this principle must be upheld by all states that sign the Convention. But victims of abuses of economic and social rights are not given protection under the 1951 Convention. Article 31 states that no penalties can be placed on those who 'on account of illegal entry or presence, on refugees who ... enter or are present in their territory without authorisation, provided they present themselves ...to the authorities and show good cause for their illegal entry...'

For more: Office of the UN High Commissioner for Human Rights - www.unhcr.org/pages/49da0e4 66.html and www.unhcr.org/3b66c2aa10.html

---

International Covenant on Civil and Political Rights (1966)

> Article 9: 'Everyone has the right to liberty and security of person...' and "Anyone...deprived of his liberty by arrest or detention shall be entitled to take proceedings before a court, in order that the court may decide without delay on the lawfulness of... detention and order...release if the detention is not lawful"

In 1982 the UN Human Rights Committee held that the right to a court review provided for in article 9.4, is applicable to all types of arrest or detention, including in cases of immigration control and has also found that any detention should be open to 'periodical review' to 'reassess the necessity of detention' and detention 'should not continue beyond the period for which a State Party can provide appropriate justification'.

The Committee specified that when considered together with illegal entry, certain factors - such as the risk of flight or lack of cooperation - may justify detention for a period of time but that 'without such factors detention may be considered arbitrary, even if entry was illegal'.

For more: Office of the UN High Commissioner for Human Rights - www.ohchr.org/EN/ProfessionalInterest/Pages/CCPR.aspx and www.ohchr.org/EN/HRBodies/CCPR/Pages/CCPRIndex.aspx

Convention on the Elimination of All Forms of Discrimination Against Women (CEDAW, 1979)

CEDAW Article 6 *'States Parties shall take all appropriate measures, including legislation, to suppress all forms of traffic in women and exploitation of prostitution of women'*

In its 2006 recommendations to Malaysia, the Committee on the Elimination of Discrimination against Women stated that the country should *'ensure that trafficked women and girls are not punished for violations of immigration laws and have adequate support to be in a position to provide testimony against their traffickers'*.

For more: UN Women - www.un.org/womenwatch/daw/cedaw/ and www.un.org/womenwatch/daw/cedaw/reports.htm

---

Convention against Torture and Other Cruel, Inhuman, or Degrading Treatment or Punishment (1984) and the Optional Protocol to the Convention against Torture (2002)

Article 3 *'No State Party shall expel, return or extradite a person to another State where there are substantial grounds for believing that he would be in danger of being subjected to torture'*.

For more: www.ohchr.org/EN/ProfessionalInterest/Pages/CAT.aspx and www.ohchr.org/EN/ProfessionalInterest/Pages/OPCAT.aspx

---

Convention on the Rights of the Child (1989) and the Optional Protocol on the Sale of Children, Child Prostitution, and Child Pornography (2000)

Article 37 renders detention of children a measure of last resort and for the shortest possible period of time; every child in detention is to be treated in a manner which takes into account the needs of persons of his or her age.

A child who is seeking refugee status or who is considered a refugee in accordance with law has a right to receive appropriate protection and humanitarian assistance in the enjoyment of the rights which he/she has under international law.

For more: Office of the UN High Commissioner for Human Rights - www.unicef.org/crc/index_protocols.html and www.ohchr.org/EN/ProfessionalInterest/Pages/OPSCCRC.aspx

OTHER LEGAL INSTRUMENTS:

International Convention on the Protection of the Rights of All Migrant Workers and Members of Their Families (1990)

For more: Office of the UN High Commissioner for Human Rights www.ohchr.org/EN/ProfessionalInterest/Pages/CMW.aspx and Migrants Rights International www.migrantrightsinternational.org

---

Protocol to Prevent, Suppress, and Punish Trafficking in Persons (2000) and Protocol against the Smuggling of Migrants by Land, Sea and Air (2004)

For more: Office of the UN High Commissioner for Human Rights - www.ohchr.org/EN/ProfessionalInterest/Pages/ProtocolTraffickingInPersons.aspx and UN Office on Drugs and Crime - www.unodc.org/unodc/en/treaties/CTOC/countrylist-migrantsmugglingprotocol.html
For a general overview of the issue of protection see the United Nations High Commissioner for Refugees at www.unhcr.org/pages/49c3646cc8.html

Source: Omar Grech, University of Malta

STATELESSNESS, MIGRATION AND DEVELOPMENT

According to the 2014 report The World's Stateless, even though there are over 15 million stateless people around the world, statelessness is a relatively little known phenomenon. The stateless include large sections of communities living in their own country (e.g. the Rohingya of Myanmar, Dominicans of Haitian descent, ethnic Russians of Latvia etc.) but also countless individuals scattered across the world, many in migration contexts. Some migrated to escape the trappings of statelessness, others became stateless because they migrated, and still others found out they were stateless through migration.

Stateless migrants are often the victims of large, inflexible state bureaucracies (such as immigration control) that cannot conceive of a world that does not fit into the neat boxes of the nation-state paradigm, and punishes those who fall (or were pushed) out of it. *After all, if you are not a citizen of any state, how can you be trusted?* Many stateless persons face negative stereotyping and discrimination; are pushed to the margins of society and punished for living in those very margins. This punishment can be latent and subtle – the knowledge that they will never be allowed to fulfil their true potential, and it can be blunt and harsh – detention and destitution, as futile attempts to remove them are made. It is unfair and wasteful (of lives and resources), and falls contrary to principles of human rights and of the worlds' stated development goals.

Indeed, statelessness poses a unique challenge to the international human rights framework. On the one hand, statelessness is the most extreme violation of the right to a nationality. On the other, the lack of any nationality closes down opportunities to access other rights and services and increases vulnerability to discrimination, exploitation and the violation of rights. This multiple victimisation – where one rights

violation can lead to many repeated violations over a lifetime – combined with the barriers stateless people have accessing justice and claiming their rights, makes statelessness a particularly difficult challenge to the universality of human rights.

In many ways, statelessness presents the same challenge to the world of development. The Sustainable Development Goals (SDGs), which were adopted by the UN in September 2015 (see Chapter 2) promise that 'no one will be left behind'; in the same way there is a human right to a nationality, SDG 16.9 provides a target for 2030 to '...*provide legal identity for all, including birth registration*'. What 'legal identity' entails and whether or not nationality (the solution to statelessness) comes within its scope is open to interpretation. But this goal can be seen as the development world's version of human rights obligations related to nationality, identity and birth registration. So, it follows that the SDGs must be implemented in a way that statelessness should not be a barrier to accessing development on equal terms. Consequently, goals and targets related to poverty, food, health, education, gender equality, water and sanitation, employment, reducing inequality, peace, inclusiveness, security and access to justice.

There is a disconnect though, between the obligations of human rights and ambitions of development on the one hand, and the realities of statelessness on the other. How does the development ambition that *no one be left behind* and the human rights obligation of *equality for all*, sit with the reality in practice that statelessness is often a consequence of state discrimination and the disadvantage is often intentional? Can a state which creates statelessness (because it promotes laws and policies which disenfranchise based on ethnicity, gender and other grounds) be taken seriously when it pledges to provide legal identity for all? Can a state which denies the stateless equal access to basic rights (food, shelter, education, healthcare, livelihood) on the basis that they do not belong, be expected to proactively ensure the stateless enjoy the fruits of development?

The notion of 'national sovereignty' – that a state has the power and the right to do everything necessary to govern itself, including through protecting its own borders and defining who is entitled to enter and be protected by the state – goes to the heart of this tension. While international human rights law, and development principles such as that 'no one be left behind' relate to a more universal, higher state of equality, justice and prosperity, the nation-state is often tribal, putting itself and its own above all others. While this tribalism may work to some extent in the context of 'civilised' reciprocity (where states see it in their interest to protect the

nationals of other states, just as they would expect other states to protect their own), it breaks down when there is no reciprocity involved. What benefit is there after all, to protecting those who belong nowhere? Particularly if they are unwanted? And so, stateless migrants (and indeed, those in their own country) are often accidentally overlooked, if not intentionally disadvantaged.

Breaking this cycle of discrimination, disenfranchisement and disadvantage is perhaps the most difficult thing. It does happen in isolated cases, but for it to happen sustainably, it requires not only a change in laws and policies and international commitments; but also a change in worldviews and attitudes. In other words, it requires for an adherence to human rights, not merely in law, but also in culture; in how we see ourselves and 'others'; how we define entitlement and belonging, and how far we are willing to go to be truly inclusive, to rectify the mistakes of history and level the playing field for the most vulnerable among us.

READING

Institute on Statelessness and Inclusion (2014) *The World's Stateless,* available at: www.institutesi.org

International Organisation for Migration (2015) *World Migration Report 2015*, Geneva

Henry Reynolds (2005) *Nowhere People*, Penguin, London

Peter Stalker (2008) *The No-Nonsense Guide to International Migration*, New internationalist, Oxford

UNDP (2009) *Human Development Report: Overcoming Barriers: Human Mobility and Development*, New York

UNHCR (2015) *Global Trends: Forced Displacement in 2015*, Geneva

MORE INFORMATION AND DEBATE

www.refugeecouncil.org.au – Australian Refugee Council

www.iom.in – International Organisation for Migration

www.unhcr.org – UN High Commissioner for Refugees. Case studies, trends and statistics updated daily

www.oecd.org/migration/international-migration-outlook – OECD overview of migration 2016 and www.oecd.org/migration

www.migrationpolicy.org – Migration Policy Institute

www.hrw.org/topic/migrants – NGO Human Rights Watch reports on migrant rights

'The problem is not that international trade is inherently opposed to the needs and interests of the poor, but that the rules that govern it are rigged in favour of the rich. The human costs of unfair trade are immense.'

KEVIN WATKINS AND PENNY FOWLER (2001) RIGGED RULES AND DOUBLE STANDARDS, OXFAM

CHAPTER 11

'DO AS WE SAY, NOT AS WE DO...'
– INTERNATIONAL TRADE AND DEVELOPMENT TODAY

BERTRAND BORG AND COLM REGAN

Initially reviewing the evolution of global trade since 1948, this chapter explores how the rules and practices of international trade systematically favour the interests of the rich at the expense of the poor. The issues of subsidies, the control of the international food system, food insecurity, the biofuels debate, tariff and non-tariff barriers to trade and trade related intellectual property rights are explored. Finally, the chapter examines the implications for human development of investor protection rules and the implications of current trade deals for climate change.

KEYWORDS:

GLOBAL TRADING SYSTEM SINCE 1948; BARRIERS TO TRADE; SUBSIDIES; BIOFUELS; THE WASHINGTON CONSENSUS; TRIPS; INVESTOR PROTECTION; TRADE AND CLIMATE CHANGE

Photo: Juan Antonio F Segal

INTRODUCTION

GLOBAL TRADE 1948 - 2000

In a historical overview of world development published by the UN University, Indian economist Deepak Nayyar (2009) argues that the distinction between developed and developing countries is a relatively recent creation. In 1700, Asia, Africa and Latin America accounted for three-quarters of global population and some two-thirds of world income; China and India together made up half the world's population and income. By 1820, Asia's economic decline had started, and its share of world gross domestic product (GDP) dropped from 36% in 1870 to 15% in 1950. Europe and the United States became dominant in world output, trade and wealth.

By the end of the 20th Century, this picture began to change. Brazil, China and India re-emerged, and it is now estimated that these three developing world giants could account for up to 40% of world economic output by 2050. This has major implications for the world trade regime, currently dominated by the traditional western powers.

Between 1948 and the late 1990s, trade became ever more globalised, with the General Agreement on Tariffs and Trade (GATT) expanding into the World Trade Organisation (WTO). Under this regime, participating countries agreed to remove trade barriers for certain products and services, and signed up to a legal framework designed to protect and enforce patents and intellectual property rights.

The system grew and grew. The first GATT round of 1948 was signed by 23 countries and involved around 45,000 tariff concessions affecting US$10 billion in world trade. By the time the WTO was created in 1984, an additional 100 countries had signed on, with tariff reductions and framework agreements expanded to affect hundreds of billions of dollars in trade.

By and large, this system of globalised trade has helped lift millions of people out of poverty, and contributed to improved living standards in many countries across the globe. As development statistician Hans Rosling has noted, *'the way globalisation is occurring could be much better, but the worst thing is not being a part of it.'*

But by the end of the 1990s, doubts about this trade model had erupted into full-blown anger. Riots during the WTO's Seattle round in 1999 made world headlines, and gradually the WTO model of trade began to be openly opposed by a combination of developing country governments and trade justice activists. They argued that trade deals were overwhelmingly favouring rich, developed countries, resulting in trade that was neither free nor fair. Farmers in developed countries continued to receive massive subsidies for their produce, allowing them to compete with much cheaper producers from poorer countries. Patent restrictions were upheld for several life-saving drugs (such as antiretroviral treatments used for treating HIV and AIDS), effectively preventing developing countries from making or buying generic copies of these drugs at a fraction of the price.

Even when the WTO moved to address such concerns, the resulting system was so complex that, according to the Commonwealth Secretariat, only countries which could afford full-time lawyers and trade experts as part of their delegations could keep up. The WTO is now moribund when it comes to establishing trade deals: its members have failed to reach a trade agreement in 15 years, and international trade deals are now regional – like the Trans-Pacific Partnership (TPP) and Transatlantic Trade and Investment Partnership (TTIP) - rather than global.

Its last round of negotiations, commonly called the Doha round, was set to promote development in poorer countries. But as China and India's economies grew, richer countries began arguing that they too should lower barriers and reduce farm subsidies. This attempt to shift the goalposts was met with anger, and opposition spearheaded by India has slammed the brakes on any further progress.

BARRIERS TO TRADE: WINNERS...AND LOSERS

In 2001, the Secretary General of the UN received a report from the 'High Level Panel on Financing for Development' which noted that, after eight rounds of multilateral trade negotiations:

'.... by far the main beneficiaries of trade liberalization have been the industrial countries. Developing countries' products continue to face significant impediments in rich country markets. Basic products in which developing countries are highly competitive are precisely the ones that carry the highest protection in the most advanced countries. These include not only agricultural products, which still face pernicious protection, but also many industrial products subject to tariff and non-tariff barriers.'

Report of the High-Level Panel on Financing for Development 2001:7
www.un.org/reports/financing/full_report.pdf

The UN Panel also estimated that the Third World was losing US$130 billion each year as a result of trade barriers, and reckoned that even a 50% tariff

cut on imports from developing countries could generate up to US$155 billion in extra revenue every year. Trade barriers take various forms, and range from straightforward taxation-based measures (e.g. import tariffs) to hidden costs (e.g. overly-stringent health and safety regulations).

Barriers to trade, such as import tariffs, are often discussed, but *'hidden'* trade barriers receive much less attention, often as their protectionist nature is veiled by pretexts unrelated to trade.

Trade barriers are always detrimental to the exporting nation, but this does not make them inherently bad. The problem for developing nations is that international trade regulations are too often skewed to favour the rich and powerful – trade has been effectively forced open with respect to areas that rich countries excel at (technology and services) but kept closed in areas where the rich are not so competitive (agriculture and textiles).

Reciprocal tariff reductions are reciprocal in name only, as subsidies, hidden trade barriers and the sheer financial muscle of large-scale corporations squeeze out smaller-scale operations from the developing world. The current reality was summarised neatly by authors Kevin Watkins and Penny Fowler in a 2001 report from Oxfam titled 'Rigged Rules and Double Standards':

'The problem is not that international trade is inherently opposed to the needs and interests of the poor, but that the rules that govern it are rigged in favour of the rich. The human costs of unfair trade are immense.'

SUBSIDIES: LIFELINE OR LASSO?

A subsidy is a form of financial aid (usually cash) given to a particular industry or business by government; they are typically handed out to help an industry keep its prices low, allowing it to compete with cheaper competitors. Subsidies are controversial because they tend to distort global

RECIPROCAL TARIFF REDUCTIONS ARE RECIPROCAL IN NAME ONLY, AS SUBSIDIES, HIDDEN TRADE BARRIERS AND THE SHEER FINANCIAL MUSCLE OF LARGE-SCALE CORPORATIONS SQUEEZE OUT SMALLER-SCALE OPERATIONS FROM THE DEVELOPING WORLD.

free trade. In principle, free trade should allow industries to compete against one another on an equal footing. If the US is better at producing IT software than, say, Zambia, its IT industry will get the lion's share of business. And if Zambia is better at producing cotton than the US, Zambian farmers should get most cotton business.

But what if the US decides to give its cotton farmers a subsidy? US farmers can then artificially lower their cotton prices, cancelling out Zambian farmers' competitive advantage. If a subsidy is tied to production (i.e. the more you produce, the greater the subsidy) then the market is doubly distorted, as subsidised farmers can overproduce a product and then trade it at artificially low prices.

The merits and demerits of subsidies are constantly debated by economists and public policy commentators. Those from the *laissez-faire*

OUR PREFERENCE FOR CHICKEN BREASTS AND LEGS MEANS THAT THIGHS AND WINGS ARE OFTEN FROZEN AND EXPORTED TO AFRICA, WHERE THEY ARE SOLD FOR ROCK-BOTTOM PRICES.

CHICKEN FARMERS IN SENEGAL AND GHANA USED TO SUPPLY MOST OF THE COUNTRY'S DEMAND - NOW THEIR MARKET SHARE HAS SHRUNK TO 11% BECAUSE SUBSIDISED IMPORTS ARE 50% CHEAPER.

school say subsidies artificially skew global markets and sacrifice long-term efficiency gains on the altar of short-term protectionism. On the other hand, economists from the Keynesian tradition - who believe the state has an active role to play in stimulating growth – tend to see subsidies as a 'necessary evil' which help protect jobs and entire industries. Whether subsidies do more harm than good remains a debating point; however, the problem with subsidies *vis-a-vis* the Third World is that, all too often, it's a case of two weights and two measures, a case of '*Do as I say, not as I do*'.

Agricultural subsidies in particular are a very real concern for developing countries, especially given the disproportionate role agriculture plays in their economies. The Food and Agriculture Organisation of the UN (FAO) estimates that low-income countries derive 36% of their GDP from agriculture. Contrast that to the developed world, where agriculture is a relatively marginal activity contributing an average of just 1.5% of annual GDP according to World Bank Development Indicators for 2015.

But you wouldn't be able to tell it from the subsidies developed world farmers receive. According to a 2013 OECD report (on agricultural monitoring and evaluation), farmers in Norway, for instance, make 65% of their income thanks to subsidies. According to that report and research published by the Worldwatch Institute, in 2012 (the most recent year with data), agricultural subsidies totalled an estimated US $486 billion in the top 21 food-producing countries, responsible for 80% of global agricultural value added worldwide. Agricultural subsidies remain a global reality: Asia spends more than the rest of the world combined - China pays farmers US$165 billion in subsidies; Japan US$65 billion, Indonesia US$28 billion and South Korea US$20 billion.

Amounting to more than US$50 billion, European Union Common Agricultural Policy (CAP) subsidies accounted for roughly 44% of the entire

EU budget in 2011; this figure does not include EU price supports, in which governments keep domestic crop prices artificially high to further 'incentivise' farmers. If these supports are included the EU spent over US$106 billion on agricultural subsidies. North America provides almost US$45 billion in subsidies, with the US spending just over US$30 billion and Canada and Mexico spending US$7.5 billion and US$7 billion respectively. According to the OECD report, 94% of subsidies were spent by Asia, Europe, and North America – leaving only 6% for the rest of the world.

International trade deals have lowered or removed subsidies on several products over the years, but agricultural subsidies have proven a tougher nut to crack. The international system of agricultural trade has evolved into what UN Conference on Trade and Development (UNCTAD) author Li Ching described in 2013 (in its Trade and Environment Review) as *'an awkward combination of protectionism and liberalisation'* with poorer countries obliged to loosen agricultural protections as part of the conditions attached to various trade and aid packages, with richer ones allowed to keep their agricultural subsidies and export promotions largely untouched.

The US continues to pursue its own share of distorting subsidies, with cotton perhaps being the most notorious. The US is the world's third largest cotton producer, mainly due to its tradition of heavily subsidising cotton farming. Between 1996 and 2006 the US paid out an average of US$2-3 billion per year in subsidies to cotton farmers. The injection of such massive sums of money into the cotton sector naturally comes at a price: in 2007 Oxfam estimated (in a report entitled Paying the Price) that US cotton subsidies led to an artificial collapse in the global price of cotton of between 6% - 14% and resulted in cotton farmers across West Africa earning up to 20% less than they would, were they on an equal playing field with their American competitors.

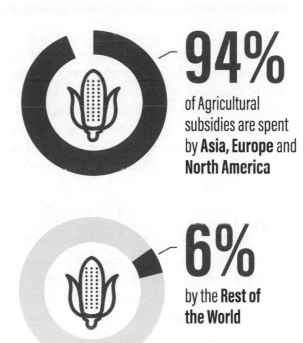

94% of Agricultural subsidies are spent by **Asia, Europe** and **North America**

6% by the **Rest of the World**

Developing countries which were by-and-large agriculturally self-sufficient up to a few decades ago are now net importers of foodstuffs, leaving them at the mercy of rising food prices (see below: *Adding biofuels to the fire*) as they are forced to import food that they once grew themselves.

According to reports from the FAO in 2003 and Action Aid in 2008, the impact can be crippling. Senegal's imports of tomato paste increased 15-fold between 1990 and 2000, and as a result local production fell by half. Vegetable oil imports 'only' doubled in Jamaica during the same period, but that was still enough to drop local production by 68%. Rich countries celebrate the market-oriented shift towards a globalised agricultural supply chain and herald it as the future of agriculture. But some of the repercussions of replacing food-producing farmers with industrialised agribusiness are already becoming clear.

Nowadays a handful of giant firms with billion-dollar turnovers control the international agricultural marketplace. 10 companies control three quarters of all the world's seeds, and the top 10 agrochemical companies sell 90% of all the world's fertiliser, pesticide and insecticide. There is a great deal of crossover between the two lists - of the top six agrochemical producers, five also feature among the world's top seed producers. Further down the supply chain, retailers are also consolidating. Nestle, PepsiCo and Kraft control 45% of all revenues generated by the world's top 10 food and beverage firms. Retailers such as Walmart and Carrefour enjoy similar dominance.

It is these giant firms, rather than small-scale farmers and landowners, who are best placed to take advantage of market liberalisation strategies. Individual farmers simply get squeezed: they are at the mercy of large firms when buying seeds and pesticides, and must then reckon with giant retailers when selling their produce.

The 'big 10' food companies in the world - Associated British Foods (ABF), Coca-Cola, Danone, General Mills, Kellogg, Mars, Mondelez International (previously Kraft Foods), Nestlé, PepsiCo and Unilever together create revenue of more than US$1.1 billion a day. Their annual revenues of more than US$450 billion are equivalent to the GDP of the world's low-income countries combined. They employ millions of people directly and indirectly in the growing, processing, distributing and selling of their products. They are part a world-wide industry valued at US$7 trillion and represent approximately 10% of the global economy. Their policies and practices have become the focus of international discussion, debate and campaigning.

(For an update on this campaign, see Oxfam (2016) The Journey to Sustainable Food)

INDIA, FOOD INSECURITY AND THE WTO

The struggle between the interests of developing country giants and the established interests of the developed world was highlighted starkly at the December 2014 meeting of the WTO in Bali. This meeting appeared to have resuscitated the WTO after many failed negotiations by concluding an agreement on *trade facilitation* - the easing and streamlining of customs rules, procedures and port and border infrastructure. But the deal was blocked

FIGURE 1 | WHO CONTROLS THE FOOD SYSTEM

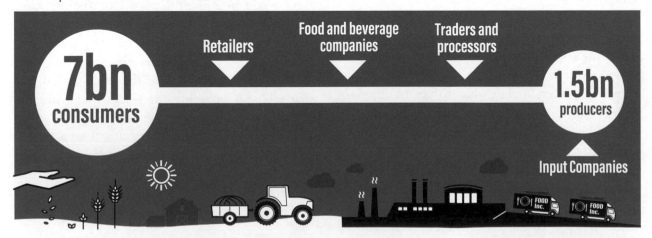

In a world with 7 billion food consumers and 1.5 billion food producers, no more than 500 companies control 70% of food choice.

The **Big 10** are the most visible industry players within the global food system and wield immense power. Collectively, they generate revenues of more than $1.1bn a day. Their annual revenues of more than $450bn are equivalent to the GDP of the world's low-income countries combined. A shift in policies and practices from the Big 10 would reverberate across the value chain.

Source: Oxfam

by India, which was concerned about its implications for food subsidy agendas deemed 'illegal' under the agreement on agriculture.

It has now been 15 years since the WTO last successfully concluded a trade round, but its agreements continue to remain vital for member countries. Central to the agenda of developing countries such as India (and many others) is the continuing inequity such agreements have generated in trade. All too often, the assumption made is that countries party to these agreements start out on an equal footing. In reality, nothing could be further from the truth.

At the heart of objections to the 2014 Bali agreement is what developing world analysts considered its uneven and unfair implementation of the agreement on agriculture. The G33 group of developing countries (which is actually composed of 48 countries which coordinate on trade and agriculture issues) had been arguing that the agreement ignored the livelihoods and, more significantly the food security agendas of developing countries. Countries such as India insisted on their right to protect, through supports, their small-scale farming sector and its needs as part of a broader campaign to address hunger.

The sticking point related to how such supports would be measured, and against which base-line year. The WTO proposed that all subsidies were to be measured in relation to 1986-88 prices and not current prices, despite the fact international agricultural prices have multiplied at least six times since that date.

The US led the charge in opposing any change to this base-line, accusing India of exceeding the allowed level of support and therefore breaching WTO rules (Thailand, Pakistan, and Uruguay were also critical of India's position, fearing 'overpaid' Indian farmers would undercut their own). Many commentators highlighted the hypocrisy of the US position: its food stamp programme amounts to

several times the value of India's total food subsidy. India's nutrition indicators are among the world's worst. In this context, India planned to expand a public procurement and distribution programme to support poor farmers, stimulate grain production and improve its distribution to the poorest. The support prices it offered small farmers were only slightly higher than current global trade prices, yet significantly higher than the base-line prices of almost three decades earlier as suggested by the WTO. Dealing with this reality is a key human development issue for India and this is what was so clearly at stake in Bali. The outcome was a so-called 'peace clause' which supposedly prevented any legal dispute against it for four years.

India is by no means isolated in its concerns; the G33 once again tabled its concerns at further WTO and G20 meetings, where South Africa echoed India's concerns arguing that the bigger risk to the multilateral trading system comes from the developed world failing to address the priority needs and agendas of developing countries.

For more on this issue, see 'World Economic Situation and Prospects' (2016, UN) and 'Rigged Rules and Double Standards' (2002, Oxfam), www.globalpolicy.org and www.ourworldisnotforsale.org

"I think we'll let our annual returns be the judge of whether our policies are right and just..."

MEAT, PULSES, BEANS, PEAS...
AND DEVELOPMENT

'How can normal consumers understand the global impact caused by their meat consumption?
How many people realize that our demand for meat is directly responsible for clearing the Amazon rainforest?
Who is aware of the consequences of industrial livestock production for poverty and hunger, displacement and migration, animal welfare, or on climate change and biodiversity?

NONE OF THESE CONCERNS ARE VISIBLE ON THE MEAT AND SAUSAGE PACKAGES IN THE SUPER-MARKET.'

The Meat Atlas (2014)

1 **DIET IS NOT JUST A PRIVATE MATTER:** each meal has very real effects on the lives of people around the world, on the environment, biodiversity and the climate that are not taken into account when tucking into a piece of meat. Worldwide meat production has tripled over the last four decades and current trade deals anticipate an increase in consumption of up to 75% by 2050 with serious implications for human health and that of the planet.

In contrast, pulses are an affordable source of protein and minerals for a large proportion of poorer populations worldwide as many varieties are drought resistant and therefore suitable for marginal environments. Pulses have a long, nutrition sustaining shelf life thus helping to minimise food waste.

2 Water, forests, land use, climate and biodiversity: **THE ENVIRONMENT COULD EASILY BE PROTECTED** by eating less meat or meat produced sustainably.

To produce one gram of edible protein, pulses consume only 19 litres of water; for an equivalent protein amount from other sources such as chicken or beef, 34 litres and 112 litres of water are required. Good soil health is the basis of food security and pulses help to increase soil microbial biomass and activity, thus improving soil biodiversity.

 3

THE MIDDLE CLASSES AROUND THE WORLD EAT TOO MUCH MEAT: not only in America and Europe, but increasingly in China, India and other emerging countries as well.

This promotes industrialised factory farming agriculture with increasing pollution through the heavy use of pesticides, herbicides and fertilisers for feed production; large-scale meat production has significant implications for world climate as animal waste releases methane and nitrous oxide - greenhouse gases that are 25 and 300 times more potent than carbon dioxide, respectively.

4

HIGH MEAT CONSUMPTION LEADS TO INDUSTRIALISED AGRICULTURE: a few international corporations benefit and further expand their market power.

Today, the 'Big 10' food giants together generate revenue of more than US$1.1 billion a day; employ millions of people directly and indirectly in the growing, processing, distributing and selling; they are part of an industry valued at US$7 trillion – equivalent to 10% of the global economy. Such companies have immense power and influence routinely to the disadvantage of small producers, ethical or sustainable purchasing and the health of the planet.

5 Compared to other agricultural sectors, poultry production has the strongest international links, is most dominated by large producers, and has the highest growth rates as **SMALL SCALE PRODUCERS, THE POULTRY AND THE ENVIRONMENT SUFFER.**

Poultry is now the fastest growing meat sector with an expected increase of some 24% by 2030 (33% in the developing world) with individual consumption highest (in 2009) in the Americas (35.9 kgs per person per year), Oceania (35.7) and Europe (21.9) as against Africa (5.5) and Asia (8.8).

Urban and small-scale rural livestock can make an important **CONTRIBUTION TO POVERTY REDUCTION, GENDER EQUALITY AND A HEALTHY DIET** – not only in developing countries.

Today, rural women produce half of the world's food and, in developing countries, between 60% and 80% of food crops, yet investment in agriculture does not reflect this reality: women working in forestry, fishing and agriculture received less than 10% of total aid in recent years. Large-scale, agribusiness continues to dominate.

7

6 **INTENSIVELY PRODUCED MEAT IS NOT HEALTHY;** as it includes the use of antibiotics and hormones, as well as the overuse of agrochemicals in feed production.

There is now considerable evidence showing that an increased intake in the 'vegetable group' (including pulses) is associated with a reduction in the risk of heart disease, diabetes, obesity, even tuberculosis and the flu.

8 EATING MEAT DOES NOT HAVE TO DAMAGE THE CLIMATE AND THE ENVIRONMENT; On the contrary, the appropriate use of agricultural land by animals may even have environmental benefits.

Alternatives already exist; apart from reducing individual meat consumption, existing initiatives and certification schemes show what different types of meat production might look like – one that respects environmental and health considerations provides appropriate conditions for animals.

 9

CHANGE IS NOT ONLY POSSIBLE; IT IS NECESSARY

Some say that meat consumption patterns cannot be changed. But a whole movement of people are now eating less meat, or no meat at all. To them it is not a sacrifice; it is part of healthy living and a modern lifestyle.

These pages are based upon pages 8/9 of the Meat Atlas edited by Christine Chemnitz and Stanka Becheva and jointly published in 2014 by the Heinrich Böll Foundation, Berlin and Friends of the Earth Europe, Brussels.

Additional sources:

UN FAO International year of Pulses 2016 (www.fao.org/pulses-2016/en/)

UNFAO Briefings (2016) Pulses Contribute to Food Security; Pulses and Biodiversity and Health Benefits of Pulses

FAO World Agriculture data 2016

Oxfam (2013) Behind the Brands: Briefing 166

WorldWatch Institute (2004) Is Meat Sustainable? (www.worldwatch.org/node/549)

R. Bailey et al (2014) 'Livestock – climate change's forgotten sector', Chatham House, London

UN FAO (2016) The state of food and agriculture: climate change, agriculture and food security, Rome

ADDING BIOFUEL TO THE FIRE

At the beginning of the 21st century, rich nations decided that biofuels could help avert the impending global warming crisis by weaning consumers off fossil fuels. As a result, billions of dollars - more than $4 billion by EU countries in 2006 alone - were poured into developing biofuel industries according to the International Institute for Sustainable Development.

Biofuels are not conjured out of thin air – they are generated from crops such as wheat, corn or soybean – and as the money started pouring into biofuel production, farmers across the globe stopped growing food and started using their land for biofuel crops instead.

A 2012 study from the International Land Coalition estimated that Africa alone has dedicated almost 19 million hectares of land to growing biofuel crops. While that figure is contested, even the lowest estimate (in 2013) from NGO GRAIN, 7.2 million hectares, gives an indication of the sheer scale of the 'biofuel revolution'.

The problem is that people still need to eat, and the sudden shift in crops had two unintended consequences. Global food prices rose as crop supply dwindled while demand continued to rise. This in turn led to even more ecologically-sensitive land being turned over to food production, as millions of hectares of rainforest and savannah were cleared to make way for more cropland. Studies on the local impact of biofuel projects remain inconclusive, in part due to the lack of clear data. But there is broad agreement that the land use shift has lifted global food prices, and in many cases (according to the UK Overseas Development Institute in 2014) it is rural women in poorer countries who end up being the biggest losers, as their primary source of food is taken away and replaced with plantations they are subsequently not employed on.

The 'biofuel revolution' is now at a crossroads. In 2013 the EU Parliament voted to cap biofuel use in transport to 6% by 2020, down from 10%. But the EU Commission blocked the proposal, and it is not clear what will happen next. What *is* clear is that the biggest winners have been the large-scale producers. Wheat prices doubled in 2008, despite the world producing an all-time record 2.3 billion tonnes of grain the previous year (FAO figures). The problem wasn't production – it was that half of all wheat was diverted away from food.

And as the world's poor struggled to put food on the table, profits at agribusiness multinationals soared. Cargill doubled its profits from fertilisers that year and saw profits from commodity trading rise by 86% in 2008. ADM, the second-largest grain trader in the world, saw its 2007 profits jump by 65% to a record US$2.2 billion - and those profits doubled *yet again* the subsequent year. According to GRAIN, fertiliser firms reported pre-tax profits at least 130% higher than the previous year's, while seed and pesticide firms saw double-digit profit increases (triple digit in Monsanto's case).

Food prices have dipped somewhat in the years since 2008, but they remain more than 50% higher than they were back in 2004. As for the mega-firms that dominate agribusiness, their profits have recently been squeezed by falling prices, yet Cargill still managed a $500m profit in 2015, while Monsanto, despite growing opposition to genetically-modified crops, began 2015 with a $243m profit.

TARIFFS AND TRADE

TARIFF ESCALATION

Tariff escalation is the raising of tariffs in line with a product's level of processing. Unrefined products (commodities) such as raw fruit and vegetables are allowed into markets tax-free, but processed variants of these, such as fruit juices or canned foods, are taxed. Moving up the product refinement cycle is in every country's interest, since higher-processed goods command a price premium and do not suffer the degree of price volatility which plagues commodities. Think of the cost of a raw leather hide, and then compare it to the price you pay for a pair of new boots in any high street, and it becomes clear that product refinement is a far more lucrative business than simply harvesting commodities.

Escalating tariffs discourage Third World countries from refining their export commodities, ensuring that this lucrative business is left to developed western states and leaving the poor where they started – exporting low-value commodities which are extremely price volatile. Nigeria drills and exports unrefined oil, only to re-import refined oil; Zambia exports copper only to re-import copper pots and pans, and Peru exports leather hides and then re-imports leather jackets and shoes.

NON-TARIFF BARRIERS TO TRADE

Historically, countries used financial tools, such as subsidies or import/export tariffs, to regulate trade flows. But over the past 25 years there has been a gradual shift towards more nuanced forms of trade discrimination. These non-tariff barriers can take multiple forms, from technical barriers (such as labelling requirements or rules about a product's shelf life) to sanitary measures (such as requiring products to undergo stringent tests before being allowed into a market) to rules of origin regulations (classifying where a product originates from for tariff purposes).

Data on the impact of such non-tariff barriers is scarce, in part due to the difficulty of measuring and quantifying such measures. Nevertheless, a 2013 UNCTAD report found a clear correlation between protectionist trade policies and the use of non-tariff barriers. The report also found that such measures restricted trade even more than traditional tariff measures, noting that:

'In the case of high-income countries, non-tariff measures add about 4 percentage points to the average tariff of about 2 per cent. In general, non-tariff measures are relatively more restrictive in high- and middle-income countries than in low-income countries.'

RULES OF ORIGIN AND REGULATORY STANDARDS

Regulatory standards are sometimes set so high that only the richest corporations can afford to gain market access. In mid-2008 the EU announced that by December 2010 all clothing manufacturers importing into the EU would have to comply with its 2008 REACH regulatory standards, which require manufacturers to identify and quantify the chemicals present within the garment to an accuracy of 0.1%. The EU calculated that meeting these new regulations would likely cost EU companies alone €2.3 billion over 11 years. Needless to say, small-scale firms within the developing world stand little chance of clearing this regulatory hurdle.

Similarly, EU 'Rules of Origin' restrictions are often used as a hidden tariff barrier. Rules of Origin are used to determine *where* a product originates, for the purposes of international trade. A product may be classified in a preferential tariff band, or conversely be penalised with higher tariffs, depending on its Rules of Origin classification. The EU's Rules of Origin system is sometimes so restrictive as to verge on the farcical. To illustrate: pineapple juice made with Ghanaian pineapples and juiced, bottled and exported by Ghanaian companies could not be considered Ghanaian (for Rules of Origin purposes) if the sugar used came from elsewhere. The result is the juice being denied duty-free entry into EU markets.

In some cases, obtaining rules of origin classification can be so expensive that it is simply cheaper for exporters to pay tariffs, or to divert their trade from cost-efficient locations to circumvent rules of origin barriers. Stringent regulatory standards leave developing country producers in a Catch-22 situation: they need access to affluent markets to source the capital needed to meet costly regulatory requirements, but they must meet these requirements if they are to be granted access to affluent markets.

It can be very difficult to argue against such hidden barriers to trade, especially because they are often presented as health and safety regulations – and it takes a brave woman (or man) to argue *against* health and safety regulations. But all too often, EU health and safety regulations adopt what is known as the 'precautionary principle', meaning that precautions should be taken even if there is no scientifically proven causal relationship between the product and the risk.

TRIPS, PATENTS AND THE KNOWLEDGE SOCIETY

TRIPS (the Agreement on Trade-Related Aspects of Intellectual Property Rights) continues to be one of the WTO's most controversial policies. TRIPS deals with the copyrighting and patenting of intellectual property, with the aim of protecting the creative rights of innovators (be they of an artistic, scientific, engineering or other nature) and encourage further ingenuity. Intellectual property rights and human development, however, often do not make for the best bedfellows, with innovators given a time-limited monopoly over their creation/s, effectively allowing them to control the sales, price and distribution of their creation as they please. When patents and exclusivity are placed on

RAW COCOA BEANS (No tax)

COCOA BUTTER +10% TAX

COCOA POWDER +10% +5% TAX

CHOCOLATE OVER 20% TAX

THE MORE VALUE THE POOR ADD TO THEIR GOODS, THE MORE IMPORT TARIFFS INCREASE

This explains why Germany processes more cocoa than Ivory Coast, the world's largets producer; and why Britain grinds more cocoa than Ghana.

life-saving medicines, or indigenous peoples are told that they must now pay for their centuries-old medicinal remedies, a number of significant ethical questions arise.

Perhaps the most publicised TRIPS and human development issue relates to anti-retrovirals (ARVs), the drugs used to treat HIV and AIDS. Until early into the 21st Century, pharmaceutical companies who owned ARV patents sold the drugs at extremely high cost – the average cost of a year's worth of ARVs was around US$15,000 per patient (as reported in research published in the Journal of the International AIDS Society in 2011).

Faced with a growing HIV and AIDS epidemic, developing nations stumped up the cash and subsidised ARVs as best they could. But by 2001, Indian, Thai and Brazilian pharmaceutical companies were producing generic ARV 'copies' and selling them at a fraction of the price – in blatant disregard of TRIPS. As a result, TRIPS was amended in 2001 to state that its regulations were supportive of *'access to medicines for all'*, and Least Developed Countries were subsequently granted permission to disregard TRIPS regulations when it comes to pharmaceuticals. Nowadays, the most commonly used generic ARV treatment costs a patient as little as US$67 per year.

TRIPS does not distinguish between traditional, community-based knowledge and industry-generated knowledge. As a result, large numbers of western companies have piggybacked on the traditional knowledge of the world's poor in order to profit. RiceTec, a US firm, has a patent on a variety of basmati rice, effectively preventing Thai and Indian farmers from growing it themselves; the Cameroonian pygeum tree, which has been used for centuries by locals as an anti-inflammatory, is now patented by a European pharmaceutical and sold as Tadenan, raking in US$150 million a year in profits; in India, a US company (W.R. Grace & Company) patented an insecticide that locals had used for thousands of years – a derivative of the neem tree.

Pharmaceutical firms have long pressed the point that patents provide a necessary financial incentive to invest in the research and development of new drugs. But while that may be true in developed nations, a 2012 study by Kyle and McGahan found that *'the introduction of patents in developing countries has not been followed by greater R&D investment in the diseases…most prevalent there.'*

CORPORATIONS, INVESTOR PROTECTION, AND WHAT IT MEANS FOR DEVELOPMENT

As world trade has become increasingly globalised, its prime beneficiaries have become ever more powerful. No single company today is as powerful (or as wealthy) as the Dutch East India Company of the 1700s, but corporations in general have more economic clout than ever before. According to UK-based Global Justice Now in 2015, of the 100 largest economic entities in the world, 69 are corporations and only 31 are countries; the world's top 10 corporations – a list that includes Walmart, Shell and Apple – have a combined revenue of more than the 180 'poorest' countries combined in the list which include Ireland, Indonesia, Israel, Colombia, Greece, South Africa, Iraq and Vietnam; if the Fortune 500 were a country, it would be the world's largest economy, and according to the 2015 IMF World Economic Outlook, the gap between it and other world economies has been steadily growing.

Just as large companies use their deep pockets to try and influence trade policies within countries, they do much the same when it comes to international trade agreements. A key provision in many recent multilateral trade and investment deals has been the inclusion of arbitration clauses allowing corporations to 'sue' governments when they make policy decisions that hurt, or may hurt, company profits. As argued by Thomas McDonagh of the Democracy Centre (2013):

> *'Under the current investment rules regime, public policies such as the denial of a mining permit or stronger public health warnings on cigarettes can give corporations grounds to take legal action against governments, not only based on what they invested in the country, but based on what they claim they could have potentially earned on that investment over years, even decades.'*

These are not hypothetical concerns. The number of arbitration cases at the World Bank's investment dispute tribunal has, as noted by McDonagh, skyrocketed from 26 in 1996 to over 400 in 2014.

Corporations argue that investor-state dispute settlement (ISDS) clauses encourage foreign investment and encourage governments to adhere to democratic principles and policies. And there have been cases where governments have seized private assets with little justification – as was the case when Bolivia nationalised its largest energy provider, despite the majority shareholder being British firm Rurelec.

But this argument is somewhat discredited by the growing legal protection corporations can now benefit from. As the Washington-based Institute for Policy Studies has shown, multilateral investment treaties now often contain clauses that give corporations:

- The right to bypass domestic courts.
- The right to demand compensation for policy decisions which could indirectly affect profits.
- The right to avoid capital controls.

The human development consequences of such clauses are obvious in the following examples:

- A private firm sued El Salvador for the right to mine its land for gold.
- Mexico was forced to pay a private firm $15.5 million after community opposition prevented it from building a hazardous waste facility in an ecologically sensitive area.
- 20,000 Ugandans were evicted from their homes to make way for a plantation run by the UK-based New Forests company.
- The government of Guatemala was cowed into not closing down a gold mine run by Canadian firm Goldcorp, despite widespread citizen protests and an Inter-American Human Rights Commission recommendation to do so, out of fear of ISDS litigation.

- After passing a tobacco control law in 2010, Namibia's government received multiple threats of litigation from Big Tobacco. It took a further 4 years for the government to finally implement parts of the law.

Rich nations also risk running foul of ISDS clauses – tobacco giant Phillip Morris sued the Australian government after it introduced plain packaging for all tobacco products, and Germany was sued by an energy firm after it decided to renounce the use of nuclear power – but it is overwhelmingly poorer nations which are damaged by ISDS clauses. The number of cases filed against Middle-Income countries was 74%, with 19% against low-Income countries and just 1.4% against G8 countries. The cases won by investors totalled 36% and cases settled out of court with compensation for investors amounted to 34% (for more, see S. Anderson and S. Grusky (2007) Challenging Investor Rule, International Policy Institute and Food and Water Watch).

TRADE DEALS, FOOD, ENERGY AND CLIMATE CHANGE

The headlines from COP 21 in Paris suggest that the West is finally getting serious about climate change. One of the key requirements of a serious approach to climate change is that all policies and practices adopted by world governments are coherent. This coherence must include trade and agricultural policies - and here there is considerable cause for concern, if not outright alarm, because governments are effectively ignoring the contradictions between trade and climate agendas.

For example, current EU trade deals with Canada (under the Comprehensive Economic and Trade Agreement – CETA 2014) and with the US (under the Transatlantic Trade and Investment Partnership – TTIP, secretly negotiated in 2009) imply significant increases in European fossil fuel imports from North America. Trade deals are also bad news as regards food and climate change; under the current agribusiness-dominated model, the global food chain accounts for approximately 50% of greenhouse gas emissions. Far from reducing emissions, proposed food-focused trade deals will actually increase them.

The meat and dairy sectors are among the food industry's greatest polluters in terms of greenhouse gases. Yet they are also key beneficiaries of new trade deals. The EU-Vietnam free trade agreement will open up Vietnamese markets to European meat exports. TTIP is expected to open Europe's border to more US beef. Australia's dairy exports to China (up 300% in the past eight years) are a big reason why the two countries just signed a trade pact. The flow of cheap imports resulting from these deals will play a part in increasing global consumption of meat by an estimated 76% by 2050 according to research from UK-based Chatham House.

Trade agreements also favour food production from intensive farms and large-scale plantations. When China joined the WTO and opened its market to soybean imports, the result was a dramatic expansion of soybean plantations in the forests and savannahs of the southern cone of Latin America and a corresponding rise in intensive pig production in China, fed on the imported beans. Current EU economic partnerships with Africa threaten to undercut traditional backyard poultry (perhaps the lowest carbon-emitting source of meat on the planet) with frozen cuts of industrial chicken from Europe, which are higher up on the emissions scale. The US has just retaliated against attempts by South Africa to protect its own local poultry industry.

Some of the most serious impacts from trade deals result not so much from the immediate lifting of trade restrictions but through the longer-term changes in behaviour, including what – and how – people eat. Once Mexico began implementing the North American Free Trade Agreement (NAFTA), investment from foreign food companies and retailers increased rapidly with processed foods

(high on the emissions scale) becoming increasingly popular.

Trade deals also contain measures that allow food companies to challenge popular initiatives that are good for the climate but impinge on their profits; 'buy local' programmes, with their obvious benefits to fighting climate change, are generally considered 'discriminatory and trade distorting' under free trade doctrine. As noted by European network of civil society groups Solidar in 2015, the TTIP, for instance, may seek to forbid initiatives to support the use of local foods in public services like schools and hospitals.

The same is true of initiatives to support 'green' purchasing, or favouring purchases from small- and medium-sized enterprises: corporations can use investor-state mechanisms in trade deals to contest such policies as discriminatory.

In the field of energy, the TTIP is designed to pave the way for the exploitation of toxic tar sand crude oil – with potentially devastating results for both people and planet, especially the poor. While presented as a 'free trade' agreement, the core objective of TTIP is to remove 'non-tariff barriers'. Announced in 2013, the Partnership seeks to eliminate regulations that prevent high-polluting tar sand crude oil from entering Europe. This objective relates directly to the EU's desire to reduce dependence on Russia and secures the interests of the powerful oil lobby and its supporters in the US, Canada and the UK. The agreement targets the EU's Fuel Quality Directive (which is intended to lower transportation carbon emissions) and the USA's 40-year ban on crude oil exports: two pieces of legislation the powerful oil lobby would gladly strike off the books.

Tar sands oil is abundant in Canada, where mining has damaged indigenous communities, forests, water supplies and increased toxic pollution. 2011 research carried out in Stanford University suggests that tar sands extraction and refining (undertaken in the US) leads to an estimated 23% higher greenhouse gas emissions than average EU fossil fuels. While claiming to seek the phasing out of fossil fuels by the end of the 21st Century, the energy component of TTIP reveals a different agenda.

Far from being an example of European versus US interests, the struggle is, as so often between the interests of transnational big business and the people and the planet.

WHICHEVER WAY YOU MEASURE PROGRESS - LIFE EXPECTANCY, EDUCATION, FINANCIAL WEALTH, GENDER EQUALITY OR ANY OTHER MEASURE - LIFE IN GENERAL IS SIGNIFICANTLY BETTER NOW THAN IT WAS 100 YEARS AGO.

CONCLUSION

Given all of the above, it would be easy to crumple into a heap of despair and conclude that things are inevitably going to get worse for the world's poorest. But there is reason for hope.

Whichever way you measure progress – life expectancy, education, financial wealth, gender equality or any other measure – life in general is significantly better now than it was 100 years ago. The share of people living on less than US$1 a day has fallen from 42% in 1981 to 14% today. Life expectancy has risen by 50% in less than a century. Two centuries ago, only one in 10 people could read. Nowadays, more than eight out of 10 can.

When it comes to trade, there is also cause for (measured) optimism. Following several years of lacklustre growth, foreign direct investment inflows were expected to rise in 2015 (figures for that year were not yet available at the time of writing), with developing countries taking ever-growing shares of Foreign Direct Investment inflows.

International organisations have also learnt from past mistakes. The Washington Consensus prescriptive policies – it would not be unfair to characterise them as *'liberalise and be damned'* – which crippled countries such as Malawi and Bolivia, have faded into the background. Even the IMF no longer insists on austerity *a priori*: nowadays it is the one pushing for the Euro-group to restructure Greece's debt and ease austerity measures.

When it comes to access to medicines, the world is a far fairer place now than it was at the turn of the century, when multinational pharmaceutical firms were still fighting tooth and nail to limit the production and availability of generic medicines in developing markets.

The globalisation that allowed corporations to mushroom into the all-powerful entities they are today has also made it easier than ever for exploitation to be made public – a public relations crisis is always just one Facebook video away.

Improvements in education are narrowing the knowledge gaps that exist between developed and developing countries. It is often noted that the Democratic Republic of Congo only had a handful of graduates when it achieved independence. Nowadays, the University of Kinshasa alone has over 25,000 students enrolled.

Perhaps most encouragingly, there are more global citizens who are interested and willing to act on issues of trade justice than ever before. Concerns about trade deals such as the TTIP and TPP have galvanised thousands into reading about trade issues and questioning shibboleths that were previously taken for granted – and that can only be a good thing for those disenfranchised by the existing status quo.

READING

Naomi Klein (2007) *The Shock Doctrine: the Rise of Disaster Capitalism*, Allen Lane

Christine Chemnitz and Stanka Becheva (eds., 2014) *The Meat Atlas*, Berlin and Brussels, Heinrich Böll Foundation and Friends of the Earth Europe, Brussels

Wayne Ellwood (2015) *No-Nonsense Globalization: Buying and Selling the World*, New Internationalist, Oxford

Oxfam (2013) *Behind the Brands,* Briefing 166

Joseph Stiglitz (2012) *The Price of Inequality*, Penguin, London

Angus Deaton (2013) *The Great Escape: health, wealth and the origins of inequality*, Princeton University Press, London

MORE INFORMATION AND DEBATE

www.gfintegrity.org   a programme of the US based Centre for International Policy

www.unctad.org – *United Nations Conference on Trade and Development site*

www.odi.org.uk – the Overseas Development Institute, UK

www.worldwatch.org – Washington-based Worldwatch Institute (see Vital Signs)

www.fairtrade.net – site for Fairtrade International with producer and seller guides

www.iisd.org/business/issues/trade – International Institute for Sustainable Development on trade

www.tradejustice.ca – environmental, civil society, student, Indigenous, cultural, farming, labour and social justice NGO-led site on trade issues

www.pambazuka.org – pan-African NGO site; contains articles on many trade issues

ARMS AND HUMAN DEVELOPMENT

'BECAUSE OF THE IMMENSE HAVOC WEAPONS AND AMMUNITION CAN WREAK, ANY GOVERNMENT THAT DECIDES TO EXPORT THEM MUST REALISE THE PROFOUND INTERNATIONAL RESPONSIBILITY IT HAS FOR EVERY TRANSFER IT AUTHORISES. CONVERSELY, A GOVERNMENT IMPORTING OR PROCURING FROM NATIONAL PRODUCTION MUST ENSURE THAT IT WILL USE THESE WEAPONS ONLY TO PROVIDE FOR THE SAFETY AND SECURITY OF ITS CITIZENS AND THAT IT HAS THE CAPACITY TO SAFEGUARD ALL WEAPONS AND AMMUNITION WITHIN ITS POSSESSION THROUGHOUT THEIR LIFE CYCLES.'

SMALL ARMS AND LIGHT WEAPONS: REPORT OF THE SECRETARY-GENERAL, UN SECURITY COUNCIL, APRIL 2015

TOP 10 ARMS EXPORTERS BY COUNTRY
2001-15 | PERCENT OF GLOBAL SHARE

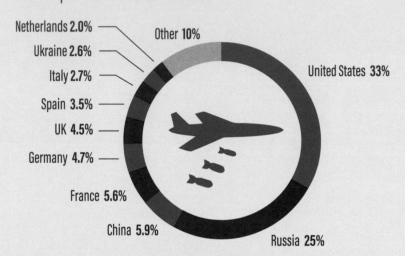

Netherlands **2.0%**
Ukraine **2.6%**
Italy **2.7%**
Spain **3.5%**
UK **4.5%**
Germany **4.7%**
France **5.6%**
China **5.9%**
Other **10%**
United States **33%**
Russia **25%**

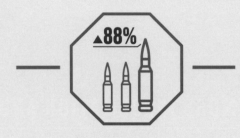

▲**88%**

US, Russian and Chinese arms exports in 2011–15 were, respectively, 27%, 28% and 88% higher than in 2006–10; between 2006–10 and 2011–15 arms imports by states in Africa increased by 19%, Asia and Oceania by 26%, and the Middle East by 61%

TOP 10 ARMS IMPORTERS BY COUNTRY
2001-15 | PERCENT OF GLOBAL SHARE

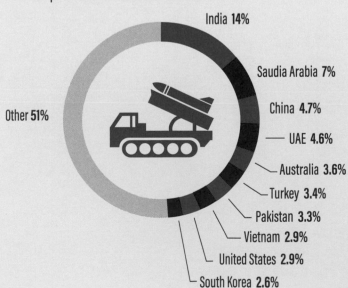

India **14%**
Saudia Arabia **7%**
China **4.7%**
UAE **4.6%**
Australia **3.6%**
Turkey **3.4%**
Pakistan **3.3%**
Vietnam **2.9%**
United States **2.9%**
South Korea **2.6%**
Other **51%**

$1676 BILLION

World military expenditure was $1676 billion in 2015 with total spend increasing by 1% in 2015, the first increase since 2011 (but there were very significant regional variations); the 5 biggest spenders were the USA, China, Saudi Arabia, Russia and the UK.

163

A landmark Arms Trade Treaty (ATT), regulating the international trade in conventional arms – from small arms to battle tanks, combat aircraft and warships – entered into force in December 2014 and, as of May 2016, has been signed by 163 states and ratified by 83.

In 2001, the UN adopted the Programme of Action to Prevent, Combat and Eradicate the Illicit Trade in Small Arms and Light Weapons in All Its Aspects; through it governments agreed to take measures to improve national laws, import and export controls, stockpile management of small arms (an industry estimated to be worth at least US$7 billion per year) and in 2005 they adopted the International Tracing Instrument, which requires governments to ensure that weapons are properly marked and therefore traced.

WHAT COULD THE REALLOCATION OF GLOBAL MILITARY SPENDING ACHIEVE?

The annual cost of the UN's Sustainable Development Goals (SDGs) as a share of total global military expenditure in 2015

$1676 BILLION
MILITARY SPENDING 2015

No poverty and hunger — SDGs 1 & 2
13%

Agriculture & food security — SDG 2
4%

Health — SDG 3
5%

Education — SDG 4
12%

Water & Sanitation — SDG 6
3%

Modern energy — SDG 7
11%

Telecommunications — SDGs 9 & 11
12%

Transport — SDGs 9 & 11
5%

Ecosystems & biodiversity — SDGs 14 & 15
2%

Emergency & humanitarian work — Necessary for many SDGs
1%

Sources:
Human Security Report Project (2013) Human Security Report 2013: The Decline in Global Violence: Evidence, Explanation, and Contestation, Vancouver, Human Security Press
SIPRI (2016) Trends in International Arms Transfers Factsheet

SIPRI (2016) Trends in World Military Expenditure Factsheet
SIPRI (2016) Military versus Social Expenditure: The Opportunity Cost of World military Spending

I watched as the Lamb opened the first of the seven seals. Then I heard one of the four living creatures say in a voice like thunder, "Come!" I looked, and there before me was a white horse! Its rider held a bow, and he was given a crown, and he rode out as a conqueror bent on conquest. (Conquest)

When the Lamb opened the second seal, I heard the second living creature say, "Come!" Then another horse came out, a fiery red one. Its rider was given power to take peace from the earth and to make men slay each other. To him was given a large sword. (Conflict)

When the Lamb opened the third seal, I heard the third living creature say, "Come!" I looked, and there before me was a black horse! Its rider was holding a pair of scales in his hand. Then I heard what sounded like a voice among the four living creatures, saying, "A quart of wheat for a day's wages, and three quarts of barley for a day's wages, and do not damage the oil and the wine!" (Famine)

When the Lamb opened the fourth seal, I heard the voice of the fourth living creature say, "Come!" I looked, and there before me was a pale horse! Its rider was named Death, and Hades was following close behind him. They were given power over a fourth of the earth to kill by sword, famine and plague, and by the wild beasts of the earth. (Death)

BOOK OF REVELATION, CHAPTER 6

CHAPTER 12

FOOD IS **POWER**

MICHAEL DOORLY AND PATRICK HAYES

This chapter examines the long and complex relationship between conflict and food. It highlights the history of food as a weapon of war, it recognises the role conflict plays as a driver of acute hunger today and argues that while we have made significant progress in reducing world hunger, political and moral leadership that is courageous, far-sighted and grounded in the values of human rights are still needed if we are to end hunger and conflict.

KEYWORDS:

CONFLICT; HUNGER; NUTRITION; FOOD AS A WEAPON OF WAR; SCORCHED EARTH; 'NEW WARS'; SYRIA; INTERNATIONAL HUMANITARIAN LAW; INTERNATIONAL COMMUNITY; POPULATION DISPLACEMENT; HUMANITARIAN AID; SUSTAINABLE DEVELOPMENT GOALS; AGENDA 2030

INTRODUCTION

Even to the non-believer there is something unnervingly accurate about the story of the four horsemen of the apocalypse. A conqueror looks to expand and solidify his power. This leads to conflict with the oppressed, which leads to hunger or famine, which ultimately leads to disease and death. There may be different versions of the story but this is the general pattern. Conflict changes everything. It threatens the existence of society itself. It disrupts agricultural seasons, displaces or annihilates communities and destroys transportation infrastructure. Rules, laws, restrictions and cultural norms all break down. The aim of conflict is to harm, to maim and to kill. While there are rules of war which attempt to regulate conflict, the truth is they are ignored. The winners write history and in conflict each side (or sides) will try to win by any means necessary.

Access to the means of production - and the means of destruction - of food are useful weapons to have in one's armoury. Since the beginning of the history of conflict food has been used as a weapon of war; a unique, ironic and cruel weapon that has a huge psychological as well as physical cost.

When famine or acute hunger occurs today, it is usually the result of armed conflict. According to the 2015 Global Hunger Index, of the 780,000 people who died worldwide due to violence, 27% died from hunger and disease due to conflict. Just 7% died as a direct consequence of war. Dominic MacSorley, chief executive of NGO Concern Worldwide stated in 2016 that:

Conflict is the antithesis of development. It separates families from each other and from their livelihoods; from their land and access to markets. It sends economic growth into reverse, forcing people out of their jobs and normal lives and into exile and poverty. It diverts resources into the hands of armies and militias, who frequently deprive populations of access to food as a deliberate tactic.'

Irish Times January 21st 2016

The human impact of conflict is growing at an alarming rate. The Centre for Research on the Epidemiology of Disasters (CRED) indicated that in 2013, 172 million people were affected by 33 conflicts across 25 countries. Globally, 50% of the world's poor now live in conflict-affected and fragile states, and that figure is set to rise to more than 80% by 2025. Much of this predicted increase, according to CRED, will be due to the continued rise in intrastate wars classified as 'low intensity' conflicts. It should be noted however that despite recent terrorist attacks, the Arab Spring, Iraq, Syria, Congo and Palestine, the Human Security Report 2013 (p. 3) maintains that, in its current stage of development the continually expanding system of global security governance remains *'inchoate, disputatious, inefficient and prone to tragic mistakes. But, as previous Human Security Reports have argued, the evidence suggests that it has also been remarkably effective in driving down the number and deadliness of armed conflict.'*

The 2015 Global Hunger Index, *Armed Conflict and the Challenge of Hunger*, reports that there are 59.5 million people displaced by conflict and persecution worldwide (The UNHCR Global Trends 2016 Report has updated this figure to 65.3 million people). Displaced people now spend on average 17 years in camps or with host communities in a crowded 'no-mans' land. Conflict creates much higher levels of malnutrition and reduced access to education and opportunity than stable countries of similar economic standing.

The good news is that on a global scale hunger has decreased significantly in recent years with levels of hunger in developing countries falling by 27% since the year 2000. Although hunger remains alarmingly high in a number of countries, gone are the days of the 'calamitous famines' (those that cause more than 1 million deaths) like Ethiopia in the 1980s, and the reduction to near vanishing point of 'great famines' or those that cause more than 100,000 deaths (see de Waal 2015, Devereux and Howe 2004). Although climate change and population growth present very serious food security challenges, there is a positive trajectory in terms of nutrition and mortality, except, that is, in countries that are affected by conflict.

The bad news is that according to Project for the Study of the 21st Century the number of conflicts and conflict-related deaths has increased from an all-time low in 2006 (while still remaining below long term averages). Between 2013 and 2014 the 20 most conflict-afflicted countries saw violent fatalities rise by 28.7% from 127,134 to 163,562. The nature of conflict has also changed, with an increasing incidence of proxy conflicts, greater numbers of non-state actors and with indiscriminate violence and the violation of International Humanitarian Law (IHL) becoming the norm. While causes of these conflicts are 'complex' (usually intrastate involving a number of stakeholders and therefore much more difficult/complex to resolve), their consequences are uniformly tragic.

In the horror that is Syria, the Yarmouk refugee camp is the deepest circle of hell.

UN Secretary General, Ban Ki-moon

The International Community is not short on rhetoric when it comes to ending conflict, however words without committed action are of little help to those caught up in 'the deepest circle of hell'. The world we live in does not conform to grand gestures; governments by no means have the monopoly on violence. Conflicts are becoming more protracted, most cannot be separated into good versus bad. Most cannot even be separated into one side against another but many different sides involved in many different conflicts within one overarching conflict; Syria and Democratic Republic of Congo (DRC) as examples. One conflict can now involve state armies, insurgents, paramilitaries, ethnic militias, criminal gangs, mercenaries and international forces. These kind of conflicts have been termed 'New Wars' (Mary Kaldor, New and Old Wars, 1999) and, although less lethal than conventional wars, they are often intractable, random, erratic and anybody is a target. In such situations it would be naive to think that the actors will comply with international laws and rules of engagement.

Global death toll from great famines, 1870s-2010

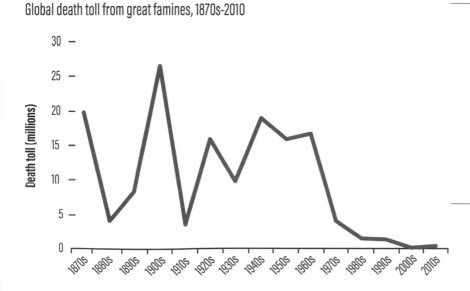

THE GOOD NEWS IS THAT ON A GLOBAL SCALE HUNGER HAS DECREASED SIGNIFICANTLY IN RECENT YEARS WITH LEVELS OF HUNGER IN DEVELOPING COUNTRIES FALLING BY 27% SINCE THE YEAR 2000.

Note: Each great famine killed more than 100,000 people.
Source: World Peace Foundation (2015)

BROKEN PROMISES...ANTIQUATED STRUCTURES,

In 2015 almost US$20 billion was needed to meet the joint humanitarian appeals for aid but only 52% was received. This lack of action on the part of the international community meant that half of identified humanitarian needs were not met. It had unacceptable consequences; cutbacks in food rations, children being deprived of education, girls forced into early marriages and people compelled to use destructive coping strategies.

International Humanitarian Law (IHL) allows for conflict-afflicted non-combatant populations to access humanitarian assistance, but this assistance remains beyond the reach of millions of civilians across many conflict areas. The current culture of impunity is evident, where siege and starvation tactics are regularly used and has facilitated an open disregard for IHL and the protection of civilians.

The United Nations Security Council and other international structures that were put in place to prevent conflict are either antiquated or have become overly politicised, and are in need of 'root and branch' reform if not outright change. The complexity of the conflict in Syria, in particular, leads many to be defeatist about the prospects for peace. However the experience of Northern Ireland and the Balkans, amongst other conflicts, where external political intervention was a major catalyst for peace, should not be forgotten.

In championing the vision of the Sustainable Development Goals (SDGs), Ban Ki Moon stated that we will *'leave no one behind and will reach the furthest away first'*. These goals however will never be achieved if we do not deliver real transformative change that tackles the root causes of conflict

Unsurprisingly it is children, women and the elderly who are the most frequent victims of hunger in conflicts. Their age or gender status can leave them relatively powerless and unable to access regular food sources or even food aid which leaves them at higher risk of malnutrition and illness. In Somalia in 1992, it is estimated that up to 90% of children under 5 died (Ellen Messer, *Conflict as a cause of hunger*). In

the ongoing conflict in Syria a report by Save the Children stated that people in all 22 focus groups interviewed said *'they had to cut the number of meals they eat in a day by half or more. In 32% of the groups (7) people said they are sometimes unable to eat even one meal a day, with four of the groups reporting that local children have died for lack of food.'* (Childhood Under Siege, Save the Children, 2016)

A government immersed in conflict will naturally divert increased amounts of financial resources to the military, such as in the Sudan, where the government in 1990 sold grain reserves to fuel their military, but refused to declare a food emergency or allow relief into starving opposition areas. Both government and opposition forces created famine as a tool to control territories and populations, and restricted access to food aid (often by attacking relief convoys) as an instrument of ethnic and religious oppression.

In most cases, the longer term economic and social costs of war are far costlier in terms of lives lost than in the numbers killed in the actual conflict itself. Between 1998 and 2007 some 5.4 million people died in the Democratic Republic of Congo's conflict(s). Approximately 90% of the victims died from war-exacerbated disease, malnutrition, or other nonviolent causes. Overall, it is estimated that by 2007 less than 1% of war-related fatalities were directly due to violence (International Red Cross, Mortality in the Democratic Republic of Congo: An Ongoing Crisis, 2007).

For those 'fortunate' enough to find safety and shelter in their own or in a neighbouring country the struggle for adequate food and a decent livelihood continues. After visiting Syrian refugees in Lebanon in 2016, Dominic MacSorley of Concern wrote;

'In Lebanon, increasing rent prices and decreasing food rations from the WFP mean that many families are falling into a spiral of unpayable debt. This is leading to more negative coping mechanisms such as survival sex, and early marriage. When I was in Lebanon I spoke to a young woman. She's 15 years old and she told me that

before she left Syria, she dreamed of becoming a doctor. Now all she wants is to get married as fast as possible so that she can care for her mother.

We are failing this young woman. We are failing her and every other young woman who is forced to turn to negative coping mechanisms because they are exiled and impoverished by a war without end.'

In post conflict situations, food shortages take years to reverse due to destruction of infrastructure, economic trade sanctions, loss of knowledge due to death or displacement, inability to farm land due to landmines, and loss of fertile land due to scorched earth policies and chemicals. This has led countries such as Iraq, Ethiopia, Eritrea and the states of the former Yugoslavia completely dependent on food aid for many years.

> *'Nobody in this world, no matter who he is, deserves to die from hunger.'*
>
> Kassem Eid (Syrian Opposition Activist), CBS, 60 Minutes 'War and Hunger'

The Food and Agriculture Organisation's (FAO) report *Crop Prospects and Food Situation (March, 2016)* estimates that globally 34 countries including

27 in Africa are in need of external assistance for food, highlighting the fact that *'civil conflicts continued to severely affect the food security of a number of countries, while adverse weather curbed production in others'*. For countries unfortunate enough to be caught up in both conflict and adverse weather due to climate change the likelihood of adequate crop yields are doubly low.

Overall, for many countries particularly in Africa, the FAO report makes for grim reading. Of the Central African Republic (CAR) it states that agricultural activities are severely hampered by the widespread conflict, which resulted in massive population displacements, caused input shortages and depleted households' productive assets that were already inadequate. In Nigeria over 1.8 million people have been displaced in the northeast region of the country, with 105,000 seeking refuge in Niger and 57,000 in Cameroon straining the already limited resources of the hosting communities. As a result the number of food insecure people in Cameroon is now estimated at 2.4 million, more than two times the level of 2015. Meanwhile, in Sudan cereal harvest is 4% below the average of the previous five years, largely due to the effects of El Ñino.

FROM THE ANCIENT TO THE MODERN:
A STRATEGY OF SCORCHED EARTH

PERSIAN EMPIRE:

The Persian Empire faced many of the same problems as other ancient empires – how to deal with nomadic tribes. For King Darius I it was the Scythians that were the thorn in his side. He believed that the Persian Empire could never feel secure as long as it had not reduced the Scythians to submission. The Scythians valued the ability to roam over the luxuries of settling in cities. According to Herodotus: *We Scythians have neither towns nor cultivated land, which induce us, through fear of their being taken or ravaged, to be in any hurry to fight with you.'*

They did not have cultivated lands or towns that could be beneficial to feed Darius' army. On top of this, the Scythians carried out a scorched earth policy as Darius' forces chased after them. They understood the importance of food as a weapon of war, starving the Persian army by burning the land. The effects would take their toll both physically and mentally.

Although Darius is known as 'The Great', in this case he was just Darius I. His ignorance of his enemy and the terrain was his downfall. Like the land, the Persian's were physically and psychologically burnt out as the Scythians began a hit and run campaign which earned them a historic victory.

IRELAND – THE LESS GREAT HUNGER:

In the late 16th and early 17th century (Elizabethan era) food was used as a weapon by the English to defeat Irish rebellions. During the Desmond rebellion in Munster the English carried out a scorched earth policy resulting in famine. While scorched earth was common practice in 16th century warfare, the English mission to civilise, Anglicise and convert the Irish resulted in a much

more prolonged use of this tactic. In six months it is estimated that 30,000 people died of famine. Edmund Spenser, who fought the rebels, wrote: *'The open enemy having all his country wasted, what by him, and what by the soldiers, findeth succour in no places. Towns there are none of which he may get spoil, they are all burnt; Country houses and farmers there are none, they be all fled; bread he hath none, he ploughed not in summer; flesh he hath, but if he kill it in winter, he shall want milk in summer, and shortly want life. Therefore if they be well followed but one winter, ye shall have little work to do with them the next summer.'*

And: *'yet sure in all that war, there perished not many by the sword, but all by the extremity of famine.'*

A Short History of Ireland, John O'Beirne

When the rebellion was put down the Crown confiscated over 500,000 acres of FitzGerald land in Munster. Food was also used as a weapon during the nine years war which resulted in the Flight of the Earls.

WORLD WAR I AND THE BRITISH BLOCKADE OF GERMANY:

While many of us associate WWI with trench warfare, one of the most decisive events took place at sea. The British blockade from 1914 – 1919 sought to prevent Germany from importing goods with the intent of starving the German people and military into submission. The blockade is considered to be the tactic that broke Germany's spirit. Germans were being starved and the shortage of food caused prices to rise to such an extent as to be unaffordable to millions. This was compounded by widespread crop failure in 1916 due to adverse climate conditions. 1917 saw metal and munition workers strike, millions waiting in ration lines, and massive demonstrations and riots increasing in frequency and intensity. Winston Churchill, then First Lord of the British Admiralty stated: '*The British blockade treated the whole of Germany as if it were a beleaguered fortress, and avowedly sought to starve the whole population – men, women and children, old and young, wounded and sound – into submission.*'

HOLODOMOR - UKRAINE:

During 1932 – 1933 Joseph Stalin designed a famine in the Ukraine as the Ukrainians were seeking independence from the Soviet Union. Stalin imposed a system of collectivisation which resulted in the seizure of all privately owned farmland and livestock. At the time 80% of Ukrainians were farmers. He declared the kurkuls (a rich or supposedly rich peasant class) enemies as they were successful farmers and deported them to remote areas such as Siberia where many died. Mandatory quotas of foodstuffs to be shipped to the Soviet Union were excessively increased until no food remained in the Ukraine. Excess wheat was sold on international markets to fund Stalin's modernisation plans and to pay for his military build-up. He then sealed off the borders of Ukraine preventing any food from entering. All food was considered state property and anyone found stealing from the fields would be imprisoned or shot, children included. Approximately 4 million people died from starvation and up to 7.5 million died altogether. It is known in the Ukraine as *Holodomor*, extermination by hunger.

BIAFRA - NIGERIA:

The Nigerian civil war started seven years after Nigeria had gained independence from Britain when the oil rich south-eastern region of Biafra declared independence. In 1968 estimates of up to a thousand children a day were dying of starvation in Biafra. Nigeria blockaded the new 'nation' by land and by sea, not allowing food or medicine in. Nigeria's representative to abortive peace talks declared: '*Starvation is a legitimate weapon of war and we have every intention of using it.*'

The blockade created a huge humanitarian crisis which led to the creation of many INGOs including Concern. Biafra wasn't accessible by land or sea so a humanitarian airlift began. It was known as the Biafran air bridge, was carried out entirely by NGOs and at its peak delivered an average of 250 metric tonnes of food a night.

During the war, there were 100,000 military casualties and between 500,000 and two million civilians' deaths from starvation. It is not known if all these deaths were due to the Nigerian blockade or if some were due to the Biafran leaders diverting food meant for civilians to their military.

SHOCK AND AWE - IRAQ:

On Friday, March 21st 2003 at 9pm local time, the US military began its assault on Iraq. It was termed 'Shock and Awe' and consisted of 29,200 air strikes. Also known as rapid dominance, *Shock and Awe*, is a military doctrine based on the use of overwhelming power and displays of force to destroy the enemy's will to fight and induce a state of helplessness. The doctrine was written in 1996 by Harlan K. Ullman and James P. Wade.

In their introduction they state; '*Rapid Dominance must be all-encompassing. It will imply more than the direct application of force. It will mean the ability to control the environment and to master all levels of an opponent's activities to affect will, perception, and understanding. This could include means of communication, transportation, food production, water supply, and other aspects of infrastructure as well as the denial of military responses and this means that physical and psychological effects must be obtained.*'

In chapter one the authors write; '*Shutting the country down would entail both the physical destruction of appropriate infrastructure and the shutdown and control of the flow of all vital information and associated commerce so rapidly as to achieve a level of national shock akin to the effect that dropping nuclear weapons on Hiroshima and Nagasaki had on the Japanese.'*

In chapter five they go on to say the shock and awe must cause *the threat and fear of action that may shut down all or part of the adversary's society.*

Shock and Awe: Achieving Rapid Dominance
National Defence University. Ullman & Wade. 1996

SANCTIONS AND EMBARGOES:

The sanctions against Iraq consisted of a trade and financial embargo imposed by the United Nations Security Council (UNSC) spearheaded by the UK and US. The sanctions lasted from 1991 until 2003 (officially ending only in 2010). Their purpose was to force Saddam Hussein to withdraw from Kuwait and to end his Weapons of Mass Destruction (WMD) programme.

Although essential foods and medicines were explicitly excluded from the embargo, the poor had less access to nutrition and medicine because cut-backs in petroleum and other items essential for moving food, and higher prices for now-scarcer foods and medicines, were magnified by their reduced earning power. In Iraq everything was evaluated on a case by case basis by a Sanction Committee in secrecy. Anything they considered to be dual use would be denied without having to give any further information.

A decrease in imported food and medicine, an inability to produce enough of their own food due to a ban on imported fertiliser, a huge increase in unemployment, low salaries and high inflation meant that prices were much higher and the poor suffered the brunt of the sanctions.

A study by the Food and Agriculture Organisation claims that as many as 576,000 children may have died due to the sanctions, a figure that Madeline Albright, US Secretary of State stated *'is worth it.'* It should be noted that this figure is contested.

FOOD AS A WEAPON OF THE 'WEAK' IN WAR:

When we think of food in conflict we generally think of widescale destruction of crops, land and animals to bring a people to it's knees. However, food, or the refusal of it, has often been used as a weapon of protest during conflict resulting in the physical destruction of the individual in the hope of destroying a system.

During the early 20th century imprisoned women of the suffragette movement went on hunger strike to protest against the unwillingness of the British government to recognise their right as political prisoners. This was a tool in their armoury in the fight for their right to be seen as equals and given their right to vote.

In 1917 twelve Republican prisoners died while on hunger strike protesting their right to be seen as Prisoners Of War (POW), something the British government refused. In 1972 forty IRA prisoners went on hunger strike which ended when the British government granted them Special Category Status, similar to POW status. In 1981 ten Republican prisoners starved themselves to death again protesting their right to be given Special Category Status.

In 2012 approximately 2,000 Palestinian detainees in Israeli prisons went on a mass hunger strike to protest against administrative detention (detention without charge or trial), to end solitary confinement and to demand more family visits. Seven prisoners were on hunger strike for more than 75 days. The hunger strikes sparked widespread protests across the West Bank and Gaza and there was a fear that if one of the hunger strikers died the demonstrations could turn violent. After a month Israel agreed to end solitary confinement, allow more visits and to release the prisoners held in administrative detention at the end of their current detention.

CASE STUDY:

SYRIA

Yarmouk camp, a district of Damascus, began life as an unofficial Palestinian refugee camp in 1957. It is just under one square mile, had a thriving market place and was home to almost a million Palestinian and Iraqi refugees as well as Syrians.

In 2012 rebels entered and stayed in Yarmouk and so the Syrian regime began to bomb the neighbourhood. The Palestinians split with some supporting the rebels and some supporting the regime, putting everybody in Yarmouk in a very dangerous position. The regime controlled access to the north and the rebels to the south and 20,000 people were stuck in the middle. From August through December 2013 nothing got in or out of Yarmouk. Malnutrition, dehydration and disease killed over a hundred people. A truce was brokered in December 2013 allowing for a limited humanitarian corridor. However, this broke down when extremists moved back into the area and the siege began again.

Madaya is a small town high in the mountains and close to the border with Lebanon. It was once famous for its pure spring water, fresh fruit and vegetables and healthy climate. Now it is famous for images of starving people, including children. Some 42,000 people have been living under siege since July 2015 by the Syrian regime and Lebanese Hezbollah forces. 46 known deaths from starvation have occurred since December 2015 according to MSF but the figures could be much higher.

Yarmouk and Madaya continue to live under siege with aid intermittently allowed in. According to OCHA (Office for the Coordination of Humanitarian Affairs) they are two out of a total of nineteen areas under siege in Syria, approximately 486,700 people. However, the word siege is politically loaded as it is the Syrian government that allows aid in and the government has a say in what areas the UN declares to be under siege or not. Yarmouk was taken off the siege list even though no humanitarian aid went in for four months, it is now back on the list. Nothing escapes the complex politics of Syria, everything is game. There are estimates that the total number of people living under siege is closer to 2,000,000.

There are also fears that areas are being besieged so as to be used as bargaining chips. That when humanitarian aid is allowed in it is not because the government or the rebels are feeling generous but so as to make a swap, *'I'll give you your people, you give me mine'*. This is leading to a Sunni/Shia swap, dividing areas along ethnic lines.

Another worry is that when the aid gets in it could be the rebels or government forces that control its distribution, ending up on the black market for prices out of the reach of the people who really need it. In many cases starvation is not so much a consequence of conflict but its goal.

'Kneel or Starve' - Graffiti on wall in Madaya, Syria

In conflict everything is political, everything is complex, everybody has an opinion or view and things rarely go according to plan. This includes humanitarian aid. What sounds like a simple idea, get aid to those who need it, is often a much more complicated process; obtaining permissions, vehicles, space, coordinating procedures to avoid duplication, battling time, getting to those who need help most. There can be very deep moral and philosophical questions surrounding humanitarian aid in conflict.

EVERY HUMAN HAS A RIGHT TO FOOD

> ## THE RIGHT TO ADEQUATE FOOD IS INDIVISIBLY LINKED TO THE INHERENT DIGNITY OF THE HUMAN PERSON AND IS INDISPENSABLE FOR THE FULFILMENT OF OTHER HUMAN RIGHTS, IT IS INSEPARABLE FROM SOCIAL JUSTICE.
>
> UN COMMITTEE ON ECONOMIC, SOCIAL AND CULTURAL RIGHTS

There have been many plans for ending hunger, but implementation has often been ineffective or incomplete.

Universal Declaration of Human Rights Article 25 states: *Everyone has the right to a standard of living adequate for the health and well-being of himself and of his family, including food, clothing, housing and medical care and necessary social services, and the right to security in the event of unemployment, sickness, disability, widowhood, old age or other lack of livelihood in circumstances beyond his control.*

Article 11 of the International Covenant on Economic, Social and Cultural Rights declares: *The States Parties to the present Covenant, recognizing the fundamental right of everyone to be free from hunger, shall take, individually and through international co-operation, the measures, including specific programmes, which are needed:*

(a) *To improve methods of production, conservation and distribution of food by making full use of technical and scientific knowledge, by disseminating knowledge of the principles of nutrition and by developing or reforming agrarian systems in such a way as to achieve the most efficient development and utilization of natural resources;*

(b) *Taking into account the problems of both food-importing and food-exporting countries, to ensure an equitable distribution of world food supplies in relation to need.*

Olivier De Shutter, former United Nations Special Rapporteur on the Right to Food defined the right to food as: *The right to have regular, permanent and unrestricted access, either directly or by means of financial purchases, to quantitatively and qualitatively adequate and sufficient food corresponding to the cultural traditions of the people to which the consumer belongs, and which ensure a physical and mental, individual and collective, fulfilling and dignified life free of fear.*

Additionally, Article 24 of the Convention on the Rights of the Child states that: *State parties shall take appropriate action to combat disease and malnutrition, including within the framework of primary health care, through, inter alia, the application of readily available technology and through the provision of adequate nutritious foods and clean drinking-water, taking into consideration the dangers and risks of environmental pollution.*

Specifically, when it comes to conflict, Article 54 of Protocol I of the 1977 Geneva Conventions states that: *It is prohibited to attack, destroy, remove, or render useless objects indispensable to the survival of the civilian population, such as foodstuffs, agricultural areas for the production of foodstuffs, crops, livestock, drinking water installations and supplies, and irrigation works, for the specific purpose of denying them for their sustenance value to the civilian population or to the adverse Party, whatever the motive, whether in order to starve out civilians, to cause them to move away, or for any other motive.*

By ratifying these treaties States are required to report to a U.N. committee on their progress towards **respecting, protecting** and **fulfilling** their citizens' right to adequate food.

NUMBER OF HUNGRY PEOPLE IN THE WORLD

795 MILLION

The United Nations Food and Agriculture Organisation estimates that about **795 million people** of the 7.3 billion people in the world, or **one in nine,** were suffering from chronic undernourishment in 2014-2016.

780 MILLION

Almost all the hungry people, **780 million,** live in developing countries, representing 12.9%, or **one in eight,** of the population of developing counties.

11 MILLION

There are **11 million people** undernourished in developed countries (FAO 2014; for individual country estimates, see Annex 1. For other valuable sources, especially if interested in particular countries or regions, see Global Hunger Index 2015).

PROGRESS IN REDUCING WORLD HUNGER

 - 42% According to the Food and Agriculture Organisation (FAO) the vast majority of hungry people live in developing regions, which saw a **42% reduction** in the prevalence of undernourished people between 1990–92 and 2012–14.

 13.5% Despite this progress, about one in eight people, or **13.5% of the overall population**, remain chronically undernourished in these regions, down from 23.4% in 1990–92. As the most populous region in the world, Asia is home to two out of three of the world's undernourished people.

 1 in 4 There has been the least progress in the sub- Saharan region, where **more than one in four people remain undernourished** – the highest prevalence of any region in the world. Nevertheless, the prevalence of undernourishment in sub-Saharan Africa has declined from 33.2% in 1990– 92 to 23.2% in 2014–16, although the number of undernourished people has actually increased.

 276 million Hunger continues to take its largest toll in Southern Asia, which includes the countries of India, Pakistan and Bangladesh. The estimate of **276 million chronically undernourished people** in 2014–16 is only marginally lower than the number in 1990– 92. Eastern Asia (where China is by far the largest country) and South-eastern Asia (including Indonesia, Philippines, Mynamar, Vietnam and others) have reduced undernutriton substantially.

 Latin America has the most **successful developing region record** in increasing food security.

Source: The State of Food Insecurity in the World, FAO, 2015

Undernourishment trends: progress made in almost all regions, but at very different rates

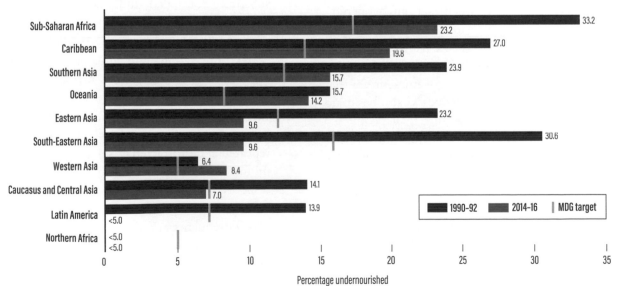

Region	1990-92	2014-16
Sub-Saharan Africa	33.2	23.2
Caribbean	27.0	19.8
Southern Asia	23.9	15.7
Oceania	15.7	14.2
Eastern Asia	23.2	9.6
South-Eastern Asia	30.6	9.6
Western Asia	6.4	8.4
Caucasus and Central Asia	14.1	7.0
Latin America	13.9	<5.0
Northern Africa	<5.0	<5.0

Legend: 1990–92 | 2014–16 | MDG target

Percentage undernourished

We have already talked of Syria and how some towns under siege are not reporting as such. The problem is do you go against the government's wishes, highlighting the full extent of atrocities, which could lead to the government refusing permission or do you obey the government, declare the situation to be less worse than it is and get some aid to people? These are not easy questions to answer.

WHAT CAN BE DONE?

The only way to prevent food being used as a weapon of war, or to prevent people going hungry during conflict, is to prevent conflict through diplomacy, before the spark turns into a raging fire, with civilian's interests at heart rather than strategic interests. Syria is a case in point for both. According to some analysts, only about a third of the population in Syria and Libya were in favour of regime change. The protests and initial anger were the spark, the vast weaponry supplied to opposition forces outside of Syria caused the fire to rage. In November 2011, 5,000 people were killed, a large number in and of itself but small compared to the estimated 400,000 now deceased or 4.9 million who have had to flee as refugees. This could have been hugely minimised if not prevented all together.

International humanitarian law is the body of rules that govern armed conflict and many of its provisions are food-related. But international humanitarian law is designed to prevent atrocities from happening. What happens when they are ignored? In reality, in non-international conflict, peace trumps justice and war crimes can be rewarded. In Syria, opposition forces blockade one area, the government another, the humanitarian community does what it has to do, and both are rewarded by getting their people out of the besieged areas and receiving humanitarian aid. In many countries where rebels have committed war crimes they are rewarded with high positions in government for the sake of peace.

For atrocities to be prevented, war criminals of today must be held to account. Those who use food as a weapon of war, who intentionally starve a population must face justice. In the short term there will be suffering but in the long term it is the only possibility to deter others from doing likewise.

The internationally agreed *Agenda 2030* made up of the Sustainable Development Goals is a hugely ambitious and daunting task. By changing the language from 'Goals' to 'Rights' we can go some way to achieving the agenda ; the right to have enough to eat, the rights of equality, freedom from fear, persecution and violence, the right to access health services and to a job. Concern's chief executive, Dominic MacSorley, in an address to the World Humanitarian Summit in Istanbul stated: *'Language is important, if we talk of these goals as rights, we move from aspiration to obligation from ambition to action.'* We will need that rigour and accountability if we are to deliver on the promise of leaving no-one behind.

In a document prepared for the World Humanitarian Summit, 2016 Concern Worldwide called on world leaders to adopt the following:

1. Remove the power of veto from permanent members of the United Nations Security council in relation to Humanitarian Crises.
2. Expand UN Resolution 2286 intended to prevent attacks on medical staff and facilities to include all humanitarian aid workers and hold to account those who violate the resolution.
3. Humanitarian aid should not be used as a substitute for failed diplomacy or a lack of political ability or will to find solutions.
4. A new deal for refugees that allows them better integration and greater rights and opportunities to work and contribute to their countries of refuge.
5. Invest development funding into resilience programming in situations of predictable, repeated and protracted crises, to save lives and minimise the need for major humanitarian response.
6. Raise public and political awareness of the causes and consequences of displacement, to enhance public empathy and help reduce growing levels of intolerance and discrimination.

READING

Alex de Waal (2015) *Armed Conflict and the Challenge of Hunger, is an end in sight?*, in Global Hunger Index 2015

Concern Worldwide (2016) *Seize the Opportunity, Turning Ambition into Action for the World's Most Vulnerable People*, World Humanitarian Summit, Istanbul

Human Security Report (2014) *The Decline in Global Violence: Evidence, Explanation and Contestation*, Human Security Press, Vancouver

International Food Policy Research Institute (2015) Global *Hunger Index 2015: Armed Conflict and the Challenge of Hunger*, IFPRI, Concern Worldwide, Welt Hunger Hilfe, Washington

Mary Kaldor (1999) *New and Old Wars; Organised Violence in a Global Era*, University Press, Stanford

Tristam Stuart (2009) *Waste: Uncovering the Global Food Scandal*, Penguin, London

UN FAO (2015) *The State of Food Insecurity in the World*, Rome

Wayne Roberts (2013) *No-Nonsense Guide to World Food*, Oxford, New Internationalist

MORE INFORMATION AND DEBATE

www.fao.org – food security, nutrition issues and challenges at the international UN agency Food and Agriculture Organisation (FAO), Rome

www.ifpri.org – International Food Policy Research Institute

www.worldwatch.org – Washington-based Worldwatch Institute

www.tni.org – Amsterdam-based Transnational Institute which is an international research and advocacy institute committed to building a just, democratic and sustainable world

www.foodfirst.org – US-based NGO that is a 'people's think tank' working to end the injustices that cause hunger and helping communities to take back control of their food systems.

www.socialwatch.org – international NGO network research and news site based in Uruguay

THE COSTS OF CONFLICT

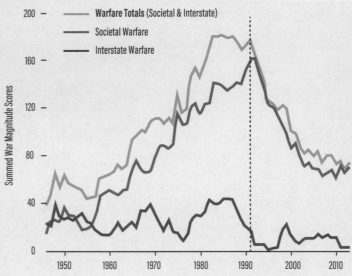

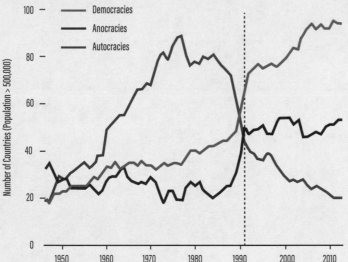

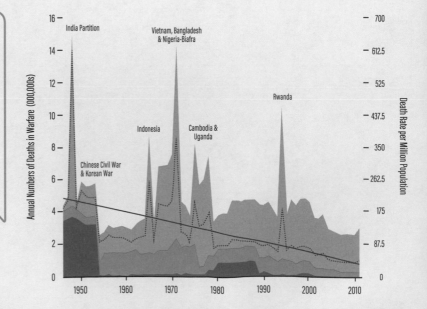

Non-Combatant Deaths
Informal Combatant Deaths
Formal Combatant Deaths

Right Axis (per million population)
Death Rate
Average Death Rate

GLOBAL ECONOMIC IMPACT OF VIOLENCE

WHICH IS EQUIVALENT TO

13.3%
OF WORLD GDP

$13.6 TRILLION

WHICH IS EQUIVALENT TO

$5 PER PERSON GLOBALLY PER DAY

WHY?

Losses from crime and interpersonal violence
$2.5 trillion

Internal security spending
$4.2 trillion

Loses from conflict
$742 billion

Military spending
$6.2 trillion

$742 billion

Economic losses from conflict

$167 billion (22% of the cost of conflict)

Total ODA, gross disbursement

$15 billion (2% of the cost of conflict)

Peacekeeping and peacebuilding

COMPOSITION OF GLOBAL VIOLENCE CONTAINMENT, 2015
The majority of expenditure for violence containment is for the military and internal security.

Homicides

Fear

Small arms

Peacebuilding

Deaths from internal conflict

UN Peacekeeping

CRIME AND INTERPERSONAL VIOLENCE

Violent and sexual crimes

Refugees and IDPs

CONFLICT

GDP losses

Terrorism

Private security services

Police and prison

Military expenditure

MILITARY

INTERNAL SECURITY

Sources:
Human Security Report Project (2013) Human Security Report 2013: The Decline in Global Violence: Evidence, Explanation, and Contestation, Vancouver, Human Security Press
Institute for Economics and Peace (2016) Global Peace Index: Ten Years of Measuring Peace
Monty G Marshall and Benjamin R. Cole (2014) Global Report, Conflict, Governance and State Fragility, Center for Systemic Peace
Stephen Pinker (2011) The Better Angels of Our Nature, Penguin

CHAPTER 13

BASIC NEEDS, POPULATION AND DEVELOPMENT

BEATRICE MAPHOSA

Basic human needs remain a priority; their realisation is fundamental to human dignity, human rights and human development. This chapter provides an overview of key aspects of the basic needs agenda - health, literacy, education, water and sanitation with a particular focus on South Africa and Africa. Having then summarised the contours of population growth today and in the future, it explores three upcoming challenges and debates – Africa's youth bulge; women, contraception and population and, finally, the ongoing debate on feeding the world.

KEYWORDS:

BASIC NEEDS; HEALTH; EDUCATION AND SCHOOLING; WATER AND SANITATION; POPULATION; CITIES AND SLUMS; AFRICA'S YOUTH BULGE; WOMEN'S RIGHTS; CONTRACEPTION; FEEDING 9+ BILLION

INTRODUCTION

The concept of human development has been underpinned by three core measures: life expectancy, education and income. The three are interlinked in their individual and complementary contributions, yet the dominant development story continues to focus primarily on income and economic growth. While the realisation of an adequate income provides both individuals and households access to basic human needs, in an increasingly unequal world, significant disparities remain, (and often become entrenched) and as such should be a higher priority agenda item than at present. True, there has been significant progress but too many remain marginalised and excluded.

The lived realities of many in the developing world evidence the growing need for a continued and direct focus on basic needs, not as an outcome of economic growth but as a basic primary focus for society in its own right. As outlined in Chapter 1, countries and societies that have advanced most with regard to basic needs are not necessarily those that have grown most economically (and vice versa). As stated in the 2015 Human Development Report, the United Nations Development Programme (UNDP) expresses concern over the economic focus of development indicating that:

'For too long, the world had been preoccupied with material opulence, pushing people to the periphery. The human development framework, taking a people-centred approach, changed the lens for viewing development needs, bringing the lives of people to the forefront'

(UNDP 2015)

A direct concern for people needs to remain at the core of development debates today and the rhetoric of the international community needs to be more fully backed up with effective action agendas. Human development must not be relegated to being a by-product of economic growth and development; this argument is at the core of basic needs agendas and approaches. Despite the progress of recent decades, the realisation of basic needs is now threatened by a number of patterns and trends including current and anticipated urbanisation (especially in Africa), extreme inequality, the continued marginalisation of women and population growth agendas in that context; conflicts over access to key resources such as water and, of course, climate change (see Chapter 9).

BASIC NEEDS, HUMAN DIGNITY AND HUMAN DEVELOPMENT

What was previously known as the 'Basic Needs Approach' to development (directly influenced by the work of psychologist Albert Maslow in the early 1940s) has now been effectively incorporated into the Human Development Index (HDI) and its accompanying debates. Originally, the basic needs perspective and strategy grew out of the work of the International Labour Organisation (ILO) in the 1970s with its focus on employment, placing work, people and basic human needs at the centre of any approach to development as directly applied to the context of developing countries. Its particular concern was to focus on the needs of the poorest 20% of the population who found it extremely difficult, if not actually impossible, to get beyond the most basic dimensions of human development. It represented a direct challenge to the focus on economic growth as the driver of human development and, much as human development debates today do, highlighted the exclusion of those *'left behind'*. (For an extended discussion on the ILO and basic needs, see D.P Ghai and others (1980) The Basic Needs Approach to Development, ILO).

Basic needs can best be described as a basket of goods and services necessary for human survival and a dignified existence. The focus on basic needs emerged in development thinking and practice as part of the need to 'dethrone' GNP as the dominant measurement tool and as an explicit focus on the needs of the poor rather than solely the needs of an economy. Essentially, those who have consistently focused on a 'basic needs approach' argue that certain key human needs are more immediately urgent than others and cannot (and should not) wait on more general economic and social development for their realisation. Basic needs should be addressed directly through both targeted and specific interventions and not indirectly via broader development strategies and plans. Directly addressing basic needs immediately will not only improve the lot of the poorest but will also contribute to broader economic and political goals and strategies and will be less costly than if delayed or approached indirectly.

The lives and realities of many at the margins of developing world experiences of development attest to the pressing need for a renewed focus on basic needs; far too large a percentage of the population in poorer countries remain recipients of charity (of one sort or another) and humanitarian assistance amidst national priorities which do not prioritise sufficiently the nutrition, housing, health and education needs of the poorest.

For example, in South Africa, one of the world's 'emerging economies' (and now a member of the G20 Group) the ongoing realities of basic needs are clear and significant: according to a 2012 UNICEF Report, South Africa is now one of the world's most unequal societies with 19 million children bearing the brunt of that inequality. The report highlighted that some 1.4 million children lived in homes that routinely rely on dirty streams for drinking water, 1.5 million have no flushing lavatories and 1.7 million live in shacks without adequate bedding, cooking or washing facilities. 4 in 10 children lived in homes where no one was employed and, in cases of extreme poverty, the figure rose to 7 in 10.

The overall situation was summarised in a Stellenbosch University study published by the South African Human Rights Commission in 2014:

> *'Two decades after the dismantling of apartheid, widespread inequality still exists in South Africa. The country's poverty is all the more glaring because it coexists with striking affluence and retains strong racial dimensions. While some children in South Africa live in relative luxury and have access to world class education and health services, others face threats to their development in the form of poor living conditions, poor nutrition and poor access to basic services.'*
>
> South African Human Rights Commission (2014:17) Poverty Traps and Social Exclusion Among Children in South Africa

Recent research by Oxfam, in addition to the evidence of the 2015 UNDP Human Development Report, suggests that if effective measures are not implemented to address the situation, South Africa will continue to have approximately 17% of its population living in extreme poverty. The evidence from South Africa illustrates the crucial importance of a priority focus on basic needs.

The pages immediately following present a graphic summary of a range of data related to basic needs.

① BASIC NEEDS - HEALTH

The graphics and evidence on this page and the page opposite highlight significant recent improvements globally as regards agreed health-related Millennium Development Goals (MDGs) with the targets for HIV and AIDS and drinking-water achieved (as have been the targets for both malaria and tuberculosis reduction).

Additionally, substantial progress has been made in terms of reducing child undernutrition (by four fifths), child mortality (by two thirds) and maternal mortality (by three fifths) and in increasing access to improved sanitation (by three fifths). Substantial progress was also made towards achieving the target of halving the tuberculosis mortality rate.

However, as the World Health Organisation observes, the gains made in different regions of the world have been very uneven with health inequities still widely prevalent with a number of additional new challenges emerging – the growing impact of non-communicable diseases and changing social and environmental contexts.

BETWEEN 1990 AND 2015 UNDER-FIVE MORTALITY RATES DECLINED BY OVER 45%; as a result, an estimated 19,000 fewer children died every day in 2015 than in 1990 - described as one of the greatest success stories of international development. Despite this the MDG target was not achieved in most countries by 2015.

GLOBALLY, THE MATERNAL MORTALITY RATE FELL BY NEARLY 44% OVER THE PAST 25 YEARS, to an estimated 216 per 100,000 live births in 2015, from 385 in 1990. The annual number of maternal deaths decreased by 43% from approximately 532,000 in 1990 to an estimated 303,000 in 2015. The approximate global lifetime risk of a maternal death fell considerably from 1 in 73 to 1 in 180. However, of the 89 countries with the highest maternal mortality ratio in 1990, 13 made insufficient or no progress at all, with an average annual decline of less than 2% between 1990 and 2015.

IN 2014, 23.8% OF CHILDREN UNDER AGE 5 WORLDWIDE (JUST UNDER 1 IN 4) HAD STUNTED GROWTH. Between 1990 and 2014, the prevalence of stunting globally declined from 39.6% to 23.8% and the number of children affected fell from 255 million to 159 million. In 2014, just over half of all stunted children lived in Asia and over one third in Africa.

THE NUMBER OF MALARIA DEATHS GLOBALLY FELL FROM AN ESTIMATED 839,000 IN 2000 TO 438,000 IN 2015, A DECLINE OF 48%. The number of malaria cases fell from an estimated 262 million globally in 2000 to 214 million in 2015, a decline of 18%. Malaria prevention and treatment measures are estimated to have averted more than 650 million malaria cases between 2001 and 2015. Despite this it is estimated that there were 395,000 malaria deaths in Africa in 2015 and in 2014 in sub-Saharan Africa, some 269 million people at risk of malaria lived in households without a single insecticide treated net while some 28 million pregnant women in the same region did not receive preventive treatment.

Global Maternal Mortality Ratio
(deaths per 100,000 live births)

380 — 1990
330 — 2000
210 — 2013

'Despite this progress, every day hundreds of women die during pregnancy or from childbirth-related complications. In 2013, most of these deaths were in the developing regions, where the maternal mortality ratio is about 14 times higher than in the developed regions. Globally, there were an estimated 289,000 maternal deaths in 2013, equivalent to about 800 women dying each day. Maternal deaths are concentrated in sub-Saharan Africa and Southern Asia, which accounted for 86 per cent of such deaths globally in 2013... Most of these deaths are preventable' UNICEF State of the World's Children 2016

Sources: UNICEF State of the World's Children 2016; WHO, UNICEF, UNFPA, World Bank Group and the United Nations Population Division Trends in Maternal Mortality: 1990 to 2015; WHO World Malaria Report 2015

Table 13.1 | Global and Regional Progress on Health-related MDGs (World Health Organisation regions)

	Target	Global	Africa	Americas	South East Asian Region	European Region	East European Region	Western Pacific Region
Target 1.C: Halve, between 1990 and 2015, the proportion of people who suffer from hunger								
Percent reduction in proportion of underweight children under five years of age, 1990–2013	50	40	27	60	43	86	36	79
Target 4.A: Reduce by two thirds, between 1990 and 2015, the under-five mortality rate								
Percent reduction in under-five mortality rate, 1990–2013	67	49	49	64	60	63	46	71
Measles immunization coverage among 1-year-olds a (%), 2013	90	84	74	92	78	95	78	97
Target 5.A: Reduce by three quarters, between 1990 and 2015, the maternal mortality ratio								
Percent reduction in maternal mortality ratio, 1990–2013	75	45	49	37	64	59	50	60
Births attended by skilled health personnel b (%), 2007–2014	90	74	51	96	68	98	67	96
Target 5.B: Achieve, by 2015, universal access to reproductive health								
Antenatal care coverage (%): at least one visit, 2007–2014	100	83	77	96	77	-	78	95
Unmet need for family planning (%), 2012	0	12	24	9	13	10	18	6
Target 6.A: Have halted by 2015 and begun to reverse the spread of HIV and AIDS								
Percent reduction in HIV and AIDS incidence, 2001–2013	>0	46	59	24	45	20	<-50	21
Target 6.C: Have halted by 2015 and begun to reverse the incidence of malaria and other major diseases								
Percent reduction in incidence of malaria, 2000–2013	75	30	34	76	49	100	39	69
Percent reduction in mortality rate of tuberculosis (among HIV-negative people), 1990–2013	50	45	40	69	54	11	15	74
Target 7.C: Halve, by 2015, the proportion of the population without sustainable access to safe drinking-water and basic sanitation								
Percent reduction in proportion of population without access to improved drinking-water sources, 1990–2012	50	54	32	60	70	60	13	76
Percent reduction in proportion of population without access to improved sanitation, 1990–2012	50	32	8	40	27	22	32	53

◼ Met or on track   ◼ Substantial progress   ◼ No or limited progress   ☐ Date not available or not applicable

Source: World Health Organisation (2015) World Health Statistics, p.12

RATIO OF UNDER-FIVE MORTALITY RATE FOR CHILDREN BY RESIDENCE, WEALTH QUINTILE AND MOTHER'S EDUCATION, 2005-2013

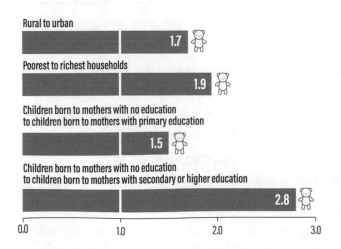

Rural to urban
1.7

Poorest to richest households
1.9

Children born to mothers with no education to children born to mothers with primary education
1.5

Children born to mothers with no education to children born to mothers with secondary or higher education
2.8

0.0   1.0   2.0   3.0

Research indicates that children from poorer households remain more vulnerable compared with those from the wealthiest households; on average, under-5 mortality rates are almost twice as high for children in the poorest households as for children in the richest.

Mortality is also more likely to strike children in rural areas who are about 1.7 times more likely to die before their 5th birthday as those in urban areas. Mothers' education remains the most powerful determinant of inequality; children of mothers with secondary or higher education are almost three times as likely to survive as children of mothers with no education (for more see WHO 2015 World Health Statistics).

② BASIC NEEDS - SCHOOLING AND LITERACY

The key importance of literacy and schooling is captured well in the following quote which reviews what illiteracy can mean:

'In developing countries, it's the story of a person who has to live amongst the poorest of the poor, often in very remote places. You're a mother and want your children to have a better life. You want them to be educated. But your husband says they should help with farming or take care of younger siblings so you're free to help eke out a meagre income.

Even if you win agreement to send them to school, the nearest one is hours away, on foot, through inhospitable terrain. Depending on which country you live in, it could be miles of steep mountains, desert scrub or rivers that often flood, cutting off access. If they get there, a willing but untrained teacher has to manage a class of at least 50 children of varying ages. The school building (if there is one) is in poor repair and exposed to the elements. There are few textbooks and other resources. And if you're in a country with more than one national language, guess which one is used in class? Alas, the one your children don't speak.'

Source: World Literacy Foundation (2015) The Economic & Social Cost of
Illiteracy: a snapshot of illiteracy in a global context

Apart from its cost in the lives of those directly affected, the overall economic cost of illiteracy remains high: when estimated as a percentage of GDP, it amounts to 2% for developed countries,

1.2% for emerging countries and 0.5% for developing countries. The current cost of illiteracy to the global economy is estimated by the World Literacy Foundation as US$1.2 trillion. Such estimates reflect a lower level of spending on social services in poorer countries.

In Dakar in 1990, an agenda of six broad education goals to be achieved by 2015 was agreed; the evidence below and on the page opposite is extracted from the Education for All 2000-2015: Achievements and Challenges Report published by UNESCO in 2015; it measured progress and change in the six agreed goals for 164 countries. The report summarises the progress:

- **Goal 1:** Progress in early childhood care and education was rapid but from a low base and highly inequitable.
- **Goal 2:** Universal primary education will not be reached by end 2015.
- **Goal 3:** More adolescents received secondary education but measuring skill acquisition among youth and adults remains limited.
- **Goal 4:** Progress in adult literacy was below the target.
- **Goal 5:** Despite fast progress, many countries have not achieved gender parity and obstacles to equality remain.
- **Goal 6:** There has been increased attention to issues of quality.

The longer-term implications of poor educational opportunities in South Africa (and, by implication elsewhere) are summarised by Nic Spaull as follows:

'Despite 20 years of democratic rule, most black children continue to receive a low-quality education, which condemns them to the underclass of South African society where poverty and unemployment are the norm. This substandard education does not develop their capabilities or expand their economic opportunities, but instead denies them dignified employment and undermines their own sense of self-worth. In short, poor school performance in South Africa reinforces social inequality and leads to a situation where children inherit the social position of their parents, irrespective of their motivation or ability. Low-quality education becomes a poverty trap from which it is almost impossible to escape. What is all the more alarming is that this situation applies to the vast majority of learners.'

Nic Spaull (2015) 'Schooling in South Africa: How low-quality education becomes a poverty trap in A, De Lannoy, S Swartz, L Lake & C Smith (eds.)
South African Child Gauge Children's Institute, University of Cape Town, p.37

LITERACY AND SCHOOLING: THE GOOD NEWS AND THE BAD NEWS

- The primary school net enrolment rate in the developing regions has reached an estimated 91% in 2015, up from 83% in 2000.

- The number of out-of-school children of primary school age worldwide has fallen by almost half, to an estimated 57 million in 2015, from 100 million in 2000

- Between 1990 and 2012, the number of children enrolled in primary school in sub-Saharan Africa more than doubled, from 62 to 149 million (from 59% in 1999 to 79%).

- The literacy rate among youth aged 15 to 24 has increased globally from 83% to 91% between 1990 and 2015. Northern Africa and Southern Asia have shown the greatest improvement in youth literacy, especially among young women.

Yet

- In the developing regions, children in the poorest households are four times as likely to be out of school as those in the richest households.

- According to 2012 estimates, 43% of out-of-school children globally will never go to school - regional disparities remain large; in Southern Asia, an estimated 57% of out-of-school children will never go to school, in sub-Saharan Africa 50%.

- Gender is still crucial – 48% of out-of-school girls are unlikely to ever go to school, compared to 37% for boys (although boys are more likely to leave school early).

- Only 17 out of the 73 countries with a literacy rate below 95% in 2000 had halved their illiteracy rate by 2015 - progress has been made towards gender parity in literacy but is not sufficient. All 43 countries where fewer than 90 women for every 100 men were literate in 2000 have moved towards parity, but none of them had reached it by the end of 2015.

- Alongside gender, household wealth, the rural/urban divide and disability remain crucial in influencing whether children access school – data from 63 countries between 2008 and 2012 indicates that children in the poorest households were four times as likely to be out of school than their peers, out of school rates were twice as high in rural than urban areas and in India, for example, more than one third of children and adolescents aged 6 to 13 who live with disabilities remain out of school.

- By the MDG 2015 deadline, 1 in 6 children in low and middle income countries – or almost 100 million – will not have completed primary school.

Sources: UNICEF State of the World's Children 2016; UNESCO Education for All 2000-2015 Achievements and Challenges

Table 13.2 | Global and Regional Progress on Health-related MDGs (World Health Organisation regions)

	Under 5 Years Mortality Rate Per 1000 live births	Moderate to severe stunting in under 5's % 2013	Total Primary Enrolment 2012 – change since 1990	Out of School Children 2012 % change since 1999	Total Secondary Enrolment 2012 – change since 1999	Adult Literacy rates 2012 – % change 2005-2012	No of countries with gender parity in primary & secondary education 2011
World	46	25	91	-45	27	84	46
sub-Saharan Africa	93	38	79	-30	125	59	0
Arab States	34	20	89	-43	40	78	2
Central Asia	35	16	95	-22	9	100	3
East Asia & Pacific	18	11	96	-42	20	95	7
South & West Asia	55	34	94	-73	58	63	0
Latin America & Caribbean	18	11	94	-6	14	92	3
North America & Europe	5	3	96	108	1	-	18
Central & Eastern Europe	12	8	96	-53	-26	99	13

③ BASIC NEEDS - WATER AND SANITATION

'Almost every day, water makes the headlines somewhere in the world. Droughts, floods and pollution are all big news, as water becomes the most precious, and most contested, essential resource...What's more, water resources are becoming increasingly fragile as populations grow, land use changes and deforestation continues. These threats will be exacerbated by the effects of climate change and have a disproportionately large impact on poor people without a safe, reliable water supply.'

Water Aid (2016) Water: At What Cost?

'Most vulnerable in a world of greater water insecurity are poor people living in informal urban settlements and those in rural areas whose livelihoods are dependent upon rainfed agriculture or the availability of grasslands and water for grazing animals. Protecting the rights of such people and avoiding elite capture of the resource and the benefits derived from it require tools that foster a more equitable allocation of scarce water resources.'

Water Governance Facility 2012

WATER: AT WHAT COST?
THE LACK OF ACCESS TO AN AFFORDABLE, CONVENIENT, IMPROVED WATER SOURCE IS ONE OF THE BIGGEST BARRIERS TO ESCAPING A LIFE OF POVERTY AND DISEASE.

The cost of water

For a poor person in the developing world water with no access to safe water at home, buying the recommended 50 litres a day can a be huge drain on their meagre salary. Many people have no choice but to compromise their health and dignity by using much less or collecting water from unsafe sources.

50 litres a day
The World Health Organisation specifies 50 litres per person per day as the recommended 'intermediate' quantity needed to maintain health, hygiene and for all domestic uses.

In Port Moresby, Papua New Guinea	In Antananarivo, Madagascar	In Accra, Ghana	In Maputo, Mozambique	In the UK
50l	50l	50l	50l	50l
£1.84	£0.50	£0.45	£0.09	£0.07
from a water delivery service	from a tanker truck	from a tanker truck	from a street vendor	from an official piped supply
54%	45%	25%	13%	0.1%
of typical low daily salary	of typical low daily salary	of typical low daily salary	of typical low daily salary	of typical low daily salary
(£3.60 a day for a snack stall-holder)	(£1.10 for a factory worker)	(£1.80 for a street food-seller)	(£0.71 for a street food-seller)	(£47 for a person on minimum wage)

Source: Water Aid (2016) Water: At What Cost?

WATER AND SANITATION; THE GOOD NEWS AND THE BAD NEWS

- The MDG target of a 50% reduction in the population without access to safe drinking-water between 1990 and 2015 was met globally in 2010; 116 countries have met the target.

- In 2015, 91% of the world's population uses an improved drinking water source, compared to 76% in 1990.

- By 2015, 91% of the world population used an improved drinking-water source, and over 55% enjoyed the convenience and associated health benefits of a piped supply on premises.

- Urban drinking-water coverage has remained high over the past two decades, and currently only 4% of the urban population relies on unimproved sources.

- Since 1990, 2.1 billion people gained access to improved sanitation (68% in 2015), and the proportion of people practicing open defecation globally has fallen almost by half.

- Since 1990, 1.1 billion people in urban areas gained access to improved sanitation (but the urban population grew by 1.3 billion).

Yet

- An estimated 748 million people still lack access with wide disparities not only between different regions but also between urban and rural areas and between socio-economic groups.

- Water scarcity affects more than 40% of the world's population and this figure is projected to rise.

- In 2011, 41 countries experienced water stress, up from 36 in 1998; of these, 10 countries - from the Arabian Peninsula, Northern Africa and Central Asia - withdrew more than 100% of renewable freshwater resources.

- Based on current trends, the world is unlikely to have met the MDG target on access to basic sanitation by end 2015, with 2.5 billion people still lacking access to improved facilities; 1 billion people (14% of world population) with no access to toilets, latrines or any form of sanitation facility.

- According to the Global Risks Report 2015, the water crisis is the number 1 global risk in terms of potential impact (ahead of infectious diseases and weapons of mass destruction).

Top 10 countries with the greatest % of people without safe water access and with largest numbers of people without safe water access, 2015

Rank	Country	%	Rank	Country	Millions
1	Papua New Guinea	60	1	India	75.8
2	Equatorial Guinea	52	2	China	63.1
3	Angola	51	3	Nigeria	57.8
4	Chad	49	4	Ethiopia	42.2
5	Mozambique	49	5	Democratic Republic of Congo	33.9
6	Madagascar	48	6	Indonesia	32.2
7	Democratic Republic of Congo	47	7	Tanzania	23.2
8	Afghanistan	45	8	Bangladesh	21.0
9	Tanzania	44	9	Kenya	17.2
10	Ethiopia	43	10	Pakistan	16.0

Source: World Health Organisation/UNICEF Joint Monitoring Programme for Water Supply and Sanitation (2015)

REASONS PEOPLE STRUGGLE FOR ACCESS TO WATER

Not enough money or political priority: the biggest barrier to improving access to water, sanitation and hygiene has too often been the chronic under-funding of these vital services and the lack of political will to prioritise clean water and toilets for all. In many developing countries, spending on water, sanitation and hygiene services is minimal compared to health and education, and the share of aid flows going to water and sanitation also remains low, having risen only slightly in the past ten years to 4.4% of all overseas aid.

Government inability to deliver: in many poor countries, although water infrastructure may be in place, effective institutions and management regimes are lacking, making it difficult to find engineers, managers and other skilled staff who can keep services running. In fragile states, the problems can be more acute, with water infrastructure and systems destroyed and needing to be rebuilt from scratch.

Deep inequalities: those in remote and rural locations are much less likely to have a reliable water source. However, even in cities, the poorest people are often socially excluded, and rarely consulted or involved in decisions about water services. Health conditions, age, disability, gender, ethnicity or caste can marginalise a person even further. 'Slums' and informal settlements are often not served at all and, where residents are regularly facing eviction attempts, even informal water connections are difficult to maintain.

Source: Water Aid (2016) Water: At What Cost? The State of the World's Water

Top 10 countries for rural women's water insecurity
(ODI study)

1. Democratic Republic of Congo	6. Nepal
2. Malawi	7. Senegal
3. Ethiopia	8. Gambia
4. Burkina Faso	9. Tanzania
5. Madagascar	10. Nigeria

Source: Helen Parker et al (2016) Gender, Agriculture and Water Insecurity, ODI Insights

WOMEN, WATER AND INSECURITY

71%	The burden of collecting water for households that falls on women and girls in sub-Saharan Africa
200 million	The average number of hours women in sub-Saharan Africa spend each day collecting water
40 billion	The estimated hours per year spent by women in sub-Saharan Africa collecting water

Source: Lakshmi Puri, deputy executive director of U.N. Women quoting 2012 UN Millennium Development Goals Report

A 2016 study by the UK's Overseas Development Institute, focused on women, water and insecurity, identified three key ways in which women farmers can be differently affected by water insecurity, variability and drought, forcing them to be especially creative in adapting where possible:

- First, women are often at the 'pinch point' of water-related tasks in the home and on the farm, with pressure intensifying around seasonal periods of scarcity in many developing countries.

- Second, compared to men, women may have less access to or control of assets that can be used to buffer against the effects of rainfall variability (for example, the equipment, land, and access rights needed for small-scale irrigation).

- Third, women often have fewer opportunities to pursue off-farm work or migrate to urban areas as a temporary coping strategy for seasonal food and income shortages, or for shortages caused by droughts and floods. In rain-fed areas, during the lean season or when harvests fail, migration provides an option to find food and employment. However, social norms, limited assets, and fewer marketable skills often mean women are less able than men to exploit off-farm opportunities. Female-headed households are therefore particularly vulnerable to climate shocks.

2050: A WORLD OF 10 BILLION?

WORLD POPULATION ESTIMATES 2015 AND 2050 (MILLIONS)

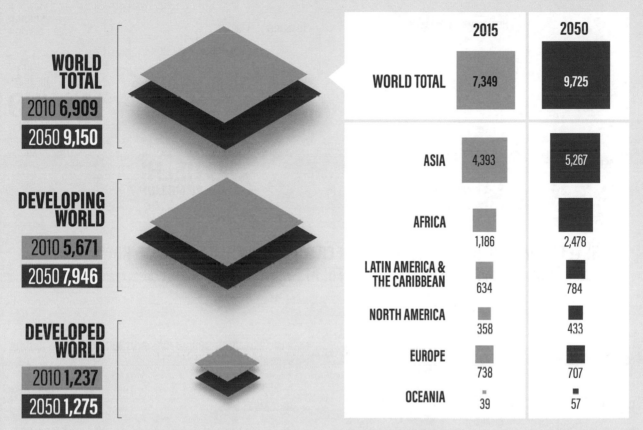

WORLD TOTAL
2010 **6,909**
2050 **9,150**

DEVELOPING WORLD
2010 **5,671**
2050 **7,946**

DEVELOPED WORLD
2010 **1,237**
2050 **1,275**

	2015	2050
WORLD TOTAL	7,349	9,725
ASIA	4,393	5,267
AFRICA	1,186	2,478
LATIN AMERICA & THE CARIBBEAN	634	784
NORTH AMERICA	358	433
EUROPE	738	707
OCEANIA	39	57

SELECTED POPULATION FACTS:

- **Currently, world population** continues to grow though more slowly than in the recent past; it is now growing annually by 1.18%, an additional 83 million; world population is projected to reach 8.5 billion in 2030, 9.7 billion in 2050 and 11.2 billion by 2100 (based on best current estimates).

- **Africa is the fastest-growing** region and more than half of world population increase between now and 2050 is expected to occur there; as a result, 1.3 billion of the additional 2.4 billion growth expected in world population by 2050 will be African. Asia will be the second largest contributor to future population growth; Europe is projected to have a smaller population in 2050 than In 2015.

- **Between 2015 and 2050,** half of the world's population growth is expected to be concentrated in just nine countries (in order) - India, Nigeria, Pakistan, Democratic Republic of the Congo, Ethiopia, United Republic of Tanzania, United States of America, Indonesia and Uganda.

- **Recent rises in life expectancy** at birth and reductions in child mortality rates especially in the Least Developed Countries have contributed significantly to population growth.

- **Populations in many regions** are still young - in Africa, children under age 15 account for 41%of population in 2015 and those aged 15 to 24 account for a further 19%; reduced fertility rates in Latin America and the Caribbean and Asia have led to smaller percentages of children (26% and 24%) and similar percentages of youth (17% and 16%).

- **Globally, population aged 60** or over is the fastest growing, the number of older people 60+ is projected to be 1.4 billion by 2030 and 2.1 billion by 2050, and could rise to 3.2 billion in 2100.

Source: United Nations, Department of Economic and Social Affairs, Population Division (2015). World Population Prospects: The 2015 Revision. New York: United Nations

10 LARGEST CITIES (2015)

3 SHANGHAI 23 MILLION

9 NEW YORK 18.6 MILLION

10 CAIRO 18.4 MILLION

7 OSAKA 20.1 MILLION

8 BEIJING 19.5 MILLION

4 MEXICO CITY 20.8 MILLION

1 TOKYO 37.8 MILLION

6 MUMBAI 20.7 MILLION

2 DELHI 25 MILLION

5 SAO PAULO 20.8 MILLION

'HE LET HIS MIND DRIFT AS HE STARED AT THE CITY, HALF SLUM, HALF PARADISE. HOW COULD A PLACE BE SO UGLY AND VIOLENT, YET BEAUTIFUL AT THE SAME TIME.' NIGERIAN AUTHOR **CHRIS ABANI** 2004

REGION	Numbers living in Slums (millions)	% of Urban Population Living in Slums
Developing World	863	32.7
North Africa	12.7	13.3
sub-Saharan Africa	213.1	61.7
Latin America & The Caribbean	113.4	23.5
East Asia	206.5	28.2
Southern Asia	200.5	35.0
South East Asia	79.9	31.0
Western Asia	35.7	24.6
Oceania	0.57	24.1

- Since 2007, **more people live in urban areas** than in rural areas globally.

- In 1950, more than 70% lived in rural areas, **by 2014, this figure was 54%.**

- Levels of urbanisation vary greatly regionally - in 2014, **80% or above in Latin America, the Caribbean and North America; Europe 73%, Africa 40%, Asia 48%.**

- Over the coming decades, the **level of urbanisation is expected to increase in all regions,** with Africa and Asia urbanising faster than the rest.

- By 2015, Africa will have **332 million slum dwellers,** a number that will continue to double every fifteen years.

Sources: UN Habitat (2013) State of the World's Cities; UN Department of Economic and Social Affairs Population Division (2015) World Urbanization Prospects: the 2014 Revision; Mike Davis (2006) Planet of Slums, London, Verso

DEBATING POPULATION: 3 ISSUES

AFRICA'S YOUTH BULGE

The world has never been so young and Africa is no exception – in 1950, approximately 10% of the world's children lived in Africa, within 50 years, that figure doubled and is projected to double again by 2050 producing a demographic 'bulge' of almost a billion younger than 18 (37% of world total) prompting two divergent responses – is this bulge a 'dividend' or a 'disaster'?

Two key drivers of this growth are the rapidly rising numbers of births and falling rates of child mortality; 1.8 billion births are projected by 2050 due to high fertility rates and the resultant increasing numbers of women of reproductive age. The average fertility rate for Africa currently stands at 4.7 children per

woman of reproductive age (15 - 49 years), far above that of Asia and globally; the number of women of reproductive age has risen fivefold between 1950 and 2015 and will likely increase to 607 million by 2050.

In addition, African women also have some of the longest lifetime period for births globally because of the high rates of adolescent fertility (currently 98 births per 1000 for girls aged 15 - 19 years, double the worldwide average). Child survival has also contributed to Africa's child population increase – in 1990, almost 1 in 6 children died before age 5; this had fallen to 1 in 11 in 2012 yet rising birth rates in some countries (in West and Central Africa)

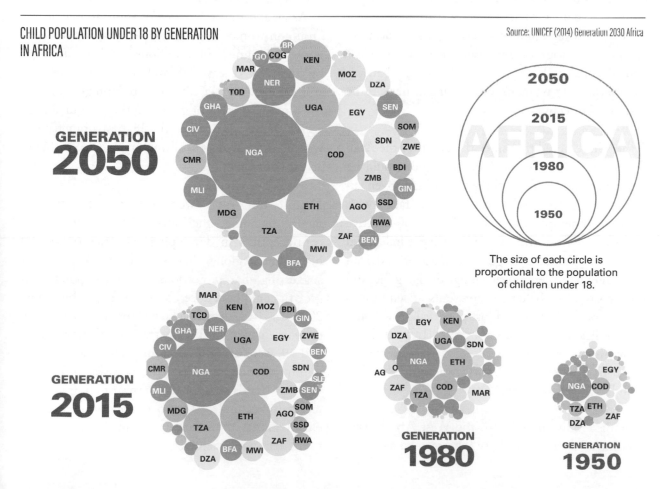

CHILD POPULATION UNDER 18 BY GENERATION IN AFRICA

Source: UNICEF (2014) Generation 2030 Africa

The size of each circle is proportional to the population of children under 18.

has tempered this pattern leading to static or rising numbers. This reality is compounded by poverty (African countries with average fertility rates greater than six children per woman of reproductive age - Chad, Mali, Niger, and Somalia – are amongst the poorest) and women in the poorest households tend to have more children (2 to 4 more) than women in wealthier households. Conflict and state 'fragility' is also an issue with such states tending to exhibit higher fertility.

For many commentators, investment in Africa's youth, in their physical and environmental health and wellbeing, their education, inclusion, and participation will be fundamental and not only from a rights perspective. Such an investment could give Africa the opportunity of realising a potential demographic dividend as youth dependency declines and the working population expands. Vital to realising such a dividend is the empowerment of Africa's girls and young women; issues such as child marriage, girls' education, access to appropriate reproductive health services and the cultural, social, and economic barriers that perpetuate women's subordination need to be addressed directly.

Others have noted that since the events of the Arab Spring in 2011, the sub-Saharan region could be the next context for political uprisings given an increasing number of educated youth faced with pervasive unemployment, the absence of effective political opportunities and increasing rural-urban migration. While a large percentage of African youth remains unemployed alongside rising fuel and food costs, the challenge represents an enormous cost to society in terms of lost potential growth and de-stabilisation (according to the ILO, in 2013, more than one-third (37.8%) of even employed youth in the developing world were living on less than US$2 per day in 2013).

Alcinda Honwana refers to the West Africa term 'youthman' to describe those who may be age-wise described as adults are still '*waiting to attain the social markers of adulthood: earning a proper living, being fully independent, establishing families and becoming taxpayers*'.

Sources: UNICEF (2014) Generation 2030 Africa; Jeffrey O'Malley et al (2014) Africa's child demographics and the world's future' The Lancet, August 12th; Julius Agbor et al (2012) sub-Saharan Africa's Youth Bulge: a demographic dividend or disaster? In Foresight Africa: Top Priorities for the Continent, Brookings Institute; ILO (2015) Global Employment Trends for Youth

RIGHTS AND MEANS: WOMEN, CONTRACEPTION AND POPULATION

In 1994 at the International Conference on Population and Development, world leaders pledged their commitment to ensuring universal access to family planning, re-affirmed it again in 2004 and most recently again in September 2015. Yet, as of 2015 according to UN Department of Economic and Social Affairs data, 22% of African and 10% of Asian and Latin America/ Caribbean married or 'in union' women have 'unmet' contraceptive needs with very significant variations on those averages by country. At least 225 million single or married women who would like to avoid pregnancy and use a modern form of contraception, are unable to access them. Africa has the highest unmet need, with an estimated 24% of women in 2015 unable to access contraception.

Despite this, more women than ever now use family planning; the number of women using contraceptives in developing countries (especially in poorer regions) has soared to record levels suggesting that projections for global population growth could be reduced by as much as 1 billion by 2030. In 2015, an estimated 64% of married women, or women living with a partner, aged between 15 and 49, were using modern or traditional forms of family planning (in 1970, the rate was just 36%). Current trends suggest high rates of contraceptive use in, for example, Africa over the coming decades – the region with the largest demand but least access to modern contraceptives.

According to Jagdish Upadhya of the UN Population Fund, quoted in the UK Guardian newspaper, March 2016:

'...If by 2030 the average family size is just one child fewer, then by 2030 the world population is estimated to be approximately 8 billion rather than 9 billion... evidence shows that women who have access to family planning choose to use family planning, often resulting in smaller families, higher educational achievements, healthier children [and] greater economic power as well as influence in their households and communities ... if all actors can work together to provide women in every country with the means, which is their right, to voluntarily exercise yet another right to freely determine their family size, then we are likely to see a significant slowing of global population growth.'

The implications are clearly demonstrated in the case of Nigeria (expected to experience one of the largest population growth rates over the next few decades and with a contraceptive prevalence rate of just 16% in 2015) where an increase of one percentage point in the use of modern contraceptives would mean about 426,000 more women would be using family planning. More broadly, the issue of family planning is also closely related to maternal and infant health and survival as well as overall development. WHO evidence clearly indicates that family planning can help prevent one third of maternal deaths by allowing women to delay motherhood, space births, avoid unintended pregnancies and unsafe abortions and stop childbearing when desired. According to the African regional report of WHO in 2014, spacing births also reduces child malnutrition and infant mortality.

Despite this, the use of contraception remains low and routinely unmet in many parts of Africa; in recent surveys (between 2005 and 2012) of married women aged 15 to 49 years, one quarter reported an unmet need for family planning. This translates into more than 47 million women without access to family planning in the region, a number considerably higher than that reported in other parts of the world. A modest increase in the contraceptive prevalence rate was registered in the region between 2007 and 2012 (from 23% to 27%) while the total fertility rate (the number of births a woman would have by the end of her reproductive life) dropped from 6.2 to 4.8 between 1990 and 2012.

Sources: WHO Regional Office for Africa (2014) The Health of the People: What Works; UNFPA 2015 State of World Population; Liz Ford, 'Rise in use of contraception offers hope for containing global population', Guardian March 9th, 2016; WHO (2014). The health of the people: What works. The African Regional Report, World Health Organisation, Regional Office for Africa

FEEDING 9+ BILLION?

In recent decades, the traditional Malthusian arguments regarding population growth and the ability of the planet to feed projected numbers have been proven unfounded; predictions of widespread hunger and famine have not been realised despite rising population and it is now generally accepted that the world has the capacity currently to feed some 9 billion people. Although written in the context of continuing hunger for many millions (an economic and political issue rather than a resource issue); increasingly pressing environmental limits; current (over)consumption patterns and extensive food waste, two UN Food and Agriculture Organisation reports argue that feeding the world is entirely possible *'if bold decisions are made'* (2009, How to Feed the World in 2050 and 2012 Towards the Future We Want: end hunger and make the transition to sustainable agricultural and food systems). And, it is in this latter comment that the challenge lies, especially in an environmentally constrained future, one that will impact significantly on agriculture and the world's poor and hungry.

This issue was reviewed in a 2010 study published by Oxfam and the UK's Overseas Development Institute which notes:

'Feeding nine billion persons by 2050 will require the production of another one third to a half of current cereals output, and 43% to 85% more meat. This can be done, mainly from intensification, with yields rising by around 50%, with perhaps 10% more land used. Much of the potential for this increase appears to lie in temperate OECD countries rather than tropical developing countries. Diet is, however, a key variable: will future generations consume animal products on the scale that many populations in the industrialised world do, or will there be the reduction in consumption per person of animal products - and vegetable oils - that many doctors would like to see on health grounds? Owing to the high demand of livestock for feed grains, meeting the needs of the future becomes much easier if future diets contained more grains, pulses, fruit and vegetables, and fewer animal products.'

The report notes that overall assessments are optimistic that projected world population can be adequately fed but that increased production, whether by intensified agriculture or an expansion of farmed land or tilled areas, will lead to increased greenhouse gas emissions. The report also addresses two additional questions – those of distribution and food waste; if food is not more equitably distributed and if large quantities continue to be unnecessarily wasted, then more food will need to be produced *'if the hungry are to eat'*.

Rather than focusing on the 'global' issue of feeding rising populations, the report's authors argue that while the issue is *'hugely complex'* it needs to be tackled at local, national and regional levels as this will recognise local agro-climatic conditions, land use patterns, food systems and structures, the impact of climate change and how to mitigate it, as well as local socio-cultural and political contexts. The report concludes *'if attention is paid at lower scales, the 'global' problem may well take care of itself'*.

(For more on this issue, see Tristam Stewart (2009) Waste: Uncovering the Global Food Scandal, London, Penguin and Paul McMahon (2013) Feeding Frenzy: The New Politics of Food, Profile Books, London)

CONCLUSION

There have been many criticisms made of the MDG agenda and the framework it was based upon; while a basic needs perspective has much in common with the MDGs, it also offers a critique. For commentators such as Vijay Prashed (The Poorer Nations, 2014, Verso), what was missing in the 'accountancy' of the MDGs was the principle of universal access by every person to certain basic needs. For Prashad and others, what is required is that the demand for basic needs must be 'institutionalised' and not incrementalised. Such institutionalisation remains a political issue (not an economic one) and thus two issues arise – the need for a political movement to champion universal access and a specific role for UN agencies in monitoring such access.

... IF FOOD IS NOT MORE EQUITABLY DISTRIBUTED AND IF LARGE QUANTITIES CONTINUE TO BE UNNECESSARILY WASTED, THEN MORE FOOD WILL NEED TO BE PRODUCED 'IF THE HUNGRY ARE TO EAT.'

READING

FAO (2015) *The State of Food Insecurity in the World, Meeting the 2015 International Hunger Targets: Taking Stock of Uneven Progress*, UN Food and Agriculture Organisation, Rome

Johan Galtung (1978), *The Basic Needs Approach*, WIP 20. Available from https://www.transcend.org/galtung/papers.php

UN Population Fund (2016) *State of World Population 2016*, New York

UNDP (2015) *Human Development Report 2015 Work for Human Development*, UNDP, New York

UNICEF (2016) *State of the World's Children*, UNICEF, New York

UN Water (2014) *International Decade for Action 'Water for life' 2005-2015*, UN Department of Economic and Social Affairs

WaterAid (2016), *Water: At What Cost? The State of the World's Water 2016*, WaterAid, London

WHO (2013) *Women's and Children's Health: Evidence of Impact of Human Rights*, WHO, Geneva

World Health Organisation *(2015) Trends in Maternal Mortality: 1990 to 2015: estimates by WHO, UNICEF, UNFPA, World Bank Group and United Nations Population Division,* Geneva,

World Health Organisation (2015) *World Health Statistics*, Geneva

MORE INFORMATION AND DEBATE

www.unfpa.org - UN Population Fund site

www.www.unicef.org - UNICEF site

www.unhabitat.org - UN Human Settlements Programme

www.pambazuka.org – pan-African NGO community network news site

www.socialwatch.org - international NGO network based in Uruguay

'ODA remains woefully inadequate to the tasks of contributing to the elimination of extreme poverty and significantly reduction of other forms of poverty and vulnerability. It is in urgent need of reform to meet the challenges of the SDGs.'

BRIAN TOMLINSON, REALITY OF AID REPORT 2016

CHAPTER 14

DEBATING AID
– MOVING BEYOND PANTOMINE

MARY ROSE COSTELLO AND COLM REGAN

The argument on aid continues unabated, it has long been the subject of intense debate and vigorous disagreement, particularly as regards its purpose, effectiveness, impact and value in development terms. Yet, aid has become big business at all levels, of government, the private sector, philanthropy, NGO, academia and celebrity culture; it has convinced critics and convinced defenders and remains the subject of much misinformation and myth-making on both sides. This chapter summarises and reviews many of the debates and much of the evidence.

KEYWORDS:

NEGATIVE AND POSITIVE DUTIES; OPTION OR DUTY; MULTILATERAL AND BILATERAL AID; HISTORY OF AID; REAL AID; IMPACT OF AID; PRIVATE AID; SOUTH-SOUTH AID; NGO AID; AID: CRITICS AND DEFENDERS.

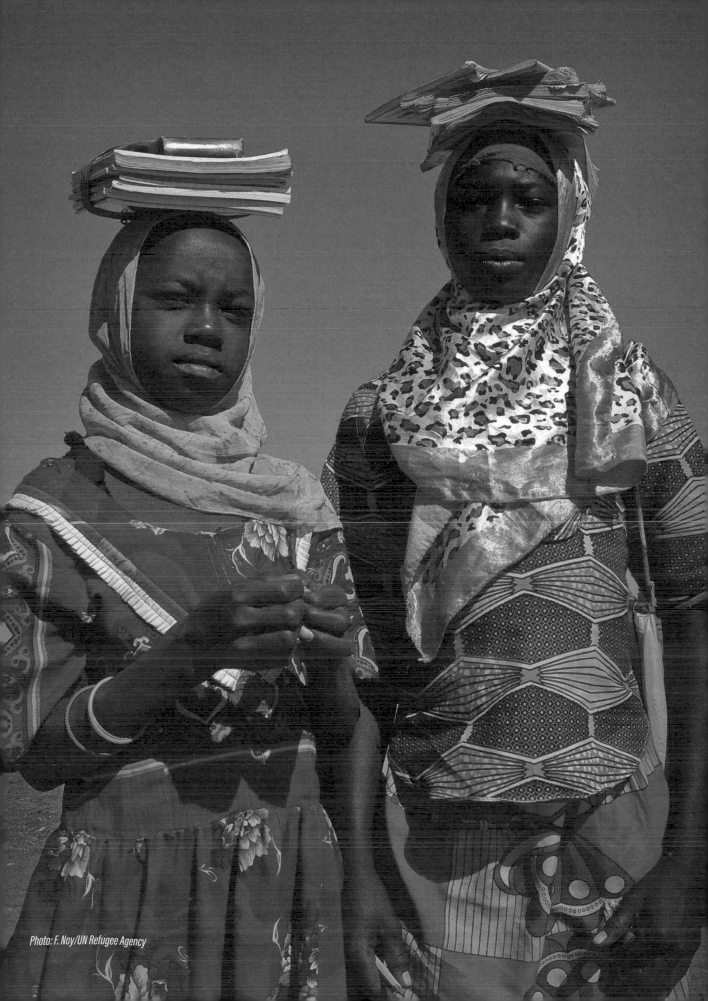

INTRODUCTION

The contexts and priorities of the aid landscape have changed significantly in the last decade; while official government aid remains dominant, private aid (from a variety of diverse sources and regions worldwide) has mushroomed and has generated different patterns and ways of working (and thinking). Meanwhile, aid from developing countries to other developing countries has taken on a new significance – not all of it deemed positive; China, India and some Gulf States have continued to emerge as aid players. While addressing traditional issues of hunger and poverty remain central to aid, other agendas have become priorities, most notably the impact of current growth and consumption-driven models of development on the planet's environmental capabilities and limits. Additionally, the increasing impact of extreme inequality in undoing key dimensions of progress in human development in recent decades threatens aid, its assumptions and impact.

Finally, the economic crisis generated in industrialised countries in the period 2007 – 2008 has had very considerable impact in developing countries and has also fuelled an increasingly narrow and inward-looking public perspective, often hostile to the needs of the world's poor and to our aid obligations. The 'business as usual' model of economic growth-led development continues to generate and sustain the very poverty and exclusion aid seeks to address.

DUTY OR OPTION: 'AID' AND THE BIGGER PICTURE

The literature on aid is voluminous and detailed; the arguments of those who criticise aid as well as those who defend aid are addressed below but first, in any serious discussion on the issue, it is necessary to address some of the bigger ideas, values and contexts underpinning the debate (which remains significantly dominated by narrow and often technical issues) including those of, for example Peter Unger (1996), Peter Singer (2002), Thomas Pogge (2008), Garrett Cullity (2004), Amartya Sen (2009), Richard Dworkin (2011) and, most recently Deaton (2013).

These broader contexts include:

- We are all a part of a bigger world picture and we are now connected to others in a bewildering series of ways. These connections have implications (both positive and negative) and it is impossible for us to cut ourselves off from them (even if we wished) or to isolate ourselves from them. As a result, we have duties to others, even others we do not know and are unlikely ever to meet – for example, the duty to acknowledge that our actions (and inactions) in trade, environment etc., routinely impact on others (and vice versa) and we ignore such impacts at everyone's cost, including our own. The challenge remains to figure out what those duties are, how far they extend and what are their (reasonable) limits?

- The rights which we proclaim for ourselves imply corresponding duties, such as the responsibility that such rights apply to all, without exception. Therefore, we have a duty to promote the rights of all; either rights apply to everyone or the very concept of rights is meaningless.

- Some commentators argue that the traditional stricture 'love thy neighbour as thyself' means literally what it proclaims. Human thought, rationality and emotion go beyond the merely 'individual' and embrace some element of a 'universal' or bigger picture. This implies that we should give equal weight to the interests and needs of others as we would give to our own. While 'self-interest' is a key motivating and ethical framework by which to live one's life, it is, nonetheless insufficient, as all of us recognise interests and needs outside those of pure self-interest.

- Part of our condition as human beings, in fact the essence of being human, is our capacity to reason and to act *reasonably* and to search for and constantly re-assess what *reasonableness* means at any point in time or in any context. This essence places us under an obligation to others – we have a duty to *go as far as we can reasonably go*.

While the implications of these debates are explored more fully in other chapters (especially chapter 5) it may be useful here to summarise a number of important implications for the aid debate *per se*.

- Some philosophers argue that not only do we have a duty to support those in need but this duty is *absolute* – development aid, they argue, can be a way of countering international injustice, just as the welfare state seeks to redress local injustices. For philosophers, such as Emmanuel Kant, humankind's moral choices had to uphold what he termed a *categorical imperative* – an absolute and universal moral standard which all human beings have an obligation to uphold. For Kant (writing over 300 years ago), acts of charity are not about benevolence but rather duty because universal morality demands that we act to right an injustice even if we did not promote that injustice.

- Such a perspective has significant implications – if charity is a duty, then *giving to the poor* is no longer a good-spirited, voluntary deed (an act of optional charity) but rather an issue of social justice with corresponding duties placed upon both the individual and the state. In this context, a rich government (society?) which knowingly does nothing to help reduce poverty (and not just at home) is morally culpable. The priority to assist should not be determined solely by nationality but rather by need – a dying child at the other end of the world is no less important than one at the end of our street.

- Many argue that if it is in our power to prevent something bad from happening, at little cost to ourselves, then we have a moral duty to do so. Using arguments about *bad* aid to dismiss all aid is akin to dismissing all music on the basis of poor musicians.

- Against this, many argue that while people have mutual obligations to each other, such obligations are neither absolute nor universal – they are a matter for individuals and governments since each person/state has a right to dispose of personal property as they see fit.

- Thus, even if helping the poor is morally right, it cannot and should not be enforced and even if an individual is indifferent to the plight of the poor, they should not be forced into assisting or punished for not doing so as an enforced morality is no morality at all.

Writing in 2010, Ghanaian economist and activist Charles Abugre (echoing the arguments of many others) extends the discussion on aid even further through exploring what he calls *reverse aid* (the resource transfers from poor to rich countries), the scale of which he describes as *staggering*. Arguing that developing countries have been net-capital providers to rich countries (as illustrated earlier in Chapter 7) Abugre (and others) argue that aid from rich countries ceases to be a discussion about 'charity' or the scale and impact of aid; it becomes a key part of the wider debate on international injustice (on this issue see the essays by Hickel and Sriskandarajah in Sumner and Kirk (eds., 2014) The Donors' Dilemma: Emergence, Convergence and the Future of Foreign Aid).

Debates about aid which avoid the broader contexts in which aid operates (international economics and politics, trade, finance, conflict etc.) and which have significant impact on aid itself and its potential impact are incomplete and ideological at best.

DEFINING OFFICIAL DEVELOPMENT ASSISTANCE
(OR OFFICIAL AID)

The Organisation for Economic Cooperation and Development (OECD) defines official aid as *'grants or loans to countries and territories'* on the Development Assistance Committee (DAC) list of recipient countries and to international organisations which are:

- Undertaken by the official (state or international organisation) sector
- With the promotion of economic development and welfare as the main objective
- At concessional financial terms (if the aid is a loan, it must have a grant element of at least 25%)
- In addition to financial flows, technical co-operation is included in aid
- Grants, loans and credits for military purposes are excluded
- Transfer payments to private individuals (e.g. pensions, reparations or insurance pay-outs) are in general not counted either.

Multilateral aid is made up of contributions to international institutions for use in, or on behalf of, developing countries, and in financial aid and technical co-operation by an international institution to developing countries. Bilateral aid is ODA provided on a country-to-country basis.

DIFFERENT TYPES OF AID

Main aid mechanisms	Programme aid including overall recipient government budget support (general or sector specific e.g. education or health); project support to or via NGOs (local and international); support to or via public-private partnerships and technical assistance.
Main types of 'flow'	Grants, concessional loans, debt relief, equity purchase.
Varied stated objectives of aid	Short-term human development results; capacity strengthening (institutional and human); policy change; economic growth and (income) poverty reduction; climate and other international public goods; research and technological advance and security concern.
Four motivations of aid	Donor benefit (primarily motivated by the interests of the contributor); mutual benefit (in which the contributor hopes to benefit as well as the recipient); recipient benefit (charitable, no immediate benefits sought for the contributor, although long-term benefits expected from safer/wealthier world); global or regional spill-over benefits (benefits beyond specific borders of one country).
Aid supports different sectors (OECD categories)	Social services and infrastructure (education, health, water, government and civil society, peace and security); economic services and infrastructure (transport, communications, energy, banking); production (agriculture, industry, trade, tourism); commodities and general programme support (food, general budget support); debt relief, humanitarian and unspecified.

Source: The US$138.5 Billion Question: When Does Foreign Aid Work (and When Doesn't It)? Jonathan Glennie and Andy Sumner, Center for Global Development Policy Paper 049, November 2014:15/16

Note from source authors: '... there will be plenty of overlap between the categories (in the diagram above) – they are meant primarily to illustrate the diversity of intervention which complicates the apparently simple question, does aid work? At one extreme, some interventions might be quite short term, local, and with empirically verifiable outcomes (such as an attempt to reduce the prevalence of malaria in a particular geographic location). At the other, some aid interventions may be intended to support long-term change nationally, making progress hard to measure (such as general budget support). There is no reason, a priori, why all types of intervention should or shouldn't work in general.'

AID: THE HISTORY OF AN IDEA

1945-1960: A NEW BEGINNING

Though aid to poorer countries existed in different forms before World War II - mostly via religious and voluntary agencies – it wasn't until the late 1940s that aid giving became part of ongoing government and *'development'* policy. After the War the United States provided a relief package known as the *'Marshall Plan'* to help rebuild Europe and to ensure Europe remained a US ally.

1960-1970: A DECADE OF DEVELOPMENT

The United Nations branded the 1960s as the *'Development Decade'* and it became characterised as the *'glory years'* for development aid; support for aid was strong and the amount of aid made available was growing. There was evidence to suggest that aid was actually working, with the rates of growth increasing in the economies of some of the poorest countries, including those in sub-Saharan Africa. Official aid continued to increase and, in 1969, the General Assembly of the UN agreed an international aid target of 0.7% of GNP for donor countries.

1970S-1980S: AID IN DECLINE

By the start of the 1970s commitment to official aid was beginning to decline. Increases in ODA had come to a halt, and aid, as a percentage of GNP, fell as compared with previous levels. The situation was compounded by an international recession and the oil crisis. Official aid began to increase again towards the end of the decade, in real terms to US$27 billion by 1980, however, this growth in real terms masked a decline in aid as a percentage of GNP to half of the 0.7% agreed. The 1970s also witnessed the growth in the size and influence of nongovernmental organisations.

1980S-1990s: THE LOST DECADE OF DEVELOPMENT

The 1980s began with the continued negative consequences of the global recession for development aid, with aid levels stagnating and in many cases declining. A focus on development aid and economic growth became the main theme of the decade and, despite recommendations against such policies, there was an increase in the number of *'conditions'* attached to aid; policies associated with neo-liberal economics led to the introduction of Structural Adjustment Programmes (SAPs)[1], which included increasing the role of the *'free market'* and cutting social expenditure. These policies had direct impact on areas such as health and education expenditure in developing countries with resulting negative impact on the poorest.

1990-2000: THE DEPENDENCY DEBATE

By 1992 debates around the notion of *'aid dependency'* grew in importance. This debate coincided with an all-time low in ODA as a percentage of GDP; in 1990 ODA was at an average of 0.33% but by the end of the decade it had dropped to just 0.22% and, with a worsening situation for the world's poorest, the aid debate again moved away from promoting economic growth to directly alleviating poverty.

2000-2015: NEW MILLENNIUM - NEW GOALS

The new century began with a positive start with the biggest ever meeting of heads of state committing to the 8 Millennium Development Goals (MDGs) and now the Sustainable Development Goals (SDGs). Debates moved away from the *'does aid work'* agenda to that of making aid more effective. By 2015, total net ODA from members of the OECD's Development Assistance Committee (DAC) increased in real terms to US$ 131.6 billion, representing 0.31% of DAC members' combined gross national income. The largest donors by volume were the United States, France, Germany, the UK and Japan. Only five countries exceeded the United Nations ODA target of 0.7% of GNI: Denmark, Luxembourg, the Netherlands, Norway and Sweden. Accompanying these trends was the considerable rise of South to South aid, a large increase in the scale and impact of private aid and the continuing importance of the voluntary sector in the delivery of aid.

---

1   Neo-liberal economics – an economic school of thought which considers the free market to be the best, most efficient route to economic growth and which seeks to transfer control of the economy from the public to the private sector. In development, neo-liberal economics were typified by the so-called Washington Consensus (a list of 10 policy proposals) adopted by the IMF and World Bank in the 1990's.

AID AT A GLANCE

'THE ODA LANDSCAPE HAS CHANGED MARKEDLY OVER RECENT YEARS IN RELATION TO HOW MUCH AID IS PROVIDED, BY WHOM, TO WHICH COUNTRIES, THROUGH WHICH MODALITIES, AS WELL AS THE PURPOSES TO WHICH IT IS PUT'

KEY ISSUES AND TRENDS

- While official aid rose in 2015 to US$131.6 billion, much of the increase was due to rising expenditure on refugees in host countries representing an average of 0.30% of OECD country GNI (overall aid has risen by 83% since the MDGs were agreed in 2000), only six of 28 OECD Development Assistance Committee (DAC) countries – Denmark, Luxembourg, The Netherlands, Norway, Sweden and the United Kingdom – met the agreed UN target of 0.7% of GNI.

- ODA rose in 22 countries in 2015 (the biggest increases in Greece, Sweden and Germany), six countries reported lower ODA (steepest in Portugal and Australia); of several non-DAC members (who report their aid flows to the OECD body), the United Arab Emirates posted the highest ODA/GNI ratio in 2015 at 1.09%.

- Approximately 1.5 million refugees claimed asylum in OECD countries in 2015 (>1 million in Europe) and DAC rules allow member countries to count certain refugee-related expenses as ODA for the first year after their arrival. Three countries (Australia, Korea and Luxembourg) do not count refugee costs as ODA. Others (Austria, Greece, Italy, the Netherlands and Sweden) saw refugee costs account for more than 20% of their ODA in 2015.

- Bi-lateral country to country aid made up approximately two-thirds of all aid in 2015.

- Final figures for 2013-14 indicate that US$18 billion of official aid was channelled through Civil Society Organisations (NGOs).

- Non OECD DAC Aid for 2013-14 amounted to a total of US$23.5 billion (from 27 countries) with 4 countries dominating – China US$6 billion, Saudi Arabia and United Arab Emirates US$11.1 billion , Turkey US$3.3 billion and India.

- According to OECD data, there has been a consistent overall trend in aid allocations away from the poorest countries towards more (upper)middle-income countries.

- There are now 3 clear groups of DAC donors: those donating above US$15 billion per capita include, in order of magnitude, the US, the UK and Germany (all increased their aid in 2014); a second group of those between US$5 billion and US$10 billion including France, Japan, Sweden, the Netherlands and Norway (the first 3 reduced their aid in 2014) and a third group with below US$5 billion includes Australia, Canada, Italy, Switzerland, Denmark and Belgium (the first two donors in this group reduced their aid in 2014; the others increased theirs).

Official Development Assistance from non-DAC Countries 2015 (preliminary data)

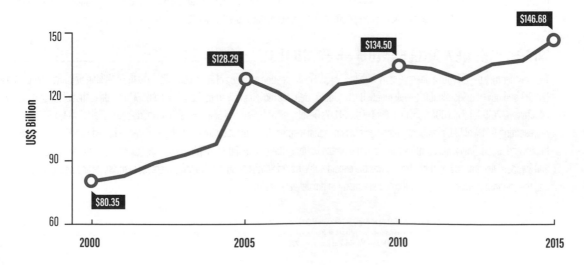

Official Development Assistance as percent of GNI (2015)

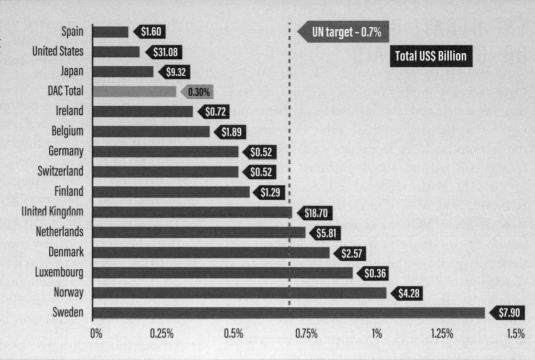

UN target – 0.7%

Total US$ Billion

Country	US$ Billion
Spain	$1.60
United States	$31.08
Japan	$9.32
DAC Total	0.30%
Ireland	$0.72
Belgium	$1.89
Germany	$0.52
Switzerland	$0.52
Finland	$1.29
United Kingdom	$18.70
Netherlands	$5.81
Denmark	$2.57
Luxembourg	$0.36
Norway	$4.28
Sweden	$7.90

0%   0.25%   0.5%   0.75%   1%   1.25%   1.5%

Official Development Assistance from non DAC Countries 2015

UN target – 0.7%

Total US$ Million

Country	US$ Million
Croatia	$51
Estonia	$33
Hungary	$152
Israel	$207
Latvia	$23
Lithuania	$44
Malta	$14
Russia	$1140
Turkey	$3930
UAE	$4839

0%   0.2%   0.4%   0.6%   0.8%   1.0%   1.2%

Estimates of South – South Aid (millions of US$, 2013 unless stated)

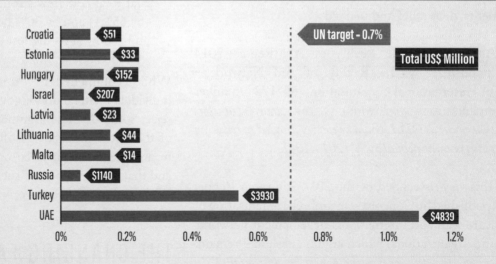

■ Brazil 900   ■ India 850   ■ Taiwan 273   ■ South Africa 217   ■ Kuwait 149

TOTAL AID
23,951

CHINA	Saudi Arabia	United Arab Emirates	Turkey
7,100	5,683	5,091	3,276

THE DEBATE ON 'REAL' OR 'GENUINE' AID

Over the past number of decades, there has been ongoing debate about what should and what should not, be included in 'official aid'; what financial transactions could be legitimately classified as aid (particularly as understood publicly). According to the OECD definition of aid, donors are able to include a number of financial flows that, in the view of many NGOs and commentators do not genuinely contribute to human development and therefore should not be included. Items they argue should be excluded in any definition of 'real' or 'genuine' aid include spending on developing world students in the donor country, spending on refugees in the donor country, repayments of interest on concessional loans and future interest on cancelled debts, debt relief and tied aid.

As stated in the Reality of Aid Report 2014 (published by the Reality of Aid Network – an international organisation of 172 member organisations worldwide): '*...the resource transfers that count as ODA should be clearly directed to reducing poverty and inequality...*' (2014:134).

This view is echoed by the 2014 Aidwatch Report (published by Concord – an umbrella organisation of European and international development networks and organisations) which argues aid should remain: '*an effective tool for fighting poverty and inequality'. In order to ensure this, official policies and practices on aid should avoid ...the securitisation of aid, certain forms of support to the private sector which do not promote development, climate finance and tax rebates*' (2014:6).

According to Aidwatch, using this definition of aid:

- Just 3 European Union countries (Luxembourg, Ireland and the UK) pursued 'genuine' aid agendas in 2013.

- While Official EU state aid figures for 2013 amounted to approximately €53.6 billion, if the Real Aid definition is used the amount declines to approximately €48.4 billion or the amount of aid provided by EU states decreased to 0.38% of their collective GNI.

- Aidwatch argues, for example that bilateral aid from Greece was completely composed of 'inflated' aid; over one-third of all bilateral aid provided by France and Spain was inflated while bilateral aid in Malta, Hungary and Latvia was inflated by 90%, 55% and 40% respectively.

- Despite this, the Reality of Aid Network reports that while Real Aid grew strongly from 2000 to 2010 (by 65%+) and was at its highest level since 2000, at US$127.5 billion in 2015, the value of Real ODA remained largely unchanged since 2010' (Reality of Aid Report 2016).

- Despite this, the Reality of Aid Network reports that Real Aid grew strongly from 2000 to 2010 (by 65%+) and by 30% between 2005 and 2010 and is now at its highest level since 2000.

While commentators from the OECD and individual bilateral donor government organisations reject some of these arguments, they accept many of the criticisms made of official aid (especially as regards debt, technical co-operation and tied aid) and that the definition of such aid needs significant modification to better serve human development directly.

THE CHANGING FACE OF AID

As indicated at the outset of this chapter, the context and landscape of aid is changing and the following section briefly explores a number of aspects of this change – the strengthening role of 'South-South' aid; the ongoing debate on China's role and the scale and impact of growing 'private' aid.

South-South cooperation

International development cooperation is commonly viewed in the context of North-South relations. The UNDP Human Development Report 2013 points to the seismic changes happening at a global economy level: *'For the first time in 150 years, the combined output of the developing world's three leading economies – Brazil, China and India – is about equal to the combined GDP of the longstanding industrial powers of the North – Canada, France, Germany, Italy, United Kingdom and the United States.'*

Traditionally, aid flowed from donor countries in the North to recipient countries in the South. This placed the balance of power in the North leaving developing country governments (and civil society) with little room for manoeuvre and dependent on Northern aid flows, fashions and demands. More recently, the aid environment has experienced significant change in this regard; strong Southern economies have emerged as big players on the world stage including Brazil, India, Saudi Arabia, Venezuela and, most notably, China. With the rapid growth of development assistance from so-called *'emerging donors'* from the South, there is increasing interest in South-South Cooperation especially within official government circles.

Southern donors argue they can bring elements of a common history (often of colonialism and imperialism), a feeling of potential mutual understanding when providing aid and can avoid some of the mistakes made in the past by Northern donors. However welcome their arrival on the aid scene may be, it is not without significant problems. New donors tend to be outside of the established norms and practices of older established donors (this is, of course, not negative per se), but as a result it remains difficult to establish what exactly is happening with this new aid; what its parameters are and what strings (or otherwise) might be attached. Just as many NGOs have been critical of the (mis) use of aid from the developed world, so too are they raising questions regarding the new donors. Their presence and potential impact has stimulated debate about both old and new issues in development co-operation – the place of geo-politics in aid; the place of commerce and resource extraction; human rights

observance, environmental issues and issues around transparency, accountability and monitoring.

For more information on South-South Development Cooperation, see Reality of Aid Network 2010 *South-South Development Cooperation: A challenge to the aid system?*

THE GROWTH OF PRIVATE AID

In 2006, US investor and businessman Warren Buffett announced that he was earmarking 85% of his wealth (about US$44 billion today) for 6 foundations – the single biggest known philanthropic gift. Since then the importance of private sector 'aid' has increased massively (some estimates suggest between a four and six-fold increase) to an estimated US$60 billion annually. Such aid includes not just gifts from philanthropists such as Bill and Melinda Gates but also funds from foundations, corporations, private voluntary organisations, universities, and religious groups (the latter having strong historical roots). The scale of such funding for human development is now very significant and geographically widely spread with

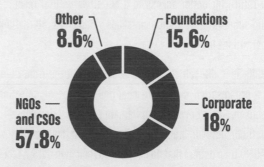

Largest source countries: US, UK, Germany, Canada, Australia and now also includes Brazil, South Africa, Thailand and China

Sources: *OECD DAC Development Cooperation Report 2015 and preliminary data 2016; Development Initiatives Investment to End Poverty 2013; Overseas Development Institute Financing Development Blog Series 2014; Center for Global Prosperity Index of Global Philanthropy and Remittances 2013; Reality of Aid Report 2014; Aidwatch 2014, Aid Beyond 2015, Concord*

CHINESE AID IS A LIGHTNING ROD FOR CRITICISM

China is fast becoming a major source of aid in Asia, Latin America and most notably Africa. Estimates vary as to how much aid China is actually giving but speculation places it between US$1 and US$2 billion with up to half going to Africa, although exact figures cannot be accessed.

China sees Africa as a growing market for its goods and in 2013, Chinese-African trade surpassed US$200 billion for the first time, making China Africa's biggest trading partner. An AFRODAD report points out that Chinese firms are building roads, rehabilitating infrastructure, and bringing in wireless communication systems where landlines have not worked, especially in rural areas.

In theory, Chinese aid comes with no political or economic strings attached, but with little transparency and accountability concerns about issues such as human rights, corruption and environmental responsibility are widespread. It's *'no questions asked'* aid policy makes Chinese aid very attractive to countries with unstable or undemocratic governments, most notably China's involvement in countries like Sudan and Zimbabwe. Critics say this strategy of not interfering in African domestic affairs is employed by China in return for better access to a country's natural resources and support for its stance on issues voted on at international institutions like the UN.

While it is difficult to explore exact aid figures from China, the organisation AidData (a coalition of three organisations focused on development finance) has developed a methodology for Tracking Under-Reported Financial Flows (TUFF) from donors that do not publish their own data. A recent AidData report argues that much of the controversy about Chinese 'aid' results from a failure to distinguish between China's Official Development Assistance (ODA) and more commercially-oriented sources and types of state financing. They conclude that the allocation of Chinese ODA is driven primarily by foreign policy considerations and findings do not

IN THEORY, CHINESE AID COMES WITH NO POLITICAL OR ECONOMIC STRINGS ATTACHED, BUT WITH LITTLE TRANSPARENCY AND ACCOUNTABILITY CONCERNS ABOUT ISSUES SUCH AS HUMAN RIGHTS, CORRUPTION AND ENVIRONMENTAL RESPONSIBILITY ARE WIDESPREAD.

support critics of China who claim its aid, in the strictest sense of the term (i.e., ODA), is predominantly motivated by natural resource acquisition interests. They conclude that Chinese aid allocation practices are not too dissimilar from those of Western donors.

AidData provides evidence that Beijing also considers humanitarian needs when making allocation decisions. They point out that Chinese ODA flows to Africa are strongly oriented towards poorer countries with the highest levels of Chinese official finance going to the Democratic Republic of Congo, Sudan and Ethiopia respectively. However, these countries, while undoubtedly some of the poorest in Africa, are viewed by many as unstable or corrupt; others argue that Chinese aid, directly or indirectly, fuels political violence and sustains pariah states in Africa, thus reinforcing poverty for the poorest people. As the debate continues, the counter-argument insists that none of this is new but reflects key aspects of aid as practiced by Northern donors traditionally.

For more, see African Forum and Network on Debt and Development, 2010 'Assessing the growing role and developmental impact of China in Africa: An African Perspective' in Reality of Aid Network *South-South Development Cooperation: A challenge to the aid system?* Dreher, Axel et al (2015) 'Apples and Dragon Fruits: The Determinants of Aid and Other Forms of State Financing from China to Africa'.

considerable impact (although difficult to measure). It has also begun to change the international aid landscape. Within this context, private aid from civil society groups and non-governmental organisations remains the largest component at an estimated 58% of total in 2011.

The discussion on why private aid has expanded so rapidly since the 1990s suggests a number of contexts – increasing globalisation expanding markets, influence and profits, the expansion of increasingly democratic governance (with a recognition of the value/need for a greater civil society voice) and information technology. A new generation of 'entrepreneurial' philanthropists has also emerged promoting a business model for international human development beyond economics. Alongside these trends, there is a growing scepticism and weariness with ODA and much of its bureaucracy and inefficiency. Finally, there has been an explosion of celebrity-led 'aid', human rights and development activity. Essentially, there is now a growing impatience with traditional models of aid.

However, there are also growing challenges associated with private aid including the need for greater transparency and accountability (individuals with vast fortunes to spend can have massive (and not always positive) impact; the need for enhanced information on such aid and its impact; the need to avoid increasing fragmentation and duplication of activity and the need for greater democratic control of such aid especially in recipient communities and locations (see, for example Development Initiatives Investment to End Poverty 2013).

CSOs, NGOs, INGOs AND AID

While official aid is by far the largest source of aid to developing countries, civil society continues to increase its involvement with human development internationally. The term includes a very broad range of organisations, networks, associations, interest groups and 'movements' that are independent of government. For example, it is now estimated that there are some 2 million NGOs in India and 1.5 million in the US. International NGOs (INGOs) now include some household names such as Oxfam, Greenpeace and Médecin Sans Frontières.

According to 2015 data from the OECD DAC, US$19.6 billion of official development assistance was allocated to and through civil society organisations by its members amounting to 11.6% of total gross ODA in 2013. In the same period, some 15.4% of total bilateral aid was channelled through these organisations (in addition, NGOs based in DAC member countries raised, at least, US$29.7 billion from private sources). There is considerable variation in the share of official aid that DAC members allocate this channel ranging from a high of 40% in Ireland to just 1% in France.

According to the Reality of Aid Report for 2014, civil society organisations (mainly but not exclusively from DAC countries) are now managing some US$65 billion in aid overall making them increasingly significant actors in development cooperation worldwide. Globally, the Center's estimate for total privately-raised CSO flows is US$48 billion, including US$366 million from philanthropists in Brazil, China, India and South Africa. A report from the Turkish aid agency TIKA, estimated that US$200 million was provided in aid through Turkish CSOs, mainly to Africa.

A particular concern in recent years as regards the work of CSOs and NGOs has been the 'securitisation' of aid in the wake of the 'war on terror' with increasing repression of civil society and a general deterioration in political, administrative and legal conditions for organisations. Under the guise of 'security, transparency and accountability', NGOs have experienced legal restraints on registration, restrictions on receipt of foreign funds, direct and indirect attacks on human rights' defenders plus increasingly limited access to policy discussions at governmental and regional level.

Studies show that most NGOs allocate aid and development funding largely according to the needs of their beneficiaries and poverty consistently appears as the main determinant of resource allocation. This contrasts with Official Development Assistance (ODA), which tends to be allocated according to political, economic and strategic considerations. In 1997 an OECD study concluded that 90% of all NGO projects achieved their immediate objectives and in 2003 a 25-year review of EU support to over 8,000 NGO projects found that 60% of projects were rated as either satisfactory or excellent. Despite this, many commentators make the valid point that the overall impact of the work of NGOs is really just a drop in the ocean by comparison with the scale and nature of the challenge.

On the role of NGOs in development, see Michael Edwards 2004 *Future Positive* (Polity Press), Roger Riddell 2005 *Does Aid Really Work* (Oxford University Press), Ian Smillie 1995 *The Alms Bazaar: Altruism Under Fire - Non-Profit Organisations and International Development* (ITDG Publishing, London) and Daniel Korten 1990 *Getting to the Twenty First Century: Voluntary Action and the Global Agenda* (Kumerian Press, Virginia).

DOES AID WORK: THE DEBATE RUMBLES ON...

Perhaps the central question in all discussions and debates about aid is whether or not it 'works' and what that phrase actually means. Is aid designed to stimulate economic growth or to tackle specific social issues; does it have long-term results or is it inevitably short term focused? Certainly the popular conversation on aid is now routinely divided into two polar opposite camps – the 'Yes, aid does work' and the 'No, it does not work'.

This debate led researchers Johnathan Glennie and Andy Sumner to undertake a review in 2014 of recent published literature on the evidence in the debate. The authors identify a number of challenges associated with assessing the impact of aid - causality (what claims can be made for aid itself given all the other influences and trends at work); what are the links between the micro-level where the impact of aid can be more easily measured and the macro-

level where this is much more difficult and how do we deal with bias in the studies undertaken given that most studies are carried out by 'aid agencies' of one type or another?

Overall, the authors conclude that the contribution of aid to overall development remains modest: *'The idea that aid 'works' can be questioned by interested parties, both informed and uninformed; assertions that aid is wholly or in part responsible for impressive improvements in human development in the past couple of decades are questionable. It is also not difficult to find examples where aid has been detrimental to countries and communities and where there may be trade-offs in terms of positive and negative impacts. More modesty is needed in any claims for how aid can contribute to development. However, the evidence... does suggest that aid has contributed in many countries and, despite its many flaws, can continue to do so' (2014:7).*

In the course of their review Glennie and Sumner note:

- The majority of (more recent) studies on aid are positive, but the impact of aid is often modest; the evidence at the moment places aid sceptics in the minority.

- As regards social development, while there are relatively few studies, those that focus, for example, on education, monetary poverty and health are generally positive in impact terms.

- The evidence suggests that the context in which aid works is crucial to its success or otherwise - the characteristics of the recipient country and its policies are important as are aid management issues (for both donor and recipient).

For more, see: The US$138.5 Billion Question: When Does Foreign Aid Work (and When Doesn't It)? Jonathan Glennie and Andy Sumner, Center for Global Development Policy Paper 049, November 2014.

READING

Bertrand Borg, Mary Rose Costello and Colm Regan (2010) *Debating Aid: a Development Education Resource*, 80:20 Educating and Acting for a Better World, Bray

Stephen Browne (2006) *Aid and Influence: Do Donors Help or Hinder?* Earthscan, London

Angus Deaton (2013) *The Great Escape: health, wealth, and the origins of inequality*, Princeton University Press, Oxford

Development Assistance Committee (2016) *Development Co-Operation Report*, Paris

William Easterley (2007) *The White Man's Burden*, Oxford University Press, Oxford

Jonathan Glennie and Andy Sumner (2014) *The $138.5 Billion Question: When Does Foreign Aid Work (and When Doesn't It)?*, Center for Global Development Policy Paper 49

Daniel Korten (1990) *Getting to the Twenty First Century: Voluntary Action and the Global Agenda*, Kumerian Press, Virginia

Reality of Aid Network (2016) *Reality of Aid Report*, Quezon City

Roger Riddell (2005) *Does Aid Really Work*, Oxford University Press, Oxford

Peter Singer (2015) *The Most Good You Can Do: How Effective Altruism Is Changing Ideas About Living Ethically*, Yale University Press, London

MORE INFORMATION AND DEBATE

www.oecd.org/dac – Development Assistance Committee of the OECD

www.realityofaid.org – main NGO site for analysis of aid issues

www.aidwatchers.com – The Aid Watch blog maintained by the Development Research Institute, New York University (contains the views of critic William Easterley)

www.concordeurope.org – European Confederation of NGOs for relief and development

www.guardian.co.uk/global-development – development section of the Guardian newspaper, London

https://www.odi.org/programmes/aid-public-expenditure – UK Overseas Development Institute themed section on aid and international development assistance issues

'...much that is written is not readily available or is presented in technical and academic language that does not speak to the lived situation of the reader. The real person...seems to disappear. Instead, we are left with concepts, ideas, statistics, theories and models, but we lose sight of the real human person that these are all about. As a result, we often put away the book or article, agreeing with all that it says, but not affected enough within ourselves to want to do something about changing things for the better...

The challenge for each one of us is: can I be satisfied that it should remain so? If not, then what am I going to do about it?'

MICHAEL J. KELLY, LUSAKA 2010

CHAPTER 15

'WE ARE ALL ACTIVISTS NOW'
MAKING CHANGE: IDEAS, EXPERIENCES AND ARGUMENTS

TONY DALY, GRACE McMANUS AND CIARA REGAN

This chapter seeks to explore some of the difficult questions of the nature of the world and our place in it – how as individuals and communities we fit into that world and how we define ourselves in relation to it. It seeks to stimulate refection – and ultimately action – in considered and appropriate ways.

Part one examines the arguments and debates about how change comes about, our roles and duties in such change processes at personal, professional and political levels. Part two presents a range of case studies making the argument that in our contemporary world, we are all activists now.

KEYWORDS:

ACTION; ACTIVISM TIMELINE; ANTI-SLAVERY MOVEMENT; 'BLOCKADIA'; CSR; HOW CHANGE HAPPENS; #ILLRIDEWITHYOU; PUBLIC JUDGEMENT; THEORIES OF CHANGE; WHY ACTIVISM

INTRODUCTION

Posing tough questions, as Michael J. Kelly does on the title page to this chapter, on the lived realities of '*the real person*' and thinking about how we might change this, and based on the cartoon from Martyn Turner opposite present fundamental questions for everyone. Given the character of our 80:20 world today, how do we understand that world, our place in it and our consequent duties? Are we satisfied with how things are and, if not, what can/should we do about it? For the majority of commentators today, activists and philosophers, these questions remain not just relevant but increasingly urgent given the challenges before us.

80-20 Development in an Unequal World is not simply about the details and dimensions of inequality and injustice in the world; it is not simply about arguments for and against particular theories or understandings of it; it is ultimately about the nature of that world and our place in it. It is about how we, as individuals and communities *fit* into that world and how we define ourselves in relation to it. It is about the fundamentally unjust character of our world and our connections to that absence of justice.

This chapter explores some of these difficult questions and seeks to stimulate reflection (and, ultimately action) in considered and appropriate ways. It examines the arguments and debates about how change comes about, our roles and duties in such change processes at personal, professional and political levels. It avoids prescribing a set of *correct* actions from whatever source – it seeks to stimulate reflection and debate on what *action* is, how it relates to each of us and what options or *duties* it places before us. It also seeks to make the argument that in the contemporary world *we are all activists now.*

Harking back to the evidence on human development today in chapter 1, the progress achieved in recent decades and the increasing challenges remaining, a series of questions inevitably arise:

- *Is this reality inevitable and unavoidable?*
- *Is it the result of factors beyond human intervention or control?*
- *Is it the result of purely domestic decisions and problems in developing countries?*
- *Is it our responsibility or concern or is it for others to engage with?*
- *Are the realities a matter for welfare and charity or are they issues of justice and duty?*
- *Are the problems and challenges an intrinsic part of modern corporate-driven globalisation or a by-product?*
- *Are they simply a legacy of the past, of slavery or colonialism?*
- *Are they the outcome of a profoundly unjust and unfair international system that condemns the many and favours the few?*
- *Who is responsible and who should be held accountable?*

How each of us understands and responds to these questions has profound implications for our concept of change (and the scale of change) and our role in such change. One conclusion that is unavoidable is that change is inevitable; things never remain the same but are constantly being re-shaped and re-formed. This chapter explores different understandings of change and the degree of challenge they present; it explores some of the key components of the change process itself and it reviews and debates the nature of 'activism' in the contemporary world.

When confronted with the scale of the change needed or proposed, most of us feel overwhelmed and confused, doubting the possibility of real change or the potential impact of individuals and groups. In this context it may be worth considering the perspective on the campaign against slavery offered by one of its pre-eminent historians, Adam Hochschild:

'If you had proposed, in the London of early 1787, to change all of this, nine out of ten people would have laughed you off as a crackpot. The 10th might have admitted that slavery was unpleasant but said that to end it would wreck the British Empire's economy. It would be as if, today, you maintained that the automobile must go. One in ten listeners might agree that the world would be better off if we travelled instead by foot, bicycle, electric train, or trolley, but are you suggesting a political movement to ban cars? Come on, be serious! Looking back, however, what is even more surprising than slavery's scope is how swiftly it died. By the end of the 19th century, slavery was, at least on paper, outlawed almost everywhere. Every American schoolchild learns about the Underground Railroad and the Emancipation Proclamation. But our self-centred textbooks often skip over the fact that in the superpower of the time slavery ended a full quarter-century earlier. For more than two decades before the Civil War, the holiday celebrated most fervently by free blacks in the American North was not July 4 (when they were at risk of attack from drunken white mobs) but August 1, Emancipation Day in the British Empire.'

Adam Hochschild (January/February 2004) *Against All Odds*,
Mother Jones, California

ARGUING ABOUT CHANGE – 5 DIVERGENT APPROACHES

Broadly speaking, it is possible to identify five approaches to change within the context of human development prescriptions today; these are briefly explored below and include:

- That of the World Bank and of those who argue that change can and should be accommodated within the current dominant economic and political system.

- Those, such as Professor Jeffrey Sachs, who argue that radical and urgent reform is necessary and immediately possible at a variety of levels but largely within the current economic and political system.

- Those, such as Peter Singer, who support far-reaching action at individual and collective level – action which would radically transform the current economic system.

- Those, such as Thomas Pogge, who emphasise a 'rights perspective' and the need to immediately transform structures and processes that harm the world's poor.

- Those, such as Indian activist and environmentalist Vandana Shiva, who reject the current economic and political model of development, describing it as a 'war' on the planet and who advocate alternatives such as Earth Democracy.

For many, the changes required in order to deliver a more equal and just world are essentially incremental and supportive of the current economic and political world order, although with a focus on degrees of urgent reform. For example, the World Bank's World Development Report 2010 outlines the case for integrating development and climate concerns without fundamentally challenging or damaging the current international trade regime (World Development Report 2010: 251-255). The World Development Report from 2009 talks of countries 'lagging behind' and of the need for greater 'integration' of poorer countries into world markets (see chapter 9 of the Report for example). However, in a 2016 study published by the Bank, *Shockwaves: Managing the Impacts of Climate Change on Poverty*, a more radical set of measures are proposed by the authors in terms of directly addressing both poverty and climate change.

In a similar vein, the Adam Smith Institute continues the argument insisting that *'free markets'* are the only viable engine of growth and that state regulation is anathema to development.[1] Many of these arguments are also echoed in Professor Paul Collier's *The Bottom Billion: Why the Poorest Countries are Failing and What Can Be Done About It* (2007) in which he examines four key development traps – conflict, resources; being landlocked and having bad governance. Collier argues for a series of solutions including free trade with preferential access for the exports of 'bottom billion' countries while also arguing against, what he terms, the 'headless heart' approach to change. As with all of those summarised in this section, Collier's views have been the subject of debate and criticism; see, for example Michael Clemens's article *Smart Samaritans* in the magazine Foreign Affairs (September/October 2007) or Erik S. Reinert's book review '*The Bottom Billion': Defending neoliberalist shock therapy* on Pambazuka News (2011).

In recent years, one of the most cited arguments for what needs to change and for what can readily change has come from Professor Jeffrey Sachs (Director of the Earth Institute at Columbia University and closely associated with the UN MDG agenda and Sustainable Development Solutions Network) who has identified four great challenges – environment, demography, poverty and global politics and has championed a change agenda on world poverty and sustainable development.

---

1 For example, see the Institute's briefing papers by Marc Sidwell (2008) Unfair Trade; Sam Bowman (April, 2010)'An international development policy that works' and Dalibor Roháč (May, 2011) 'Does inequality matter?'

In *Commonwealth: Economics for a Crowded Planet* (2008), he insists that the *'relentless acceptance of the status quo is not acceptable in the face of the challenges we confront'* and critiques a negativism based on a *'state of mind, not a view based on facts'*. In a chapter entitled *'The Power of One'*, he outlines (following the arguments of economist Albert Hirschman) an *'unholy trinity'* of reaction to the possibility of radical change:

- Futility: the course of reform cannot work because the problem is insoluble.
- Perversity: attempting to solve the problem will actually make matters worse.
- Jeopardy: attempting to solve the problem will take attention and resources away from something even more important.

In rejecting these 'resistances', he insists on the responsibility of individuals and offers an agenda of change focused around learning, interculturalism, social action and engaging at the personal, professional and political level. Sach's analysis and interventions have been the subject of much debate and criticism (see, for example the reviews of Sach's book *The End of Poverty, Economic Possibilities of Our Time* by William Easterley in the Washington Post and by Professor Michael Blim in the journal Logos in 2006) yet his agenda for change, especially in the context of the SDGs, remains persuasive and highly influential.

Taking the argument one stage further, one of the most controversial commentators on wealth and poverty in the world and the responsibilities of each *individual* is Australian philosopher Peter Singer, whose views have already been analysed in chapter 5. Singer's conclusions regarding our responsibility as individuals to effect change in the world are far-reaching and startling; he concludes that we do have a *duty* to respond to human suffering in the world for a variety of reasons – such suffering is evil; people *must* respond to relieve it whenever they are in a position to do so (and it is morally wrong not to do so) and affluence places very considerable demands on the affluent. In a well-known article in the New York Times in September 1999, Singer argued:

> *'In the world as it is now, I can see no escape from the conclusion that each one of us with wealth surplus to his or her essential needs should be giving most of it to help people suffering from poverty so dire as to be life-threatening. That's right: I'm saying that you shouldn't buy that new car, take that cruise, redecorate the house or get that pricey new suit. After all, a $1,000 suit could save five children's lives...*

> *...If we don't do it, then we should at least know that we are failing to live a morally decent life - not because it is good to wallow in guilt but because knowing where we should be going is the first step toward heading in that direction.'*

Singer's arguments on the moral obligations of affluence and on the options open to affluent individuals are developed more fully in his 2009 book *The Life You Can Save: Acting Now to End World Poverty* (an argument extended further in his 2015 book *The Most Good You Can Do: How Effective Altruism Is Changing Ideas About Living Ethically*, published by Yale University Press). His arguments have been the subject of much debate and criticism on a number of grounds – such as overstating the responsibility and potential of individuals; overstating obligations to those we do not know or who live distantly and offering an 'extreme' scenario in terms of how far one's obligations to others go. As noted in chapter 7, an extended critique of Singer's position is offered by Gareth Cullity in his 2004 work *The Moral Demands of Affluence*.

At a *community* level, commentators have advocated for economic system changes for many decades. More recently, commentators such as Naomi Klein, Jason Hickel, Arturo Escobar and Noam Chomsky have challenged dominant models of progress and development that undermine democracy, such as 'globalisation', and looked for alternative methods, tools, critiques and ways of reading the world to, ultimately, change it. By consolidating alternative approaches, these advocates have argued that communities should look to build enough pressure and civil unrest on the centres of wealth and power, whether the state, a company, or another institution, so that they are compelled to respond. Commenting on social change in the US in 2013, Chomsky argued:

> 'Some things are going on quietly in the country which potentially have revolutionary implications such as the growth and development of co-operatives, the worker-owned enterprises, for example. It's not on a huge scale but it's on a significant scale and is spreading. Those could be the germs of a new society; a very different society that undermines capitalist economic and social relations. On all sorts of fronts there are things that can be done and sometimes they are successful.'

Arguments about the compelling need for fundamental change are taken a significant step further by philosopher Thomas Pogge of Yale University (and co-founder of Academics Stand Against Poverty) who asserts that people in wealthy Western democracies are currently simply not doing enough to tackle poverty but are actually harming the world's poor through support for, and participation in, the current dominant economic and political system. The world's poor are being actively and unjustly harmed by an international system of political and economic policies and practices that are disproportionately shaped by and for wealthy Western societies (see chapter 5 for his discussion of the nature of 'radical inequality'). His analysis suggests that not only is individual charitable action required, but so too is individual and collective political action to address this international system of harm.

For Pogge, eliminating poverty is easily achieved – in a 2007 essay, he observed:

> 'The collective annual consumption of the 2,735 million people reportedly living (on average 42%) below the World Bank's \$2/day poverty line is about \$440 billion and their collective shortfall from that poverty line roughly \$330 billion per year. This poverty gap is less than 1% of the gross national incomes of the high-income countries, which sum to \$35,142 billion in 2005 (World Bank 2006: 289). These countries contain 15.7% of the world's population with 79% of the global product. The global poor are 42% of the world's population with 1% of the global product. At market exchange rates, the per capita income of the former is roughly 200 times greater than that of the latter... Eradicating severe poverty (relative to the \$2/day poverty line) is a matter of raising the income of the poor from currently 2.3% of the average human income to 4%.'

Thomas Pogge (2007) *Poverty and Human Rights*, UN Office of the United Nations High Commissioner for Human Rights

When confronted with such facts, citizens of the rich countries should recognise that we, the world's affluent, should (and could) do a lot more to help the poor. For Pogge, the issue is that the majority in the West continue to see this as a '*demand of humanity or charity – not as a demand of justice*' and certainly not as a moral and political '*duty*' imposed on us by our acceptance of the principle of human rights. Pogge argues that '*...the rich countries' response to world poverty is mainly rhetorical...and even the rhetoric is appalling*' and insists that we have both negative duties (to not do '*harm*') but also positive duties (to ensure the rights of others). He rejects western arguments of '*innocence*' and '*powerlessness*' when faced with the current international system and argues that the benefits and advantages western populations (and, by implication, developing world elites) gain from this system must be fundamentally challenged, as a matter of fulfilling our human rights obligations.

Pogge's analysis has been criticised on a number of

grounds – that the current world order is *'imperfect'* rather than *'unjust'* (as asserted by Pogge); that his definition of *'harm'* in relation to the poor is overstated; that the scale of demands his analysis places on individuals as regards positive duties are too high (or low); which causal factors should receive greatest weight (and who decides this) and that his proposals are unworkable. For an extended discussion of Pogge's work (and his robust response), see Alison Jaggar (2010, ed.) *Thomas Pogge and his Critics*, Cambridge, Polity Press.

One of the most far-reaching analyses of the change that is required has come from the creator of the concept of Earth Democracy, Indian environmental activist and eco-feminist, Vandana Shiva, who argues that the current international economic, political and social system amounts to little more than *'a war against the planet'*. For Shiva, this war is rooted in an economy that fails to respect either *'ecological or ethical limits'* – limits to inequality, limits to injustice, limits to greed and economic concentration. In her speech on receipt of the Sydney Peace Prize in 2010, she argued:

> *'A handful of corporations and of powerful countries seeks to control the earth's resources and transform the planet into a supermarket in which everything is for sale. They want to sell our water, genes, cells, organs, knowledge, cultures and future.'*

Shiva highlights three levels of violence that characterise non-sustainable development – the first is the violence against the earth, which manifests itself as the ecological crisis; the second is the violence against people, which is expressed as poverty, destitution and displacement. The third is the violence of war and conflict, as the powerful reach for the resources that lie in other communities and countries for their limitless appetites. The richer the world becomes, the poorer we are ecologically and culturally; the growth of affluence, measured in money, is leading to a growth in poverty at *'the material, cultural, ecological and spiritual levels'*.

Respecting the earth and essentially *'making peace'* with the earth was, for Shiva, always an ethical and ecological imperative but today it has become *'a survival imperative for our species'*, as she chillingly comments *'…dead soils and dead rivers cannot give food and water'*. In her book *Earth Democracy: Justice, Sustainability and Peace* (2005), she argues against what she describes as our increasing *'monoculture of the mind'* where both our society and our science and technology force us to think and act in one frame of reference only and where we have a growing *'inability to appreciate diversity'* to our own disadvantage but also that of millions of the poor and of the earth itself. She argues that we *'must change the paradigm of who we are'* because we are effectively *'shrinking citizenship'* by disenfranchising vast groups of people and perpetuating injustice.[2]

As is clear from the brief reviews above, the debates about change worldwide are not simply about deciding which particular economic, social or political (or technical) response will address the problem. The debates are concerned about the nature, scale, and the *'fundamentals'* of the issue. As Amartya Sen argues: the *'atrocity of poverty'* will not correct itself:

> *'Quiet acceptance – by the victims and by others – of the inability of a great many people to achieve minimally effective capabilities and to have basic substantive freedoms acts as huge barrier to social change. And so does the absence of public outrage at the terrible helplessness of millions of people…We have to see how the actions and inactions of a great many persons together lead to this social evil, and how a change of our priorities – our policies, our institutions, our individual and joint actions – can help to eliminate the atrocity of poverty.'*

> Amartya Sen (2008) Preface in D. Green *From Poverty to Power*, Oxfam International

---

2 In this context also see UNDP Speech by Ela Bhatt June 27, 2011 Tarrytown, NY

UNDERSTANDING CHANGE

Blending practical experiences and activism with insight and analysis from research in many disciplines, Duncan Green (of Oxfam) has explored some of the key elements and lessons on how change happens in a recent book. Green's analysis assesses international experience and ideas on the change process in the context of promoting progressive change. What follows is a brief summary of some of his key arguments – it offers one effective 'guide' to the change process.

In thinking about change, Green argues that we need to focus on three key core issues:

1. SYSTEMS, POWER AND SOCIAL BEHAVIOUR

Systems

Ways of thinking are helpful when discussing change; thinking about complex systems, power and social norms helps us understand how and why change happens. Human systems are complex and cannot be reduced to 'cause and effect' simplicity. Change in complex systems occurs in slow steady processes (such as demographic or technological shifts), punctuated by sudden, unforeseeable jumps (such as crises, conflicts, failures and scandals).

Power

Power is central to change and will always face resistance at three levels – institutions, ideas and interests. Understanding this is essential in trying to influence change as it can help identify potential allies. Too often, activists default to working with 'people like us', ignoring new potential alliances with, for example, corporations, traditional leaders, faith groups, academics.

Social Norms

Change often begins at a deeper level 'within' as people organise for basic needs and rights, often inspired by profound shifts in social ideas and behaviour e.g. understandings of the rights of marginalised groups, including women, children or people with disabilities, hence the importance of such issues/campaigns for activism.

'...HISTORY SHOWS US THAT THE STATUS QUO IS FAR LESS FIXED THAN IT APPEARS...'

2. INSTITUTIONS

Understanding how institutions work; their history, politics and internal structures can be the key for activists as they are routinely not immune to change.

States

States are central as drivers of change; they constantly change as conflict, bargaining and power relations impact on them. In recent years, non-violent civic coalitions have been significant. Since the 1980s, waves of civil society protest have contributed to the overthrow of military governments, the downfall of Communist and authoritarian regimes, the removal of dictators, the end of apartheid, and the upheavals of the Arab Spring. Their tactics have included boycotts, mass protests, blockades, strikes, and civil disobedience.

The Law

The law – courts, police services, customary and international law - is often underestimated by activists; the law also changes, not only are old laws replaced by new, but the interpretation of laws evolves, often promoting human rights and equality and addressing privilege and discrimination.

Political Parties and the Media

Political parties, the media, and 'accountability' initiatives are other checks and balances that offer opportunities for activists.

'...MANY OF THE MOST PRESSING CHALLENGES FACING HUMANITY ARE 'COLLECTIVE ACTION PROBLEMS' THAT CANNOT BE SOLVED BY SINGLE COUNTRIES ALONE...'

The International System

The international system is a success story; each day sees extensive interchange between nation states under a fairly loose system of governance – norms, rules, procedures and institutions – without any recognised world government. This system has a critical role in shaping society's norms and beliefs. As many of the most pressing challenges facing humanity are 'collective action problems', they cannot be solved by single countries alone.

Transnational Corporations (TNCs)

Activists try to influence TNCs with strategies that run from cooperation to confrontation; NGOs sit with corporate executives, academics and government officials on problems like climate change or food security. Activists also use litigation or public shaming to oblige governments to act. Understanding the traditions and mindsets of TNCs and the variety of ways they can be influenced is important for change.

3. THE ROLE OF ACTIVISM

Citizen Activism and Civil Society

Citizen activism is important as it includes political activism alongside any action with social consequences – collective activity, participation in faith groups or neighbourhood associations, producer organisations and trade unions, village savings and loan groups and funeral societies.

Most day-to-day efforts of citizens' associations are more mundane than the overthrow of governments, but they are equally important. Factory workers, state employees and small-scale farmers have organised to build bargaining power. Trade unions, producer associations, cooperatives, small business associations and the like can win fairer wages, prices or working conditions; many take up lobbying for state regulation or other measures to limit the excessive but hidden power of vested interests.

Leaders and Leadership

From the village committee or women's savings group to great nation-builders, leaders reinforce group identity and cohesion and mobilise collective effort toward shared goals. Grassroots leaders are often shaped by experiences of travel, struggle and conflict, and are thrust forward by the historical moment while many are inspired by faith.

Advocacy

When it comes to campaigning, the playbook was pretty much written two centuries ago, by the campaign to end slavery; the abolitionists invented virtually every modern campaign tactic, including posters, political book tours, consumer boycotts, investigative reporting and petitions.

Critical junctures, coalitions and alliances

Critical junctures – windows of opportunity created by failures, crises, changes in leadership, natural disasters or conflicts, play a major role in advocacy and change processes. One of the skills of a good advocate is knowing how to construct effective alliances – and to distinguish powerful engines of change; bringing together 'unusual suspects' is fast becoming a core skill for activists.

For more see: Duncan Green (2016) How Change Happens, Oxford University Press

---

'DESPITE SETBACKS AND THE GRIM FILTER OF THE EVENING NEWS, THAT STORY IS OVERWHELMINGLY POSITIVE. THE EXPANSION OF THOSE FREEDOMS OVER THE LAST CENTURY HAS BEEN UNPRECEDENTED: MILLIONS, EVEN BILLIONS OF HUMAN BEINGS LEADING HEALTHIER, BETTER EDUCATED LIVES, FREEING THEMSELVES FROM POVERTY AND HUNGER, EXPANDING THEIR RIGHTS, LIVING RICHER, MORE REWARDING LIVES. FOR ME, NOTHING GIVES LIFE MORE MEANING THAN BEING AN ACTIVIST, DOING WHAT WE CAN TO SUPPORT THAT HISTORIC STRUGGLE.' (P.258)

PUBLIC JUDGEMENT AND CHANGE

As noted by many commentators on change processes (such as Amartya Sen or Duncan Green earlier in the chapter), one key element in the mix is that of public perceptions, beliefs and knowledge – Sen particularly highlights the *'lack of public outrage'* at the plight of millions worldwide in addition to the impact of public action (and inaction). This issue of how the public becomes aware of issues such as human development challenges; how it comes to public judgement on them and how public resistances play a key role has been analysed in detail over many years by US commentator Daniel Yankelovich.

It appears to be a truism that if 'better off' people knew more about how, for example, the poor suffer, they would develop the public outrage sought by Sen. However, in terms of engaging with key social issues, Yankelovitch notes that people come to such questions with *'...a lifetime of prejudice, convictions, personal experience, information and misinformation...'*, all of which often lead to a set of *'resistances'* that information and facts alone (especially those coming from the 'top downwards') cannot address. These 'resistances' include public preoccupation with a variety of more dominant domestic issues such as suspicion of leaders' priorities and motives and the perception or conviction that money is being wasted. Simply informing people through emphasising the facts of any given situation is, for Yankelovich and others insufficient.

In a 2010 book *Towards Wiser Public Judgement*, Yankelovich and Friedman observe (page 15): *'To assume that public opinion is invariably improved by inundating people with information grossly exaggerates the role of information and underestimates the importance of values and emotions.'*

CONSCIOUSNESS RAISING

...largely media-driven, and news events are a major factor in expediting the process...

1 **Awareness** – becoming aware that an issue deserves public attention

2 **A Sense of Urgency** – recognition that an issue or challenge needs to be addressed as a matter of some urgency

WORKING THROUGH

...largely a social process as individuals work problems through in discussion with others until they ultimately achieve resolution for themselves...

3 **Reaction** – once people come to feel that a problem is urgent, they want to hear about possible solutions; this step begins once people begin to react to proposed solutions

4 **Resistance** – a critical moment and one that is often least understood. Only when people have been exposed to specific policy ideas are their emotional resistances engaged with effectively; this step is one where individuals, groups and communities as well as countries confront and try to work through 'resistance'

5 **A Sense of Urgency** – recognition that an issue or challenge needs to be addressed as a matter of some urgency

RESOLUTION

...people sign on, having 'worked through' both their emotional resistances and the cognitive weighing of pros and cons... People choose a course of action and are prepared to accept its likely consequences...

6 **Cognitive stand** – after 'choicework' people usually reach tentative conclusions, largely cognitive (own reasoning and thinking) in character

7 **Judgement** – in this final moment people add strong elements of emotional and moral conviction to their cognitive conclusions

In the latter context, they argue that it is necessary to provide positive reasons for wanting, for example, aid to continue and to succeed; to argue a combination of national and personal interest reasons as well as altruism (e.g. mutual well-being, the security of future generations and of the planet – *regardless of location, we are all in this together*' etc.). Changing models of communication becomes hugely important, not bombarding people with facts devoid of context or linkages; linking local and global challenges and avoiding much of the jargon and elitist language of development, human rights, environmentalism etc. and nurturing public dialogue are vital.

Yankelovich offers a framework for public judgement – a typology of learning 'moments' in the journey to judgement. Moving through these steps can take time - weeks, months, even decades but it can also be catapulted onwards by events and is also dependent in part on our actions and strategies.

PUBLIC JUDGEMENT: SOME KEY ELEMENTS AND LEARNING FROM EXPERIENCE

Time Variability: the environmental movement made significant progress after a period of some 30 years of consciousness-raising but, for HIV and AIDS, the process took less than a decade. North-South charity dates from the days of the anti-slavery movement, some 200 years ago, and has gone through various phases e.g. 'starving babies' (hunger emergencies), the Congo a century ago, China half a century ago, in Biafra, Ethiopia, Somalia etc. – 'little seems to have changed'.

While the broader international development movement is much younger – roughly 50 years – it is old enough to have made more headway than has been the case.

Publicity: in order to arouse concern for action people must be aware of an issue – messages must be clear and unambiguous, and quantity is an essential feature, both in getting the message across and in reinforcing it. Publicity needs many dimensions and strategies and not just one that is 'top down'.

Where quantity is concerned, public messages on development are virtually non-existent compared with the bad news provided by the media and the frequently self-serving PR and fund-raising of NGOs (and governments) - there are alternatives (see the Dóchas World's Best News project www.dochas.ie/our-work/worlds-best-news).

Credibility: lack of credibility is a serious impediment. A great many opinion polls show that governments have especially low credibility where development assistance is concerned - the public just doesn't believe what they are told and for good reason.

Although NGOs survive on public donations, the giving public is not the same as the entire public. Questions about credibility of NGOs as a source of information show that they too can have credibility problems.

 The Cogency or Power of Events: 'Nothing advances consciousness-raising as powerfully as events that dramatise the issue.' All too often, the events that dramatise development are usually portrayed in the media as a series of disconnected tragedies, having little to do with each other or with North–South relations. 'Blame' is apportioned to mismanagement, corruption or 'natural' events.

This has led to 'simplistic' and often wholly inappropriate 'solutions' and temporary measures – unpredictable aid programmes, peacekeeping, volunteerism and charity alone.

 Perceived Relevance to Self: the women's movement has proved itself to have direct relevance to the large majority of people worldwide - people understand it in clear, personal terms. In the case of HIV and AIDS and some environmental issues, personal relevance has been fundamental to a readiness to grapple with solutions.

While sometimes development is marketed in 'self-interest' terms or from that of a 'global village' (a dangerous term?) yet it remains distant in the lives of most people in rich developed countries.

 Concreteness and Clarity: development messages from the media, from NGOs and from government agencies are confusing, self-serving, contradictory, and, more often than not, negative.

Although Yankelovitch is writing about public understanding of global warming, his argument resonates on development – 'An inherently abstract and difficult issue has been made even more difficult by treating it in a fragmented way with confusing and misleading semantics.'

Sources: Daniel Yankelovich (1991) *Coming to Public Judgement: Making Democracy Work in a Complex World,* Syracuse University Press; Yankelovich, D. and W. Friedman (2010) *Toward Wiser Public Judgement,* Nashville, Vanderbilt University Press; Colm Regan and Scott Sinclair (2005) *Engaging Development - learning for a better future,* 80:20 Development in an Equal World 5th Edition, 80:20 Educating and Acting for a Better World, Bray and Tony Daly, Ciara Regan and Colm Regan (2015) *Doing Development Education: ideas and resources - a starter guide,* www.develpmenteducation.ie

'WE ARE ALL ACTIVISTS NOW...'

From quick actions such as recycling and ethical shopping to mass protests on the world's streets; from supporting a women's rights issue to joining the environmental movement; from making a personal choice on an important issue to publicly advocating on that issue - having an ethical conscience or perspective is becoming part of our daily lives. Even when choosing not to discuss or act, in choosing *not to become involved*, we are making choices.

In an era of changes in climate, of corporate-led globalisation and consumerism, of ongoing and (regionally) bloody conflicts, of forced migration and the rise of intolerance, it is well-nigh impossible to declare 'neutrality'. US writer and film maker Susan Sontag argues that *'no one after a certain age has the right to this kind of innocence, of superficiality, to this degree of ignorance, or amnesia.'* In each region of the world, individuals and communities face a range of challenges some of which are specifically 'local' or 'regional' while others are part of a series of larger, international challenges which need to be faced collectively.

Traditional understandings and definitions of activism tend to emphasise particular forms of activism such as writing letters to newspapers or to politicians, political campaigning, engaging in rallies, marches, strikes, sit ins or joining movements, organisations or political parties. It can include economic activism such as taking part in boycotts or opting to support 'ethical' companies or pension providers. Consumer action has always been an important component of activism but has increased in importance in recent decades.

The emergence of social media has impacted significantly on activism, on the role of the individual and increasingly on business and the state. Mass (and significantly unrestricted) communications have enabled millions of individuals to engage with issues at a very 'personal' yet 'public' level. Writing in the Huffington Post in August 2012, Mark Pfeifle commented on social media's role:

> 'People are using social media to hunt down war criminals, win the White House, defeat an American House Speaker, change banking regulations, and overthrow dictators in Libya, Egypt and Yemen. In each instance, it was social media that facilitated broad-based social activism and empowered the aspirations of millions. Its power has just begun to be tested, but the evidence so far indicates that social media has successfully re-invented social activism.'

Apart from social media, recent decades have also witnessed the international growth of altruism of various types to accompany an expanding 'world view'; these trends have been analysed in some detail recently by Peter Singer in his 2015 book *The Most Good You Can Do: How Effective Altruism Is Changing Ideas About Living Ethically* - see especially chapter 2. Singer concludes:

> 'Effective altruism is an advance in ethical behaviour as well as in the practical application of our ability to reason. I have described it as an emerging movement, and that term suggests that it will continue to develop and spread.' (2015:181)

More recently, Duncan Green reflects on the role of activists as follows:

> 'Progressive change is not primarily about 'us' activists: it occurs when poor people and communities take power into their own hands; shifts in technology, prices, demography and sheer accident can be far more important than the actions of would-be change agents.
>
> That said, activists do play a crucial role. We put new questions into the endlessly churning stream of public debate, and we can help those on the sharp end raise their voices, shifting some degree of power from those who have too much to those who have too little.'

POVERTY, HUNGER, INEQUALITY, SUSTAINABILITY – 10 ARGUMENTS ON WHY WE SHOULD BOTHER

1 **FOR ECONOMIC REASONS** – our current model of economic development is not sustainable; it places little or no value on nature and its bounty; it takes nature for granted and assumes its renewability; it takes little account of 'blowback'; it values short-termism and sees the bigger challenges as the responsibility of others; does not contemplate long-term 'economic' security and it equates the economy with the society and with nature.

2 **FOR POLITICAL REASONS** – current development denies too many, too much; it routinely blames the victim for their condition; it is based on elite capture of resources and opportunities; it puts huge numbers of people at risk; it increases the cost of containing violence and of policing the world; it is anti-democratic and therefore is a threat to overall human security.

3 **FOR ECOLOGICAL REASONS** – the planet is incapable of sustaining ever-expanding growth; we have already over-used our resources base; the renewability of nature annually is now at fundamental risk; we have intergenerational obligations to those following; we have a duty to pass the planet on with enough for all and in as good a condition as we received it.

4 **FOR HUMAN RIGHTS REASONS** – if human rights have any meaning they must have meaning and impact for all, not just for some; otherwise, there are no human rights with inevitable consequences for each and every one of us; denying the rights of some (selected) people based on race, disability, gender or sexual orientation, culture, beliefs etc. means that all human rights can be denied and that discrimination is acceptable.

5 **FOR MORAL AND ETHICAL REASONS** – the human consequences of current development models are immense and the suffering of those excluded intense; concepts such as dignity (and indignity), welfare (and ill-fare), well-being (and ill-being), security (and insecurity) demand a response from each of us as thinking and feeling human beings; to deny the needless suffering of huge numbers of people undermines the idea of humanity itself, the idea of human development and human flourishing.

6 **FOR SOCIAL AND CULTURAL REASONS** – current and projected demographic trends imply internationalisation; communications, travel and media generate multiculturalism and interculturalism; living in a 'mono-culture' is not feasible given the nature of our own societal needs; valuing and respecting diversity makes us richer at every level and embraces the inevitability of change; this enriches all our lives.

7 **FOR HUMAN SECURITY REASONS** – the constant making and remaking of the world cannot simply be based on enforcement; the price of exclusion and subordination is far too high; militarisation threatens every one; protecting the wealth and privilege of some through force leaves all at risk; the exclusion of millions offers the continuing prospect of violence; when people have no reasonable alternative we are all left insecure and fearful.

8 **FOR EDUCATIONAL AND JUDGEMENT REASONS** – we are thinking and emotional beings capable of reasoning and acting reasonably; our own innate humanity explores, questions, probes and seeks questions and answers; a response to despondency and despair is vital; we need to build public awareness and public judgement around a host of challenges; our emotional intelligence needs to challenge our 'emotional resistance'; making sense of ourselves and our place in the world.

9 **FOR REASONS OF INEVITABLE CHANGE** – change is ongoing and unavoidable; small and large scale change has and will happen; things have changed and, routinely, for the better; struggles can be won and lost; much change is now global with massive local implications; we are all implicated in change and need to face the question 'what kind of change'?

10 **AND, FINALLY BECAUSE IT IS THE RIGHT AND JUST THING TO DO**

POVERTY HUNGER INEQUALITY SUSTAINABILITY

A TIMELINE OF **ACTIVISM**

LAW 1: An object at rest will remain at rest, and an object in motion will remain in motion with the same speed and direction unless it is compelled to change that state by external forces impressed on it.

LAW 2: The time taken to change the momentum of an object is equal to the force acting on the object. The greater the mass (of the object being changed) the greater the amount of force needed to accelerate the object.

LAW 3: For every action, there is an equal and opposite reaction.

NEWTON'S LAWS OF MOTION*

This timeline highlights selected actions for change from a variety of contexts worldwide. Sometimes, change can take decades; other times just minutes. Most change occurs locally but, as the clamour for change grows, it often spills across borders as it links with other actions and movements.

LAST 60 YEARS

1960s

THE ACTIVISM OF STEVE BIKO

In the 1960s Steve Biko helped to found the South African Students Organisation and would be made president by 1968. The SASO would eventually evolve into the Black Consciousness Movement which promoted a new identity and politics of racial solidarity.

1962

SILENT SPRING

Rachel Carson wrote the book that launched a global environmental movement by documenting what then seemed like massive declines in bird populations. The silence Carson referred to came from fewer birds singing due to the negative effects of pesticides like DDT on bird populations.

1965

SELMA TO MONTGOMERY FREEDOM MARCHES

Sunday, March 7th, 600 people attempted a freedom march after the shooting dead of a young African-American while demonstrating against the opposition to black voter registration. Multiple attempts to march were met with violent resistance by state and local authorities. Protesters finally completed their march under protection of National Guard troops. It took 3 days to walk the 54 miles to Montgomery to raise awareness of the difficulties faced by black voters in the South, and the need for a Voting Rights Act, subsequently passed later that year.

1968

POLITICAL ACTIVISM AT THE OLYMPICS

At the Mexico City Games, US athletes Tommie Smith and John Carlos were expelled for giving 'Black Power' salutes on the winners podium. In an interview 40 years after, John Carlos told the Guardian *'I had a moral obligation to step up. Morality was a far greater force than the rules and regulations they had.'* The image of the two athletes raising their fists became one of the most iconic of the Civil Rights Movement and Olympic history.

1972

REGISTRATION OF THE SELF EMPLOYED WOMEN'S ASSOCIATION

The Self Employed Women's Association (SEWA) is a trade union movement which pioneered the empowerment of self-employed women and of women employed in informal economy enterprises (small, unregistered enterprises) and informal economy jobs (no secure contracts, worker benefits or social protection) where 93% of India's female labour force is employed. Membership now spans more than 1.75 million women in 12 states, 50 districts and 700 villages with 66% originating from rural areas.

1974

WANGARI MAATHAI PLANTS HER FIRST TREE

Founder of the environmental conservation Green Belt Movement, Wangari Maathai plants her first tree in 1974 in Kenya.

1976

THE GRAMEEN BANK PROJECT

In 1976, Muhammed Yunaus founded the Grameen Bank following an action research project to examine the possibility of designing a delivery system to provide banking services to the rural poor. In October 1983, the Grameen Bank project was transformed into an independent bank by government legislation. Borrowers of the Bank own 90% if its shares, while 10% is owned by the government.

1984

FREE NELSON MANDELA

Influenced by South African music with upbeat, ska rhythm melodies, the song "Free Nelson Mandela" is launched by UK band The Specials. Against the backdrop of the international sports, cultural and academic boycott of South Africa, the song scored well in the music charts, prompting a whole generation to become aware of the horrors of apartheid.

*ON LOAN TO ACTIVISTS AS THREE POSSIBLE LAWS FOR ACHIEVING SOCIAL CHANGE.

1977
NESTLÉ BOYCOTT

This campaign began in response to Nestlé's 'aggressive marketing' of breast milk substitutes especially in developing countries. Organisations such as International Baby Food Action Network (IBFAN) echo the arguments of the WHO and UNICEF who encourage the practice of breast feeding and oppose the idealisation of infant formula in many advertising campaigns. The boycott has been cancelled and renewed on the basis of reports on actual Nestlé practises and continues to this day.

1977
THE MOTHERS OF THE PLAZA de MAYO

During the military dictatorship in Argentina from 1976 to 1983, many people were 'disappeared' as a direct consequence of state terrorism. Mothers of the disappeared began investigating and coming together to protest at the Plaza de Mayo in Buenos Aires, in front of the Casa Rosada – the Presidential palace, in defiance of the state and its laws. Their apparent 'simplicity', methods of organisation, their use of symbols and slogans, and, above all, their silent weekly protests grabbed the attention of the world. Their work continues today.

1978

MAIDEN VOYAGE OF RAINBOW WARRIOR

Greenpeace launch world's first purpose built environmental campaigning ship

1995
BEIJING PLATFORM FOR ACTION

At the Fourth World Conference on Women in September 1995 in Beijing, the Beijing Platform for Action was adopted – an historical roadmap for women's empowerment requiring commitment from all 189 governments involved. It flagged 12 key areas where urgent action was needed to ensure greater equality and opportunities for women, men, girls and boys. It is seen as the most progressive blueprint ever for advancing women's rights.

1997
MINE BAN TREATY

Historically, armed force personnel, 'security experts' and even governments argued that the use of landmines was justified despite collateral civilian casualties. The International Campaign to Ban Landmines mobilised public opinion over two decades and eventually built up a network of NGOs, International Organisations, United Nations agencies and governments committed to the ban. This objective was achieved in 1997.

1998
GOOD FRIDAY AGREEMENT

The Good Friday Agreement, negotiated and signed by leaders of the British and Irish governments and eight political parties or groupings from Northern Ireland, brought to an end the 30 years of sectarian conflict in Northern Ireland known as 'The Troubles'. It was ratified in a referendum in May 1998. The agreement set up a power-sharing assembly to govern Northern Ireland by cross-community consent.

1999
GLOBAL TRADE RULES PROTESTS

Massive civil society protests of 40,000 people in Seattle, Washington, helped shut down international free trade negotiations and spotlight the environmental and social shortcomings of the World Trade Organisation.

2000
WATER WARS – BOLIVIA

In response to the privatisation of water services and sharp increases in the cost of water in Cochabamba, Bolivia, local citizens formed the Coalition in Defence of Water and Life in January 2000; they issued a declaration for the protection of universal water rights for all citizens and an end to privatisation. Their demands were rejected, protests continued and finally the government was forced to back down. The US company which had been given the water contract, Bechtel, left Bolivia and filed a lawsuit against Bolivia demanding $50 million in compensation; protests continued for four years and in 2006, Bechtel settled for a token 30 cent payment.

2000
MDGS

189 countries came together to sign up to the Millennium Development Goals (MDGs) at the Millennium Summit in September 2000 at a landmark moment to insist that they would not tolerate the extreme inequality in the world and would do all in their power to eradicate extreme poverty and hunger by 2015.

2002
INTERNATIONAL CRIMINAL COURT ENTERS INTO FORCE

Efforts to establish a global criminal court spans more than a century, including in 1872 that of Gustav Moynier (one of the founders of the International Committee of the Red Cross) who proposed a permanent court in response to the crimes of the Franco-Prussian War. Other calls followed to try war criminals after both WWI and WWII, establishing codes recognising crimes against humanity and genocide and the campaigning work of the Coalition for the International Criminal Court which included 2,500 organisations in 150 countries.

2003
THE WORLD MARCHES AGAINST WAR

On the 15th of February, an estimated 30 million people across the world protested against the war in Iraq, including 2 million people in London and across 800 cities. In Dublin, at least 100,000 people marched. For active citizens this is an indication of how many people were prepared to join others to make their feelings heard.

A TIMELINE OF **ACTIVISM**

LAST 10 YEARS

2004
POLLUTION DATA

The European Union issues it's first-ever pollution register containing a wealth of data on industrial emissions and representing a "landmark event" in public provision of environmental information.

2007
BAMBOO BICYCLES

The Ghana Bamboo Bikes Initiative is founded: a youth led non-profit enterprise committed to the economic empowerment of youth by taking advantage of the abundant bamboo raw materials in Ghana to manufacture and assemble high quality bamboo bikes – suitable for the road conditions and terrain in Ghana, affordable and carbon free.

2008
THE APOLOGY

Following campaigning since the early 1980s, the Australian PM Kevin Rudd issues a formal apology in parliament for the past wrongs caused by successive governments on the indigenous Aboriginal population forcibly removed from their families from 1909 until the 1960s.

2010
ENDING TRADE IN CONFLICT MINERALS

Multinational firms such as Apple, Intel and Motorola were unwittingly buying conflict minerals to make products such as smartphones and laptop computers. US activists successfully pressured democrat and republican lawmakers to pass legislation. Section 1502 in the Dodd-Frank Act compels US companies to audit and disclose publicly on their supply chains to ensure that they are not using conflict minerals — particularly gold, coltan, tin and tungsten from artisanal mines controlled by the Democratic Republic of Congo's murderous militias, armed groups and the army.

2011
ART AS ACTIVISM IN EGYPT

Art historian Bahia Shehab has long been fascinated with the Arabic script for 'no.' *'I am a quiet person. I don't know how to scream. My contribution to the revolution was to paint on walls, was to be an artist.'* Her message was simple: 'no.' No to military rule, no to emergency law, no to stripping the people, no to burning books, no to violence and more. She has painted this message around Cairo in many forms.

2013
WOMEN DRIVERS

Women in Saudi Arabia are subjected to various restrictions, including needing a male guardian's consent in almost every aspect of their lives, including being banned from driving. More than 30 women staged a driving demonstration to challenge the driving ban law on women, following two demonstrations in 1990 and 2011 when dozens of women drove in opposition to the ban.

FAIRTRADE

2013
EQUAL VOTING RIGHTS FOR PRODUCERS AND SELLERS

The Fairtrade General Assembly brought together representatives from national Fairtrade markets (Europe, North America, Oceania) and producer networks (Asia, Africa, Latin America) and is the highest decision-making body in Fairtrade. Since 2013 producers have half of the votes, giving farmers and workers an equal say in all major decisions creating a truly global cooperative that tackles inequalities through fairer trade, wages and ownership.

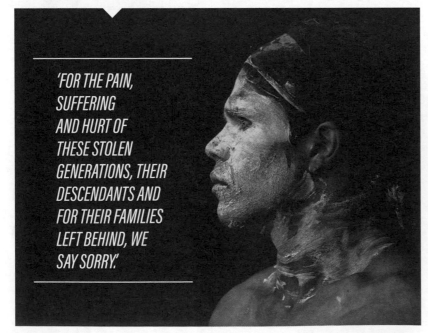

'FOR THE PAIN, SUFFERING AND HURT OF THESE STOLEN GENERATIONS, THEIR DESCENDANTS AND FOR THEIR FAMILIES LEFT BEHIND, WE SAY SORRY.'

2013

UN 'WOMEN NEED TO' CAMPAIGN

A series of ads which used genuine Google searches to reveal the widespread prevalence of sexism, stereotyping and discrimination against women. Developed by Memac Ogilvy & Mather Dubai/UN Women.

2013

THE ARMS TRADE TREATY

In April 2013, the UN General Assembly voted overwhelmingly to support an Arms Trade Treaty which entered into force in December 2014 with 87 states signing and ratifying it. It followed a long campaign by NGOs and civil society groups. The Treaty seeks to regulate the international trade of conventional weapons in order to contribute to international peace and to promote co-operation, transparency and responsible action in a notoriously secretive trade.

2015

10,000 SHOES IN PARIS

In November 2015, 10,000 pairs of shoes were left at Place de la Republique in Paris by people who were to take part in a planned Climate Change protest, but were unable to due to a terrorist attack the previous week.

2015

LISTENING TO THE WORLD

SUSTAINABLE DEVELOPMENT GOALS

The Sustainable Development Goals, adopted by countries across the world at the UN on September 25th 2015, aim to end poverty, protect the planet, and ensure prosperity for all as part of a new sustainable development agenda. Extending the MDGs agenda, each goal has specific targets to be achieved over the next 15 year and follow the UN's largest pubic consultation exercise in history involving more than 8.5 million people worldwide.

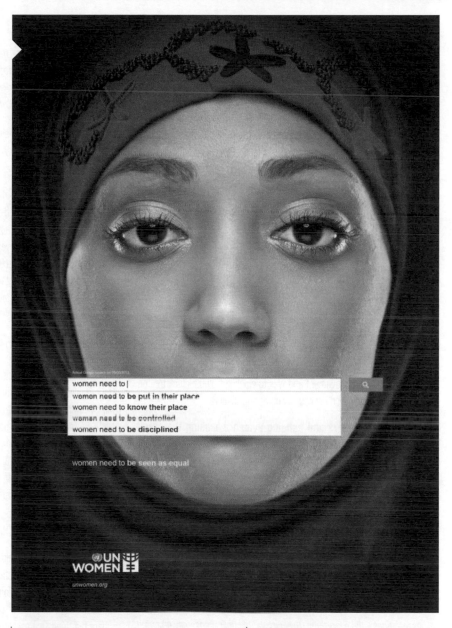

women need to |
women need to be put in their place
women need to know their place
women need to be controlled
women need to be disciplined

women need to be seen as equal

UN WOMEN

unwomen.org

2015

MARRIAGE EQUALITY IRELAND

YES EQUALITY.

Following a popular grassroots campaign for civil marriage equality in Ireland involving families, the support of businesses, young people registering to vote and 500,000 YES EQUALITY badges, 62.4% of people voted in favour of the referendum. More well known for being socially conservative, Ireland is the first country to vote by national referendum in favour of marriage equality for all its citizens.

2016

SAVING LIVES IN THE MEDITERRANEAN

At 18 years old Yusra Mardini and her sister fled their home in Damascus and boarded a dinghy to cross the Aegean sea. When their boat began to take on water, Yusra Mardini, her sister and two others jumped into the sea and pushed the boat for three hours, saving the lives of 20 people on board. Mardini went on to compete in the women's 100 meter butterfly and freestyle swimming races in the Olympic Games in Rio in August 2016.

AGAINST ALL ODDS: FROM THE CAMPAIGN TO ABOLISH SLAVERY

The first great human rights campaign – the movement to end slavery in the British Empire – had no business succeeding. In the late 1700s over three-quarters of the people on earth were in bondage at the time in one way or another. Yet by 1807 the British parliament had banned the slave trade, and on 1 August 1838 almost 800,000 slaves throughout the British Empire became free when slavery itself was abolished. Presented below are seven of the many learning lessons from the campaign to abolish slavery:

1. Personal testimonies put issues into the public domain: Nothing is of more use to a cause than a person who seems to embody it, as, in our own time, the cause of freedom in Tibet has seemed embodied by the Dalai Lama or in apartheid-era South Africa by Nelson Mandela. The tens of thousands of Britons who read Olaudah Equiano's book or heard him speak got to see slavery through the eyes of a former slave. Writing a dozen forceful letters to London newspapers, praising new anti-slavery books, defending abolitionist friends and protesting a pro-slavery speech he had heard from the House of Lords visitors' gallery, he also signed more than a half-dozen joint letters about slavery from groups of black men in London.

2. There is no substitute for face-to-face interactions: Having penned an essay while in college on the immorality of the slave trade, Thomas Clarkson instigated the first meeting that was to become the launchpad for the movement and was to clock up 56,000 kilometres on horseback as he toured the country gathering support.

3. Campaign posters and building evidence 'making the case': Clarkson purchased examples of the equipment used to contain and torture slaves - leg shackles, thumbscrews and surgical instruments used to pry open the mouths of those on hunger strike. Key to his armoury was a diagram of the slave ship Brookes, which became one of the most enduring images of the horrors of the slave trade. Over the course of the campaign this image was printed over 700 times.

4. The women's societies were almost always bolder than those of the men: former schoolteacher and Quaker Elizabeth Heyrick called for immediate, not gradual abolition. One well known male activist noted that there were more than 70 women antislavery societies: *'Ladies associations... did everything. They circulated publications: they procured the money to publish; they dunned & talked & coaxed & lectured... they carried round petitions & enforced the duty of signing them... In a word they formed the cement of the whole Antislavery building.'*

5. Industries under assault try to defend themselves: for instance, there were moves in Parliament to try to regulate the treatment of slaves, the planters hastily drew up a lofty-sounding code of conduct of their own and insisted no government interference was necessary. They considered other PR techniques as well. *'The vulgar are influenced by names and titles,'* suggested one pro-slavery writer in 1789. *'Instead of SLAVES, let the Negroes be called ASSISTANT-PLANTERS; and we shall not then hear such violent outcries against the slave-trade.'*

6. Hitch campaigns onto other political wagons: in the spring of 1792, the House of Commons had approved a bill that limited aspects of the trade. The House of Lords, however, rejected the bill, but when war with France broke out the next year it proved to be the abolitionists' saviour. When it was discovered that British ships were supplying slaves to French colonies in the Caribbean, it enabled abolitionists to argue that the slave trade was helping the enemy. That turned the tide, and both houses of Parliament voted to ban the slave trade entirely.

7. People power and boycotts: over tens of thousands of pamphlets, newsletters and petitions united the sense of outrage felt by the public, despite most people not being eligible to vote. In 1792, for example, more than 350,000 people in Britain – including a third of the population of Manchester – signed a petition calling for the abolition of the slave trade. Journalist Clare Goff points out that at the height of the campaign grassroots supporters began a boycott of sugar, one of the key products produced by slaves. In total around 300,000 people abandoned sugar; and manufacturers who offered the product *produced by the labour of freemen* labelled their products as such.

THREE QUESTIONS FROM THE PAST FOR TODAY

Historian Adam Hochschild notes that the abolitionists succeeded because they managed to effectively draw connections between the near and the distant. We have long lived in a world where everyday objects embody labour in another corner of the earth. Often we do not know where the things we use come from, or the working conditions of those who made them.

1. Were the shoes or shirt you're wearing made by children in Indonesian sweatshops? Or by prison labour in China?

2. What pesticides were breathed in by the Latin American labourers who picked the fruit on your table?

3. And do you even know in what country the innards of your computer were assembled?

Adapted from: Adam Hochschild (2012) Bury the Chains: Prophets and Rebels in the Fight to Free an Empire's Slaves, Pan Books, London (a highly recommended read); Adam Hochschild (2015) The interesting narrative, The Slate; Clare Goff (2007) Anti-slavery pioneers, New Internationalist issue 398; Mark Hertsgaard (2010) What climate activists can learn from the anti-slavery movement, Grist Magazine.

EXPLORING HOW CHANGE HAPPENS - CASE STUDIES

FEMALE GENITAL MUTILATION

'This has been seven years of hard work, we had so many obstacles to overcome and struggles at the beginning too because it was so taboo. It was fighting against something people were in denial about, it was hard for people to understand our point of view and for people in the community to be able to come out and say I am against this, too.'

Fahma Mohamed, The Guardian, 2016

Fahma Mohamed is 19 years old and lives in Bristol. Being from a small Somali Muslim family, she has seen first-hand among her friends and family the devastation caused by Female Genital Mutilation (FGM). It has been estimated that there were approximately 66,000 victims of FGM in the UK with more than 25,000 girls under the age of 15 at risk. It was these figures and her own experiences which inspired Fahma and her classmates to campaign for the education system to do more on FGM. Despite previous government promises to stop FGM, experts had warned that not only are girls still being taken abroad to be cut during the holiday 'cutting season', but some are even being cut in Britain.

In 2014, Fahma began a campaign to urge the then British Education Secretary, Michael Gove, to write to all of the heads of primary and secondary schools highlighting the dangers of FGM before the summer holidays of that year, when girls are at greatest risk. She gained support from British newspaper, The Guardian and began a petition on change.org which gathered well over 250,000 signatures. After a meeting with Fahma, Gove agreed to write to all schools on the issue.

'If every single head teacher was given the right information, we could reach every single girl at risk of FGM. We could convince these families not to send their daughters abroad and help those girls that are at risk.'

The campaign also called for better data on how many victims there are in the UK, leading the government to announce that hospitals would begin to keep records of how many of their patients have undergone FGM. The campaign culminated in compulsory training for all public sector workers to help teachers, medical professionals and social workers identify and assist girls at risk.

CONAKRY HAIRDRESSERS

In a large number of communities around the world, from the Caribbean community in Brixton, London, to the compounds in Lusaka, Zambia, beauty salons and hairdressers have become more than just a service provider. They are a community outlet, whether women (and men) are attending for their usual treatments or something more, such as receiving advice on contraception.

Guinea, in West Africa, has one of the lowest rates of modern contraceptive use in the world, with women having an average of five children. According to UN report World Contraceptive use 2015, only 7.5% of married or cohabiting women use any form of contraception. Traditionally, a Guinean woman would go and live with her mother for a few years after every time she gave birth. This was in order to prevent becoming pregnant too soon after.

In Conakry, the country's capital, Tata Sylla and her twin sister, Mbalia run a hair salon together called Jumelle Coiffure. They are very much aware of the lack of knowledge in young women around contraception. Their salon, along with 4 others in Conakry, is part of an initiative born out of Jhpiego's work in Guinea on contraception (a health organisation affiliated with Johns Hopkins University in the US). The project's aim is to dispense family planning advice to women while they have their hair braided, in the popular, busy salons.

> *'It is better to go to where they do braids, because that is what traditionally women want. A woman who is straightening or washing her hair has more money and more access to information.'*
>
> Yolande Hyjazi, Jhpiego's director in Guinea

The hairdressers and their employees strike up the usual conversations with their clients about the weather, the weekend but gradually become more personal asking if they are in a relationship or married. This then leads them to asking if they know of ways of avoiding getting pregnant.

Jhpiego has trained some of the apprentice hairdressers as community health workers, to discuss issues such as breastfeeding and talking about the different forms of contraception. They are even able to sell the contraceptive pill, receiving commission on any pills and condoms they sell, as an incentive.

The trial originally began in 2013, but stopped during the Ebola outbreak. It is now back on track and looking to expand to new locations such as tailors.

> *'I never knew about this before coming here – they taught me how. I got the injection, and since then I have been able to control the number of children I have. I already have four and I don't want any more. My husband can't afford it, school fees are so high.'*
>
> Kouma, who first heard about family planning at Jumelle Coiffure

Source: Ruth Maclean (12 August 2016) Conakry hairdressers dispense cut-and-dried contraceptive advice to women, The Guardian (UK)

#ILLRIDEWITHYOU

On December 15th 2014, an Iranian-born cleric living in Australia, entered a cafe in Sydney during the morning rush hour and took the staff and customers hostage. Almost 24 hours later, the siege was over, two hostages were killed and the hostage-taker himself.

Following concern that people wearing Islamic dress would be harassed after the armed man, claiming links to Islamic State, took the hostages, local people used twitter to offer to travel with them spreading a message of solidarity and humanity. One woman started what soon blossomed into a social media campaign to stand in solidarity with the city's Muslims.

Tessa Kum, a TV content editor and writer living in Sydney, acted after seeing a tweet that shared

> **Rachael Jacobs**
> 1 hour ago
>
> ....and the (presumably) Muslim woman sitting next to me on the train silently removes her hijab

> **Rachael Jacobs**
> 1 hour ago
>
> ...I ran after her at the train station. I said 'put it back on. I'll walk with u'. She started to cry and hugged me for about a minute – then walked off alone

Rachel Jacobs' comments on Facebook in support of a Muslim woman removing her hijab riding the train with her. Seeing this tweet, Tessa Kum offers her company to anyone in religious attire on her route. Fellow twitter users swiftly joined in, offering their support…and actions.

According to Twitter Australia, there were 40,000 tweets in just two hours using the hashtag #illridewithyou. In four hours 150,000 tweets were posted. Social Media 'clicktivism' on its own may not be transformative, but as an amplifier of voice it helps to build community conversations and many individual actions.

Sir Tessa
@sirtessa

If you reg take the #373 bus b/w Coogee/MartinPl, wear religious attire, & don't feel safe alone: I'll ride with you. @ me for schedule.

#illridewithyou reminds me: Muslim Woman Covers the Yellow Star of Her Jewish Neighbor with Her Veil. (Sarajev, 1941)

#illridewithyou radiates the beauty of Australian mateship. We are many, but together we are one. #sydneysiege

#illridewithyou
Sydney #biggerthanthis

If you need #illridewithyou I'll even drive you round if you need.

Practical thing: I've made a temporary sticker for my bag so people who need me can spot me #illridewithyou

THE FOOD SOVEREIGNTY MOVEMENT IN ECUADOR

Via Campesina, a transnational movement of peasant organisations and NGOs, first introduced the concept of food sovereignty at the 1996 World Food Summit. As the movement has long argued, food sovereignty represents an alternative to the food security paradigm. While food security affirms each person's right to sustenance, food sovereignty goes a step further, seeking to also democratise access and control over resources like land, water, and seeds. The food sovereignty movement has also been an advocate of redistributive land reform in several countries of Latin America, while also championing a system of international exchange based on fair trade principles and democratised and decentralised food systems.

In Ecuador, social activists have been crucial in institutionalising the principles of food sovereignty. They successfully advocated for the concept's inclusion in the country's 2008 Constitution, for example, and activists helped transform the ideal into national law in 2009. Since then, the Ecuadorian government has created state agencies, organised legislative committees, and approved local ordinances with the goal of making food sovereignty a reality. Both national and international non-governmental organisations are also involved in promoting projects on food security, agroecology, and local food systems in the name of food sovereignty.

The concept has particular resonance in Ecuador as it's often invoked as a means towards attaining Sumak Kawsay— a Kichwa indigenous cosmovision that translates roughly to Buen vivir, or *'to live well.'* Buen vivir refers to an alternative framework of development focused on building a harmonistic and synergetic relationship between diverse peoples, nature, and local communities, based on principles of social justice as well as more participatory forms of democracy. In 2008, the notion was also incorporated into Ecuador's Constitution.

Source: Karla Peña (2015) Ecuador's Quest for Food Sovereignty and Land Reform, The North American Congress on Latin America, New York

GREEN AND ART 'WASHING': THE CSR DILEMMA

As an idea, Corporate Social Responsibility (CSR), has been around since the 1950s and been open to selective interpretation by different companies; for example, it has been used progressively by companies such as Unilever (in association with Oxfam) to engage progressively with working conditions or by some supermarket chains on the issue of food waste. In other cases, it has been used as a marketing tool, adopting the 'halo effect' through aligning with a reputable non-profit organisation. By sponsoring 'the arts', oil companies appear to be socially responsible by supporting popular culture. Is it possible to sponsor your way out of unethical practices? One such example of this is the sponsorship of the arts by oil companies.

Those who protest this alignment of corporate values argue that sponsorship does not make up for the lack of ethical action by the rest of the company particularly where the environment is damaged by spills (and inaction), fossil fuel extraction projects and impact on land rights and communities, usually with financial and administrative state support. A key area of debate in CSR has been in sustainable and responsible supply chain management where CSR and company policies and practices are not aligned.

The movement against *'artwashing'* through corporations funding the arts (e.g. museums and galleries), began in the UK and extends a practice of 'culture jamming' as characterised by the Canadian anti-globalisation magazine Adbusters. Anti-artwash activities act as counter-cultural protests that typically include constructing art pieces that twist brand images and messages in public or private corporate spaces to question the ethics of the sponsorship, which art consumers are very often oblivious to the unsolicited performance. Recent examples include:

- Brazil (2011): artists spilled a pool of oil in front of the Museu de Arte Moderna in Rio de Janeiro to protest oil and mining sponsorship where museum visitors had to walk through the sponsor's product in order to view the art display. The message was clear: out of sight does not mean out of mind and appreciators of art must pay attention to where sponsorship for the arts comes from.

Amy Scaife (2011) 'Human Cost' performance by Liberate Tate, Duveen Gallery, Tate Britain. The performance took place on the first anniversary of the start of the BP Deepwater Horizon disaster Gulf of Mexico disaster. It lasted for 87 minutes, one for every day of the spill.

- Canada (2013): The Council of Canadians, Ecology Ottawa, and the Polaris Institute protested against Museum of Civilisation in Gatineau sponsorship by the Canadian Association of Petroleum Producers (CAPP). They created a snowman with a frown on his face, outside the museum. The figure held a sign that read 'CAPP pollutes snow' and Ben Powless, a Pipeline Community Organiser with Ecology Ottawa noted: *'We're concerned that the Canadian Association of Petroleum Polluters and their members are using this sponsorship to white-wash their dirty tar sands projects.'*

- In the UK, many artists, staff, and art lovers have spoken out and boycotted museums and galleries e.g. artists have organised protests at the Tate Museum in London, members have resigned and the issue of oil sponsorship from British Petroleum has become an agenda item at Museum meetings etc.

Earlier in 2015, BP was the sponsor of the British Museum's 'Indigenous Australia: Enduring Civilisation' exhibition and, within the same calendar year, had submitted its formal plan to drill four new ultra-deep-water wells in the Great Australian Bight, following extensive seismic testing that coincided with the exhibition.

Bunna Lawrie, a traditional Aboriginal owner from the Mirning people, has said, 'My greatest concern is that I cannot let BP mine oil in the Great Australian Bight ... it is the greatest whale nursery on this planet'. The British Museum was also criticised as many of the communities who lent objects to the exhibition were not told it would carry a BP logo. Art Not Oil campaigner Chris Garrard observes that BP *'are desperately trying to keep fossil fuels woven into a society that needs a cultural shift to renewable energy'*. In response to 'greenwash' and 'artwash' accusations, BP commented, *'We were the company probably first out of the blocks to recognise the potential causal link between the burning of fossil fuels and potential climate change. We've been working on that agenda pretty tirelessly for a long time.'*

According to a recent ranking, BP is Europe's fiercest corporate opponent of action on climate change regulation through its lobbying, advertising and, as part of the Oil and Gas Climate group, BP dropped a commitment to carbon pricing. Pressure from art and activist groups saw the Tate put an end to their sponsorship deal with BP, finishing in 2017.

Since the Paris summit on climate change in December 2015, a collection of artwash activism groups from France, Britain, Norway, Brazil, Canada and the US co-organised the Louvre action to launch an international collaboration to liberate museums and cultural institutions around the world from ties to fossil fuel companies and are active under the hashtag #FossilFreeCulture. In a field report on the event Jess Worth of the New Internationalist noted:

'This new and rapidly growing movement for a #FossilFreeCulture extends the successful global divestment movement into the cultural sphere, calling on cultural institutions to cancel fossil fuel sponsorship contracts, divest financial holdings in the industry, and kick oil executives and climate deniers off their boards.'

During an era of increasing 'public private partnership' models of development, these types of 'direct action' protests have managed to take what is being sponsored and turn it on its own operations and practices.

Sources: adapted from: Jess Worth (9 December 2015), *Art, oil and arrests in Paris*, New Internationalist; Chris Garrard (26 October 2015) *BBC fails to challenge BP arts sponsorship chief on kidnap and torture allegations*, The Ecologist, www.theecologist.org; Evans (2015) *Artwash: Big oil and the Arts*, PlutoPress; Cayley-Daoust (2013) *Museum's tar sands funding pollutes Snow exhibit, says snowperson*, Polarish Institute

THE PIONEERING RE-MUNICIPALISATION TOWN OF WOLFSHAGEN, GERMANY

The last decades of the 20th century have witnessed a profound experiment to increase the role of markets in local government service delivery, most acute in water and energy service provision through grand promises of investment and efficiency. This trend expanded rapidly, affecting towns and cities in the richest and poorest parts of the planet. Private-sector investment in developing countries has been falling since its peak in the 1990s, and as David Hall, Emanuele Lobina and Robin de la Motte noted in 2005 (In reviewing public resistance to privatisation in water and energy): *'multinational companies have failed to make sustainable returns on their investments, and the process of privatisation in these sectors has proved widely unpopular and encountered strong political opposition. This resistance is now generally recognised as an important factor in the failure of private investment in these sectors, by supporters and critics of privatisation alike.' (p.286)*

A 2014 report by the Transnational Institute provides examples of movements to reverse privatisation of public sector goods despite 'economic shocks' promoting such policies (pursued, for example, by the IMF as part of conditional financial support to developing countries).

Examples can be found in 180 cities in 35 countries which have returned control of their water supply to municipalities in the past 15 years, including in Uruguay (which became the first country to make water privatisation illegal by prohibiting the sale and operation of water services to private companies) and Cochabamba, Bolivia's third largest city (see timeline).

In recent years, Germany has seen a surge of reversing privatisation in the energy sector where authorities have reversed local and regional privatised contracts and reinstated public ownership. Since 2000, more than 100 contracts for energy distribution networks or service delivery in Germany have been returned to the public sector.

An oft-quoted example of *'re-municipalisation'* is the town of Wolfshagen (population 14,000) in the state of Hessen, which has won a federal government award as an 'energy efficient town'. The local town council took back the grid from the private utility E.ON Mitte in 2006. Although the original contracts were for 20 years, a break clause in the contract allowed the town to bring the network back into public ownership after 10 years. As in many parts of Germany, Wolfshagen retained a small energy-producing public company, which gave it the technical expertise both to strike a tough bargain with E.ON and to devise a new strategy to promote renewables.

The town initially had a contract with an Austrian hydroelectric supplier to produce 100% of its electricity from renewables, but Wolfshagen's aim was to be self-sufficient in renewable energy by the end of 2015, through the construction of five wind turbines and a 42,000-panel solar park, completed in 2012. Two-thirds of the town's energy now comes from wind, with the remainder from solar and biomass. The form of public ownership – part local council and part cooperative (with a community cooperative created to give local residents a 25% stake) – is also typical of the demand to share revenues and encourage greater civic engagement.

Sources: Andrew Cumbers (2016) 'Remunicipalisation, the Low-Carbon Transition, and Energy Democracy', p.279-281 in *State of the World: Can a City be Sustainable?* Worldwatch Institute, and based on Wagner and Hauenschild *The Wave of Remunicipalisation of Public Services in the EU (2014)*; Tom Lawson (2015) *Reversing the Tide of Water Privatization*, the Centre for Research on Globalisation

EXTRACTIVE INDUSTRY PROJECTS AND BLOCKADIA

Blockadia is not a specific location on a map, but rather a roving transnational conflict zone that is cropping up with increasing frequency and intensity wherever extractive projects are attempting to dig and drill, whether for open-pit mines, or gas fracking, or tar sands oil pipelines. What is clear is that fighting a giant extractive industry on your own can seem impossible, especially in a remote, sparsely populated location. But being part of a continent-wide, even global, movement that has the industry surrounded is a very different story. Blockadia is turning the tables, insisting that it is up to industry to prove that its methods are safe – and in the era of extreme energy that is something that simply cannot be done.

Western culture has worked very hard to erase Indigenous cosmologies that call on the past and the future to interrogate present-day actions, with long-dead ancestors always present, alongside the generations yet to come. As Indigenous people have taken on leadership roles within this movement, these long-protected ways of seeing are spreading in a way that has not occurred for centuries. What is emerging, in fact, is a new kind of reproductive rights movement, one fighting not only for the reproductive rights of women, but for the reproductive rights of the planet as a whole – for the decapitated mountains, the drowned valleys, the clear-cut forests, the fracked water tables, the strip-mined hillsides, the poisoned rivers, the 'cancer villages'. All of life has the right to renew, regenerate, and heal itself. Increasingly, Blockadia is also a constructive movement, actively building an alternative economy based on very different principles and values.

Blockadia activities have included:

- Europe: protecting the Skouries forest, Greece, from open-pit gold and copper mine project (2012); farmers building a protest camp in Pungesti, Romania, to prevent Chevron from launching the country's first shale gas exploration well (2013).

- Africa: the Ogoni People's fossil fuel peaceful resistance in the Niger Delta, Nigeria, to corporate oil company Shell's oil production facilities through occupying off-shore platforms, oil barges and flow stations. From 1998 the student movement joined in nonviolent dramatic demonstrations. An escalation of violence by the state and, more recently, in a more militant resistance by protestors has changed the original goals of the movement (from 1990s).

- Americas: first nations people of Elsipogtog, Canada, leading a blockade against SWN Resources from trying to conduct seismic testing ahead of possible fraction operation and associated poisoning toxins (2013); ranchers, indigenous people and others blocked construction site access and progress along the TransCanada Keystone XL oil pipelines pipe's 1,897 km proposed route from Alberta, Canada to refineries in Illinois and Texas, Oklahoma, traversing six U.S. states and cross major rivers, including the Missouri River, Yellowstone, and Red Rivers, as well as key sources of drinking and agricultural water (from 2010).

- Australia: New South Wales, where for a year and a half activists chained themselves to various entrances of the largest coal mining operation at the Maules Creek project (from 2012).

If the movement has a guiding theory, it is that it is high time to close, rather than expand, the fossil fuel frontier. Suddenly, no major new extractive industry project, no matter how seemingly routine, is a done deal.

Extracts adapted from: Naomi Klein (2014) *This Changes Everything: Capitalism vs the Climate*, p.293-336, Allen Lane, London

CONCLUSION

'ANOTHER WORLD IS NOT ONLY POSSIBLE, SHE IS ON HER WAY. MAYBE MANY OF US WON'T BE HERE TO GREET HER, BUT ON A QUIET DAY, IF I LISTEN VERY CAREFULLY, I CAN HEAR HER BREATHING.' ARUNDHATI ROY (2002) COME SEPTEMBER

Above, Indian activist Arundhati Roy asserts that a new world is in the making and that it can be seen and heard across all regions worldwide, by those who wish to see and hear it.

It can be observed in the countless movements, large and small that seek to protect our Earth and its resources; from indigenous people to women's groups to scientists, journalists and NGOs. It can be recognised in the resistances of those who proclaim human rights in the face of tyranny and conflict and who have advanced the structures and practice of human rights worldwide. It can be identified in the resilience of the poor and excluded who continue to insist that human dignity is for all and not just some. It can be seen everywhere by those who have the eyes to see it.

It can be heard in the protests of those who have taken to the streets to protect freedom in the Arab World, to defend democracy in Hong Kong and Brazil, to proclaim aboriginal rights in Australia, migrant rights in Europe, women's rights in India and Africa and water rights across Latin America. It can be heard in the dissenting voices of local leaders, youth activists, climate change activists, academics and religious leaders. It can be heard in the many movements across the planet that insist that there is an alternative to the dominant development model that exists today. It can be heard by those who take the time to listen.

But, that world *in the making* faces a daunting set of challenges that appear, at first sight, as insurmountable barriers – accelerating climate change and its consequences; extreme inequality and the powerlessness that accompanies it; the absolute poverty and exclusion of far too many

internationally (and the extreme luxury of far too few). It is inhibited by the barrage of commentary, advertising and analysis that proclaims there is no alternative. And, it faces the frequent assertion that there is little that can be done.

Yet, as this chapter has amply illustrated, change is the norm but the crucial question we all face is what kind of change? The change that is needed is not simply about deciding on an appropriate response to specific problems or issues, important as they are. The intrinsic change that is required will only be brought about once the nature, scale and fundamentals of an issue are adequately addressed. South African activist Kumi Naidoo insists that:

> *'...The future rests with all of us that have the luxury of knowledge, that we have come to understand that what is at stake here is the survival of the planet.'*

While the *simplicity* of his argument can be challenged, it's fundamental reasoning rings true. Knowledge is important yet as suggested by Yankelovich and Friedman earlier in this chapter, a more nuanced approach is required in order to 'hear' (to use Roy's analogy) this new world. For them, the assumption that public opinion is invariably improved by inundating people with facts and information grossly exaggerates the role of such information and underestimates the importance of values and emotions; an argument that is rooted in Arundathi Roy's quote above.

If we accept the arguments offered throughout this book that change is needed, occurring all the time, is natural and inevitable, then the accompanying question is unavoidable – *Where do we fit into that change?* In examining human values, human rights and the role played by photographs to tell stories and stir actions, in particular on the pain of others, American filmmaker and teacher Susan Sontag considers a number of strands within this question, reminding us that we all share in and are connected by the same time and space, both viewers and victims alike:

> *'So far as we feel sympathy, we feel we are not accomplices to what caused the suffering. Our sympathy proclaims our innocence as well as our impotence. To that extent, it can be (for all our good intentions) an impertinent – if not an inappropriate – response. To set aside the sympathy we extend to others beset by war and murderous politics for a reflection on how our privileges are located on the same map as their suffering, and may – in ways we might prefer not to imagine – be linked to their suffering, as the wealth of some may imply the destitution of others, is a task for which the painful, stirring images supply only an initial spark.'*

Susan Sontag (2003) Regarding the Pain of Others, page 91-92

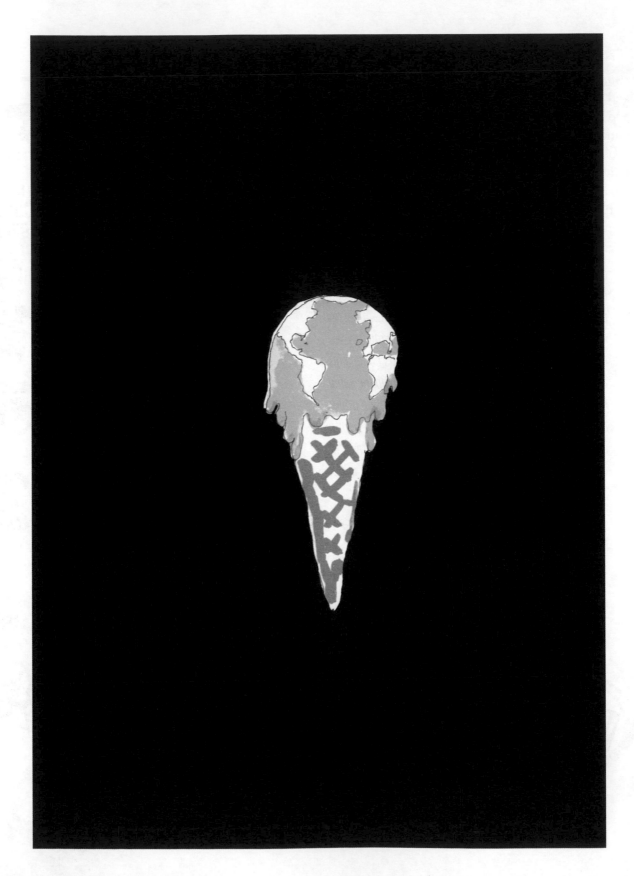

READING

Concern Worldwide (2015) *Everyday Activism*, Dublin

Duncan Green (2008) *From Poverty to Power: How Active Citizens and Effective States Can Change the World,* Oxfam International

Duncan Green (2016) *How Change Happens*, Oxford University Press

Thomas Pogge (2008 2nd ed.) *World Poverty and Human Rights*, Polity Press, New York

Jeffrey Sachs (2008) *Common Wealth: Economics for a Crowded Planet*, Penguin, London

Peter Singer (2009) *The Life You Can Save: Acting Now to End World Poverty*, Random House, New York

Danny Dorling (2012) *The No-Nonsense Guide to Equality*, New Internationalist, Oxford

Sally Blundell (2013) *The No-Nonsense Guide to Fair Trade*, New Internationalist, Oxford

Danny Chivers (2015) *NoNonsense Renewable Energy: cleaner, fairer ways to power the planet*, New Internationalist, Oxford

MORE INFORMATION AND DEBATE

www.amnesty.org – popular human rights movement NGO Amnesty International and www.hrw.org – regional monitoring and research NGO Human Rights Watch; 2 key human rights organisations

www.developmenteducation.ie – popular education on development and human rights issues and learning resources, based in Ireland, with case studies of 'actions', blogs and more

www.euromedrights.org – news, research and advocacy from network of more than 80 human rights organisations, institutions and individuals based in 30 countries in the Euro-Mediterranean

www.fairtrade.net – Fairtrade International site (see also www.developmenteducation.ie and www.ethicalconsumer.org for more on fairtrade, ethical consumption and the debates surrounding them)

www.guardian.co.uk/global-development - articles, blogs, reviews and campaigns for change; see in particular, the Poverty Matters blog on www.guardian.co.uk/global-development/poverty-matters

www.hdr.undp.org – interactive online portal to flagship thematic Human Development Reports produced annually

www.oxfam.org/en/campaigns - Oxfam International campaigns site

www.ted.com - rich site for presentations including by Sachs, Collier, Pogge and especially Hans Rosling (see, for example his 2006 talk, *The best stats you've ever seen*)

www.worldwildlife.org - World Wide Fund for Nature (WWF) site on conservation and campaigns on climate, food, forests, oceans and wildlife

www.foei.org – Friends of the Earth: the world's largest grassroots environmental network

INDEX

s = source
n = note

Abani, Chris, 254
Abdul Habib, Malim, 8
Aboriginal people, 6-7, 190, 192, 197-9, 290, 297, 300
Abugre, Charles, 263
Academics Stand Against Poverty, 108, 280
Achebe, Chinua, 41
Action Aid, 119, 145, 146, 211
Adam Smith Institute, 278
Adbusters, 296
Adiche, Chimamanda Ngozi, 150, 162
Africa Human Development Report, 158, 160
African Charter on Human and Peoples' Rights, 74, 81, 84, 87, 91
African Commission on Human and Peoples' Rights, 84
African Court on Human and Peoples' Rights, 84, 93s
African Development Bank, 133, 134
African National Congress (ANC) 114, 117
African Progress Panel, 56, 133, 135; Report, 144-5
African Union, 81, 134
AFRODAD, 270
Agarwal, Anil, 105
Agenda 2030 see Sustainable Development Goals
Aghazarm, Christine, 200
Agreement on Trade-Related Aspects of Intellectual Property Rights (TRIPS), 206, 218-9
AidData, 270
Aidwatch, 268, 273s
Al-Farabi, 78
Albright, Madeline, 234
American Academy of Political and Social Science, 195
American Convention on Human Rights, 89, 91
Amin, Samir, 30, 44
Amnesty International, 32s, 82, 83, 93s, 148, 197
ANC see African National Congress, 114
Annan, Kofi, 144, 159
Anthony, Susan B., 122
Anti-Terrorism, Crime and Security Act, 89
Antrobus, Peggy, 156
apartheid, 6, 114, 115, 119, 245, 282, 288, 292
Apple, 219, 290
Apter, David, 40

Arab Spring, 89, 125, 126, 228, 256, 282
Aristotle, 37, 78
Arms Trade Treaty (ATT), 225, 291
Art Not Oil, 297
'artwashing', 296-7
Associated British Foods, 212
ATT see Arms Trade Treaty

Badawi, Raif, 115
Baker, Raymond, 135, 137
bamboo bikes, 290
Banerjee, Abhijit, 116
Banerjee Subhabrata Bobby, 59
Banda, Fareda, 150
Banjul Charter see African Charter on Human and Peoples' Rights
Bechtel, 289
Bedjaoui, Mohammed, 87, 88
Beijing Platform for Action, 148, 156, 162, 165s, 289
Big 10, 212, 214
Big Tobacco, 220
Biko, Steve, 288
biocapacity, 72-73
biofuel, 179, 185, 206, 211, 216
Black Consciousness, 115, 288
Black Power, 288
Blockadia, 184, 299
Bomba, Briggs, 137
BP see British Petroleum
Brennan, William J., 76
Bretton Woods system, 30
BRICs, 30, 50
British Medical Association, 169
British Museum, 297
British Petroleum, 297
Brown, Lester, 200
Brundtland, Dr Gro Harlem, 65
Brundtland Commission, 60
Buarque, Cristovam, 13, 30, 107
Buffett, Warren, 269

Cáceres, Berta, 8
California State Pension Fund, 169
Campaign to Ban Landmines, 289
Canadian Association of Petroleum Producers (CAPP), 297
Canadian Center for Policy Alternatives, 151
CAP see Common Agricultural Policy
Caparrós, Martín, 13
CAPP see Canadian Association of Petroleum Producers
Cargill, 216
Carlos, John, 288

Carrefour, 57, 212
Carson, Rachel, 288
Castles, Stephen, 190
CDVI see Climate Demography Vulnerability Index
CEDAW see Convention on the Elimination of All Forms of Discrimination Against Women
censorship, 82, 92
Center for Systemic Peace, 241
Centre for Research on the Epidemiology of Disasters (CRED), 228
Césaire, Aimé, 48
CETA see Comprehensive Economic and Trade Agreement
Chabal, Patrick, 117
charity, 74, 78, 87, 94, 96, 101, 245, 263, 276, 280, 285
Chatham House, 215s, 221
Chevron, 105, 299
childbirth, 103, 157, 161, 246
Chomsky, Noam, 76, 279, 280
Christian Aid, 90, 146
Churchill, Winston, 233
Cicero, 78
Civicus State of Civil Society Report, 115, 119, 124
Civil Rights Movement, 115, 288
Clarkson, Thomas, 292
Clemens, Michael, 278
Climate Accountability Institute, 105
climate change, 14, 16; 2014, 29; 30, 43, 44, 50, 52, 57, 104; 106, 107, Paris 2015, 123; 130, costs, 13-33; 151, women, 153; displacement, 160; gender equality, 162; development, 166-87; marine species, 188; sea temperature, 189-9; migration, 193, 196, 200; trade, 206; livestock, 214; trade deals, 220-1; food security, 229, 231; development, 244; water supply, 250; food supply, 258; *Shockwaves: Managing the Impacts of Climate Change on Poverty*, 278; TNCs, 283; protests, 291 (see also Paris Agreement), 297, 300
Climate Demography Vulnerability Index, 105
climate injustice, 94, 97, 102, 104
climate justice, 101, 104, 133, 166, 169, 177, 178, 179, 181, 186
Coalition in Defence of Water and Life, 289
Coca-Cola, 212
Cold War, 36, 40, 41, 77, 80, 90, 108
Collier, Professor Paul, 125, 278
Collins, Daryl, 116

Committee to Protect Journalists, 92
Common Agricultural Policy (CAP), 210
Commonwealth Fund, 143
Commonwealth Secretariat, 108
Comprehensive Economic and Trade
   Agreemen (CETA), 220
Concern Worldwide, 228, 230, 233, 238, 239s,
contraception, 242, 256-7, 293, 294 see also
   family planning
Convention Against Torture and Other
   Cruel, Inhuman, or Degrading Treatment
   or Punishment, 33, 83, 202
Convention on the Elimination of All
   Forms of Discrimination Against Women
   (CEDAW), 202
Convention on the Rights of the Child, 202,
   236
Convention Relating to the Status of
   Refugees, 201
Cook, John, 170
COPs, 180, 184; COP15, 186; COP21,
   220 see also United Nations Framework
   Convention on Climate Change
   (UNFCCC)
Corporate Social Responsibility (CSR), 296
Council of Europe, 81
The Cry of the Earth, 104
CSR see Corporate Social Responsibility
Cullity, Gareth, 98, 99, 100, 102, 111s, 262,
   279
'culture jamming', 296

DAC see Development Assistance
   Committee
Dalai Lama, 74, 292
Danone, 212
de la Motte, 298
de Shutter, Olivier, 236
death penalty, 33, 83
Deaton, Angus, 31s, 262
Declaration on the Right to Development,
   74, 85
Democracy Centre, 219
dependency theory, 34, 41
Development Assistance Committee (DAC),
   133, 264, 265, 266, 267, 269, 271, 273
Development CooperationReport, 269
Development Initiatives Investment to End
   Poverty, 269s, 271
Dóchas World's Best News Project, 285
Dodd-Frank Act, 290
domestic violence, 33, 157
driving demonstration, Saudi Arabia, 290
Duflo, Esther, 116
Dutch East India Company, 219
Dworkin, Richard, 262

ecosystem, 58, 61-63, 104, 188, 225 see
   ecological footprint

E.ON Mitte, 298
e-waste, 64, 65
Earth Democracy, 51s, 187s, 278, 281
Earth Institute, 278
Earth Overshoot Day, 29, 73
ecological footprint, 68-69, 72-73
ecology: 'Development, Ecology and Women',
   37; agroecology, 183, 295; Ecology Ottawa,
   297
Economic Causes of Civil Conflict and their
   Implications for Policy, 125
education, 14, development, 17-9, 21, 22, 28,
   30, 32, 36, 58, 66s; human rights, 80, 81,
   84, 85, 97; finance, 116, 121, 122, 123, 126,
   135, 141, 142, 144, 145; women, 148, 151-
   63; migration, 199, 203, 204; progress, 222;
   spending, 225; access, 228, 230; 242, 244-5,
   247, 248, 249, 252, 256, 257, 264, 265, 272,
   285s, 287, 293
Economic Justice Network, Malawi, 145
Edwards, Michael, 272
Edward, Peter, 26
Eid, Kassem, 230
Eisenstadt, Shmuel, 40
El Niño, 63, 231
Emancipation Proclamation, 277
Escobar, Arturo, 31s, 49, 50, 51s, 279
Esteva, Gustavo, 49
Eurodad, 140
European Convention on Human Rights, 74,
   81, 84, 89, 91
European Court of Human Rights, 81, 84, 92
European Network on Debt and
   Development, 144
European Parliament, 69
Exxon-Mobil, 105

Fairtrade, 9, 290
family planning, 157, 159, 247, 256-7, 294
   see also contraception
Fanon, Franz, 42, 48
FAO see United Nations Food and
   Agriculture Organisation
FDI see foreign direct investment
female genital mutilation, 157, 159, 162, 165s,
   293
feminism: feminist perspective on
   development, 36, 49; movement, 115;
   feministing.com, 123; 165s; eco-feminism,
   280
FGM see female genital mutilation
Financial Transparency Coalition, 146
fishing, 54, 56-7, 64, 132, 133, 138, 215
food security/insecurity, 12, 31s, 56, 104, 153,
   161, 176, 181, 206, 213, 214, 215, 225, 229,
   231, 237, 239s, 259s, 283, 295
Forced Migration Review, 200
foreign direct investment (FDI), 131n, 135,
   137, 144, 146, 222

Fortune 500, 219
Fossil Free Campaign, 169
fossil fuel, 9, 49, 60, 104, 169, 171, 172, 178,
   181, 183, 185, 186, 187s, 216, 220, 222,
   296, 297, 299
Foundation for Climate Justice, 186
'Four Freedoms', 79, 80
Fowler, Penny, 206, 209
Frank, Andre Gunder, 41
Freedom House, 31s, 32s, 82
Freedom in the World Report, 16, 31s, 32, 82
Freedom on the Net Report, 83
Freire, Paulo, 99
Friedman, W., 284, 285, 300
Fuel Quality Directive, 221
Fuller, Linda K., 153,
FUNAI, 123
Future Positive, 272

G8, 146, 220
G20, 213, 245
G33, 213
G77, 49
Gaia hypothesis, 59, 60
Galeano, Eduardo, 46, 51s
Gandhi, Mahatma, 116
Gates, Bill and Melinda, 269
GATT see General Agreement on Trades and
   Tariffs
Gay Rights Movement, 115
Gazprom, 105
Gender Development Index, 66 see also
   Gender Inequality Index
Gender Inequality Index, 19, 23 see also
   Gender Development Index
General Agreement on Trades and Tariffs,
   208
General Mills, 212
Geneva Conventions, 236
genocide, 92, 93s, 101, 198, 289
Georgetown University, 169
GFI see Global Financial Integrity
Giddens, Anthony, 170
Glasgow University, 169
Glennie and Sumner, 260, 264, 272
Global Financial Integrity (GFI), 103, 130,
   133, 134, 135, 136-7, 139s
Global Footprint Network, 67, 68, 69, 73
Global Hunger Index, 228, 237, 239s
Global Industry Analysts Report, 103
Global Justice Now, 182, 219
Global Justice Programme, 14, 214
Global Peace Index, 240-1
Global Resources Dividend, 108
Global Risks Report, 251
'Global South', 30, 42, 48, 49, 51s, 52, 128,
   135, 187s
Global Trade Rules Protests, 289
Global Wealth Report, 31s

Global Witness, 119, 133, 146, 186
Goff, Clare, 292
Goldcorp, 220
Going Offshore, 144
Good Friday Agreement, 289
Gove, Michael, 293
Graeme, Professor H., 199
GRAIN, 216
Grameen Bank, 116, 288
Grayling, A.C., 98
GRD see Global Resources Dividend
Great Australian Bight, 297
Green, Duncan, 118, 282, 283, 284, 286
Green, Ronald M., 106
Green Belt Movement, 288
Greenpeace, 271, 289
Grown, Caren, 36
Gudynas, Eduardo, 50

Hall, David, 298
Happy Planet Index, 69, 70
HDI see Human Development Index
Health Poverty Action, 143
Heede, Richard, 105
Heltberg, Rasmus, 125
Herodotus, 232
Hettne, Bjorn, 46
Heyrick, Elizabeth, 292
Hickel, Jason, 13s, 29, 53, 183, 263, 279
Higgins, Michael D., 7, 152
High Level Panel on Financing for
    Development, 209
Hirschman, Albert, 279
HIV and AIDS, 21, 146, 151, 152, 153, 157,
    160, 208, 218, 219, 246, 247, 285
Ho Chi Minh, 48
Hobbes, 79
Hochschild, Adam, 277, 292
*Honest Accounts: The True Story of Africa's
    Billion Dollar Losses*, 128, 132s, 133
Honwana, Alcinda, 256
Horn-Phathanothai, Leo, 178, 187s
Human Development Index, 17, 18, 19,
    20, 22, 23, 28, 42, 66, 69, 244; Inequality
    Adjusted, 18, 19
Human Development Reports see United
    Nations Development Programme
human rights, 6-7, 16, 18, 26, 30, 36, 37, 47,
    74-94; NGOs, 104; 108, 111s, 112-22; IFF,
    135; trafficking, 139; women, 148-52, 159-
    60, 162; climate change, 168, 177, 179-82,
    186; migration, 192-3, 196, 197, 199, 200-
    5; 220; hunger, 226, 236; 242, 245, 259s;
    aid, 269, 270, 271; change, 280, 282, 285,
    287; slavery, 292, 300-1 see also African
    Charter, European Convention, European
    Court, International Covenant, OHCHR,
    United Nations Commission, Universal
    Declaration, World Conference

Human Rights Fifty Years On: A Reappraisal,
    76
The Human Rights Reader, 37, 78
Human Security Report, 16s, 225s, 228, 239s,
    240, 241s,
humanitarian, 38, interventions, 76, 90;
    Summit, 152, 238, 239s; crises, 159-61,
    199; assistance, 202; policy group, 205s;
    spending, 225; International Humanitarian
    Law, 226, 229, 230, 238; 233, 235, 238, 245,
    264, 270
Hussein, Saddam, 234

IBFAN see International Baby Food Action
    Network
ICCPR see International Covenant on Civil
    and Political Rights
ICESCR see International Covenant on
    Economic, Social and Cultural Rights
The Idea of Justice, 263
IFF see Illicit Financial Flows
IHL see International Humanitarian Law
Ikeda, Daisaku, 47
Illicit Financial Flows (IFF), 130, 133, 134,
    135, 137, 146
ILO see International Labour Organisation,
    39, 120, 122, 125, 244, 256
IMF see International Monetary Fund
IMR (Infant Mortality Rate) see mortality
Indigenous People's Movement, 115
Institute for Policy Studies, 220
Intel, 290
Intended Nationally Determined
    Contributions, 181
Inter-American Human Rights Commission,
    84, 220
Intergenerational Justice or the Rights of
    Future Generations, 81, 106
Intergovernmental Panel on Climate Change
    (IPCC), 29, 104, 166, 170-2, 183, 184s,
    187s
International Baby Food Action Network
    (IBFAN), 289
International Bank for Reconstruction and
    Development, 39 see also World Bank
International Committee of the Red Cross,
    239s, 289
International Conference on Population and
    Development, 256
International Convention on the Protection
    of the Rights of All Migrant Workers and
    Members of their Families, 202
International Council of Voluntary Agencies,
    195
International Court of Justice, 87
International Covenant on Civil and Political
    Rights (ICCPR), 80, 89, 90-1, 201
International Covenant on Economic, Social
    and Cultural Rights (ICESCR), 80, 236

International Covenant on Human Rights, 80
International Criminal Court, 289
International Energy Agency, 174, 185
International Humanitarian Law (IHL), 226,
    229, 230, 238
International Institute for Sustainable
    Development, 179, 216
International Labour Office, 26 see also
    International Labour Organisation
International Labour Organisation (ILO), 39,
    120, 122, 125, 244, 256
International Land Coalition, 216
International Monetary Fund (IMF), 24, 39,
    42, 50, 51s, 103, 120, 131s, 135, 139s, 140,
    141, 145, 185, World Economic Outlook,
    219; 222, 259s, 265n, 298
International Organisation for Migration
    (IOM), 143, 144, 195s, 200
International Science Academies, 171
International Tracing Instrument, 225
investor-state dispute settlement (ISDS), 220
IOM see International Organisation for
    Migration
IPCC see Intergovernmental Panel on
    Climate Change
IRA, 234
International Rescue Committee, 230
ISDS see investor-state dispute settlement
Ishay, Micheline, 37, 78, 93s
IUCN see World Conservation Union
Iversen, Katja, 162

Jacobs, Rachel, 294
Jaggar, Alison, 100, 281
Jiping, Chen, 186
Journal of the International AIDS Society, 218
justice: access to, 203; distributive, 102, 107;
    ecological, 49; economic, 120, 145; gender,
    165s; global, 86, 93s, 120; intergenerational,
    81, 106; just society, 99; natural, 79;
    rectificatory, 102; regulative, 102; social
    justice, 47, 263; tax, 8-9, 135, 144, 145;
    trade, 111s, 208, 222;
Kaba, Maria Leusa, 123
Kälin, Walter, 200
Kant, Emmanuel, 263
Keating, Paul, 197
Kellogg, 212
Kelly, Michael J,. 274, 276
Kenny, Charles, 30
King, Martin Luther, 8, 116
Kissinger, Henry, 12
Klein, Naomi, 183, 184, 279
Kraft, 212
Kubuabola, J.Y., 141
Kum, Tessa, 294
Kyle and McGahan, 219
Kyoto Protocol, 175, 180

La Via Campesina, 47
Laczko, Frank, 200
Lalla-Maharajh, Julia, 162
League of Nations, 38
Lehmann Brothers, 140
life expectancy, 17, 19, 22, 23, 27, 28, 29, 32, 58, 68, 69, 70, 96, 157, 198, 222, 244, 253
Limits to Growth, 61, 62
literacy, 16, 19, 23, 32, 36, 42, 45, 157, 242, 248, 249
Living Blue Planet Report, 188
Living Planet Index, 54, 57, 64, 66, 68, 69
Living Planet Report, 57, 64,
Lobina, Emanuele, 298
Loch Erne declaration, 146
Locke, John, 106
Lovelock, James, 59, 60
LPI see Living Planet Index

Maathi, Wangari, 114, 115, 122, 288
Mack, Andrew, 240
MacSorley, Dominic, 228, 230, 238
'Majority World', 48, 49
malaria, 146, 177, 246, 247, 264
Malawi Economic Justice Network, 145
Malembeka, Godfrey, 151
Manby, Bronwen, 205s
Mandela, Nelson, 116, 119, 242, 288, 292
Mar Dieye, Abdoulaye, 159
march against war in Iraq, 289
Mardini, Yusra, 291
Markham, Susan, 153
Marriage Equality Ireland, 291
Mars, 212
Marshall Plan, 265
Maslow, Albert, 244
Maules Creek project, 299
Mbeki, Thabo, 134
McClelland, David, 40
McDonagh, Thomas, 219-20
McInturff, Kaye, 151
McKibben, Bill, 29, 104
MDG see Millennium Development Goals
The Meat Atlas, 214-5
Médecins sans Frontières (MSF), 235, 271
migration, 74, 90, 131, 133, 142-4, 177, 190-205, 214, 252, 256, 286
Migration Policy Institute, 193
Milanovic, Branko, 26
Millennium Declaration, 14
Millennium Development Goals, 12, 13, 23s, 24, 34, 43-4, 52-3, 130, 131, 145, women's rights, 148, 151, 156, 162, 165s, 237; health, 246, 247; schooling, 249; sanitation, 251, 252s; 258; aid, 265, 266; 278, 289, 291; Annual Reports, 24, 156, 252s
Millennium Summit, 289
Miller, Mark, 190
Mo-Zi, 78

modernisation theory, 34, 40, 41
Mohamed, Fahma, 292
Mondelez International, 212
Monsanto, 216
monsoon, 63, 169
Morgan, Lewis Henry, 38
mortality, 229; adult, 19; child, 14, 16, 19, 22, 23, 32, 45, 103, 122, 246, 247, 249, 253, 255, 257; Democratic Republic of Congo, 230, 239s; Infant Mortality Rate (IMR), 19; maternal, 21, 23, 32, 45, 96, 153, 157, 158, 160, 161, 246, 247, 257, 259s; tuberculosis, 246
Mothers of the Plaza de Mayo, 289
Motorola, 290
Moynier, Gustav, 289
MSF see Médecins sans Frontières
Multi-Dimensional Poverty Index see UNDP
Museu de Arte Moderna, 296
MyWorld 2015 survey, 44

NAFTA see North American Free Trade Agreement
Naidoo, Kumi, 300
Narain, Sunita, 105
natural disasters: 108, 160, 166, 168, 177, 200, 283; bushfire, 161; hurricane, 161, 176-7; tsunami, 161
Nayyar, Deepak, 208
Nazi Germany, 6
Nehru, Jawaharlal, 48
neoliberalism, 30, 47, 49, 51s, 141, 265, 278
Nestlé, 212, 289
New Forests, 220
New Internationalist, 9, 139s, 292s, 297
'New Wars', 229
Nkrumah, Kwame, 116
North American Free Trade Agreement (NAFTA), 221
Norwegian State Pension Fund, 169
Nuremberg Tribunals, 79

OCHA see Office for the Coordination of Humanitarian Affairs
OCHRH see United Nations High Commissioner for Human Rights
ODA see official development assistance
OECD, 104, Development Assistance Committee Report, 133, 135, 136, 138, 139, 141, 142, 143, 193, 195, 210, 211, 258, 264, 265, 268, 269s, 271, 272, 273s
Office for the Coordination of Humanitarian Affairs (OCHA), 235
official development assistance, 136, 137, 241, 265-8, 270-2
Ogoni Nine, 8
Ogoni people, 299
Oil and Gas Climate Group, 297
Olympic Games, 288, 289

Optional Protocol on the Sale of Children, Child Prostitition, and Child Pornography, 202
Optional Protocol to the Convention against Torture, 202
Oxfam, 16, 24, 29, 35, 111s, 178, 206, 209, 211, 212s, 215s, 245, 258, 271, 281, 282, 296
Oxford University, 169

Pan Africa Energy Company, 145
Pankhurst, Emily, 122
Paris Agreement, 166, 175, 180-3, 185, 186, 187s, 220, 291, 297 see also United Nations Climate Change Conference
Parks, Bradley, 104, 105
Parks, Rosa, 122
Patriot Act, 89
The People's Test on Climate, 182
PepsiCo, 212
Pew Research Centre, 27
Pfeifle, Mark, 286
Pinter, Harold, 46
Plato, 78
Pogge, Thomas, 11, 13s, 14, 93s, 99, 100, 101, 108, 111s, 262, 278, 280, 281
population, 20, 22, 24-27, 61-62, 67-68, 72-73, 107, 109, 122-123, 142, 163, 178 179, 238, 253-258, 280, see United Nations Population Fund
The Politics of Climate Change, 170
polluter pays, 107, 178
pollution register, 290
Poor Economics, 116
Pope Francis, 104
PPP see Purchasing Power Parity
Prashed, Vijay, 258
Prato, Stefano, 44
Prisons Care and Counselling Association, 151
Programme of Action to Prevent, Combat and Eradicate the Illicit Trade in Small Arms and Light Weapons in All Its Aspects, 225
Project for the Study of the 21st Century, 229
Protocol Against the Smuggling of Migrants by Land, Sea and Air, 202
Protocol Relating to the Status of Refugees, 201
Protocol to Prevent, Suppress, and Punish Trafficking in Persons, 202
Purchasing Power Parity, 20, 25, 28, 121,

Rainbow Warrior, 289
rainforest, 63, 214, 216
rape, 33, 139, 157, 160 see also sexual harassment
Rawls, John, 106
REACH, 217

Reality of Aid, 268, 269, 270, 271, 273s
Reinert, Erik, 278
Reynolds, Henry, 199
RiceTec, 219
Rist, Gilbert, 34, 37, 39, 45, 46, 51s
Roberts, J. Timmins, 104, 105
Robinson, Mary, 104, 106, 186
Rodney, Walter, 39, 42
Rome Declaration on World Food Security, 12
Roosevelt, Eleanor, 93s, 122
Roosevelt, Franklin, 79, 80
Rosling, Hans, 208
Rostow, Walt, 40, 41
Roy, Arundhati, 300
Rousseau, 79
Rudd, Kevin, 197, 290
rules of origin, 217-8
Rurelec, 220

Sachs, Jeffrey, 45, 51s, 116, 273s, 278-9
Sachs, Wolfgang, 36, 51s
Samson, James, 105
Sandel, Michael, 111s, 183
SAP see Structural Adjustment Programme
Saro-Wiwa, Ken, 8
Sauvy, Albert, 48
Save the Children, 230, 235, 239s
Schumacher, E.F., 59, 60
Scott, James C., 117, 119
SDG see Sustainable Development Goals
Self Employed Women's Association (SEWA), 288
Sen, Amartya, 31s, 42, 43, 51s, 98, 99, 100, 111s, 117, 121, 122, 152, 262, 281, 284
Sen, Gita, 36
Senegal, 28, 54, 56, 57, 210, 252
September 11 Attacks 2001, 88
SEWA see Self Employed Women's Association
sexual harassment/violence, 33, 157, 158, 159, 161 see also rape
Shehab, Bahia, 290
Shell, 219, 299
Shiva, Vandana, 29, 37, 51s, 59, 104, 184, 187s, 278, 281
Shock and Awe, 233-4
Shock Waves: Managing the Impacts of Climate Change on Poverty, 168, 177, 278 see also World Bank
Silent Spring, 288
Singer, Peter, 97, 98, 100, 101, 106, 107n, 111s, 262, 278, 279, 286
Singh, Manhoman, 141
slavery, 57, 90, 91, 100, 101, 118, 138, 276, 277, 283, 285, 292
Smith, Tommie, 288
Social Unrest Index, 125

Social Watch, 31s, Spotlight on Sustainable Development, 44; 51s, 52, 151,154, 166s
Solidar, 221
Sontag, Susan, 286, 301
South African Human Rights Commission, 245
South-South Development Cooperation, 193, 260, 268, 269, 270
Spaull, Nic, 248
Spenser, Edmund, 232
Sriskandarajah, Dhananjayan, 263
Stages theory, 40
Stalin, Joseph, 233, 239s
Stanford University, 169, 221
Stanner, Bill, 7
Structural Adjustment, 119, 265
suffragette movement, 115, 234
Sumner, Andy, 26, 260, 264s, 272
Sunni/Shia, 235
sustainable development, 36, 44, 51s, 52, 59-69, 106, 130, 175, 183, 186, 187s, 278, 281
Sustainable Development Goals, 8, 11, 13, 34, 37, 43-5, 52-3, 130, 151, 152, 156, 158, 165s, 166, 176, 203, 225, 226, 230, 238, 265, 279, 291
Sustainable Development Solutions Network, 45, 278
SWN Resources, 299
Sydney Peace Prize, 281

Taliban, 8
Tanner, Thomas, 178, 187s
tax havens, 24, 128, 137, 144-6
Tax Justice Network, 135, 144, 145
'Third World', 17, 31s, 34, 39, 41, 46, 48, 49, 51s, 59, 101, 187s, 209, 210, 217
TIKA, 271
TNC see Transnational Corporations
torture, 33, 74, 80, 83, 89, 90, 91, 198, 202, 292, 297
Toubia, Nahld, M.D., 162
Toynbee, Arnold, 78
TPP see Trans-Pacific Partnership
Tracking Under-Reported Financial Flows, 270
Trade and Environment Review 2013, 211
trafficking: drugs, 137, 139; human, 139, 159, 160, 196, 202, 205s
Trans-Canada Keystone XL, 299
Trans-Pacific Partnership (TPP), 208, 222
Transatlantic Trade and Investment Partnership (TTIP), 208, 220, 221, 222
'Transforming our World: the 2030 Agenda for Sustainable Development' see Sustainable Development Goals
Transnational Corporations, 283
Transnational Institute, 298
Transparency International, 135

TRIPS see Agreement on Trade-Related Aspects of Intellectual Property Rights
Trócaire, 176, 187s
Truman, Harry S., 36, 39
TTIP see Transatlantic Trade and Investment Partnership
TUFF see Tracking Under-Reported Financial Flows

UK Overseas Development Institute, 51,195, 216, 252, 258, 269, 273s,
Ul Haq, Mahbub, 19, 42
Ullman and Wade, 233-4
Umbrella Movement, 124
UN see United Nations
UNCTAD see United Nations Conference on Trade and Development
Underground Railroad, 277
UNDESA see United Nations Department of Economic and Social Affairs
UNDP see United Nations Development Programme
UNEP see United Nations Environment Programme
UNESCO, 248, 249s, 20s, 32s
UNFCCC see United Nations Framework Convention on Climate Change
UNFPA see United Nations Population Fund
Unger, Peter, 98, 111s, 262
UNHCR see United Nations High Commissioner for Refugees
Unicef, 19, 23, 31s, 32s, 103s, 157s, 162, 165s, 202s, 245, 246s, 249s, 251s, 255s, 256s, 259s, 289
UNIFEM, 151
Unilever, 212, 296
United Nations, 13, 30; establishment, 36, 38, 39, 78; Preamble to the Charter, 79-80; human rights, 77, 80; 122; Report of the Secretary General, 131; 138, 141; 168; 265; agencies, 289
United Nations Agenda for Sustainable Development, 186 see also Sustainable Development Goals
United Nations Climate Change Conference, 123 see also Paris Agreement
United Nations Commission for Social Development, 88
United Nations Commission on Human Rights, 80 see also Universal Declaration of Human Rights
United Nations Committee on Economic, Social and Cultural Rights, 236
United Nations Conference on Sustainable Development, 195
United Nations Conference on Trade and Development (UNCTAD), 30, 133, 176, 211, 217

United Nations Convention against Torture, 33, 83, 202

United Nations Declaration of Human Rights see Universal Declaration of Human Rights

United Nations Department of Economic and Social Affairs (UNDESA), 32s, 40, 157, 159, migration, 192, 193; 256, 259s; Population Division, 19, 157s, 246s, 253s, 254s, 259s; Population Fund, 160, 257; *World's Women: Trends and Statistics*, 32s, 157s, 159

United Nations Development Programme (UNDP), 17, 24, 29, 42, 43, 86, 104, 135, 141, 143, 166, 192, 196, 244, 281n; Human Development Reports, 16s, 18, 20, 22, 23s, 28s, 31s, 32s, 37, 42, 47, 51s, 86, 112, 114, 117, 120, 121, 144, 153, 158, 166, 169, 176, 187s, 193, 195, 199, 244, 245, 259s, 268; Multi-Dimensional Poverty Index, 19, 27

United Nations Economic Commission for Africa, 135

United Nations Environment Programme (UNEP), 180, 185, 187s

United Nations Equator Prize, 123

United Nations Family Planning Agency, 159, 160, 161s

United Nations Food and Agriculture Organisation (FAO), 12, 13, 31s, 39, 56, 57, 103, 152, 210, 211, 215s, 216, 231, 234, 237, 239s, 257, 259s

United Nations Framework Convention on Climate Change (UNFCCC), 175, 180-1, 184, 187s see also COPs

United Nations General Assembly, 80, 159, 192, 265, 290, 291; Declaration on the Elimination of Violence Against Women, 159

United Nations High Commissioner for Human Rights (OHCHR), 24, 86, 93s, 201, 202, 280, 281

United Nations High Commissioner for Refugees (UNHCR), 32, 83, 160, 193; Refugee Convention, 197; 198, 201, 202, 205s; Global Trends 2016 Report, 228

United Nations Human Rights Committee, 201

United Nations Human Rights Council Universal Periodic Review of Australia, 199

United Nations International Day of Zero Tolerance for Female Genital Mutilation, 159

United Nations Office on Drugs and Crime, 139s, 146, 202

United Nations Population Fund (UNFPA), 157s, 160, 161s, 165s, 246s, 257, 259s

United Nations Rapporteur of Food Security, 104

United Nations Report on World Contraceptive Use, 293

United Nations Resolution 2286, 238

United Nations Review on Small Island Developing Nations, 169

United Nations Secretary General, 131, 159, 160, 192, 196, 200, 209, 229, 230

United Nations Security Council (UNSC): Report on *Small Arms and Light Weapons*, 224; 230; Iraq, 234; 238

United Nations Special Rapporteur on the Right to Food, 236

United Nations Special Representative of the Secretary General for Disaster Risk Reduction, 160

United Nations Special Representative of the Secretary General on the Human Rights of Internally Displaced Persons, 200

United Nations Women: *Progress of the World's Women 2015-2016*, 153; 202, 291

United Nations Working Group on Enforced Disappearances, 83

United Nations World Economic Situation and Prospects Report, 130, 131, 213

United States Bill of Rights, 84

Universal Declaration of Human Rights, 74, 77, 78, 80, 81, 85, 93s, 114, 119, 236

UNSC see United Nations Security Council

US Energy Information Administration, 173s

US National Research Council's Board on Sustainable Development, 58

USAID, 153

Vervynck, Mathieu, 144

Via Campesina, 47, 295

Vieira, Marco, 30

Voting Rights Act, 288

vulture funds, 140

W.R. Grace & Company, 219

Wahlstrom, Margareta, 160

Walmart, 57, 212, 219

war crime/criminal, 79, 238, 286, 289

'Washington Consensus', 49, 206, 222, 265n

waste, 61, 106-107, 188-189, 214-215, 257, see e-waste

Water Aid, 250, 252s

Water Governance Facility, 250

water stress/insecurity, 169, 176, 251-2

Watkins, Kevin, 206, 209

WCED see World Commission on Environment and Development

Weapons of Mass Destruction, 234, 251

Weiss, Edith Brown, 106

WESCO see World Employment and Social Outlook

The Whispering in our Hearts, 199

White Helmet workers, 9

'white man's burden', 38, 278s

WHO see World Health Organisation

WMD see Weapons of Mass Destruction, 234

Women Deliver, 162

Woodward, David, 13s, 27, 30, 94

Woolstonecraft, Mary, 122

World Bank, 11, 13s, 17, 19, 24, 25s, 27, 29, 30, 39, 42, 43, 47, 51s, 60, 88, 103s, 120, 122, 131s, 133, 135, 138, 140, 144, 145, 146, 153, 157s, 174, 192, 196, 199, 219, 246s, 259s, 265n, 278, 280; Development Indicators for 2015, 210; Migration and Development Brief 20, 195, 199; *Shock Waves*, 168, 177, 278; World Development Report, 31s, 64s, 66s, 125, 278;

World Commission on Environment and Development (WCED), 58, 59, 60

World Conference on Human Rights, 77

World Conference on Women, 151, 289

World Conservation Union (IUCN), 65, 66

World Council of Churches, 169s

World Development Report, 125 see also World Bank

World Economic Forum, 162, 163; *World Risk Report*, 168; *Global Gender Gap Report*, 157s, 165s

World Economic Situation and Prospects Report, 131

World Employment and Social Outlook Report, 120

World Energy Outlook Special Report, 174

World Food Conference, 12

World Food Summit, 14, 47, 295

World Health Organisation (WHO), 23, 32s, 83, 103, 133, 139, 142, 143, 153, 157, 159, Air Quality Guideline, 174; 177, 103s, 246, 247, 249, 257; water, 250, 251s; family planning, 257; 259s, 289

World Humanitarian Summit, 152, 238

World Literacy Foundation, 248

World Migration Report, 193, 195

world military expenditure, 224-5, 241

World Protests 2006-2013, 120

World Resources Institute, 152

World Risk Report, 168, 200

World Trade Organisation (WTO), 42, 60, 208, 212, 213, 218, 221, 289

World Wide Fund for Nature (WWF), 66, 68, 72

The World's Stateless, 32, 203, 205s

Worldwatch Institute, 51s, 210, 214s, 298s

WTO see World Trade Organisation

WWF see World Wide Fund for Nature

Yankelovich, Daniel, 284, 285, 300

Yousafzai, Malala, 116, 122

Yunaus, Muhammed, 288

Ziegler, Jean, 179

Zucman, Gabriel, 146

New Internationalist

Challenging injustice
Changing perspectives

New Internationalist is an award-winning, independent media co-operative. Our aim is to inform, inspire and empower people to build a fairer, more sustainable planet.

We publish a global justice magazine and a range of books, both distributed worldwide. We have a vibrant online presence and run ethical online shops for our customers and other organizations.

Independent media: we're free to tell it like it is – our only obligation is to our readers and the subjects we cover.

Fresh perspectives: our in-depth reporting and analysis provide keen insights, alternative perspectives and positive solutions for today's critical global justice issues.

Global grassroots voices: we actively seek out and work with grassroots writers, bloggers and activists across the globe, enabling unreported (and under-reported) stories to be heard.

> **❛For decades New Internationalist has been at the forefront of offering an alternative to the mainstream media's neoliberal hegemony.❜**
> **Noam Chomsky**

Our books bring a greater insight and sensitivity to subject areas that we believe are poorly served elsewhere. They contribute to and influence public debate and the discourse around controversial subjects.

And we celebrate and promote cultural diversity, bringing world fiction and literature to new audiences.

newint.org